SAGE was founded in 1965 by Sara Miller McCune to support the dissemination of usable knowledge by publishing innovative and high-quality research and teaching content. Today, we publish over 900 journals, including those of more than 400 learned societies, more than 800 new books per year, and a growing range of library products including archives, data, case studies, reports, and video. SAGE remains majority-owned by our founder, and after Sara's lifetime will become owned by a charitable trust that secures our continued independence.

Los Angeles | London | New Delhi | Singapore | Washington DC | Melbourne

BRITISH RULE IN INDIA

Thank you for choosing a SAGE product!
If you have any comment, observation or feedback,
I would like to personally hear from you.

Please write to me at **contactceo@sagepub.in**

Vivek Mehra, Managing Director and CEO, SAGE India.

Bulk Sales

SAGE India offers special discounts
for purchase of books in bulk.
We also make available special imprints
and excerpts from our books on demand.

For orders and enquiries, write to us at

Marketing Department
SAGE Publications India Pvt Ltd
B1/I-1, Mohan Cooperative Industrial Area
Mathura Road, Post Bag 7
New Delhi 110044, India

E-mail us at **marketing@sagepub.in**

Get to know more about SAGE

Be invited to SAGE events, get on our mailing list.
Write today to **marketing@sagepub.in**

This book is also available as an e-book.

BRITISH RULE IN INDIA

Pandit SUNDERLAL

Los Angeles | London | New Delhi
Singapore | Washington DC | Melbourne

Copyright © Popular Prakashan, 2018

All rights reserved. No part of this book may be reproduced or utilized in any form or by any means, electronic or mechanical, including photocopying, recording, or by any information storage or retrieval system, without permission in writing from the publisher.

First published in 2018 by

SAGE Publications India Pvt Ltd
B1/I-1 Mohan Cooperative Industrial Area
Mathura Road, New Delhi 110 044, India
www.sagepub.in

SAGE Publications Inc
2455 Teller Road
Thousand Oaks, California 91320, USA

SAGE Publications Ltd
1 Oliver's Yard, 55 City Road
London EC1Y 1SP, United Kingdom

SAGE Publications Asia-Pacific Pte Ltd
3 Church Street
#10-04 Samsung Hub
Singapore 049483

Popular Prakashan Pvt. Ltd
301, Mahalaxmi Chambers
22, Bhulabhai Desai Road
Mumbai 400026
www.popularprakashan.com

Published by Vivek Mehra for SAGE Publications India Pvt Ltd, typeset in 10/13 pt Bembo by AG Infographics, Delhi and printed at Chaman Enterprises, New Delhi.

Library of Congress Cataloging-in-Publication Data Available

ISBN: 978-93-528-0802-1 (PB)

Contents

Foreword by Amar Farooqui   vii

1. End of the Second Maratha War   1
2. The First Lord Minto (1807–1813)   15
3. Deliberate Destruction of Indian Industries and Trade   37
4. The War with Nepal   63
5. Some Other Achievements of Lord Hastings   79
6. The Third Maratha War   85
7. Lord Amherst (1823–1828)   117
8. Lord William Bentinck (1828–1835)   135
9. Charter Act of 1833   149
10. National Education under British Rule   161
11. The First Afghan War   181
12. Annexation of Sindh   199
13. Ellenborough's Action Against Indian Rulers   221
14. The First Sikh War   233
15. The Second Sikh War   249
16. The Second Burmese War   263
17. Usurpations   273
18. Before the 1857 Revolution   291
19. Greased Cartridges—'Fat in the Fire'   311
20. Reprisals   329
21. Jhansi and Oudh   343

22.	Punjab—Its Importance and Reaction	355
23.	On the March to Delhi	365
24.	Delhi–Its Emperor and People	369
25.	First Battles for Delhi	373
26.	March of the Revolution and Its Repercussions	379
27.	Slaughter of Innocents	385
28.	Fall of Delhi	393
29.	Delhi After Its Fall	407
30.	Lucknow–Oudh–Rohilkhand	415
31.	Bihar	441
32.	Rani Lakshmibai of Jhansi	455
33.	Ineffectual Outbreaks in the South	467
34.	Oudh's Last Bid for Freedom	475
35.	Tatya Tope's Final Efforts	485
36.	A Retrospective View of the Revolution	495
37.	After 1857—England's Reaction	503

Epilogue	522
Bibliography	525
Annals	527
Index	528
About the Author	536

Foreword

British Rule in India is the second and final volume of one of the most important and widely read texts published during the last decades of colonial presence in India, as an indictment of the entire history of British rule. Its author, Pandit Sunderlal (1886–1981), was a very prominent freedom fighter, civil rights activist, scholar and journalist. His political career spanned more than seven decades. Sunderlal was a prolific writer and published extensively, writing mostly in Hindi. *British Rule in India*, along with its companion volume, *How India Lost Her Freedom*, is perhaps the most well known of his writings. *Bharat Mein Angrezi Raj*—a massive work of which these two books together are the English translation—was originally published in 1929. It was written over a period of nearly three years against the backdrop of the anti-colonial mass movements, led by Gandhiji, in which Pandit Sunderlal himself was an active participant and a leading organiser.

The struggle against colonial rule entered a new phase in the years following the end of the First World War. This phase was marked by the radicalisation of the freedom struggle and mass mobilisation, inspired by Gandhiji's leadership. This was precisely the period when communal mobilisation became a pronounced feature of politics in India. Throughout his political life, Pandit Sunderlal remained a staunch opponent of communalism and was unwavering in his commitment to secularism. *British Rule in India* is as much an indictment of colonial oppression as it is of the cynical policy of 'divide and rule'. Practices of colonial governance created conditions that promoted and sustained divisions in Indian society along communal lines. This book seeks to expose the divisive character of the colonial regime.

In the period after the First World War, communal politics emerged as the dominant form of the politics of religious identity in colonial India. Although historically, there are numerous instances of religious conflict in the pre-colonial period, and also in the late 18th and early 19th centuries, it is from the late 19th century onwards that political mobilisation based on aggressive assertions of religious identity began to emerge in several parts of the British Indian Empire.

The most significant feature of communal politics, involving the blatant use of religion for purely political purposes, was the emphasis on the distinctiveness and separateness of 'Hindu' and 'Muslim' identities. The interests of the two communities were supposedly so different and antagonistic that there was no possibility of their having any shared concerns. This, it was alleged, rendered their imagined differences irreconcilable. For the British, communalism was a convenient instrument for furthering their policy of 'divide and rule'. Communal politics became prevalent in India with a helping hand from the colonial state.

Pandit Sunderlal was able to argue convincingly and forcefully that roots of the communal trend in early 20th century politics could be traced back to the beginnings of British rule and the initial conquests of the East India Company. In fact, the lengthy introductory part of *How India Lost Her Freedom* is a critique of the falsification of the history of the late pre-colonial and early colonial periods in colonial historiography, and a consideration of how people of diverse religious persuasions fared in polities of the Indian subcontinent which had rulers predominantly of the Muslim faith. The thrust of Sunderlal's argument was that colonial rule had been responsible for disrupting the harmonious relationships that had existed among religious communities prior to the Company's ascendancy.

British Rule in India commences with the closing phase of the Second Anglo-Maratha War (1802–1805) and takes the story up to the brutal suppression of the revolt of 1857. Richard Wellesley (Governor-General, 1798–1805) turned his attention to the Marathas immediately after the defeat of Tipu Sultan and the conquest of Mysore (1799). The Second Anglo-Maratha War substantially reduced Maratha power. The Third Anglo-Maratha War (1817–1818), which began shortly after Britain had settled scores with Napoleon and defeated his forces decisively at the Battle of Waterloo (1815), completed the process of subjugating the Marathas. There then followed nearly four decades of war and conquest by the British against Nepal, Burma, Afghanistan, Sindh and Panjab, leading to the subjugation of the entire Indian subcontinent and southern Burma (though not of Afghanistan and Nepal) by the 1850s. This was achieved by inflicting bloody wars on the people of South Asia by an aggressive British colonialism invigorated by its success over France and strengthened economically by the Industrial Revolution. The history of this conquest is narrated by Pandit Sunderlal in detail, laying bare the violent and oppressive character of colonial rule. A little less than half of the text is devoted to the revolt of 1857. It should be borne in mind that the colonial version of the history of the revolt, disseminated and popularised through writings published on a massive scale for over 70 years, had made it virtually impossible to challenge this version. *British Rule in India* challenges and undermines, very effectively, the colonial narrative of the revolt.

This is a book written in anger—anger over the long history of oppression and ruthless exploitation under British rule. It is a scholarly work and is also a powerful political text. The political significance of the book was immediately grasped by the colonial state which promptly imposed a ban on it. Although the State did not delay taking action in this matter, 1,700 of the 2,000 copies, which had been published, were already in circulation by the time the book was proscribed. This ensured that several hundred copies circulated underground, and the political message of the book reached a large audience. Soon after the Congress established its control over several provincial governments following the 1937 elections, the ban on the book was revoked by these provinces. A new edition, containing some very minor modifications, was published in 1938 with a print run of 10,000 copies. Even as the edition was being prepared for the press, 14,000 orders had been received for the book. *Bharat Mein Angrezi Raj* was indeed a bestseller and continues to be relevant and in demand. SAGE is to be commended for taking up the publication of its English translation, *British Rule in India*.

Amar Farooqui
Professor, Department of History
University of Delhi

1

END OF THE SECOND MARATHA WAR

(Marquess Wellesley Recalled— Lord Cornwallis—Sir George Barlow)

Holkar and Sindhia Unite

The English had lifted the siege of Bharatpur and made peace with its Raja. But Maharaja Jaswantrao Holkar was still undefeated and the various disputes with Maharaja Doulatrao Sindhia were still outstanding.

On leaving Bharatpur, Holkar went to Sabalgarh where Sindhia was encamping. The two rulers agreed to unite against the English and marched with their combined armies to Kotah, and from Kotah to Ajmer. The union of Sindhia with Holkar unnerved the English completely. Marquess Wellesley directed Gen. Lake to march in pursuit of Sindhia, but on 24th April, 1850, Lake wrote back saying "It would be impossible for me to pursue Sindhia" because of "the intense heat" and the "scarcity of water". An additional reason given by him was "There is no vile act these people are not equal to; that inhuman monster Holkar's chief delight is in butchering all Europeans."

As a matter of fact, both Holkar and Sindhia had proved themselves to be courageous military leaders of a very high order and Lake, who only knew how to use his "secret" methods, was naturally anxious to avoid an armed conflict in the open with either of them.

Marquess Wellesley, too, seemed to agree with Lake, and wrote to him on 17th May, saying that an armed conflict with Sindhia was to be avoided as long as possible, and in the meanwhile all disputes with Holkar were to be settled without fighting, if that was at all possible. It would, however, appear that Marquess Wellesley had suggested the peaceful approach only to gain time by lulling Holkar and Sindhia into inaction for the time being.

At the moment, Marquess Wellesley was hard up for money, and on account of the rainy season any military operation was out of the question. This is borne out by what Marquess Wellesley went on to say in the same letter:

> "... The troops ... should be completely ready to commence active operations as soon as the season will permit and

arrangements will, of course, be adopted by Your Lordship for collecting supplies, etc., and for completing every other preparation which may be necessary to enable Your Lordship to destroy Sindhia at an early period of the ensuing season ... the possible contingency of our being compelled to attack Sindhia, or to operate against Holkar, about the month of August, or as soon as the violence of the rainy season may have subsided." (Marquess Wellesley's official and secret letter to General Lake, 17th May, 1805.)

He further directed Lake to keep four detachments ready for the attack on Holkar and Sindhia—one in Gohad, at the expense of the Raja of Gohad, another in Bundelkhand, a third at Agra and Mathura and a fourth between Delhi and the northern Doab.

To meet the huge expenditure involved, he "arranged" for a fresh loan from the Nawab Wazir of Oudh. In July, 1805, he again wrote to Gen. Lake: "Great danger must inevitably be produced by our abstaining from the prosecution of hostilities at the earliest practicable period of time ... against the confederated forces in every quarter of Hindustan and Deccan."

But on 29th July, Lord Cornwallis arrived at Calcutta and replaced Marquess Wellesley as Governor-General of India the following day.

Repercussions in England of English Reverses

War had been going on for two years and its second year was marked by the reverses suffered by the English again and again. The monetary losses, particularly in the implementation of Lake's "secret" methods of bribery and corruption in which money had been spent like water, had led to intense dissatisfaction to the rulers of England and the Directors of the Company. The shareholders of the Company, too, had been losing their dividends and joined in the clamour for the removal of Marquess Wellesley from the Governor-Generalship of India and so he was recalled.

It must not be forgotten that the English were a commercial nation and as such could least put up with any loss of money. Their possessions in India were of use so long as they were a source of quick-made fortunes. According to Mill (Vol.VI, p. 471):

> "If India affords a surplus revenue which can be sent to England, thus far is India beneficial to England."

But by that time, the financial position of the East India Company had been reduced to near-bankruptcy. Its treasury in India was empty. In addition, Marquess Wellesley had borrowed heavily in the name of the Company. The loans included 20 lacs of rupees from the Nawab Wazir of Oudh, who was being pressed by Marquess Wellesley for another loan of ten lacs, as Lord Cornwallis wrote (to Lord Castlereagh) on 1st August, 1805, only two days after taking over as Governor-General. On 9th August, Lord Cornwallis again wrote to Lord Castlereagh:

> "Lake's army, the pay of which amounts to about five lacs per month, is above five months in arrears. An army of irregulars, composed chiefly of deserters from the enemy, which with approbation of Government, the General assembled by proclamation, and which costs about six lacs per month, is likewise somewhat in arrears."

On the 14th, he wrote to Colonel Malcolm, saying that the Company had to maintain an army for the control of the Emperor Shah Alam and the defence of Delhi and that the Company did not receive a copper from anywhere to help in its maintenance. In England, too, the indebtedness of the Company was mounting steadily because for eight years nothing had been remitted to England by the English Government in India. The following quotation is from the speech of M. Paul delivered to the Members of the British Parliament on 25th February, 1806:

> "By the Act of 1793, after the payment of the military and civil establishment, the Act enjoins that a sum not less than one million pounds sterling shall be applied for commercial purposes, and remitted to Great Britain to form part of its national wealth. Since 1798, no sum whatever has been applied to commercial purposes, and the law has been violated in this single instance to a sum exceeding eight millions. To this

extent and to this amount has this commercial nation been deprived of ..."

Lord Cornwallis Governor-General Again

So far as imperialist ambitions about India were concerned, there was no difference between Lord Cornwallis and Marquess Wellesley. After the Second Maratha War had started and Generals Lake and Wellesley had been successful against Sindhia and Berar, Lord Cornwallis had written to Marquess Wellesley from England on 30th April, 1804:

> "The important and glorious achievements of my friends, Generals Lake and Wellesley, have afforded me the most sincere satisfaction ... I earnestly hope that, in every part of the globe, its (my country's) interests will be promoted by as able statesmen, and its armies conducted by as meritorious generals, as those who have of late been entrusted with the preservation of our Asiatic Empire."

But the difficult circumstances under which he assumed office made it imperative for him to take steps for the immediate cessation of hostilities with the Marathas. He left Calcutta for the north-west region on 8th August and on 19th September, wrote a long letter to Lake. At that time there were four important matters under dispute between Maharaja Doulatrao Sindhia and the English, which may be summarised as follows:

(i) Sindhia had put under arrest the English Resident Jenkins at his court on account of Jenkin's most objectionable behaviour, and the English wanted the latter's release,

(ii) Gwalior Fort and Gohad were still occupied by the English and Sindhia was demanding their restoration,

(iii) the English had not restored to Sindhia, as provided in the last treaty, the districts of Dholpur, Bari and Rajkeri and were still collecting revenues there, and

(iv) the English were collecting from the Maharaja of Jaipur the annual tribute of three lacs of rupees which was due and payable to Sindhia by the Maharaja of Jaipur.

In the letter to Lake, Lord Cornwallis stated very plainly his readiness to conclude peace with Sindhia on the following terms:

(i) the question of Jenkin's release will not be raised at all,
(ii) Gwalior and Gohad will be immediately restored to Sindhia,
(iii) Dholpur, Bari and Rajkeri districts will also be given up to Sindhia and an account rendered to him of the revenues collected by the English, and
(iv) the tribute collected from Jaipur by the English will be refunded to Sindhia provided the latter breaks off completely from Jaswantrao Holkar and arranges a maintenance allowance of two to three lacs of rupees to be paid to the Rana of Gohad.

In the same letter, Lord Cornwallis informed Lake of his willingness to make peace with Jaswantrao Holkar too, even if all the latter's territory seized by the English had to be restored to him.

But Lord Cornwallis was not destined to get the credit for ending the war. Within three months he suddenly died at Ghazipur in October, 1805. He was buried there and a mausoleum was erected on his grave with money subscribed by Indians.

A Notable Incident

An incident illustrative of the way in which wealth was being drained from India occurred during Lord Cornwallis' brief tenure of office as Governor-General. Some bullion from England was on its way to China for the purchase of merchandise which England wanted to import. The ships carrying it touched Madras. Lord Cornwallis seized the bullion and used it to liquidate the arrears into which the pay of the Company's armies had fallen to such an extent that a revolt by the soldiers was feared. On 9th August, Lord Cornwallis wrote to the Company's Directors assuring them that the Company would not be put to any inconvenience or loss by the seizure of its bullion as he would recoup the Company by obtaining from China free of cost all the merchandise which the Company had intended to buy with the money.

In those days China was importing from India opium, cotton and other merchandise to the tune of 40 lacs of rupees per year. The price of these commodities in China was increasing and the Chinese were keener than ever to import them from India. Lord Cornwallis' plan was to supply these free to the Chinese at the cost of India in return for a free supply by the Chinese to England of the merchandise needed by the latter. The sufferer would be India as it would add to the burden of the million pounds sterling payable every year to England as mentioned before.

Sir George Barlow as Governor-General

It will be recalled that on 12th July, 1803, a senior member of the Governor-General's Council had presented a memorandum to Governor-General Wellesley in which he had pressed the view that "...... no native state should be left to exist in India, which is not upheld by the British power, or the political conduct of which is not under its absolute control."

On the death of Lord Cornwallis, Sir George Barlow succeeded him as Governor-General of India. He gave top priority to the achievement of a break between Sindhia and Holkar and he succeeded.

A Fresh Treaty with Sindhia

Sindhia and Holkar were both at Ajmer. But Sindhia had never trusted Holkar completely. He was also no longer enthusiastic about his union with Holkar or about the continuation of hostilities with the English. Finally the terms offered by Lord Cornwallis were irresistibly attractive. Munshi Kamalnain, Sindhia's Principal Adviser, was with Sindhia when Holkar went from Bharatpur to Sindhia at Sabalgarh. Sometime after, Kamalnain suddenly left Sindhia and went to Delhi to contact Lake, who used him as the channel of negotiations for peace with Sindhia. Thanks very largely to Kamalnain's efforts, Sindhia ultimately agreed to break away from Holkar and to enter into a separate treaty with the English which was signed on 23rd November, 1805.

Its terms very materially changed the provisions of the earlier treaty of 1803. The new treaty provided for:

(i) The freedom of Sindhia from the yoke of the Subsidiary Alliance.
(ii) The restoration to Sindhia of the Gwalior Fort and the province of Gohad.
(iii) The acknowledgement by the English that the Rajputana States of Jaipur, Jodhpur, Kotah, etc., were the Tributaries of Sindhia and the undertaking by the English that the latter will not have direct political relations or negotiate any separate treaty or engagements with any of these States.
(iv) The declaration that the river Chambal was the boundary of Sindhia's territory.
(v) The restoration to Sindhia of some of the Doab districts seized by the English and the undertaking by the latter to pay Sindhia 4 lacs of rupees every year in return for such districts as were not to be restored.

Sindhia won all along the line and his prestige had never been so high. As a gesture, he set free the English Resident Jenkins.

Rejection by Holkar of the English Offer of Peace

The Governor-General's Council in Calcutta had been pressing Lake to conclude peace with Holkar somehow. An offer was made to Holkar that in return for a treaty of peace, all of his original territory would be restored to him.

Jaswantrao Holkar faced a difficult situation. Sindhia had deserted him and he had no other ally. He had long been in exile from his country and his financial resources had dwindled to such an extent that he was unable to pay his soldiers. But even so, he would not give in and declined even to consider the very attractive terms for peace. As a penance for his siding with the English at the beginning of the Second Maratha War, he was determined to carry on his struggle for ridding India of the English menace. Led by hopes of enlisting the support of Maharaja Ranjit Singh of Lahore and other Punjab Chiefs and *Sardars*, he left Ajmer with the faithful remnants of his adherents and proceeded towards Punjab. He had hopes even of an alliance with other Asiatic rulers, particularly with the King of Kabul who had already threatened the English with an invasion of India and who was still the titular Suzerain of Maharaja Ranjit Singh and several other Rajas in the Punjab.

Lake followed Holkar and got quite close to him near the river Beas. Amir Khan, who was still with Holkar, records in his Autobiography (p. 286) "...... the General (Lake) saw himself that if Ranjit Singh, with the Patiyala chief and other Sirdars of this country, were to make common cause with the Maharaja (Holkar), a new flame would be lighted up, which it would be difficult to extinguish." He accordingly "...... looked out for an intelligent skilful negotiator to be sent to Holkar's camp, and to be made the channel for an overture ......"

The English had established friendly contacts with Maharaja Ranjit Singh and other Sikh Rajas whose political position in the Punjab was very largely due to the help received by them from the English. The latter had been pressing the Sikhs to break away completely from Kabul and to abstain from helping the Marathas. Ranjit Singh could not afford to go against the English and as desired by them refused to help Holkar and pressed him to make peace with the English. Incidentally, a legend still persists in the Punjab to the effect that in reproaching Ranjit Singh for his attitude, Holkar asked the latter: "Is this treatment of a compatriot and a guest in dire distress, who has sought your protection and help, consistent with your duty?" and added "your rulership will die with you, whilst my descendants will continue to be rulers."

Holkar's Treaty with the English

It was impossible for Holkar to go on to Afghanistan through a hostile Punjab. Further, an English Agent, Sir John Malcolm, had succeeded in stirring up civil strife in Afghanistan and so no help could be expected from the King of Kabul. Frustrated and isolated, Jaswantrao Holkar agreed to a peace treaty with the English on the terms proposed by Lord Cornwallis. The treaty was signed on 24th December, 1805, and under its provisions Holkar's entire territory in the south of the Godavari and Tapti rivers, which the English had recently seized and occupied, was restored to Jaswantrao Holkar, who was further acknowledged as the sole and independent ruler of all his original dominions. In other words, the treaty did not in the least affect Jaswantrao Holkar's status as an independent ruler of the area of his territory.

Some Reflections on the Second Maratha War

The treaty with Jaswantrao Holkar ended the Second Maratha War, but the war had failed to end the political power of the Maratha rulers involved in it, which was Marquess Wellesley's objective in starting it. It had, however, given the Maratha power a very severe blow, from which the Maratha rulers never recovered fully. The Peshwa had been entrapped in the Subsidiary Alliance with the English and he as. well as Sindhia and Berar had lost to the English for ever some of their most fertile and prosperous regions. This was the sum-total of the English gains.

The war had indeed proved the English to be skilful intriguers and adepts in subornation by bribery; it had also shown that so far as courage on the battlefield or the technique of warfare was concerned, the English could not stand any comparison with the Maratha and other Indian military leaders and soldiers.

Thanks very largely to the "cunning despotism" which used "native soldiers to maintain and extend native subjection" (Herbert Spencer), the Indian statesmen who took part in the war failed to check the progressive strengthening of the foundations of British rule in India. Also, the Indian people, by and large, lacked nationalist sentiments, and the rulers were either short-sighted or distrusted one another. The only bright exception was the Raja of Bharatpur who stuck to his principles, bravely fought for them and won.

It is perhaps idle to speculate now on what might have been, but it does appear extremely doubtful that the English would have been able to defeat Sindhia or Bhonsle of Berar, at Assaye, Argaon or Lasvari, had not Jaswantrao Holkar sided with them and abstained from giving any help to Sindhia or Bhonsle. He discovered after Sindhia and Bhonsle had been defeated, that the English had duped him for their own ends and intended to destroy him too. He then went all out to retrieve his blunder in having trusted the English and inflicted on them defeat after defeat for a whole year. Had he not done so, Marquess Wellesley would have continued to "heap kingdoms upon kingdoms" in Rajputana, Central India and even Punjab under one false pretext or another. The Sikhs were not at that time powerful enough to resist.

As the Irish Military Commander, George Thomas, had written to Marquess Wellesley, it would have been quite easy to conquer and annex Punjab. Had the Raja of Bharatpur and Jaswantrao Holkar not fought the English so courageously and so unremittingly, it is very probable that out of the six or seven hundred big and small Indian States that existed in 1929 not one would have been left, and the map of India would have been completely covered with the English colour within the first decade of the 19th century. It is unlikely that the treatment of the people of India by the English would have been different from that meted out by other colonial powers of Europe to the natives of their colonies. But after repeated defeats at the hands of Indians, the English had to treat them differently and with wholesome respect. Also the hypnotism of the Indian mind generated by the much-vaunted English superiority was dispelled.

Sir George Barlow's Policy of Dividing The Rajputana Chiefs

The Rajputana Chiefs had helped the English against the Marathas and, in return, Marquess Wellesley and Gen. Lake had entered into separate treaties with each of them and had promised that if any one of them was attacked by an outsider, the English would give all help to the attacked. Contrary to the friendly spirit of these treaties, Sir George Barlow, as soon as he took over, proceeded to sow deliberately discord and incite disputes among the Rajas themselves. He followed "... a policy, which declaredly looks to the disputes and wars of its neighbours as one of the chief sources of its security, and which if it does not directly excite such wars shapes its political relations with inferior states in a manner calculated to create and continue them" (*Political History of India* by Sir John Malcolm).

We quote another eminent Englishman, Lord Metcalfe:

> "The Governor-General, in some of his despatches, distinctly says that he contemplates in the discord of the native powers an additional source of strength; and, if I am not mistaken, some of his plans go directly and are designed to foment discord among these states." (Footnote Kaye's *Selections from the Papers of Lord Metcalfe*, p. 7)

No comments are needed.

Zealous Propagation of Christianity In India

The Madras Presidency at that time offered the most promising field for the conversion of Indians to Christianity. Lord William Bentinck was then the Governor of Madras and Sir John Craddock was the Commander-in-Chief of the Company's forces there. Both were very zealous propagators of Christianity. Lord W. Bentinck commissioned Abbe Dubois, a French clergyman, to write a book on the religious and social customs of Indians and paid him Rs. 8,000 out of the Indian Exchequer. The book reviled Indians to the limit and pictured them as a barbarous people whose only hope of salvation lay in Christianity and English rule in the country. The book was widely published in England and East India Company rewarded a life pension to Abbe Dubois when he retired and went to France (*Encyclopaedia Britannica*, Vol. VIII, p. 624, 11th Edition).

In Madras all sorts of privileges and facilities were given to the Christian missionaries. Their proselytising pamphlets, appeals and literature were printed free by the Government presses and very widely distributed. Special facilities were provided to the missionaries to preach Christianity to the Indian soldiers of the Company in and outside its forts and cantonments in the Presidency. Free grants of large areas of land were made to the missionaries for carrying on their proselytising work. (Note—These statements are based on what the

Rev. Sydney Smith has written in "The Edinburgh Review" for 1807 on "The Conversion of India").

The Mutiny at Vellore

The root-cause of the Vellore mutiny was the brazen English attempt to convert the Indian soldiers to Christianity under the guise of military discipline. Instructions to the Madras sepoys in 1806 ordered every sepoy, Hindu or Muslim:

> "... not (to) mark his face to denote his caste, or wear earrings, when dressed in his uniform; and it is further directed that at all parades, and upon all duties, every soldier of the battalion shall be clean-shaved on the chin".

The sepoys were also ordered to change their traditional turbans for the kind of head-dress adopted by Indian converts to Christianity.

The sepoys at the Vellore Cantonment mutinied in July 1806. They collected in front of the Main Guard Room, then surrounded the residence of Col. Fencourt, their Commanding Officer, and shot him dead. They then proceeded to kill all their Christian officers and the white soldiers in the Cantonment. The revolt was put down and its ringleaders had to pay the penalty under the Military Code. Governor Bentinck and Commander-in-Chief Craddock were both dismissed. Tipu's sons who were then under detention in the Vellore Fort and were suspected of being implicated, were removed to Bengal. The enthusiasm of the Company's Christian officers for the propagation of Christianity in India cooled down very considerably. Lord Minto was appointed the Governor-General of India; Sir George Barlow was appointed Governor of Madras.

2

THE FIRST LORD MINTO (1807–1813)

Situation in India

When Lord Minto took over as Governor-General, the English position in India had deteriorated considerably. Their prestige was at a very low ebb. So was the financial condition of the East India Company. The Indian rulers had lost all faith in the honesty of the English and no longer trusted the latter's profuse protestations of goodwill and friendship or their lavish promises made only to be broken after the English ends had been served. The ungrateful way in which the English had treated the Rana of Gohad and the Rajas in Rajputana who had helped them against the Marathas was a warning taken to heart by all the other Rajas and rulers. The English had no friend left amongst them. Sindhia, Berar and Holkar were still as strong and independent as ever. The possibility of all the Indian rulers combining against the English for the recovery of all the territories lost to the English could not be ruled out completely.

The people in the regions ruled by the English were also in great distress which they rightly attributed to the English. The latter had increased the land revenue assessments enormously to an unheard-of extent, the like of which could not be found in any Indian-ruled part of the country. Thus there were grounds for fearing a revolt by the Indian ryots too.

Maintenance of Law and Order By the English

Perhaps as an antidote to the ryots' intense discontent with their English rulers, the latter would appear to have deliberately abstained from giving any protection to the people from the decoities, murders and other atrocities rampant in English-ruled Bengal. It is better to quote some Englishmen, including Lord Minto himself, on the law and order situation as it had been allowed to develop. "The crime of dacoity," wrote the distinguished judge, Sir Henry Strachey, "has, I believe, increased greatly, since the British administration of justice". The Divisional Judge of Rajashaye recorded in 1808:

> "That dacoity is very prevalent in Rajashaye has been often stated ... Yet the situation of the people is not sufficiently attended to. It cannot be denied that, in point of fact, there is no protection, either of person or of property."

In 1809, Mr. Dowdswell, the Secretary to the Government, wrote, "To the people of India there is no protection, either of person or of property." Lord Minto, in a private letter to his wife, stated:

> "They (the dacoits) have of late come within thirty miles of Barrackpore. The crime of gang robbery ... has been much greater in this civilised ... part of India than in the wilder territories adjoining, which have not enjoyed so long the advantages of a regular and legal government; and it appears at first sight mortifying to the English administration of these provinces, that our oldest possessions should be the worst protected against the evils of lawless violence."

Mill (Vol. V, p. 387) wrote:

> "This class of offences ... increased under the English Government, not only to a degree of which there seems to have been no example under the Native Governments of India, but to a degree surpassing what was ever witnessed in any country in which law and government could with any degree of propriety be said to exist."

It cannot be urged either that the English Government lacked adequate means of protecting the people. As Mill says, "the military strength of the British Government in Bengal ... could exterminate all the inhabitants with ease" (Vol. V, p. 410). Lord Dufferin, speaking at Calcutta on 30th November, 1888, thus commented on the regime of Lord Minto:

> "... in his time whole districts within twenty miles of Calcutta were at the mercy of dacoits, and this after the English had been more than fifty years in the occupation of Bengal."

It might well be asked why the dacoits were not put down and why dacoity and other crimes against the people were allowed to flourish and increase in British India to a degree of which there was no example in any other part of India ruled by Indians. Was it because it was one way of intimidating the people and making them weak so that no resistance to the oppressive rule of the English could be apprehended? That the people of Bengal did lose "their martial habits and character" and did become "timid and enervated" was admitted by Lord Minto in the letter to his wife.

Death of Jaswantrao Holkar and After

The English did not yet consider themselves completely immune to the Maratha menace. Although peace treaties had been entered into by them with Sindhia, Berar and Holkar, yet none of them had been so reduced as to cease to be a danger, individually or collectively, to the future of the English in India. Jaswantrao was the one most feared by the English. Captain Grant Duff (*History of India,* p. 606) has thus described Jaswantrao Holkar:

> "The character was that hardy spirit of energy and enterprise, which though, like that of his countrymen, boundless in success, was also not to be discouraged by trying reverses. He was likewise better educated than Marathas in general..."

In 1808, Jaswantrao became insane and this gave the English a chance to acquire an indirect hold on the administration and affairs of his State. Two parties had sprung up in Holkar's *Durbar,* each trying to carry on the government during Holkar's insanity. The Marathas constituted one party and the Pindaris, led by Amir Khan, constituted the other. The two parties ultimately agreed, probably with the "friendly" mediation of the English, that Amir Khan was to carry on the administration of the State on behalf and in the name of Maharani Tulsibai, wife of the insane Maharaja. Jaswantrao died shortly afterwards and his widow, Maharani Tulsibai, adopted as son and heir to her deceased husband, Malharrao, a boy of four. The administration continued to be, as before, entirely in the hands and under the control of Amir Khan.

Amir Khan has been mentioned before more than once and we would now quote from Nolan's *History of the British Empire* (pp. 510, 521):

> "Among the chiefs who received favours from the English was one Amir Khan ... This person had, in spite of previous treaties, a considerable portion of Holkar's territory made over to him by Lord Minto, and a formal treaty sealed the bond of amity between this desperate robber and murderer and the East India Company ... The intrigues between the English and Amir Khan against the integrity of Holkar's dominion were not honourable to our nation. In connection with them ... perjury, perfidy, abduction, assassination, murder, plunder, revolt and civil war rent and stained realms which had owned the sovereignty of the once far-renowned Holkar."

Deliberate Incitement

After Holkar, the English apprehensions centred round Sindhia and Berar. During the war, some of their regions had been seized and occupied by the English. The territories of both adjoined areas under English rule. The English apprehension was that either of them might make an armed attempt to get back from the English the regions occupied by them during the war. The financial condition of the Company ruled out the enlisting of an army large enough to guard all the borders between English territory and that of Sindhia or Berar. To get over the difficult situation, recourse was had by the English to intrigues. They sent secret agents to incite revolts in the territories of the Maratha Chiefs and armed clashes between the Chief themselves. The English also incited and encouraged the Pindaris to pillage the Maratha territories. To quote Grant Duff once again:

> "It was expected that their (the Maratha Chiefs') domestic wars, the plunder of their neighbours, and the fear of losing what they possessed would deter them from hostile proceedings against the British Government."

The Pindaris

Before proceeding with our narrative, we would like to describe the Pindaris. They were South Indian Pathans whose main profession was soldiering. They served as horsemen in the armies of many rulers in South India and provided their own mounts. Thousands of them served under the Maratha rulers who considered them to be the most courageous and trustworthy of all men in their armies. Their loyalty to their employer was evidenced by the fact that although they were Muslims, they fought tenaciously for the Marathas against the Moghal Emperor, Aurangzeb. A Pindari chief, Nasroo Khan, was a trusted commander in Shivaji's cavalry. The Peshwa Bajirao I conquered Malwa mainly with the help of his Pindari horsemen. Some 15,000 horsemen under the Pindari chief, Hool Khan, fought on the side of the Marathas in the Third Battle of Panipat.

The entire Pindari tribe was composed of separate military groups, each under its own elected head called *Durray* or *Labbar*, elected unanimously by the group. Vacancies in the office of the *Durray* were filled also by unanimous election. Hindus were also freely enlisted in the Muslim Pindari military groups, who fought side by side with the Marathas against their co-religionists. In this connection, we would quote an English writer:

> "No great religious enmity would ever appear to have existed between the Marathas and Mohammadans. The same language is common to both, many of their customs are the same and the former have adopted many of the titles of the latter. The Generals of Sindhia, and the other Maratha chiefs, are often Mohammadans; and Brahmans frequently govern the Courts of Mussalman Princes." (*Origin of the Pindaris* by an Officer in the Service of the Honourable East India Company, 1818, p. 149)

The terms on which the Pindaris served the Maratha Princes were unusual and interesting. As instances may be quoted the free grants of lands made to the Pindaris by the Sindhia and Holkar *Durbars* along the Narmada river in return for military service. The Pindaris settled down in thousands on these lands and earned their livelihood in times of peace by agriculture. They kept ponies and bullocks for transporting their produce to the market. Those settled on Sindhia's lands were called "Sindhia Shahi," whilst those on Holkar's land were called "Holkar Shahi." In times of war every able-bodied male Pindari horseman joined the colours with his horse for service in the army of the Prince on whose land he had been settled. Thousands of Pindari horsemen were in this way always at the beck and call of Sindhia and Holkar whenever either of them went to war. Two well-known Pindari chieftains, Cheetoo Khan and Kareem Khan, had received from Doulatrao Sindhia *Jagirs* and the title of "Nawab". Similarly Amir Khan was the noted Pindari chieftain with Jaswantrao Holkar.

Pindaris as English Tools

Marquess Wellesley had realised at the very start that most of Jaswantrao's military strength lay in his Pindari horsemen, and had consequently made overtures to Holkar's Pindari chief, Amir Khan. As mentioned before, the latter had been won over but only to the extent that suited Amir Khan. Marquess Wellesley adopted other means too for reducing Holkar's potential strength which he might derive from the Pindaris and established friendly relations with some Pindari chieftains, whom he incited and helped to raid and plunder the territories of some Indian rulers. Fighting was in the Pindari blood and the Pindaris readily agreed to tow the English line. General Wellesley too tried to get the Peshwa to employ the Pindaris and enlisted some 3,000 Pindari recruits to be absorbed in the Peshwa's army. The use to which these recruits were to be put in case the Peshwa refused to employ them is clearly set fourth in the letter which General Wellesley wrote to General Stuart on 29th March, 1803:

> "If he (the Peshwa) should not approve of retaining them, they may either be discharged, or may be employed in the plunder of the enemy without pay ... and at all events, supposing His Highness should refuse to pay their expenses ... the charge to the Company will be trifling in comparison with the benefit which this detachment must derive from keeping this body of Pindaris out of Holkar's services." (Duke of Wellington's *Despatches*, Vol. I, pp. 120, 121)

The English relations with the Pindaris became so friendly that, according to Grant Duff, even an unarmed lone Englishman could pass unmolested through the Pindari raiders' camps. The East India Company paid money to the Pindaris and encouraged them to raid the Indian rulers' territories. That and the inciting of the Pindaris to revolt against their Maratha masters were at that time an integral part of the Company's settled policy. It led, however, to such an increase in the power of the Pindaris that the English decided to reduce it, and with that end in view they started dividing the Pindari chieftains by promoting dissensions and fights among them. The Company also stopped further payments of money to several of them. The Pindaris retaliated by raiding the English territories too. That, however, did not seem to bother the English as they considered it to be in their interests that their Indian subjects should live in perpetual fear of raids and thereby lose courage and character.

The most powerful of all the Pindari chieftains was Amir Khan who was at the zenith of his strength and political influence as the virtual ruler of the deceased Jaswantrao Holkar's State. The English had befriended him and paid large amounts of money for their own ends and Amir Khan had been of immense service to them. But now that their purpose had been served, they considered their erstwhile tool a menace, and adopted a double-faced policy towards Amir Khan, which is best illustrated by the English-engineered Amir Khan's attack on Berar.

Attack on Berar

Besides their aim of reducing Amir Khan's power, the English also wanted to place the Raja of Berar in serious difficulties so that he felt compelled to enter into the Subsidiary Alliance with the English. The latter had been 'trying for some years to rope him too into the notorious Subsidiary Alliance. On 24th March, 1805, Marquess Wellesley had informed the Company's Directors that the English Resident at Nagpur (Berar's capital) had been repeatedly pressing the Raja and his Ministers to conclude the Subsidiary Alliance with the English and pointed out to him the likelihood of Holkar attacking Berar after his (Holkar's) war with the English. If the attack materialised, the Raja was told, the English would help him if he was already in alliance with them. But the Resident's efforts had failed and so "it appeared to be more advisable," wrote Marquess Wellesley, "to leave the Raja to the operation of events on his mind."

How the Attack was Engineered

The English got the Nizam to offer monetary and military help to Amir Khan if the latter attacked Berar under an excuse which was suggested and later used by Amir Khan. It was alleged that when Jaswantrao was at Nagpur, some very valuable jewellery of his was retained by the Raja of Berar for safe custody. Amir Khan as the head of the administration in the deceased Jaswantrao's State demanded the jewellery from the Raja and, getting no "satisfactory" reply from him, started preparations for an invasion of Berar's territory. The English had, in their treaty with Jaswantrao, given an undertaking that they would not in any way interfere in the internal affairs and administration of Holkar's State and, more particularly, in Holkar's disputes with Berar. Relying on this treaty, Amir Khan marched on Berar and reached its border in January, 1809.

Amir Khan Betrayed

On reaching Berar's border, Amir Khan was astounded to find the Company's army facing him and barring his progress. It would appear that the Raja of Berar had also been duped into believing that the Nizam and Amir Khan, both Mussalmans, had conspired to attack the Maratha Raja of Berar's territory adjoining the Nizam's dominion and to bring it under Amir Khan's rule. It is to be noted that even so, the Raja of Berar had not asked for the Company's help or for its troops to be sent for the "defence" of his border. Nor was there any agreement between him and the English to the effect that the latter would give military help to the Raja. It is evident, therefore, that Lord Minto sent these troops only to fight Amir Khan. We will quote Prof. H. H. Wilson on the situation and on Amir Khan's reaction:

> "He appealed with unanswerable justice, although with no avail, to the stipulation of the existing treaty with Holkar …

which engaged that the British Government would not in any manner interfere in his affairs; ... he argued that the conduct of the Government was a manifest infraction of the treaty, and a breach of the solemn promises made to Jaswantrao, that it would not meddle with his claims upon the Raja of Berar. These representations were no longer likely to be of any weight." (Mill, Vol. VII, p. 210)

Amir Khan retired from Berar's border and the English considered it inadvisable to pursue him.

Lord Minto's Policy with Regard to Indian Rulers

This was the kind of policy followed by Lord Minto for minimising the chances of any opposition by their own Indian subjects and by Indian rulers like Holkar, Sindhia, Bhonsle and others. The Company's troops were also sent against the Raja of Bundelkhand and against Travancore in the south, where there was some desultory fighting. Ultimately all of them were subdued and subjected to the English will.

Background of Lord Minto's Foreign Policy

We have to go back a decade to the regime of Marquess Wellesley for the background, as Lord Minto's foreign policy was conditioned by it and was in certain respects more important and far-reaching in its effects than his domestic policy.

Marquess Wellesley's Foreign Policy

Zaman Shah was then the King of Afghanistan and the *Subas* (rulers) of Punjab and Sindh were his tributaries. Reports had been persistent for some time about his projected invasion of British possessions in

India. Marquess Wellesley took certain steps to nip the trouble in the bud. He incited the rulers of Punjab and Sindh against Zaman Shah. He also sent secret agents to bribe King Baba Khan of Iran and get him to invade his co-religionist Zaman Shah's neighbouring territory. On 8th October, 1798, Marquess Wellesley wrote to the Hon. J. Duncan, Governor of Bombay:

> "I concur with you in thinking that the services of the native agent, whom you have appointed to reside at Bushire may be usefully employed for the purpose mentioned in the letter; and as the probability of the invasion of Hindustan by Zaman Shah seems to increase, I am of opinion that Mehdi Ali Khan cannot too soon commence his operations at the Court of Baba Khan ... It would certainly be a very desirable object to excite such an alarm in that quarter as may either induce Zaman Shah to relinquish his projected expedition, or may recall him, should he have actually embarked on it."

Mehdi Ali Khan was an Iranian noble domiciled in India. From Bushire he wrote many letters to King Baba Shah of Iran and incited him against Zaman Shah on religious grounds. Baba Shah was a Shia Muslim, whilst Zaman Shah was a Sunni. The perpetual hostility between the Shia and Sunni sects of Islam is proverbial, and Mehdi Ali took advantage of it. In his letters to Baba Khan, he described imaginary atrocities committed by the Sunnis on the Shias of Lahore at the instance of Zaman Shah and alleged that the latter had to flee from Lahore and seek refuge in British India. An attack on Zaman Shah, urged Mehdi Ali, would, therefore, be a service rendered to the Shia faith. As an instance of downright lies unhesitatingly resorted to by Mehdi Ali in his letters to Baba Khan may be mentioned his statement that 300,000 of Siraj-ud-daula's soldiers had been routed by only 700 of the Company's brave men (*History of Persia* by Lt. Col. P. M. Sykes, Vol. II, p. 397). It would appear that Mehdi Ali's letters did have some effect on Baba Khan, the King of Iran, who in the autumn of 1799 invited Mehdi Ali to his court at Teheran. Mehdi Ali went and made lavish presents in cash and kind, at the cost of the Company's Indian Exchequer, to King Baba Khan and his courtiers. He then returned to Bushire.

To carry on the good work commenced by Mehdi Ali to consolidate the hostility engendered by him between King Baba Khan of Iran and King Zaman Shah of Afghanistan, Marquess Wellesley formally deputed his special envoy, Capt. Malcolm (later Sir John Malcolm) to the Court of Persia. The purpose of Capt. Malcolm's mission is clearly set forth in the Governor-General's letter of instructions to John Malcolm dated 10th October, 1799, from which we quote the following:

> "At Bombay you will be furnished by the Governor-in-Council with copies of all the correspondence which has passed between him and Mehdi Ali Khan, a native agent employed for some time past by Mr. Duncan, under the instructions of the Governor-General, in opening and conducting a negotiation at the Court of Persia with a view to preventing Zaman Shah from executing his frequently renewed projects against Hindosthan."

> "You will apprise the Court of Persia of your deputation as soon as possible after your arrival, either at Basrah or at Bagdad, intimating, in general terms, that the object of it is to revive the good understanding and friendship which anciently subsisted between the Persian and the British Governments. It is not desirable that you should be more particular with any person who may be sent to meet you, or to ascertain the design of your mission; but if much pressed on the subject you may signify that, among other things, you have been instructed to endeavour to extend and improve the commercial intercourse between Persia and the British possessions in India."

Nothing could more plainly indicate the truly sinister activities which Capt. Malcolm was instructed to be engaged in than the above-suggested cloak for covering the same. The letter proceeds:

> "The primary purpose of your mission is to prevent Zaman Shah from invading Hindostan; ... The next objective of His Lordship is to engage the Court of Persia to act vigorously and heartily against the French in the event of their attempting at any time to penetrate to India by any route in which it may be practicable for the King of Persia to oppose their progress."

Malcolm was further given the authority:

> "to engage to prevent Zaman Shah, by such means as shall be concerted between His Majesty and Captain Malcolm, from invading any part of Hindostan, and in the event of his crossing the Attock, or the actual invasion of Hindostan by that prince, the King of Persia to pledge himself to the adoption of such measures as shall be necessary for the purpose of compelling Zaman Shah to return immediately to the defence of his own dominions".

Apparently, Marquess Wellesley considered it necessary to tempt King Baba Shah with money in order to induce him to fight his co-religionist. Malcolm was instructed to undertake that:

> "the Company would arrange to pay to the King of Persia for his service, either an annual fixed subsidy of three lacs of rupees during the period that the proposed treaty shall continue in force, or a proportion, not exceeding one-third, of such extraordinary expense as His Majesty shall any time actually and *bona fide* incur for the specific purposes stated in the foregoing article of the proposed treaty".

The letter proceeded to instruct Capt. Malcolm that:

> "In considering the different means by which Zaman Shah may be kept in check during the period required, you will naturally pay due attention to those which may be derived from the exiled brothers of that Prince, now resident in Persia under the protection of Baba Khan."

The exiled brothers of Zaman, Shah were Mahmood and Shah Shuja.

Finally, the letter instructed Capt. Malcolm as follows:

> "You will endeavour during your residence at the Court of Baba Khan to obtain an accurate account of the strength and resources of Zaman Shah, and of his political relations with his different neighbours, and to establish some means of obtaining hereafter the most correct and speedy information on the subject of his future intentions and movements."

(Governor-General's letter of instructions to John Malcolm, dated 10th October, 1799)

Success of the English Intrigues Against Zaman Shah

Within two years of Capt. Malcolm's arrival in Iran, internal strifes and disorders leading to bloodshed and revolts became rampant in Afghanistan. In 1801 Mahmood, the step-brother of Zaman Shah, deposed, blinded and imprisoned Zaman Shah and seized the throne for himself. But Mahmood himself was deposed by the third brother, Shah Shuja, who released Zaman Shah and himself occupied the throne. Shah Shuja was a creature of the English and it suited them to have him as King of Afghanistan. It would thus appear that Capt. Malcolm had been sent to Iran not so much for the purpose of establishing close friendly relations with Baba Khan, as for preparing the ground for an English attack on Afghanistan by sowing internal dissensions in that country. Marquess Wellesley also sent his special agents to Sindh and Punjab for getting the rulers there to combine in a conspiracy against the King of Kabul.

Situation When Lord Minto Took Over

The English fear of an invasion of their possessions in India had disappeared completely but its place had been taken by the probability of a combined invasion by Russia and France from the west. The 1807 Treaty of Tilsit between the Emperors of Russia and France appeared to be the forerunner of such a joint invasion with the aim of acquiring and dividing the English possessions between Russia and France. To defeat this objective the British Government sent Sir H. Jones as England's Ambassador to Iran and Lord Minto also sent Sir John Malcolm as his envoy to help Sir H. Jones. The latter negotiated a treaty with Iran, pledging English non-interference in any future hostilities between Iran and Afghanistan. At the same time another English envoy, Elphinstone, was sent to Afghanistan to negotiate a treaty with the King of Afghanistan, promising English support and help to the King in case the latter attacked Iran. This double-faced policy indicates that whilst the English, on the one hand, considered it essential for the security of their newly-acquired Indian empire to keep Iran and Afghanistan on their side, in case the joint Russian-French invasion materialised, on the other, they considered it necessary to keep Iran and Afghanistan at loggerheads with each other.

Lord Minto's Treaties with Sindh

The Company's trade with Sindh had been at a standstill for some seven years following the expulsion in 1802 of the Company's trade agent from Sindh due to his intolerable maltreatment of Sindhi craftsmen. Lord Minto sent Capt. Seaton as his special envoy to Hyderabad, the capital of Sindh. Seaton made the Amir at Hyderabad believe that Shah Shuja was plotting to dethrone the Amir and replace him by a former deposed Amir, Abdul Nabi, then in exile. Seaton offered to the Amir English help for defeating this plot. The simple Amir believed the story and agreed to negotiate a treaty with the Company. But when the Amir wanted it to be expressly provided in the treaty that the English would help him if the King of Afghanistan attacked him, the negotiations were held up, because at that very time the English were negotiating a treaty of friendship with Afghanistan.

At this juncture, Iran not only offered help to the Amir of Sindh against Afghanistan, but actually dispatched a detachment to render that help. This was intolerable to the English and Capt. Seaton hurriedly signed a treaty with the Amir, providing for mutual help against the respective enemies of the English and the Amir. Lord Minto, however, did dot ratify this treaty as it jeopardised the friendly relations of the English with Afghanistan which he was anxious to preserve and promote. He, therefore, sent another envoy, Smith, from Bombay to Hyderabad (Sindh). Smith succeeded in persuading the Amir to rescind the treaty made with Capt. Seaton and to enter into a fresh treaty of "perpetual friendship" with the Company on 23rd August, 1809. It provided for the re-establishment of trade between the Government of Sindh and the Company and for the mutual exchange of trade agents of both. It also provided that no

Frenchman was to be permitted to reside in Sindh. The stationing of the Company's trade agent in Sindh permanently was designed to facilitate (i) the promotion of dissensions between Sindh and Afghanistan and (ii) the future English intrigues in Sindh itself.

Maharaja Ranjit Singh

We must go back to the regime of Marquess Wellesley for the events preceding Lord Minto's treaty with Maharaja Ranjit Singh.

Ranjit Singh was the ruler of the Indian territory beyond the river Sutlej and was supposed to be a tributary of the King of Afghanistan. He was a very capable military leader and had the ambition of throwing off even the titular suzerain of Afghanistan and of carving out a fully independent kingdom for himself. This suited the policy of Marquess Wellesley of maintaining a buffer state between Afghanistan and the Marathas, which could be used against either of them as and when it became expedient. He, therefore, encouraged Ranjit Singh's ambitious plans and plotted with him and some other Sikh chieftains against the Marathas. It was mainly because Ranjit Singh trusted and relied upon the friendship of the English, that he not only refused to help Jaswantrao Holkar but actually co-operated with the Company's troops pursuing Jaswantrao when the latter left Lahore. It has been narrated earlier that the English had won over Patiala and other Sikh chieftains to their side during the Second Maratha War.

Ranjit Singh could have united with these Sikh chieftains and thus established a unitary Sikh hegemony over the whole of the Punjab. But self-interest and short-sightedness led him astray and he offered to the English his help in establishing their rule over the territories of the Sikh chieftains to the south of the river Sutlej for a *quid pro quo*. His offer was communicated by Marquess Wellesley to the Company's Directors:

> "Raja Ranjit Singh, the Raja of Lahore and the principal amongst the Sikh chieftains, has transmitted proposals to the Commander-in-Chief for the transfer of the territory belonging to that nation south of the river Sutlej, on the condition of mutual defence against the respective

enemies of that chieftain and of the British nation." (Governor-General-in-Council to the Hon'ble Secret Committee, etc., 29th September, 1803)

But the English had no use of Ranjit Singh's offer, as they were directly entering into treaties with the Sikh chieftains and taking them under their "protection" one by one. One of the terms of the treaties was that if a chieftain had no son of his own, he could not adopt any and in the absence of any other lawful successor, the territory of the deceased chieftain would be merged in the Company's territory. So some states like Kaithal were annexed later. The English then proceeded to incite the Sikh chieftains under their "protection" against Ranjit Singh himself. When the latter realised that siding with the English was not paying dividends, he resolved to bring the dissident Sikh chieftains under his control and thus extend his dominion southwards right up to the river Jumna. Ranjit Singh began his march. News was brought to him that the Company's troops were assembling at the Jumna to thwart his plans and help the chieftains. He wrote to Lord Minto and sought confirmation of the news and stated that the territory on his side of the Jumna was under his rule except for such parts as were in the Company's possession. He, therefore, pressed for the maintenance of this position. Lord Minto sent Charles Metcalfe (later well-known as Sir Charles Metcalfe) as his special agent to Ranjit Singh's *Durbar*, ostensibly as a token of the English friendship for him, and at the same time directed the Commander-in-Chief to be ready to march. He wrote:

> "There is reason to believe that a considerable portion of the country usurped by Ranjit Singh is strongly disaffected, and should any grand effort be made and be crowned with success, nothing would be more advantageous to our interests than the substitution of friends and dependants for hostile and rival powers throughout the country between our frontier and the Indus." (*Lord Minto in India*, p. 154)

Metcalfe left Delhi in August 1808 and on 11th September met Ranjit Singh at Kasur. He suggested to Ranjit Singh that in view of the imminence of a French attack on the Punjab, it would be advisable for him (Ranjit Singh) to enter into a treaty with the

English. "In the course of this conversation." Metcalfe later wrote to the Governor-General, "I endeavoured, in conformity to the instructions of the Supreme Government, to alarm the Raja for the safety of his territories, and at the same time to give him confidence in our protection" (Kaye's *Lives of Indian Officers*, Vol. I, p. 394).

But it was not so easy to mislead Ranjit Singh, who wanted from Metcalfe a plain "yes" or "no" to the question: "Does the British Government recognise my sovereignty on both sides of the river Sutlej?" Metcalfe pleaded want of the requisite authority from his Government for his inability to answer the question then and there. Ranjit Singh was offended and immediately attacked several Rajas (chieftains) of that region (Doab) and exacted tributes from them.

Metcalfe continued to stay on with Ranjit Singh and later, when the English had fully completed their preparations, he sent to Ranjit Singh on 22nd September, 1808, a message that:

> "The British Government has decided that the States between the rivers Sutlej and Jumna are under British 'protection'. Those parts of the territory beyond Sutlej which were under your rule from before will continue to be so, but those which you have recently occupied will have to be given back by you to the Company. To get this decision enforced a detachment of the Company's army will be stationed on the left bank of Jumna."

Ranjit Singh was furious when he received this message but restrained himself. That very day he sent a message to Metcalfe to the effect that "the decision of the British Government is so astounding that I must consult other chieftains before I convey to you my own decision." He then left for Amritsar for consultations with his Ministers. Metcalfe went with him to Amritsar.

After consultations with his Ministers, Ranjit Singh was ready to fight the English. The latter then suggested to him that if he desired to expand his dominion, he was welcome to do so by attacking and annexing Afghanistan without any interference by them, provided Ranjit Singh left to them the territory across the Sutlej. As a part of pressure-tactics and to alarm Ranjit Singh, some detachments of the Company's army were sent from Delhi to Ludhiana under

Col. Ochterlony. Some Punjab chieftains, too, appeared to have been won over by the English. Ultimately, Ranjit Singh retired his army from the region and on 25th April, 1809, entered into a treaty with the English. Its terms embodied the decisions of the British Government as conveyed to Ranjit Singh by Metcalfe in his above quoted communication. The only concession to Ranjit Singh was that he was allowed a free hand to invade Afghanistan if he wanted to. Thus, Lord Minto succeeded in getting what he wanted, namely, an increase in the causes of hostility between the Sikhs and the Afghans, a buffer state (Punjab) between the British possessions and the latter's future invaders and lastly a clear field for the expansion of the British Empire right up to the river Sutlej.

Lord Minto and Afghanistan

In addition to his plans for stirring up war between Baba Khan (King of Iran) and Afghanistan through Malcolm, as also between Ranjit Singh and Afghanistan through Metcalfe, Lord Minto, in further pursuance of his plans, sent Elphinstone as his special agent to Afghanistan. Elphinstone's real mission was to do his very best to incite Shah Shuja (King of Afghanistan) to go to war with Iran. But it was given out that he was sent to establish close friendship with Shah Shuja as a safeguard against the projected Russian-French invasion of India.

Elphinstone avoided passing through Ranjit Singh's territory and took the circuitous route through Bikaner, Bahawalpur to Multan where he was held up because Shah Shuja and his Ministers refused him permission to enter Afghanistan. There were serious internal uprisings and revolts in Afghanistan and they could not ignore the possibility of Elphinstone encouraging and promoting the revolts. Ultimately, Elphinstone succeeded in assuring Shah Shuja that his mission was nothing but merely to establish friendship between the English and Shah Shuja. The latter then permitted Elphinstone to enter Afghanistan and received him hospitably at Peshawar on 5th March, 1809.

Elphinstone tried to alarm Shah Shuja with the imminence of the invasion of Afghanistan by the combined forces of Iran, Russia and France. At the same time he assured him of the English readiness to help him, if he co-operated with them. He was pressed to ban the entry of Iranians or the French into Afghanistan and to help the English to thwart the threatened invasion of India. But all this had little or no effect on Shah Shuja and his Ministers, who were too harassed by their own internal disorders to take any immediate precautions for warding off a future invasion. They told Elphinstone that if the English wanted to be really friendly, they should first help the Afghan King to put down the revolts:

> "The Afghan ministers, it must be admitted, argued the case acutely and not without some amount of fairness. They could not see why, if the English wished the King of Cabul to help them against their enemies, they should not in their turn help the King to resist his; but as it was, they said all the advantage was on the English side, and all the danger on the side of the King." (Sir John Kaye's *Life of Indian Officers*, Vol. I, pp. 241-42)

Elphinstone himself records his conversation with Mulla Jaffar, the Afghan Minister:

> "He said that he did not believe that we intended to impose upon the King, but he did not think that we were so plain as we pretended to be ... He frankly owned that we had the character of being very designing and that most people thought it necessary to be very vigilant in all transactions with us."

Of course, Elphinstone knew quite well that the internal disorders and revolts in Afghanistan had been deliberately brought about by English intrigues during the past decade and so all that he could offer was no more than profuse protestations of the English friendship, which cut no ice with Shah Shuja and his Ministers and Elphinstone was pressed to return to the English territory as soon as possible.

Although there was no longer any likelihood of France invading the British possessions in India, yet the bogey of Russia's intention to do so still persisted in the English mind and they decided to patch up some sort of treaty with Afghanistan by offering money to the latter. Shah Shuja promised to prevent the entry or passing through of Iranians or other enemies of the English through his territory in return for an annual subsidy which the English undertook to pay him.

Elphinstone returned to India through Punjab. He had exploited the opportunity presented by his visit to Afghanistan and collected valuable and important information about the different routes to Afghanistan from India and about the military strength of that country. He had also contacted the various Pathan tribes living alongside of these routes. Incidentally, a French writer states that the English had even then planned to annex the entire territory of Ranjit Singh after his death and therefore had incited and encouraged him to expand it by invading and annexing the adjoining Afghan territory.

Annexation of French and Dutch Islands

Some small islands in the Indian Ocean belonged to the French and the Dutch. In 1809, Lord Minto sent a naval expedition to invade the French Islands and the English occupied them in 1810. In 1811, the Dutch Islands were similarly taken. The cost of the two operations was exacted from India.

Mutiny of White Soldiers and Officers

Lord Minto's regime was, from the English point of view, eminently successful in furthering the expansion of their Indian Empire and in meeting all the exigencies of the changing situations as they arose. But he could not keep satisfied the Company's white soldiers and officers. The financial stringency had forced him to curtail expenses in all departments including the army. The numerous allowances which the European officers were till then getting, in addition to their pay, were stopped in the Madras Presidency in 1808. The European officers retaliated by an armed revolt in which the European soldiers joined them at Masulipattam, Seringapattam, Hyderabad and several other places. A revolting European battalion from Chittaldrug was on its way to Seringapattam to join the revolting European battalion there, when it clashed with a loyal European battalion. Both fired at each other. The trouble spread and became so grave that Lord Minto himself went to Madras to pacify the rebels. Some European officers from other parts of India were also sent to the Madras Presidency on the same mission. Somehow the revolt was quelled but none of the European rebels was hanged or blown off from the cannon's mouth, a penalty which as a rule, was exacted from the Company's coloured or Indian mutineers.

> "... This happened at a critical period. If Ranjit Singh had then crossed the Sutlej, and marching through the territory of the Marathas and Bundelkhand, which were not then reduced to submission, and marched to Bengal, the British power would no doubt have re-entered into the limits conquered by Lord Clive;—but the revolters of Madras soon perceived the danger and returned of themselves to their duty ... and the Government had the weakness not to shoot a single officer."
> (M. Victor Jacquemont's *Letters from India*, Vol. I, pp. 323-24)

Lord Minto returned to England in 1813.

DELIBERATE DESTRUCTION OF INDIAN INDUSTRIES AND TRADE

The Marquis of Hastings

The Marquis of Hastings succeeded Lord Minto as Governor-General and took charge on 11th September, 1813. He was also appointed Commander-in-Chief of the Company's forces in India. Of the three Governors-General—Wellesley, Hastings and Dalhousie—who expanded and established the British Empire in India on firm foundations, Hastings' contribution to it was the most important from at least one point of view. The programme of systematically destroying the old indigenous Indian industries and handicrafts and of promoting at the cost of Indians English industries and trade was initiated at the beginning of the nineteenth century. It was carried out most successfully by Hastings. Later this became the guiding factor of the policy followed by England in relation to India.

Ancient Industries and Trade of India

For thousands of years before the first Englishman set foot on Indian soil, cloth and other goods manufactured in the country were being exported to China, Japan, Ceylon, Iran, Arabia, Cambodia, Egypt, Africa, Italy, Mexico, etc. In England itself there was a "passion for coloured East Indian calicoes, which spread through all classes of the community ...At the end of the seventeenth century, great quantities of cheap, graceful Indian calicoes, muslins, chintzes were imported into England and that found such favour that the woolen and silk manufacturers were seriously alarmed" (Lecy's *History of England in the Eighteenth Century,* Vol. II, p. 158 and pp. 255–56).

The English had perhaps never dreamt of trying to sell in India textiles manufactured in England. The economic conditions in the India of those days was described thus by the noted English historian, Dr. Robertson, in 1817:

> "In all ages, gold and silver, particularly the latter, have been the commodities exported with the greatest profit to India.

In no part of the earth do the natives depend so little upon foreign countries, either for the necessaries or luxuries of life. The blessings of a favourable climate and a fertile soil, augmented by their own ingenuity, afford whatever they desire. In consequence of this, trade with them has always been carried on in one uniform manner, and the precious metals have been in exchange for their peculiar production, whether of nature or art." (*A Historical Disquisition Concerning India*, New Edition, London, 1817, p. 180)

He also confirms the fact that till the beginning of the nineteenth century, Indian international trade continued on the same lines (ibid., p. 203).

Till the second half of the eighteenth century, the weavers and craftsmen of England lagged far behind their Indian counterparts so far as the beauty, durability, cheapness and the quantities and exports of their respective products were concerned. Up to that time the only aim of the European traders reaching India was to arrange for the imports of the Indian manufacturers into their respective countries. This was the sole original objective of the East India Company too. Thousands of sailing boats and ships were used for transportation of these goods.

Contribution of the 'Plunder' from India to English Industrial Progress

According to the European writer Baines, the spinning contraptions used in England were primitive and crude and were manually operated till 1760. Watt's invention for using steam-power presented possibilities of immense progress. But the exploitation of the invention involved a huge capital outlay and the English spinners did not have any capital. Nor had their Government any money to spare.

According to Brooks Adams,

"... had Watt lived fifty years earlier, he and his invention must have perished together. Possibly since the world began, no investment has ever yielded the profit reaped from the Indian plunder, because for nearly fifty years Great Britain stood without a competitor ... Between 1760 and 1815, the growth was very rapid and prodigious." (*The Law of Civilization and Decay,* pp. 263–64)

The money to improve their sadly backward industries was found by the English through unprecedented plunder, in various ways and forms. William Digby, C.I.E. (*Prosperous British India,* p. 33) has estimated that between the Battles of Plassey and Waterloo, the total of this unadulterated "plunder" amounted to nearly a thousand million pounds sterling or over twenty-five crores of rupees per year which the Company's employees looted from the Indians and sent to England in 58 years (1757–1815). The staggering total pales into insignificance the notorious loot by Mahmud Ghazni and Mohammad Ghory in the wake of their invasions of India.

Effects of Napoleon's Domination of Europe

Napoleon Bonaparte had in the beginning of the nineteenth century become the dictator of practically the whole of Europe. England alone had been opposing him and had spent huge sums in bribes and subsidies to some European rulers in an effort to win them over against Napoleon. But the English resources were not inexhaustible and the only source of their income was their European trade, which Napoleon had banned. England was at the end of its tether so far as money was concerned and except India, there was no other country to which the English could look for recouping their heavy losses caused by the end of their European trade as also for finding more money to oppose Napoleon who was a threat to their Indian Empire too.

Coercion in Commerce

We now proceed to give instances of the ways and means adopted by the Company to loot Indian weavers. Major B. D. Basu has quoted in his book, *The Ruin of Indian Trade and Industries* (pp. 78–79), some extracts from a volume published by an Englishman, Richards, in 1813. Richards had described the way in which "business" was carried on at the Company's factory in Surat. The description is founded on events recorded in the daily journal maintained at the factory. Richards writes:

> "... the Surat investment was provided under the most rigorous and oppressive system of coercion ... the weavers were compelled to enter into engagements and to work for the Company, contrary to their own interests, and of course to their own inclinations, choosing in some instances to pay a heavy fine rather than be compelled to work ... they could get better prices from Dutch, Portuguese, French and Arab merchants for inferior goods than the Company paid them for standard or superior goods ... the object of the commercial resident was, as he himself observed, to establish and maintain the complete monopoly ... of the whole of piece-goods trade at reduced or prescribed prices ... In the prosecution of this object compulsion and punishment were carried to such a height as to induce several weavers to quit the profession; to prevent which, they were not allowed to enlist as Sepoys, or even on one occasion to pass out of the city gates without permission from the English chiefs ... So long as the weavers were the subjects of the Nawab, frequent application was made to him to punish and coerce weavers ... the Nawab was but a tool in the hands of the British Government ... Neighbouring Princes were also prevailed on to give orders in their districts, that the Company's merchants and brokers should have a preference over all others, and that on no account should piece-goods be sold to other persons ... Subsequently to the transfer of Surat to the British Government, the authority of the *Adalat* (our own Court of Justice) was constantly interposed to enforce a similar series of arbitrary and oppressive acts ... As long as the Company continued to trade in piece-goods at Surat, this was the uniform practice of their commercial servants. It may be taken as a specimen of the practice of other factories."

A letter written on 19th July, 1814, by Lord Wellesley to the Madras Government testifies to similar practices in all the Company's factories throughout the Madras Presidency.

The Bengal Enactment of 1793

The above practices were improved upon in Bengal and given a more legalised form. Weavers were inveigled into accepting from the Company some small amount of money as earnest money and part-payment of the price of the entire quantity of goods which the weavers undertook to produce and deliver to the Company within a specified period. In 1793, the English Government of Bengal enacted a law which made it an offence for any weaver owing any money to the Company or having any connection whatsoever with the piece-goods trade of the Company, to cease working for the Company, or to work for another or even for himself. Every weaver, who had unsuspectingly accepted an advance from the Company, was thus reduced to virtual slavery for the rest of his life under the Company. If a weaver was unable to produce or supply the specified quantity of goods within the specified time, then he was locked up and all his belongings including raw material and finished products were confiscated by the Company under the said law.

Atrocities on Silk Producers and Weavers

People in the silk-producing areas of Bengal where the Company had established their factories were the victims of even worse atrocities. The price of silk, raw and finished, had increased throughout Bengal in 1827. But the English chiefs of the Company reduced the prices at which they compelled the silk producers and weavers to sell to the Company (*Vide* Mr. Saunder's evidence in March, 1831 before the Parliamentary Committee).

We quote below an Englishman, Henry Grouger, about the practices of the Company relating to their silk trade:

> "The East India Company had their commercial residents established in different parts of the silk districts, whose emoluments mainly depended on the quantity of silk they secured for the Company ... The system pursued by both parties was thus: advances of money before each bund

or crop were made to two classes of persons—first, to the cultivator who reared the cocoons: next to the large class of winders who formed the mass of the population of the surrounding villages. By the first the raw material was secured; by the last the labour for working it ..."

"I will state a case of everyday occurrence ... A native wishing to sell me the cocoons he produces for the season takes my advance of money; a village of winders does the same. After this contract is made, two of the Resident's servants are dispatched to the village, the one bearing a bag of rupees, the other a book in which to register the names of the recipients. In vain does the man to whom the money is offered protest that he has entered into a prior engagement with me. If he refuses to accept it, a rupee is thrown into his house, his name is written before the witness who carries the bag, and that is enough. Under this iniquitous proceeding the Resident, by the authority committed to him, forcibly seizes my property and my labourers even at my door."

"Nor does the operation stop there. If I sued the man in Court for repayment of the money I had thus been defrauded of, the judge was compelled, before granting a decree in my favour, to ascertain from the commercial Resident whether the defaulter was in debt to the East India Company. If he was, a prior decree was given to the Resident and I lost my money." (*A Personal Narrative of Two Years' Imprisonment in Burma*, 1824–26, by Henry Grouger, p. 2)

Grouger has also asserted that the Resident had the unfettered right and authority to fix the prices payable by the Company for the silk thus acquired.

Atrocities Perpetrated

Ever since Siraj-ud-daulah's regime, the Company had been ceaselessly making all sorts of frantic efforts to secure the monopoly of the entire trade and industries in Bengal. What these efforts involved and led to is thus described by a noted Englishman, Bolts, in his book, *Considerations on Indian Affairs* (pp. 72, 74, 192–95), which was published only ten years after the Battle of Plassey:

> "To effect this, inconceivable oppressions and hardships have been practised towards the poor manufacturers and workmen of the country, who are, in fact, monopolised by the Company as so many slaves ... Various and innumerable are the methods of oppressing the poor weavers which are daily practised by the Company's agents and *gomashtas* in the country; such as by fines, imprisonments, floggings, forcing bonds from them, etc., by which the number of weavers in the country has been greatly decreased ... The weaver, therefore, desirous of obtaining the just price of his labour frequently attempts to sell his cloth-privately to others ... This occasions the English Company's *gomashta* to set his peons over the weaver to watch him, and not infrequently to cut the piece out of the loom when nearly finished.... therefore, every kind of oppression to manufacturers of all kinds of denominations throughout the whole country has daily increased; so much so that weavers, for daring to sell their goods, and dallals and pykars for having contributed to and connived at such sales, have, by the Company's agents, been frequently seized and imprisoned, confined in irons, fined considerable sums of money, flogged and deprived, in the most ignominious manner, of what they esteem most valuable, their castes ..."

> "It was not till the time of Seraj-ud-dowla that oppressions of the nature now described from the employing of *gomashtas,* commenced with the increasing power of the English Company ... in Seraj-ud-dowla's time ... above seven hundred families of weavers, in the districts round Jungalbarry, at once abandoned their country and their profession on account of oppressions of this nature, ... winders of raw silk were treated with such rigour during Lord Clive's late Government of Bengal, from a zeal for increasing the Company's investment on raw silk, that the most sacred laws of society were atrociously violated ... upon their inability to perform such agreements as have been forced upon them by the Company's agents, ... have had their goods seized and sold on the spot to make good their deficiency and have

been treated with such injustice, that instances have been known of their cutting off their thumbs to prevent their being forced to wind silk."

Manual silk-winding cannot be done without the use of the thumb.

The Cultivators' Plight

The treatment meted out to the actual tillers of the soil in Company-ruled areas was even worse. Bolts has written that the Company's commercial agents forced the cultivators to spend all their time in producing what the Company wanted to "purchase," and left the villagers with no time or money to look after or pay the rents for their fields. On the other hand, the Company's revenue-collectors harassed the cultivators to such an extent that the latter "not infrequently have by those harpies been necessitated to sell their children in order to pay their rents or otherwise obliged to fly the country" (ibid.).

Herbert Spencer on the Above Atrocities

Referring to the atrocities perpetrated by the Company from the second half of the eighteenth century to the first half of the nineteenth, the famous English philosopher, Herbert Spencer, writes:

> "Imagine how black must have been their deeds, when even the Directors of the Company admitted that the 'vast fortunes' acquired in the inland trade have been obtained by a scene of the most tyrannical and oppressive conduct that was ever known in any age or country." (*Social Statistics*, 1st Edition, p. 367)

This gives a true picture and proves that under the Company's rule, no value whatsoever was attached to the life, property, self-respect, traditions or the most sacred religious sentiments of the people, and all of them were trampled under foot most cruelly. Perhaps no other people at any period of history had been subjected to such inhuman treatment.

New Commercial Policy of 1813

We have given above the background of the Charter Act passed by the British Parliament in 1813. The previous Charter Act was passed, in 1793 which had invested the East India Company with all its powers and authority for twenty years. These were renewed and added to by the Charter Act of 1813. It initiated an era of forcing on India, by fair means or foul, the goods manufactured in England. In a way, the Act may well be called the root-cause of the widespread poverty in India and its utter helplessness. Before the Act, the East India Company alone enjoyed the monopoly of all trade and commerce between India and England. The Act put an end to this monopoly and the door was opened for every Englishman to trade with India on the pattern of the Company.

Mr. Tierney's Speech in the House of Commons

When the Bill was being debated in the Parliament, a member, Mr. Tierney, characterised it thus:

> "The general principle was to be that England was to force all her manufactures upon India, and not to take a single manufacture of India in return. It was true they should allow cotton to be brought; but then, having found out that they weave, by means of machinery, cheaper than the people of India, they would say,—'Leave off weaving; supply us with the raw material, and we will weave for you'. This might be a very natural principle for merchants and manufacturers to go upon, but it was rather too much to talk of the philosophy of it, or to rank the supporters of it as in a peculiar degree the friends of India. If instead of calling themselves the friends of India they had professed themselves its enemies, what more could they do than advise the destruction of Indian manufactures?"

Praiseworthy as Mr. Tierney's plain-speaking was, he appears to have made one slip. Subsequent events proved that the claim to be able to "weave by means of machinery cheaper than the people of India" was groundless.

Ways and Means Adopted for Ruining Indian Industries and Trade

Before taking decisions about the steps to be taken, the British Parliament appointed two Special Committees to examine some of the most prominent Englishmen who had been to India or lived or worked there, with a view to finding out the best ways and means of achieving what the Act aimed at. All the witnesses examined by the Committees declared that the Indian people did not need or want English manufactures and so an Indian market for them did not exist. The English rulers of India, nevertheless, adopted these ways and means. They were:

(i) English manufactures were imported into India either duty-free or with only a nominal import levy,

(ii) a heavy import duty was levied on the Indian manufactures imported into England so as to make it impossible for them to be sold in England at prices lower than those at which the English manufactures were selling in England,

(iii) new rules of procedure and methods of levying excise, octroi and other internal duties at new enhanced rates on Indian manufactures by the Company were framed and laid down, the object being

    (a) to facilitate and encourage and to increase the export of cotton and other raw material from India by English buyers and

    (b) to increase the Indian manufacturers' cost of production and to burden them and the Indian dealers with such difficulties and heavy duties as to make it impossible for them to produce goods for sale even in the Indian markets in competition with the imported English products, which were offered at cheaper prices, thus creating for them a virtual monopoly of the Indian consumers, and sounding the death-knell of the country's most paying and important industry.

(iv) the English traders and artisans were given special facilities and privileges as also financial help for living and working in India,

(v) the Indian artisans and craftsmen were subjected to intense pressure to make them disclose to the English or their agents their trade secrets or secret processes of finishing the goods, such as bleaching and colouring cotton fabrics. The English artisans were then instructed in the use of these processes. Exhibitions were also held in England to study the needs and the tastes of the Indian consumers and to help in finding out the jealously-guarded secret processes used by the Indian craftsmen,

(vi) railways were constructed for the quick transport of the English manufactures throughout the country, and of the raw material acquired by the English for export to England and

(vii) the British Empire was to be expanded to cover the entire country, so that the sale depots for the English manufactures could be established and run throughout India by the English.

Some Witnesses Before Parliamentary Committee

After the above measures had been taken and had been in use for about seventeen years, the British Parliament appointed a committee to inquire into and report on the extent to which they had succeeded in increasing England's trade with India.

Many witnesses were examined and asked to describe in detail the facilities provided to the English importers and merchants in India.

We summarise here a few of the statements given by some of the witnesses:

(i) Sargent, an English witness, stated that since 1814 no duty was levied on raw cotton exported from India to England, whilst the duty on the raw cotton exported from India to China was levied at five per cent.

(ii) Larpont, another English witness, stated that the rates of duties on the English manufactures had been substantially reduced to two-and-a-half per cent and that on some particular kinds of English manufactures no duty at all was levied. He also stated that land was ordered to be given on sixty years' lease to such English planters of indigo or coffee as wanted to settle down and carry on that business in India.

(iii) A third Englishman, Crawford, stated that the Charter Act of 1813 had forbidden the levy of any new duty on any English manufactures imported into India without the prior permission of the authorities in England. The latter also drew up a schedule of the existing duties with reduced rates and sent it to the Company's Government in India who promptly passed the necessary legislation to give effect to the changes.

(iv) The Glasgow Chamber of Commerce admitted in its written statement that no duty at all was charged by the Company's Government in India on woolens, metals and Other cargoes imported from England and that it placed England in a very privileged position.

Prohibitive Duties on Indian Manufactures Imported into England

The well-known historian, Lecky, states (*History of England in the Eighteenth Century,* Vol. VII, pp. 255, 256, 320) that at the beginning of the eighteenth century, the weavers in England had begun to fear the total loss of their industry because of the competition offered by the cheaper, more durable and more beautiful Indian fabrics. The English tried to stop the inflow of the Indian manufactures by levying heavy import duties, banning altogether the import of several kinds of cloth manufactured in India, and even by the passing of a law making it an indictable offence for an Englishwoman to wear a dress made of Indian woven material.

Robert Brown, an English merchant who imported Indian cotton textiles, gave details (in his evidence before a Parliamentary Committee in 1813) of the import duties levied in England on cotton textiles imported from India. One duty

(i) was charged when the goods were cleared at the port of entry, and another
(ii) when the goods reached the English markets for retail sale.

The rates at which the duties were charged were stated to be as follows:

(i) on muslins, etc.: (a) was levied at ten per cent and (b) at twenty-seven-and-one-third per cent,
(ii) on calicoes both duties totalled seventy-two per cent,
(iii) on other fabrics the sale or use of which in England was forbidden by law, was charged at sixty-eight percent, after paying which the importer had to export the goods immediately to some other country.

But even so, the calicoes, after paying seventy-two per cent import and internal duties could be sold in the English markets at prices cheaper by anything up to sixty per cent as compared to the English manufactures of the same type and quality. Till 1830, the quantity of the hand-spun and hand-woven cloth which could be had in India for Rs. 100 could not be produced, for quality, by the steam-powered machines in England and was not available there even for Rs. 450.

Besides cotton, silk and woollen textiles of different varieties and designs, many other articles of everyday use made or produced in India were imported into England. Among these may be mentioned, arrowroot, tea, sugar, soap, paper, coconut oil, wines, liquid extracts and essences, horns, ropes, mattings, articles made of leather, wood, china and clay, walking-sticks with tops or heads worked in gold or silver, etc. Between 1813 and 1832, the import duties on these were reduced or increased according to English needs. The sale in England of certain kinds of Indian textiles, particularly of silk scarfs and other articles made of silk, was banned by law till 1826. Many of these imported articles were subjected to heavy import duties ranging from one hundred to six hundred per cent. An Englishman, Richards, stated before the Parliamentary Committee in 1832 that import duty on certain articles imported from India was as high as three thousand per cent!

To sum up, whilst many English manufactures were allowed to be imported into India free of any import duty and the highest rate of import duty levied never exceeded two-and-a-half per cent, the Indian manufactures were virtually barred from entering the English market by the terrible handicaps of fiscal burdens, legal prohibitions and even of boycott by some sections of the English people.

Helplessness of India

What we have said in the preceding paragraph is borne out by an English historian whom we quote below:

> "The history of the trade of cotton cloths with India ... is . . . a melancholy instance of the wrong done to India by the country on which she had become dependent. It was stated in evidence, that the cotton and silk goods of India up to this period (1813) could be sold for a profit in the British market at a price from fifty to sixty per cent lower than those fabricated in England. It consequently became necessary to protect the latter by duties of seventy and eighty per cent, on their value, or by positive prohibition. Had this not been the case, had not such prohibitory duties and decrees existed, the mills of Paisley and of Manchester would have been stopped in their outset, and could scarcely have been again set in motion even by the powers of steam. They were created by the sacrifice of the Indian manufacturer. Had India been independent, she would have retaliated, would have imposed preventive duties upon British goods, and thus would have preserved her own productive industry from annihilation. This act of self-defence was not permitted her; she was at the mercy of the stranger. British goods were forced upon her without paying any duty, and the foreign manufacturer employed the arm of political injustice to keep down and ultimately strangle a competitor with whom he could not have contended on equal terms."
> (Mill's *History of British India*, Vol. VII, p. 385)

The English had succeeded in virtually closing the English markets to Indian manufactures and in promoting, through special privileges, the sale of the English manufactures in the Indian markets. But that was not enough. What was aimed at was the monopoly of the Indian market for the sale of English products. To achieve that, the Indian markets had to be closed for the sale of Indian products too. A way was found to accomplish that by devices which made it extremely difficult, if not impossible, for the Indian producer to take his products to and sell them in the Indian markets. One such device was the new method of collecting octroi on Indian products.

New Method of Collecting Octroi

During the Moghul regime octroi was collected in a simple way. Octroi posts were established fifty or sixty miles apart. Octroi on goods passing these posts was collected not on the value of the goods but at a flat rate on goods of all kinds. A certain fixed duty was collected per bullock-load, a little more per pony-load, a little more per camel-load, and so on, the highest being per cart-load. This system rendered it quite unnecessary for the goods to be unpacked, inspected and valued by the octroi officials before the proper amount of duty payable was calculated. Moreover, the duty charged was so nominal that no one ever tried to evade it. The producer, often illiterate, knew exactly what he had to pay per load at every post that he passed.

The simple Moghul system worked smoothly and did not impose any undue burden on the producer, dealer or consumer of Indian goods. But it was of little use to the Company for the attainment of its objectives and, therefore, had to be replaced by a new system evolved by the Company which, however, on the face of it, appeared just.

It was put into practice as follows:

(i) The country under the Company's rule was covered by octroi posts at every one of which goods were inspected and valued by the Company's underlings.

(ii) Octroi was levied and collected at these posts at different rates for different kinds of goods and on their value as estimated by the men in charge of the posts. Needless to say, very few of these men, if any, had the requisite knowledge for arriving at a fair estimate. The goods were valued in a haphazard manner and duty was collected on them accordingly.

(iii) The rates of octroi duty were fixed in such a way as to amount to several times the highest total amount which could have become payable under the Moghul system.

(iv) On payment of the octroi, the owner of the goods was given a pass or permit exempting the goods from the levy of the octroi anywhere for a year. If the goods or any portion thereof remained unsold at the end of the year, the permit expired, and the owner had to get a fresh permit at the nearest octroi post by producing the expired permit and by paying an additional charge at the rate of half-a-rupee per cent. If the owner failed to do so, then he had to pay, once again, the full amount of the octroi levied originally on the unsold goods.

(v) Check posts interspersed the octroi posts and were more numerous than the latter. At any of the check posts the goods passing it could be unpacked and tallied with the permit covering them by any petty official, who also had the authority to confiscate them at his discretion, if in his sole opinion, their quantity or value did not tally with that mentioned in the permit. If a check post intervened between the starting point of the goods and the octroi post nearest to it, then their owner was expected to go to the nearby octroi post and obtain a permit for the goods he wished to carry or transport *before the goods left their starting point.* Otherwise, the goods were liable to be confiscated at the intervening check post on the ground that they were in transit without a permit. As it was almost impossible for the owners of the goods to do so in every case, their difficulties, harassment and oppression can well be imagined.

Hon. Frederick Shore's Comments on the Company's Method of Collecting Internal Customs

We quote from Shore's *Notes on Indian Affairs:*

> "We hear loud complaints of the impoverishment of the people, the falling-off of the internal trade, and the decline instead of the increase of manufactures. Is it to be wondered at? Could any other result be anticipated from

the intolerable vexations to which merchants are exposed by our internal customs?"

He could have gone a step further and said with perfect truth that the "intolerable vexations" were deliberately calculated to bring about the "results" he deplored. The aim and objective of the "internal customs" were to discourage and dishearten the producers and dealers of Indian goods to the extent of making them give up their profession. This inevitably led to the ruin of the indigenous industries and the extinction of all competition in the Indian markets which the English manufactures would have had to face otherwise. This is evident from the fact that the English manufactures and their dealers or agents in India were entirely untouched by the "internal customs" which were applicable exclusively to the Indian producers and dealers in Indian products.

Frederick Shore has described how the shawl-dealers of Delhi and Banaras completely lost their business as a result of the intolerable vexations to which they were exposed by the ways in which internal duties were collected. He has referred to the losses suffered by the dealers of Bokhara (Russia), Peshawar and Kabul, and to the bitter complaints made by them. He has cited instances to prove that Indian industries had to pay the internal duties twice—once on the raw material and a second time on the finished products. Dealers in shawls had also to pay the duties twice, whilst the dealers in leather goods had to pay them three times; and the dealers in cotton fabrics had to pay them four times.

He concludes:

> "... if this be continued much longer, India will, ere long, produce nothing but food just sufficient for the population, a few coarse earthenware pots to cook it in, and a few coarse cloths. Only remove this incubus and the tables will very soon be turned."

Creation of English Tea-Estates

We have so far described the first three of the seven steps which, as mentioned before, England had taken to implement the policy underlying the Charter Act of 1813. The fourth step was to provide special facilities and financial help to Englishmen so as to induce them to live in India and exploit the country's resources. Accordingly, experiments were made for growing tea in India. Some Englishmen were sent to China to obtain seeds of different kinds of tea grown there. Chinese tea-growers were brought over to teach the English the know-how of the tea-growing industry. Extensive lands in the Assam and Kumaon regions were granted to the English for their tea-plantations. Huge tea-estates were thus created and to ensure that enough labour was available to the planters, the notorious indentured-labour system was introduced. It had legal sanction. In actual practice however it proved to be nothing but brutal legalised slavery. That, however, is another story.

Acquisition of Knowledge of Secret Processes used By Indian Craftsmen

This was the fifth step. For a description of the way in which it was taken, we would quote the English journalist, Major Keith (*The Pioneer,* September 7, 1891):

> "Everyone knows how jealously trade secrets are guarded. If you went over Messrs. Doultons' Works, you would be politely overlooked. Yet under the force of compulsion the Indian workman had to divulge the manner of his bleaching and other trade secrets to Manchester. A costly work was prepared by the India House Department to enable Manchester to take twenty millions from the poor of India; copies were gratuitously presented to Chambers of Commerce, and the Indian *Raiyat* had to pay for them. This may be political economy, but it is marvellously like something else."

Increase in Sales of Foreign Liquor in India

Another English product for which England created a market in India was liquor. On 24th March, 1832, a Commons Committee examined one Mr. Bracken on the promotion by Englishmen of the foreign liquor sales in India. He gleefully stated:

> "Liquors in Calcutta are now consumed in large quantities by natives who can afford to purchase them."

In answer to another question, he said:

> "I heard from a native shopkeeper in Calcutta, who is one of the largest retail shopkeepers, that his customers for wines and brandy and beer, were principally natives."

Question: What should you say was the favourite wine among the natives?
Answer: Champagne.
Question: Formerly did they not consume any wine?
Answer: Very little, I believe.
Question: Is it not contrary to their religion?
Answer: I do not know whether it is contrary to their religion, but it is contrary to their habits; ……it is not done openly, but when done it is a violation of their custom rather than of their religion.

Other English witnesses, too, joyfully declared that the Indians were increasingly taking to drinking foreign liquors and to other European ways of living luxuriously, thus creating an ever-increasing demand for the English-manufactured articles of luxury. The phenomenal increase in the demand for their products was what the English wanted and had worked for. Who cared whether or not the creation of the demand led to any deterioration of the Indian consumers' character?

End of Indian Cloth Industry and Trade

According to Sir Charles Trevelyan (1834), the textile workers and traders of Bengal had lost by 1833:

(i) the English market for their goods valued, on an average, at a crore of rupees per year, and
(ii) the home-market in Bengal for the goods produced in Bengal valued, on an average, at 80 lacs of rupees per year.

"What is to become," he pathetically asks, "of all the people who were employed in working up this great annual amount?" (Rs. 1,80,00,000).

We quote below some of the figures relied upon by Sir Charles:

(i) the value of cotton cloth exported in 1816 from Bengal to foreign countries was a little less than 166 lacs of rupees; by 1832, it had dwindled down to only a little more than eight lacs,

(ii) the value of the cloth exported in 1814 from England to Bengal was a pitiful 45 thousand rupees; by 1816, it had risen to well over three lacs of rupees and by 1828, it had shot up to nearly 80 lacs, and

(iii) not a yard of foreign cotton yarn was imported into Bengal till 1826. In 1828, the value of the English cotton yarn imported into Bengal was well over 35 lacs of rupees. This was in addition to the cloth imported from England as mentioned above.

We would supplement Sir Charles Trevelyan's figures by the figures collated for Parliamentary Papers (as quoted in Major B. D. Basu's *Ruin of Indian Trade and Industries,* pp. 70–71):

(i) in 1814, over 3,800 bales of cloth were exported from India to England. In 1824 their number was reduced by more than a half, and only 1,878 bales were exported. In 1828, the number of the bales exported to England had gone down to a mere 433;

(ii) the total value of all the cotton goods imported into India during 1814 was a little over 16 lacs of rupees (Rs. 16,15,315). During the next 14 years the value had increased, by nearly nineteen hundred per cent, to Rs. 3,01,46,615. By 1830, the value had soared up to the colossal figure of Rs. 13,10,42,240;

(iii) the value of the woollens imported into India from England during 1814 was about Rs. 6,70,700. By 1830, it had risen to well over Rs. 2,13,88,770;

(iv) the total value of all English manufactures (including cloth, iron, copper, liquor, paper and glass) imported into India in the year 1814 was Rs. 6,14,87,475; by 1830, the figure had shot up to Rs. 60,11,00,310 or nearly ten times the 1814 figure. (The figures in the Parliamentary Papers are in sterling. The rate of conversion is Rs. 15/- to the pound sterling.)

The above figures are eloquent of the degree of the success achieved by the English in writing *finis* to the cloth industry of India. It was the most important industry of the country. The other less important ones, too, did not escape English rapacity for long.

Merchant Shipping Business and Industry

W. S. Lindsay describes in his book, *History of Merchant Shipping*, Vol. II (pp. 454–55), the situation in 1789 as regards merchant shipping engaged in the Asiatic transport trade. According to him, the Portuguese had only three cargo-carrying ships stationed at Canton, the Dutch had five, the French one, the Danes one, the U.S.A. fifteen and the British East India Company had forty. All these were transporting Asiatic merchandise. The Indian people of the English-ruled regions alone had merchantmen which in numbers equalled all the above-mentioned merchantmen put together. Almost all the Asiatic cargo-carrying trade was carried on by ships built in India and owned by Indians. These ships were constantly making return-trips to China. Their trips along the Malabar coast, to and from the Persian Gulf and the Red Sea, were quite as numerous before the sea-route to Europe round the Cape of Good Hope was discovered, as they were even after its discovery.

Till 1794, however, ships built in India were not permitted to transport merchandise to and from London. In that year, because of the engagement of the East India Company's ships in the British Government's work, the overseas English governments were instructed to use the Indian-built cargo ships. The freight up to the river Thames was fixed at £16 per ton for rice and other heavy merchandise and at £20 per ton for lighter cargoes. The masters of the cargo vessels were also permitted to take on board *en route* and at their discretion any goods intended for any of the regions under the Company's rule. But this privilege was taken away, shortly after 1794, from the ships built in India when the Company's Charter was revised in 1796, and a new clause was inserted. It was that only such Indian-built and Indian-owned vessels as had been hired by the Company could be used by the English or Indian traders, or by the Company's employees for the transport of merchandise from India to England or *vice versa*.

Lord Melville has quoted as follows from a letter written by the Marquis of Hastings to the Company on 21st March, 1812:

> "It cannot be denied that the 1796 law did not prove satisfactory, at least for the ship-builders of the country." (ibid., p. 457)

This was the beginning of the end of Indian merchant-shipping trade and of the ship-building industry.

The Iron and Steel Industry

Sir George Watt states in his book, *The Commercial Products of India*, written under instructions of the British Government's Secretary of State for India, and published in 1908:

(i) that there is no doubt that the industry of smelting iron ore existed in ancient India, for references to it are to be found in the contemporary records;

(ii) that the industry began dying out in places near the railways because of the competition offered by imports of the cheaper English iron;

(iii) that the industry still showed signs of progress in parts of the Bombay Presidency and the Central Provinces of India;

(iv) that according to Syed Hussain Bilgrami, the famous Demascus blades of the Middle Ages were hammered out of the steel produced in the Nizam's territory, and

(v) that Hyderabad was still famous for its swords and daggers.

Another English writer, Valentine Ball, states in his book, *Jungle Life in India*, pp. 224–25:

(i) that furnaces for smelting iron-ore existed in almost all the villages of India, but the industry was ruined because the owners of the furnaces were forced to lease them out to Englishmen, and

(ii) that in this way hundreds of thousands of Indian smelters, steel craftsmen, iron-ore and coal workers were deprived of their livelihood.

The Paper Industry

Sir George Watt in his above-mentioned book (p. 866) states:

(i) that the English writer who has described in detail the paper-making industry of India is Buchannon Hamilton;

(ii) that the raw material used in India for making paper was flax or hemp;

(iii) that at one time, India used to import paper from China, but many Hindus and Mussalmans learned the know how of making paper by hand, and their products were sufficient to meet the whole country's demand for paper, and

(iii) that when Sir Charles Wood became the Secretary of State for India, he issued strict orders that the Government of India must not buy for its needs any other paper except that made in England.

The orders were calculated to and did strangle the growing paper industry of India.

The Sugar Industry

Sugar was the second largest commodity, the first being cloth, exported from India. Thousands of maunds of Indian sugar were shipped every year to English and European ports. By following the doctrine of "free trade", the English could not stop the import of Indian sugar into England. So they resorted to the imposition of heavy import duties. Sir George Watt, in his above-mentioned book, states that such a heavy import duty was levied on Indian sugar as to stop altogether its import into England.

According to him, the import duty on Indian sugar was eight shillings per quarter higher than that levied on sugar imported into England from her colonies. There is no doubt, Sir George goes on to say (p. 958), that a very severe blow was deliberately aimed at the Indian sugar industry; that it was intended to be mortal but India took it on its chin and its sugar industry survived it; that the Indian sugar industry would certainly have progressed still further had England continued to import raw sugar from India; that the articles of food and drink exported by England to India had a sugar content of 53.3 per cent, and that the two biggest exports from India to England were thus stopped and actually replaced by imports into India of these very commodities.

Ruin of Indian Trade and Industry Concomitant with Loss of her Independence

The two were inextricably bound up with and acted and re-acted upon each other. The members of the Parliamentary Committee (1830–32) stated that the English workmen, artisans and craftsmen were earning twenty million pounds a year through England's trade with India. This amount continued to increase in proportion to the extent to which India lost her freedom.

Major W. Sedgwick (*India for Sale: Kashmir Sold*, Newman & Co. Ltd., 1886, p. 4.) has endorsed this view as follows:

> "We do not appear to realise the fact that the loss of India will assuredly deprive us of all our Eastern trade, and yet it is easy to see that it will be so; for not only will the marts of India be closed against us if we lose it—as firmly closed against us as are those of Central Asia now—but, besides this, India, with its raw produce and its people skilled in manufactures from of old, will soon, under a system of protection, become a great manufacturing nation, will soon with its cheap labour and abundant supply of raw material supplant us throughout the East."

In further support of our views, we quote Lord Dufferin who in the course of one of his speeches said:

"Indeed, it would not be too much to say that if any serious disaster ever overtook our Indian Empire, or if our political relations with the Peninsula of Hindustan were to be even partially disturbed, there is not a cottage in Great Britain—at all events in the manufacturing districts—which would not be made to feel the disastrous consequences of such an intolerable calamity." (*Lord Dufferin's Speeches in India,* John Murray, p. 284.)

Thus it was that the forceful efforts of the East India Company fully backed by the British Government relegated the existence of the time-honoured and flourishing trades and industries of India to the pages of history text-books, and the country which, less than a century earlier, was considered to be the wealthiest in the world was dragged down to the position of the poorest in the world.

THE WAR WITH NEPAL

Its Genesis

The first military venture of Lord Hastings' regime was the invasion of Nepal. The motive was to acquire for the Company such regions in India as were suitable for the formation of British colonies in the country. The English had long been coveting for this purpose the Himalayan valleys of Dehra Dun, Garhwal and Kumaon in the Kingdom of Nepal. According to Mill:

> "if British colonies be ever formed in the East, with a chance of preserving the moral and physical energies of the parent country, it is to the vales and mountains of the Indian Alps that we must look for their existence, it will be to the Gorkha war that they will trace their origin." (*History of British India*, Vol. VIII, pp. 59–60)

Declared and Created Reason For Invasion

At one place the border-line between Nepal and India ran close to the Company-ruled Indian districts of Saran and Gorakhpur. It was not clearly or definitely demarcated and some lands along the border had often been the subject matter of boundary disputes between the Company and the Nepal *Durbar*. In the past, they had been decided by a joint commission appointed by both the parties and the decision was accepted by both.

One such dispute had arisen before Hastings took over and as usual a joint commission to decide it had been appointed. The Company's nominee and representative on the commission was Major Bradshaw. It would, however, appear that with Hastings' assumption of office, the policy of settling such disputes by arbitration was discarded and Major Bradshaw was given to understand that the Governor-General did not desire a peaceful settlement. So,

> "Major Bradshaw began using insulting and offensive language in speaking to the Nepalese commissioners when they arrived for a sitting of the commission. The Nepalese bore it all in dignified silence and found that no work to be done was put up." (*History of British India* by Mill and Wilson, Vol. VIII, p. 12)

The commission broke up *ipso facto*. Its breaking-up provided Hastings with the excuse he wanted for writing a strongly-worded letter to the Maharaja of Nepal, demanding immediate evacuation by Nepal of the disputed region. The letter was sent through the District Magistrate of Gorakhpur. He was at the same time ordered to take forcible possession of the region with the help of the Company's troops, if Nepal did not vacate it within 25 days of the dispatch of the letter.

Hostilities Begin

The District Magistrate carried out the order and, at the end of the period, marched the Company's troops into the region. The Nepalese *Durbar* had sent a civil reply to Hastings' rude demand and were taken by surprise as the attack had not been anticipated by them. The Gurkhas manning the region fell back before the Company's troops, who occupied the region, established some police posts and started on their way back to Gorakhpur. But on 29th May, 1814, before the Company's troops reached Gorakhpur, the Gorkhas evicted the Company's police posts and re-occupied the entire region. Nepal had accepted Hastings' challenge.

Hastings had probably expected that the Nepalese would take the aggression lying down. But Nepal's successful counterattack made it essential that the Company should retaliate to maintain English prestige. Hastings wanted war, but could not declare it immediately. The English merchants trading in Nepal had to be safely evacuated with all their belongings and investments and arrangements for financing the war were yet to be made.

"Loan" Taken From the Nawab Wazir of Oudh

In June, 1814, Hastings left Calcutta for northern India to activate the sinews of war. The Company had no funds and its credit in the country was pretty low. Its bills of exchange were marketable only at a discount of 12 per cent. But its old milch cow, the Nawab Wazir of Oudh, was still available. Nawab Ghaziuddin was then on the *Gadi*. He was, however, fed up with the ill-treatment he had received from the English Resident, Major Baillie, and had complained to the Governor-General, Hastings, who immediately went to Lucknow and met the Nawab Wazir.

We quote from an entry (dated 13th October, 1814) in Hastings' diary:

> "Nawab Vazier had reckoned on being emancipated from the imperious domination of Major Baillie under which His Excellency groaned every hour, but that I had riveted him in his position. Major Baillie dictated to him in the merest trifles, broke in upon him at his palace without notice, whensoever he (Major Baillie) had anything to prescribe, fixed his (Major Baillie's) creatures upon His Excellency with large salaries to be spies upon all his actions; and, above all, lowered His Excellency in the eyes of his family and his subjects by the magisterial tone which he constantly assumed." (*Private Journal of the Marquess of Hastings,* Panini Office, Allahabad, p. 97)

Somehow, the Nawab Wazir was made to feel happy with Hastings. He immediately agreed "out of gratitude" to advance a loan of 25 million rupees to the Governor-General. Major Bird, in his book (*Dacoities in Excelsis,* Chap. IV, pp. 58–76), describes the ways and means adopted to extort this huge amount of money.

Planning of the War

Having secured the money, Hastings lost no time in planning the campaign whilst he was still at Lucknow.

Hastings Plans Invasion of Nepal

The plan finalised at Lucknow was that the Company's forces were to invade Nepal at five points along the 600-mile-long border running between that country and the English possessions, from the river Sutlej in the Punjab to the river Kosi in Bihar. Accordingly, five separate units of the Company's army, each under its own Commander, were detailed for the purpose. Hastings had mobilised some 3,000 European and 20,500 Indian soldiers for the invasion.

The main unit of this invading force was commanded by General Morley. He had been assigned the attack on Kathmandu, the capital of Nepal. It was composed of about a thousand European and some 7,000 Indian soldiers and the attack was to be made from its base at Murshidabad, through the ravines of the rivers Gandak and Bagmati.

Further to the east, a unit of about 2,000 men under Major Lettre was stationed on the bank of the river Kosi opposite the Nepalese border. Major Lettre's assignment was to defend the Company's side of the border at that point and to win over the Raja of nearby Sikkim by inciting him against Nepal.

A third unit of about 1,000 European and 3,000 Indian soldiers under Major-General Wood was stationed at Gorakhpur and Banaras. Its assignment was to enter the Nepalese territory at Palpa by way of Butwal.

A fourth unit of about the same size and composition as the third was stationed at Meerut under Major-General Giliespe, whose assignment was to attack Dehra Dun, Garhwal, Srinagar and Nahan in Nepalese territory.

The fifth unit was composed of about 6,000 Indian infantry and some artillery was stationed at Ludhiana (Punjab). It was commanded by Col. Ochterlony who was assigned the invasion of the Nepalese territory from the hillocks near the river Sutlej.

As against this force of over 22,000 men, the Nepal *Durbar* could mobilise only about 12,000 by the time the hostilities began.

Hastings Starts Nepal War Before Declaring It

War began with the invasion of Dehra Dun, which was governed by Raja Amar Singh Thapa, a noted general in the army of the Nepal *Durbar*. His nephew, Balbhadra Singh, was in charge of the Dehra Dun region and had only a few hundred soldiers under him.

The Company's fourth army-unit under Major-General Gillespe marched on Dehra Dun and was helped, it is stated, along its march by some *Khesi Zamindars* and by Bahadur Singh's son, Rana Jeevan Singh. Gillespe sent most of his unit a little in advance. The detachment was commanded by Col. Mowby and entered Dehra Dun on 24th October, 1814.

The next morning Mowby laid siege to the Nepalese stronghold at Kalanga situated above the Nalapani Springs, some three and a half miles beyond Dehra Dun. He had shelled the stronghold for a whole week *before* Hastings formally declared war against Nepal on 1st November, 1814.

Defence of Kalanga Fort

It is something of a misnomer to call Kalanga a "fort", as it was nothing better than a primitive fortification on the top of Kalanga, the highest hillock in the locality. It had been hastily improvised by Balbhadra Singh. The walls of the fort were mere barricades of logs of forest-timber, re-inforced by heavy stones locally collected by the Gorkha men and women under the personal guidance of Balbhadra Singh, who established his headquarters at Kalanga. Even the barricade-walls of the "fort" were incomplete when he got news of Col. Mowby's arrival at Dehra Dun. He had only 300 men, the other inmates of the fort being women and children, the lot numbering about 600 in all. Some of the men were expert archers and were armed with bows and arrows.

Col. Mowby had reached Dehradun a little before nightfall. He could not and did not expect that a handful of men, some of them armed with primitive weapons, would have the courage or the spirit to resist a force about ten times stronger in numbers and arms. So, the same night he sent a letter by a special messenger to Balbhadra Singh calling upon him to surrender the "fort" to the English. Balbhadra Singh read the letter and instantly tore it up, throwing the pieces at the messenger. He sent through the same messenger an oral challenge to Col. Mowby, daring him to come immediately with his English force and fight for the "fort". Next morning, Kalanga was bombarded from every available direction by Col. Mowby. The defenders replied with a hail of bullets and arrows, many of which found their mark. Col. Mowby realised at the end of the day that the capture of the "fort" was not going to be an easy job and sent word to Major-General Gillespe who had stayed behind with the rest of his army unit at Saharanpur, some 45 miles away from Dehra Dun. Gillespe joined forces with Mowby at Nalapani the very next day and spent another three days in studying the terrain and evolving a fresh line of attack. He divided his entire unit into five detachments. Four were detailed to attack the "fort" simultaneously from four directions and the fifth was held in reserve. On the fourth day after the arrival of Gillespe, the "fort" was heavily bombarded and the four detachments advanced to take the fort by a simultaneous assault delivered from all points of the compass. A sizeable part of the defenders' tiny force of 300 had been killed and disabled by that time. But the shooting from the "fort" continued unabated and all the assaults were repeatedly repulsed with heavy losses. The defenders were gallantly supported by their women who stood on the walls fully exposed, shoulder to shoulder with their men, and whilst the latter were firing guns and shooting arrows, the women were raining stones and rolling down big boulders on the invaders' heads as soon as the latter appeared within striking distance. Captain Vansittart has testified (in his Notes on Nepal) that the women could be plainly seen doing it throughout the veritable hail-storm of bullets and gun-shots. Intermingled bodies of both men and women, later discovered in the ruins of the "walls" of the deserted "fort", bore mute testimony to the part played by the brave Gorkha women in fearlessly fighting the invaders.

The assaults were made again and again, day after day, but were repulsed every time. Goaded by the repeated failures, Major-General Gillespe personally led three companies of white soldiers to storm the gate of the "fort". The Gorkhas had mounted a cannon on the top of the gate, the most vulnerable spot in the "walls of the fort". Its fire swept the approach to the gate, but the gallant Gillespe braved it and continued to advance, waving to his soldiers with his drawn sword. Then a stray bullet hit him and he fell down dead.

Col. Mowby, who, after Gillespe's death, once again took over the command of the besieging force, considered it wiser to retire to a safe distance and send for help from Delhi. On arrival of the reinforcements of infantry and artillery from Delhi, the assaults on the "fort" were resumed on 25th November, 1814. But these achieved nothing and the storming parties were repulsed and had to retreat every time. The siege was, however, continued and Kalanga was subjected to heavy bombardment round the clock.

But even with hundreds dead and dying all around them and with death raining from the skies all the time, the gallant Gorkhas, now reduced to a pitiful 70, led by the indomitable Balbhadra Singh, never thought of saving themselves by an ignominious surrender. They carried on the struggle as spiritedly as ever, till fate dealt them a cruel blow. They had run through their store of water and there were no means of replenishing it as the springs from which they drew water were now in English hands. They had held out against fearful odds in numbers and weapons but could not hope to go on doing it for more than a few days without a drop of water, and with the wounded, the women and the children suffering horribly and raving wildly for it. In this desperate situation, Balbhadra Singh, preferring death to surrender, decided to fight his way out through the besieging force.

Early in the morning, on 30th November, 1814, the gunfire and the flight of arrows from the "fort" suddenly ceased. A few minutes after the gate swung open and out of it emerged Balbhadra Singh, naked sword in hand, head held high in pride. He was followed by the defenders, men and women, armed with drawn swords, shouldered guns, and their celebrated traditional *khukris* swinging from their belts. Unhurriedly, in measured steps, they marched through the besiegers, went to the water springs, quenched their thirst and disappeared in the neighbouring hills.

> "Such was the conclusion of the defence of Kulunga, a feat of arms worthy of the best days of chivalry, conducted with a

heroism almost sufficient to palliate the disgrace of our own reverses." (*Memoirs of Dehra Dun* by G. R. C. Williams)

Be it said to the credit of the English besiegers' chivalry, that not a finger was raised against Balbhadra Singh, "the Gorkha Leonidas", as Williams calls him, or against his companions from the moment of their appearance out of the "fort" till they were out of sight. The English did something more, which is rarely, if ever, done by an invader for the adversary who had discomfited him.

They raised an unassuming memorial on the bank of the nearby Rispana river, which bears to this day (1929) the inscription: "... As a tribute of respect for our gallant adversary Balbhadra Singh ... And his brave Gorkhas."

We finish the episode by relating that from Kalanga Balbhadra Singh went to the defence of Jeet Garh, another Nepalese fortress, which was under attack by the Company's detachment of a thousand men commanded by Major Belldoc. Balbhadra Singh had less than five hundred men but he had fought against far greater odds, and Major Belldoc's force had to retreat in a disgraceful rout. After leaving a small garrison in charge of Jeet Garh, Balbhadra Singh took the rest of his men to the defence of the fortress at Jaitak. We shall leave this for the present.

Hill Tribe of Jaunsar Incited to Revolt

Soldiers and guns having failed to achieve for the English a victory over the Gorkhas, the former resorted to their time-honoured "secret method" of intrigue. After occupying the abandoned empty shell of the Kalanga "fort", Mowby sent Col. Carpenter into Nepalese territory to the right of the river Jumna. Carpenter's assignment was to incite the hill tribes of the area to revolt against the Nepal *Durbar,* and he succeeded to the extent of getting the people of the Jaunsar region to rise up in an armed rebellion. They drove away the few Gorkhas manning the Nepalese post at Barath and occupied it.

Mowby himself went to Nahan, the capital of Sirmaur, a vassal state under Nepal, because Nahan offered a more important and fertile field for his intrigues. Sometime earlier, the King of Nepal had deposed the then Raja of Sirmaur and had placed the State's administration in the hands of one of his own Generals, Raja Amar Singh Thapa (the uncle of Balbhadra Singh). Mowby had heard that Amar Singh had been assigned the defence of Srinagar and had left Nahan, and that his son Ranjor Singh, who carried on the administration during his father's absence, had also been directed by his father to leave Nahan and go north to the Nepalese fortress at Jaitak. Ranjor Singh's assignment was to establish his headquarters at Jaitak and to spread out his men around the nearby hills. So Mowby had a clear field for sowing dissensions and winning over to the English side the deposed Raja of Sirmaur who was still living in Nahan.

Battle at Jaitak

On 20th December, 1814, General Martindale was given the overall command of the late Major-General Gillespe's army unit. On the 25th, Martindale invaded the Jaitak fort with the entire force under his command. As mentioned above, the fort was the headquarters of Ranjor Singh who was joined by his cousin, the heroic Balbhadra Singh. The Nepalese garrison in the fort numbered less than two thousand and were pitted against a force several times their number.

Martindale was aware of what had happened at the siege of Kalanga and his first act was to take possession of all the wells which did or could supply water to the Jaitak garrison. He divided the main body of his unit into two separate detachments and placed one under Major Ludlow and the other under Major Richards. He despatched each in a different direction to converge on the wells and seize them. But both of them were completely routed by the Gorkhas. Majors Ludlow and Richards had to beat a hasty retreat, leaving many of their officers and hundreds of their men dead on the battle-field or as prisoners in the hands of the Gorkhas. According to Prof. Wilson, General Martindale, after his ignominious defeat, did not dare to take any further action for reducing the Jaitak fort.

Thus ended the "exploits" of the army unit originally assigned to Major-General Gillespe for attacking Dehra Dun, etc. By then, quite a third of the unit which had marched from Meerut for the purpose had been liquidated.

The English Checked on Oudh-Rangpur Frontier

Two other army units, 12,000 strong, one commanded by Major-General Wood and the other by Major-General Morley, had been assigned the invasion of Nepal from the east, right up to Kathmandu. They advanced but were repulsed in all the engagements with the Gorkhas. These were the fiercest and bloodiest of all the battles till then fought by the English.

> "From the frontier of Oudh to Rangpur, our armies were completely held in check on the outside of the' forest, while our territory was insulted with impunity and the most extravagant alarms spread through the country." (Prinsep's *History of the Political and Military Transactions in India*)

Some of the commanding officers in both the units proved to be so incompetent and lacking in spirit that the Governor-General had to cashier them.

Ochterlony's Initial Success and Ultimate Failure

Of all the five Commanders of the Company's five army units, Ochterlony was the first one to achieve even a partial success initially. It was mainly due to his ability as an expert in implementing the Western policy of machinations against all enemies, present or potential. Ochterlony was stationed at Ludhiana on the far-western border of Nepalese territory, which he invaded near the river Sutlej. Three minor ranges of hills branched off from the left bank of the Sutlej and on each of these the Gorkhas had put up fortifications at Nalagarh, Ramgarh and Malam. On 31st October, 1814, Ochterlony began operations by taking his guns up the hill facing the Nalagarh fortress, which he threatened to bombard. Within less than a week, Ram Saran, the Raja of Nalagarh, a vassal of the King of Nepal, surrendered to the English and later became their most helpful ally. The historian, Cunningham, has stated in his *History of the Sikhs* that not only did Ram Saran help Ochterlony with men and supplies but also built at his own cost a road for the English cannons from Makram to Nahan.

After occupying the Nalagarh fortress and the nearby Gorkha stronghold at Taragarh, Ochterlony, on 13th November, 1814, advanced towards Ramgarh, the second Gorkha hill-fortress in that region. Unfortunately for Ochterlony, Raja Amar Singh Thapa, the distinguished Nepalese General, was personally in charge of the defence of Ramgarh. Amar Singh had less than half the number of men that Ochterlony had, and yet he not only held the latter at bay, but inflicted heavy losses on the invaders and drove them back.

It appears from a letter which Ochterlony wrote at the time to the Governor-General that he (Ochterlony) became extremely doubtful about his ability to succeed. The Governor-General sent reinforcements. Whilst waiting for them, Ochterlony got on with his intriguing activities. He won over the Raja of Bilaspur, who was a distant relative of Raja Amar Singh Thapa and some other hill chiefs who were under the suzerainty of Nepal by promises calculated to appeal to their greediness. But neither the reinforcements nor the success of his intrigues helped him in any way. He lost every single battle fought with the Gorkhas from November 1814 to April 1815, and could not take even an inch of Nepal's territory. The Gorkhas under the brilliant leadership of Raja Amar Singh Thapa, to which Prinsep had paid a great tribute, repulsed Ochterlony all along the line. But, for one reason or another, they did not follow up their victories by invading the English possessions. The English utilised the respite for the furtherance of their secret intrigues against Nepal.

Acquisition of Morang, Kumaon and Garhwal

Major Lettre, the Commander of the Company's fifth army unit, had been busy for some time in intrigues at the eastern end of the Nepal border. He succeeded in winning over the Raja of Sikkim, who helped him to annex the Nepalese region of Morang.

Kumaon and Garhwal were the next victims of the intrigues leading to their "conquest" by the English. These regions were administered by Nepal's Subedar, Chautra Bamshah. The Governor-General deputed Col. Gardiner to conspire with Chautra Bamshah against Nepal. Gardiner had been dismissed, some time earlier, from Holkar's service for traitorous activities. He was as skilful a schemer as Ochterlony. An English doctor, Rutherford, was also sent to help Gardiner. Rutherford had for some time wide contacts with the people of Kumaon and Garhwal as the Company's trade agent. To help Gardiner, he employed as his spies and secret agents many local *Pandits* and soldiers of those regions. They were used to bribe and corrupt the local officials, administrators and the people throughout Kumaon and Garhwal. He succeeded in persuading the local rulers and the people to come over to the English side. In April 1815, Hastings sent a small force under Col. Nicolls to occupy the Kumaon-Garhwal region. It was occupied almost bloodlessly and Nepal was done out of its two most fertile provinces by bribery and corruption.

Thus, within a few months, first Dehra Dun, then Morang on the eastern, Kumaon and Garhwal in the middle, Hindur (Nalagarh) and Bilaspur on the western borders were taken from Nepal, thanks very largely to "... the length of the purse" (Prinsep, Vol. I, p. 136) provided by the Nawab of Oudh. Most of the credit for the English successes must, in the opinion of some writers of history, go to the arch-schemers, Ochterlony and Rutherford, rather than to the Company's military strength or the ability of its Commanders who were worsted in every battle with the Gorkhas.

Temporary Suspension and Resumption of Hostilities

The English were unable to advance any further, and the Nepal *Durbar* had been equally unable to cope successfully with the machinations and intrigues which the English had resorted to. Thus both sides were ready for peace.

Raja Amar Singh Thapa, the Nepalese General, came to know about the Nepal *Durbar's* inclination towards peace. He sounded a note of warning in a letter which he wrote to the King of Nepal in March 1815 about a couple of months before the cease-fire. The letter stated quite plainly:

(i) that the English were not to be trusted at all in any matter,
(ii) that even after concluding peace the English would continue their efforts to weaken Nepal by secret intrigues and conspiracies with the vassal-chiefs against the *Durbar,* and
(iii) that the stationing of an English Resident at Kathmandu would be extremely dangerous as it would pave the way for the inveiglement of Nepal into the Subsidiary Alliance, thus making its complete subjugation to the English will inevitable.

Quoting the examples of the Raja of Bharatpur, Tipu Sultan and other redoubtable fighters for freedom, Amar Singh most earnestly urged his master to continue the struggle against the English rather than make peace with them by giving them concessions and a foothold in Nepal. About a hundred years later, in October 1912, Colonel Shakespeare wrote in *The United Service Journal:*

"It is also worthy of note that Amar Singh's policy of keeping out the English at all costs from Nepal, so gravely impressed by him on the *Durbar* then, is still kept up; and who shall say that he was not wise?"

But in 1815, the *Durbar* did not appear to be much impressed by Amar Singh's advice. After the suspension of hostilities in June 1815, the King sent his emissary, Guru Gajraj Mishra, the Royal priest, to the English Political Agent, Major Bradshaw, at the latter's request, to start negotiations.

The Governor-General instructed Major Bradshaw to offer peace on the terms that the Nepal *Durbar* must (a) cede to the English the Nepalese territory which the latter had till then occupied, together with some additional territory along the southern border of Nepal, (b) agree to the permanent stationing at Kathmandu of an English Resident with his armed retinue, and (c) undertake not to employ any European without first obtaining permission from the English.

The King asked the Governor-General to reconsider the above terms but it was futile. Hastings re-started hostilities in January 1816 after having reinforced his army detachments all round Nepal during the intervening six months.

End of the War

But the resumed hostilities lasted only a couple of months as both sides were tired of war. Peace was at last concluded in March 1816. By its terms, the Nepal *Durbar* was acknowledged to be a fully independent sovereign of Nepal but its sovereignty was limited to the country bounded by the Chinese Empire on one side and by the British possessions in India on the other three. Some southern Nepalese territory with an annual income of ten million rupees was ceded to the English and an English Resident was permanently stationed at Kathmandu!

5

SOME OTHER ACHIEVEMENTS OF LORD HASTINGS

Whilst the Nepal war was on, Hastings was busy with other steps for the achievement of the object he had set before himself. His *Private Journal* (p. 30) has the following entry dated 6th February, 1814:

> "Our object ought to be to render the British Government paramount in effect, if not declaredly so. We should hold the other states as vassals, in substance, though not in name ... First, they should support it with all their forces in any call. Second, they should submit their mutual differences to the head of the confederacy (our Government) without attacking each other's territories ... a system which must include the extinction of any pretension to pre-eminence in the Court of Delhi ..."

During the years 1814–19, Hastings deprived the Kutch State of its independence, annexed the minor states of Hathras and Mursan and took the initial step towards the "extinction of any pretension to pre-eminence in the Court of Delhi".

Kutch

Kutch was a fully independent State on the Arabian Sea coast of India and was situated south of Sindh. It was ruled by the Jadeja, Rajputrao. It was stated that some dacoits from Kutch had raided some outlying parts of Kathiawad, situated to the south-west of Kutch. The Rajas of Kathiawad were vassals of the Peshwa and the Gaikwad, both of whom were allies and friends of the English. This was the declared reason for the English invasion of Kutch territory from which the dacoits had raided Kathiawad. An expedition under Col. Yeast was despatched. It occupied the Kutch fortress at Anjar after some desultory fighting. Rajputrao of Kutch was then told that the Mussalman Amirs of Sindh were about to invade Kutch and that the English would have to help the Amirs, unless he agreed to submit to them and placed himself under their protection. The threat made up in force what it lacked in logic. With the Company's troops inside his territory and in occupation of his Anjar fortress, Rajputrao had no option but to execute (in 1816) the treaty dictated by the Company, whereby Kutch lost its independence for good and the English prestige in Western India went up another step.

Hathras and Musran

The Jat States between the rivers Ganga and Jumna had till then retained their independence. Principal amongst them was Bharatpur which, as already described, General Lake had twice attempted to reduce but without success. Hastings did not consider it wise to make a third attempt but the disgrace of the English reverses had to be blotted out somehow from the minds of the other Jat Rajas and the people of that region. So he decided to reduce two of the smaller States of Hathras and Musran. The fortress at Hathras was reputed to be nearly as impregnable as that at Bharatpur. Prinsep has candidly admitted the utter lack of any reason or even a plausible excuse for the English to attack Hathras but Hastings hoped to rehabilitate the English prestige by taking the Hathras fort. On 11th February, 1817, the Company's troops suddenly encircled the fortress and an almost ludicrous device was resorted to for peaceful penetration into it. A message was sent to the Raja of Hathras, Daya Ram, that as the Hathras fortress was modelled on the lines of the Bharatpur fortress, the Governor-General wanted his military officers to inspect the inner fortifications of the Hathras fortress before making another attack on the Bharatpur fortress. Perhaps the English did not know that Raja Daya Ram was a relation of the redoubtable Ranjit Singh, the Raja of Bharatpur. Anyway, Daya Ram was not as great a fool as the English had apparently taken him to be, and he promptly refused the solicited admission into the fort. The city and the fortress of Hathras were then shelled for ten days. On 23rd February, 1817, a part of the wall was breached, but Daya Ram continued to fight valiantly with his handful of men. Then on 2nd March, his magazine blew up mysteriously. The explosion may have been due to a shell from one of the besiegers' guns or to the success of the "secret method" adopted by the English now and then. With no powder left,

Daya Ram could not continue the fight. When further defence of the fortress became impossible, he left it one night. His way out of the fortress was barred by some English soldiers but he fought through them and disappeared into the night.

With the fall of the Hathras fortress, the Raja of Musran, Bhagwant Singh, lost heart completely and surrendered his fortress and State to the English without a fight.

Thus both the Jat States of Hathras and Musran were added to the Company's possessions.

Denial of Moghul Emperor's Suzerainty

Akbar Shah II was then the Emperor at Delhi. The practice till then had been that every Governor-General of the Company on taking office presented himself before the Emperor as an acknowledgement of the latter's sovereignty over the whole of India, including the Company's Government. The Company observed all the usual formal etiquette towards Royalty in all their communications, written and verbal, addressed to the Court at Delhi. The Emperor Akbar Shah II summoned Hastings to his Court, but the latter declined on the ground that the Court etiquette, which he was called upon to observe towards the Emperor, would be tantamount to an acknowledgement by the Company of the Delhi Emperor's suzerainty over the Company's Government and territory in India. In the *Private Journal of the Marquess of Hastings*, one finds the following entry dated 22nd January 1815:

> "It is dangerous to uphold for the Mussalmans a rallying point, sanctioned by our own acknowledgement, that a just title to supremacy exists in the King of Delhi."

Hastings went a step further in raising his Government's status to the level of the Emperor by creating a puppet "King". At a *Durbar* held at Lucknow in October, 1819, he elevated Nawab Ghaziuddin, the Nawab Wazir of Oudh, and had him formally proclaimed *Badshah* (King). *Badshah* was one of the titles used for the Emperor exclusively. Ghaziuddin disowned his allegiance to the Emperor and accepted the Company's suzerainty over himself and his dominions. Hastings had been careful enough to exact an undertaking from Ghaziuddin that the latter's elevation to "kingship" would not make the slightest difference to his existing relationship with the Company's Government. So Ghaziuddin had only changed his nominal master for a very real one. Hastings also wiped off the loan of twenty-five million rupees which Ghaziuddin had advanced to the Company by giving Ghaziuddin a slice of the region taken from Nepal. According to Major Bird (*Dacoities in Excelsis*), the tract given to Ghaziuddin was so barren and so unremunerative that the total annual income from it did not come up even to one-sixth of the amount which he would have received by way of dividend every year had he invested only a crore of rupees in the Company's shares.

6

THE THIRD MARATHA WAR

Hastings' Preliminary Steps for Crushing the Marathas

We have in the preceding chapter referred to other steps with which, during the war with Nepal, Hastings was busy in furtherance of his object "to render the British Government paramount" over the whole of India. The Marathas constituted the most formidable obstacle and their removal was rightly considered by Hastings to be indispensable for the attainment of British paramountcy. To that end he had, whilst the Nepal war was on, initiated several preliminary actions for the ultimate crushing of the Marathas. One of them was to enter into direct treaties with the Rajput princes who were Sindhia's vassals, whereby the princes cast off their allegiance to Sindhia and placed themselves under the Company's protection. Another was to force Sindhia to abrogate the old treaty of 1805 and to enter into a fresh treaty whereby he had to endorse the defection of the Rajput princes and to accept his own unqualified political subordination to the Company. Preparations were also taken in hand for the suppression of the Pindaris who formed the most important and strongest element in the Maratha armies. Other activities were calculated to weaken still further the Peshwa's position as the head of the Maratha Confederacy. The rift between the Gaikwad and the Peshwa was widened "to thwart every attempt of Bajirao to create fresh political ties between the Courts of Baroda and Poona" (*Baroda Gazetteer,* p. 219). The Peshwa's authority in his own State was undermined by intrigues in which his corrupt ministers indulged. Gaikwad's minister, Gangadhar Shastri, was done to death inside the Peshwa's territory and the English accused the Peshwa's minister, Trimbakji, of having instigated the murder. A fuller description of these steps follows.

Direct Political Relations with Rajput States

The Rajput princes were Sindhia's vassals and owed allegiance to him. It was expressly stipulated in the 1805 Treaty between Sindhia and the Company that the latter would never enter into any direct correspondence or any separate political relations with any of these States. As against this undertaking the Company appointed Col. Todd as its agent and representative at the *Durbars* of the five principal Rajput States of Mewar, Marwar, Jaipur, Kotah and Bundi. The agent created rifts between the Marathas and the Rajput princes and prevailed upon them to break off from Sindhia and to enter into separate subsidiary alliances with the British Government. But it was obviously necessary to obtain Sindhia's assent to such a defection. So the next step taken was to get Sindhia to accept the *fait accompli* and to recognise it formally.

Doulatrao Sindhia Coerced into Signing New Treaty

Why and how it was accomplished is summarised below by Hastings himself (Lord Hastings' Summary, pp. 97, 100):

> "One of the terms of our old Treaty with Sindhia was derogatory for us and an obstacle in our way. According to it our direct contact or correspondence of any nature with the Rajput princes was definitely barred. I deliberately committed a breach of this injurious undertaking and made all these States the subsidiary allies of the British, independently of Sindhia. These States possessed considerable military strength, but were always quarrelling amongst themselves. So there was no likelihood of their combining to offer united resistance."

> "Had Sindhia, by far the most powerful of all the Indian rulers, then taken up arms against us, the other Maratha

rulers constituting the Maratha Confederacy, too, would have felt encouraged to do likewise. The cost of fighting simultaneously on a number of fronts would have been prohibitive."

"Gwalior, Sindhia's capital, is situated in the centre of the richest region of his State. Some 20 miles south of it flows the small river Sindhu. From Sindhu to the river Chambal (in the north), Gwalior is encircled by a range of very steep hills covered by dense impassable forests. The range could be crossed by horsemen and perhaps by carts over two hilly paths. One ran along the Sindhu and the other along the Chambal. I stationed the central division of the force commanded by me at a point commanding the path along the Sindhu. Another division, under Major-General Dunkin, commanded the path along the Chambal. This made it impossible for Sindhia to get away with his army and artillery by either path. He was thus faced with the alternatives of either signing the Treaty as drawn up by me, or to leave the most valuable region of his State with his splendid artillery of over 100 brass cannons and other possessions in our hands and making good his escape through the jungles on the encircling hills with only a handful of men who could or would go with him. He chose the former course and meekly put his signature to the Treaty which I placed before him."

"The essence of the Treaty was an acknowledgement by him of his most complete political subordination to the Company, but its language covered its real intent and effect, so that Sindhia and his people may not feel that he had been humbled."

Thus it was that Doulatrao Sindhia was forced, at the point of the bayonet, to abrogate the ten-year-old Treaty of 1805 and to sign the new treaty. Its terms made no difference to his autonomy in the internal affairs of his State, nor did he thereby enter into the subsidiary alliance with the British. But he did agree to his former vassals (the Rajput princes) placing themselves under the fullest direct control of the Company. He also agreed to help the English in suppressing the Pindaris, who had till then furnished him with the best and most loyal of his horsemen.

Incidentally, the subsidiary alliance with the Rajput princes made their armies available to the English, not only for the suppression of the Pindaris, but also for the final crushing of the Marathas too.

Suppression of Pindaris

As mentioned above, the operations against the Pindaris were undertaken with the object of depriving the Marathas of the strongest component of their military strength. These operations also served as a cover for the amassing of the Company's armies for the campaign against the Marathas, as it was given out that the armies were being collected for the suppression of the growing Pindari depredations in the territories round about the Maratha States. Several English writers of history have lent colour to the stories of the depredations by describing the Pindaris as "dacoits," "brigands," "merciless murderers," etc. But Prof. Wilson has testified to their bravery, honesty and fidelity and has said that the Pindaris' behaviour in the villages through which they passed rendered them so popular with the villagers, that none of the latter would ever act as an informer against the Pindaris, or agree to help their enemies. A description of the Pindaris, their way of life, their organisation, their love of fighting and terms of their military service under Sindhia, Holkar and other Maratha rulers, has already been given in an earlier chapter. The English too had on several occasions used the Pindaris for their own ends and had employed or instigated them to raid the areas whose people the English wanted to overawe or terrorise. The entire warlike Pindari tribe was composed of separate clans, each independent of the others and under its own elected leader. As long as these clans acted in unison, it was impossible for the English to get the better of them. Consequently, they started sowing seeds of dissension among the clans through bribery, corruption and intrigues. Fights between one clan and another were successfully engineered. At the opportune time, Major Fraser attacked a Pindari clan in October, 1815. The Pindaris retaliated by raiding the Company's territory along the Krishna river. This provided the English with the needed excuse for starting their planned military operations against the entire tribe which, by now, had been terribly weakened by internecine quarrels. The English attacked each clan in turn, hemmed it in and either destroyed or dispersed it. Those who could escape sought refuge in the wilderness. Thus the Pindaris were virtually exterminated.

Activities at Peshwa's Durbar

Bajirao was then the Peshwa. He had been installed on the *Gadi* for the second time by the English to serve their own ends. He was the last of the Peshwas and was not only a puppet of the English but also a virtual prisoner in their hands. But even so, the situation was not completely satisfactory for the English as it hampered their progress towards their goal of total destruction of the Marathas as a political power. So their efforts to accomplish that continued unabated. As an illustration of these efforts, we would revert to and relate some of the English activities with regard to Bajirao since the end of the Second Maratha War.

Bajirao was profoundly religious. His high integrity has been admitted by Sir Barry Close, the Company's Resident at Poona. But he was spineless and lacked even ordinary foresight. In the game of politics and devious diplomacy he was quite an incompetent player. These shortcomings were mainly responsible for his share in bringing about the final destruction of Maratha power.

Some years earlier, General Wellesley had initiated the system of employing a number of people at the Poona *Durbar,* from Ministers down to the Palace domestics, as spies and informers. The system was continued in the years that followed. When Hastings took over, Elphinstone had been the Company's Resident at Poona for two years and had proved extremely useful in furthering Hastings' designs against Bajirao, particularly in thwarting the latter's attempts to create fresh political ties with the Gaikwad of Baroda.

It will be recalled that the Gaikwad had seceded from the Maratha Confederacy and allied himself with the English. But throughout the years that followed, the English deliberately kept fluid their political relationship with him as also his status *vis-a-vis* the Peshwa. Col. Wallace describes the position in the following words:

> "The Gaikwad state had been the utensil of the Honourable Company; it had been embraced as an ally when required and dismissed when no longer wanted; treaties had been made respecting it, in which it was not consulted; treaties had been made with it which had been abrogated when it suited the Company's convenience; sometimes it had been induced to wage war with the Peshwa as an independent State and then again, on the return of peace, it had been acknowledged as a vassal merely of the Maratha Empire; thus its external policy had been altogether dictated."

> Strictly speaking, the Gaikwad had never ceased to be a vassal of the Peshwa, even though the Company had made inroads on the Peshwa's authority and had, in actual practice, reduced him to the position of a mere titular suzerain of the Gaikwad. As early as 1802, the Company had deputed and sent Major Walker to Baroda to press the Gaikwad to enter into a direct treaty with the English, whereby he was to agree to dismiss the remnants of his own army and to place himself and his State completely under the protection of the Company's Subsidiary Army. As recorded in the *Baroda Gazetteer* (p. 210, footnote) the only function of the Peshwa as suzerain of Baroda was to instal formally on the Baroda *Gadi*, after the reigning Gaikwad's demise, the new Gaikwad nominated by the Company.

When Elphinstone arrived in Poona as the Company's Resident at the Peshwa's *Durbar,* Fatehsinh was the reigning Gaikwad and was, like his predecessor, completely under the influence of the English. Also a financial dispute between the Peshwa and the Gaikwad had been pending for a number of years. We give below some necessary particulars of the dispute as it led to very serious consequences for the Peshwa, and which also provided the English with a plausible excuse for starting the preplanned war against the Peshwa—a war which ended only when the Peshwa had been completely destroyed.

Dispute Between the Peshwa and the Gaikwad

A treaty had been executed in 1751 between Doomaji Gaikwad and Balajirao Peshwa, whereby the Gaikwad had ceded to the Peshwa half of Gujarat including the town of Ahmedabad. The Peshwa had, thereafter, granted to the Gaikwad a lease of the ceded area for a limited period. In return for the lease, the Gaikwad undertook to maintain a 10,000 strong cavalry to render military service to the Peshwa and to pay, in addition to the stipulated rent, an annual tribute of Rs. 5,25,000 to the Peshwa. Doomaji Gaikwad's successors had not paid the rent and the tribute for years and by 1811, when Elphinstone arrived at the the Poona *Durbar,* the arrears had accumulated to about a crore of rupees. The correctness of the accounts had been disputed for some time, and Fatehsinh Gaikwad, backed by the English, would make no attempt to settle them. Bajirao Peshwa had repeatedly sought Elphinstone's help in obtaining a settlement, but the latter had postponed taking any action every time. When, however, the end of the period of the lease drew near, it became necessary for the English to set about getting the lease renewed. So they got the Gaikwad to send his representative, Gangadhar Shastri, to Poona to settle the account and obtain a renewal of the lease from the Peshwa Bajirao. Gangadhar Shastri was a clever adventurer who lived and prospered by his wits and had long been in the pay of the English as their spy and secret agent. He had been planted by them in the service of the Peshwa. English writers of history have stated that the greatest help received by the English in their progressive subjugation of the Gaikwad and his State was rendered by Gangadhar Shastri, who had consequently acquired, amongst the patriotic statesmen of Baroda and Poona, the reputation of being a willing tool of the English and a betrayer of his own country's interests. Bajirao and his ministers vigorously protested to Elphinstone against their being made to deal with such a person, but the protests were ignored and Gangadhar Shastri left Baroda for Poona on 19th October, 1813, that is, about a month after Hastings had taken over at Calcutta.

Activities of Gangadhar Shastri and Elphinstone at Poona

There were at the Peshwa's *Durbar* then, two patriotic and alert politicians, who foresaw the implications of the English tactics and what they intended to accomplish. One of them was the noted Parsee statesman Khorshedji Jamshedji Modi, through whom all correspondence between the Company and the Peshwa had been carried on when Sir Barry Close was the Company's Resident at Poona. Sir Barry and Bajirao were both very happy with Khorshedji and his work. The other was the Peshwa's minister Trimbakji. Both were intensely loyal to the Peshwa and the Maratha power, and always warned Bajirao against the English designs and their, real intentions. It was Khorshedji who had given to Bajirao a very clear picture of the great harm and the immense benefit accruing to the Maratha power and the English, respectively, as a consequence of the Treaty of Bassein. Elphinstone did not take long to find that Khorshedji was a staunch partisan of Bajirao and his sincere well-wisher. That, according to Elphinstone himself, was the reason for his bye-passing Khorshedji in all approaches to Bajirao or his *Durbar,* and to contact both directly. His private letters written at the time disclose the fact that Elphinstone's treatment of Bajirao and his ministers then became progressively discourteous to the verge of contempt. Gangadhar Shastri, soon after his arrival at Poona, warned Elphinstone against Trimbakji too, and both of them set about the elimination of Khorshedji as well as Trimbakji from the scene at Poona. Khorshedji was still at Poona and Elphinstone peremptorily ordered that he be sent away. Bajirao did not have the guts to resist the order for Khorshedji's expulsion and meekly carried it out. But when Khorshedji was about to leave Poona, he suddenly died of poisoning. The English went out of their way to exculpate themselves by declaring that Khorshedji had either committed suicide or been poisoned at the instigation of Bajirao.

The main objective of Gangadhar Shastri's mission to Poona was to obtain from the Peshwa a renewal of the lease in favour of the Gaikwad. But he found that Bajirao was unwilling to renew it on account of the Gaikwad's past behaviour and his utter subservience to the English will. Then Bajirao granted the lease to his loyal minister Trimbakji. Elphinstone advised Gangadhar Shastri to return to Baroda without settling the accounts. It suited the English that the long-standing dispute should continue and the rift between Baroda and Poona be further widened and stabilised. Another reason, discovered later, would appear to be that the English wanted the lease to be granted to the Company. Anyway Bajirao and Trimbakji both realised that Gangadhar Shastri's return to Baroda at that stage would do no good to them and so they went all out in their efforts to keep him in Poona, and, if at all possible, to win him over. Gangadhar Shastri did eventually become a warm supporter of a complete reconciliation between Fatehsinh Gaikwad and Bajirao Peshwa. He could not get the lease renewed in favour of the Gaikwad, but he drew up a fair and straightforward statement of accounts and sent it to his master with the following recommendations (*vide Baroda Gazetteer,* p. 221):

(i) That the Gaikwad's total liability (inclusive of interest) to the Peshwa (amounting to Rs. 39 lacs) be accepted, and

(ii) That the Peshwa's claims to rupees one crore on account of arrears and to Rs. 40 lacs on account of the tribute, be compounded by the Gaikwad's ceding to the Peshwa a region with an annual income of rupees seven lacs.

So keen was Gangadhar Shastri on a rapprochement between Bajirao Peshwa and Fatehsinh Gaikwad, that he even solicited Elphinstone's help in getting his proposals accepted. But the Gaikwad kept his own representative's proposals pending for months, and then rejected them, doubtless under the influence of "his master's voice". The Peshwa and Gangadhar Shastri were terribly disappointed, but the latter would not give up. He stayed on at Poona and made fresh attempts for the success of the cause which he had espoused. This made him a veritable thorn in Elphinstone's flesh. The latter pressed him continuously to return to Baroda, but he would not. He went on a pilgrimage with Bajirao to the sacred place of Purandhar, where on 14th July, 1815, he was foully murdered by some unknown person. Elphinstone and his English colleagues promptly declared that the murder had been instigated by Trimbakji at the instance of his master, Bajirao. Elphinstone held an investigation of sorts and came to the foregone conclusion that Trimbakji was guilty. No motive on the part of Bajirao or Trimbakji was even alleged. Subsequent events, however, showed who the real beneficiaries were. Any rapprochement between the Peshwa and the Gaikwad became more difficult than ever because of the murder of Gangadhar Shastri on Peshwa's soil. Further, the accusation furnished plausible reasons to the English for the agitation which they now started, on religious and moral grounds, against Trimbakji and the Peshwa, amongst the latter's own people. An ambassador, who was a Brahmin too, had been foully murdered at a place held sacred by the people and they were naturally horrified. The English historian, H. T. Prinsep, has described the English attitude in the following terms:

> "We assumed the role of the avenging angel for the murder of a Brahmin ambassador and won the people's support ... When two years later the war against Bajirao started, his subjects remembered the murder which they considered to be the root cause of the war and not only remained totally indifferent right through it, but in the end accepted Bajirao's downfall as nothing but just retribution for the sin of having had an innocent and devout Brahmin murdered at a sacred place."

It must not, moreover, be forgotten that Gangadhar Shastri had been for years in the pay of the English as their spy and secret agent and had, as such, acquired knowledge of their plans and plots. According to the English thinking, he had changed sides and gone over to the Peshwa and so was most likely to divulge his knowledge of English machinations against the Peshwa. His death eliminated that risk. Trimbakji, who was accused of the murder, was a very wideawake politician devoted to the Peshwa and to the Maratha cause and so long as he was free and continued to guide Bajirao, the danger of the English plans going awry was ever present. So his removal too from the scene was definitely indicated and duly effected. After completing his investigation, Elphinstone demanded that the Peshwa deliver Trimbakji into the custody of the English. But, even if Trimbakji was guilty, his alleged crime had taken place inside the Peshwa's territory and therefore, the latter's government alone could take cognizance of it. Clearly, therefore, Elphinstone's demand was an abrogation by the English of the Peshwa's sovereignty over his subject and territory. Bajirao at first refused to surrender Trimbakji. Thereupon, Elphinstone threatened to besiege Poona with the Company's Subsidiary Army which was already quartered in the town. Bajirao did not have the courage to resist further and handed over Trimbakji to the English who confined him in their fort at Thana.

Before narrating further events on what may be called the "Maratha Front", we would deviate here to describe the overall situation as it had developed since the conclusion of the Nepal War in 1815–16.

Benefits of Nepal War to the English

The conclusion of the Nepal War and its benefits to the English had not only whetted Hastings' Empire-hunger but it had also enabled him to pursue his plans against the Marathas more vigorously than ever. It will be recalled that he had "borrowed" from the Nawab Wazir of Oudh Rs. 2.5 crores to finance the war. Not all of it had been spent. A good deal of it was still in the Company's coffers. After the end of the war, the Company's officers had subjected the regions ceded by Nepal to heavy financial levies to their heart's content. Further, the revenues from these regions had increased the Company's recurring income by about a crore of rupees. Thus the Company's financial difficulties were practically over. The suspension of hostilities sometime before May, 1815, and the end of the war a few months later, left Hastings free to devote his undivided attention and resources to his preparations for the destruction of Maratha power.

Hastings' Preparations

He began by getting together a vast army of about' 1,00,000 soldiers and put himself personally in command of about one-third of it. Then he started to station detachments of the army on all vantage points around the territories of the Maratha rulers, under the pretence that it was being done for the suppression of the Pindari "bandits", whose numerous raids were terrorising the people, because, more frequently than ever before, they sallied forth from the security of their settlements in the Maratha territories and raided the territories of the Company and its allies. He was by now also equipped with a very accurate detailed map and description of the topography of the whole of Central India completely in 1815 by Col. Todd, who had worked on it for about nine years. It might be mentioned here that one of the causes of the English failure in the Second Maratha War was that their knowledge of the geography of the region was grossly inadequate. The maps available up till 1815 were, in certain respects, ludicrously wrong and very misleading. Todd's map was of immense help to Hastings and contributed substantially to his success in the Third Maratha War. Attention may also be drawn to the fact that by now Hastings had succeeded in muzzling the most powerful of the Maratha rulers, Doulatrao Sindhia, by forcing him as mentioned before into signing a new treaty, which deprived the Maratha power of its strongest member. Thus, by the beginning of 1817, Hastings had completed his preparations to the last detail and was quite ready to start the war of extermination against the Peshwa. On 7th April, 1817, he wrote to his Army Commander, Sir Evan Napean, and alerted him to be ready to seize parts of the Peshwa's Gujarat territory and northern Konkan "as the war between the English and the Peshwa was about to begin" (*Vide* Prinsep's *History of the Political and Military Transactions,* Vol. I, p. 321). A day earlier (6th April), Elphinstone made the following entry in his Diary:

> "I think a quarrel with the Peshwa desirable."

Bajirao Again Threatened with Siege of Poona Cedes Some Forts to the Company

It would appear that by then Bajirao had somehow got wind of what was afoot and made a futile attempt to avert the impending calamity. He invited Elphinstone for a personal interview and appealed for the continued friendship and support of the English on the ground of his steadfast loyalty and submission to the Company, in proof of which he detailed his past behaviour at some length. He might have spared himself the trouble, because his appeal fell on deaf ears. Hastings had made an irrevocable decision to crush him in any case.

A few days later, it was alleged that Trimbakji had escaped from his incarceration in the Thana Fort and was hiding in the Peshwa's territory. Elphinstone promptly faced Bajirao with the demand that he should produce and hand over Trimbakji to the Company within one month and, as a guarantee for his doing so, should forthwith give into the possession of the Company his forts at Sinhgarh, Purandhar and Raigarh. The helpless weak Peshwa ruler once again yielded to Elphinstone's threats, and, on 8th May, 1817, signed away the forts in favour of the Company. His surrender, however, got him only a few weeks' reprieve.

Bajirao Coerced into Ceding Gujarat

The English had long coveted the Peshwa's Gujarat province. Like the "wolf" in the "Wolf and the Lamb" fable, they trotted up another reason for demanding from Bajirao a good deal more of his territory including Gujarat. They resurrected the dead issue of the culpability for Gangadhar Shastri's murder. Two years earlier the English Resident, Elphinstone, had, after an investigation, held Trimbakji *alone* to have been guilty of the crime. It was now declared that Bajirao too was equally culpable as the instigator of the murder and must be penalised as such. On this ground some of the Peshwa's most fertile territories, including Gujarat, were demanded from him as an indemnity. He was hemmed in at Poona by the Company's troops and, under duress, was made to sign a fresh treaty on 13th June, 1817. By this treaty the whole of his Gujarat province was ceded to the Company, *not,* be it noted, for the benefit either of the victim's family or of his employer the Gaikwad but for the sole benefit of the Company. It has been stated too that Bajirao, at the same time "admitted that he had a hand in the murder".

After the Treaty

With the loss of Gujarat, Bajirao lost completely what little spirit he had. He was utterly disconcerted and after signing the treaty he left

Poona for Purandhar and from there went on to Mahuli, a sacred place near Satara. He asked Sir John Malcolm to meet him there and related to him his woes brought upon him by Elphinstone who had surrounded him with spies to watch his every movement (*Vide* "Memorandum of Lieut.-General Briggs"). He further expressed to Sir John his eagerness to reestablish sincere friendship with the Company. Sir John suggested that Bajirao should, as an earnest token of his friendliness, get together and send an army to help the English in suppressing the Pindaris. Bajirao followed this advice but his doing so had a reaction which was totally unexpected. As soon as he began to collect the army, Elphinstone reported to the Governor-General that Bajirao was collecting an army to fight the English, and asked for an immediate reinforcement of the Company's army at Poona to meet the threat.

War Started Against Bajirao—Battle of Kirkee

On 30th October, 1817, a whole battalion of the Company's army, under Gen. Smith and Col. Burr, arrived at the Poona Cantonment. Elphinstone stationed it on an elevated place some four miles away from the city. The Peshwa now realised that the English were bent on war in spite of his having submitted to their will so far. The worm turned at last, and Bajirao went out to meet them with his army commanded by the intrepid Bapu Gokhale. On 5th November, 1817, Gokhale engaged the English enemy in a fierce battle at Kirkee. But his army was honeycombed by cells of traitors in the Company's pay and "... his troops deserted him in the hour of trial" as recorded by an English writer who was present at the battle (*Fifteen Years in India*, p. 492). The English won the day, and Bajirao had to retreat with Bapu Gokhale. But the latter's spirit was unbroken and with a handful of loyal troops he engaged the Company's troops more than once and died fighting. "It is impossible not to respect the spirit of Gokhale ... the muse of history will encircle his name with a laurel for loyalty and devotion in his country's cause" (ibid., pp. 304, 505). Bajirao lost heart completely and was further crippled by the action of the Maratha State of Satara.

The Winning Over of the Raja of Satara

Elphinstone knew that throughout Maharashtra the English were discredited and their name was mud. He had feared therefore that when the war against the Peshwa was on, the Maratha rulers might not watch the approach of the Peshwa's end without raising a finger. They might rush to his rescue and rally round his flag. To avert that calamity, he started secret negotiations in order to win over the Raja of Satara as an instrument for keeping the Marathas, in check. According to the Parliamentary Papers relating to that period, the English offered to vest the Raja of Satara, after the war, with the status, privileges, rights and authority appertaining to the office of the Peshwa. The Raja, Pratapsinh, was a young man but legally still a minor and under the guardianship of his mother. She succumbed to Elphinstone's wiles and trusted the English promise. In the name of her son, the descendant of Shivaji and so the true head of the Maratha Empire (founded by Shivaji), she issued a proclamation calling upon the Marathas everywhere to break off all connections with Bajirao and to render every help to the English in their war against him.

Bajirao Peshwa's End

In June, 1818, Bajirao again approached Sir John Malcolm and sued for peace, although he still had a force of about 6,000 cavalry and 5,000 infantry and was still in possession of his fort at Aseergarh. Sir John wrote to the Governor-General. His letter has been summarised by Kaye (*Life of Malcolm,* Vol. II, p. 24) as follows:

> "I am well acquainted with the feelings which actuate the people of this country, from prince to pauper. I can, therefore, unhesitatingly state that the good name and welfare of the British government in the country lie in Bajirao's abdication by agreement and his removal elsewhere on a pension, rather than in his incarceration or death. His death will evoke the people's pity for him and will encourage any ambitious individual to claim the *gadi* as his successor. People discontented with the foreign rule would flock to the

claimant's flag. Bajirao's imprisonment will keep alive too, the people's sympathy for him, as, also the hope in the minds of the Marathas, that some day Bajirao will effect his escape from the prison and after that, they will be able to renew their efforts to regain their country's freedom from foreign rule. But if Bajirao, of his own accord, disbands his army and abdicates, then the effect on the people's mind would be entirely beneficial to us."

The Governor-General accepted Sir John's suggestion and sent orders accordingly. Bajirao abdicated and was given a yearly pension of Rs. 8 lacs. He was sent to Bithoor on the bank of the Ganges near Kanpur, where the exiled Peshwa lived for the next 32 years till his death in 1850 at the age of 75. He left behind an adopted son, Nana Sahib Dhondupant, who afterwards became a noted figure as a leader of the 1857 "mutiny".

The Peshwa's entire territory was usurped by the Company, with the exception of a narrow strip given to the Raja of Satara. Thus ended the Peshwa regime. The conditions prevailing in the city of Poona and amongst its residents as described by an English traveller, R. Richards, will be of interest. So we quote below from his writings:

> "On a late excursion into the Deccan I was exceedingly pleased and surprised to observe the great appearance of prosperity which the city of Poona exhibited … all the principal streets and bazars were crowded with people, whose dress and general appearance displayed symptoms of comfort and happiness, of business and industry, not to be exceeded in any of our own great commercial towns. The whole, indeed, was a smiling scene of general welfare and abundance. On noticing this to the Resident, he informed me that the Peshwa (Bajirao) since his return, with a view of promoting the prosperity of Poona, had exempted it and the surrounding country from every description of tax; and to prevent the possibility of exactions unknown to himself, had even abolished the office of Kotwal."

The population of Poona at that time was about eight lacs or four times the population in 1930.

The English and Raja Bhonsle

Concurrently with his campaign against the Peshwa, Hastings was very actively carrying out his plans against the Raja Bhonsle of Nagpur. Some months before Bajirao had sued for peace, Jenkins, the English Resident at Nagpur, had on 15th March, 1818, arrested Appa Sahib, then the Raja Bhonsle, on the charge that, over a year earlier, he had ordered the murder of his predecessor on the *gadi,* who had been found dead in his bed on the morning of 1st February, 1817. We would now revert and relate the events leading up to the arrest.

Before Appa Sahib's Occupation of the Gadi

Up to the Second Maratha War, Bhonsle was known, as he in fact, was as the Raja of Berar. But following the war, the province of Berar was forcibly taken away from him by the English and given to the Nizam. Thereafter Bhonsle was the Raja of Nagpur, in fact as well as in name. At the time of the war, Raghoji Bhonsle was on the *gadi* at Nagpur, and when it was over, Elphinstone (later the Resident at Poona) was appointed as the English Resident at Nagpur. During his four years at Nagpur, Elphinstone persistently presssed Raghoji to enter into the subsidiary alliance with the Company, but Raghoji declined to do so in spite of Elphinstone's efforts, supplemented by intrigues, bribery and corruption. The following extracts from letters written at the time by General Wellesley (later the Duke of Wellington) to Elphinstone throw a good deal of light on the latter's activities at Nagpur:

(i) "In answer to your letter of the 6th, I beg you will do whatever you think necessary to procure intelligence. If you think that Jaikishen Ram will procure it for you or give it to you, promise to recommend him to the Governor-General, and write to His Excellency on the subject" (Colebrooke's *Life of the Duke of Wellington,* Vol. I, page 113.)

(ii) "Before Ram Chandra went away he offered his services. I recommend him to you. He appears a shrewd fellow, and he has certainly been employed by the Raja in his most important negotiations. I have recommended him to the Governor-General for a pension of Rs. 6,000 a year. I think he will give you useful information."

Raghoji had, besides his only son Bala Sahib, a nephew called Appa Sahib, who was a shrewd, clever and ambitious young man. Elphinstone had won him over and made him the central figure in his intrigues at the Nagpur *Durbar*. Once there was some difference between Raghoji and Appa Sahib about the latter's private *Jagir*. It was a purely internal affair and had nothing to do with Bhonsle's relations with the English. The latter, therefore, had no right to intervene. But Elphinstone did so. He espoused Appa Sahib's eause and pressed Raghoji to settle the matter according to his (Elphinstone's) wishes.

Raghoji died in April, 1816. On his death-bed he pathetically put his son's hand into the hands of Appa Sahib and said "The honour of the family and the prestige of this state is now in your hands."

Raghoji's son and heir, Bala Sahib, was stated to be incapable of carrying on the administration because he was weak in mind and intellect. So, although he ascended the *gadi,* the entire administration of the State came to be in Appa Sahib's hands. At Bala Sahib's installation, Jenkins, who had earlier replaced Elphinstone as Resident, attended the *Durbar* on behalf of the English Government and offered felicitations to both Bala Sahib and Appa Sahib.

Raghoji's death was most opportune for the English. According to Prinsep along with "the intrigues and passing occurrences of that court" it "promised equally to give the long-sought opportunity of establishing a subsidiary alliance with the Nagpur State" (*History of Political and Military Transactions*).

Treaty Signed at Midnight

Within a few weeks of Bala Sahib's installation as the Raja and of Appa Sahib's taking over the administration of the State, Jenkins, under Hastings instructions, got Appa Sahib to sign on behalf of Bala Sahib the treaty of Subsidiary Alliance. It is significant that it was signed at midnight (24th June, 1816) and that Appa Sahib was a youth of only 20.

Under the treaty the Raja of Nagpur was purported to have agreed to disband almost the whole of his army and to pay the Company Rs. 20 to Rs. 30 lacs every year for maintaining the Company's force which was to replace the Raja's army at Nagpur. The total gross revenue of the State then was no more than Rs. 60 lacs.

On receiving the Treaty, Hastings made the following entry in his Private Journal (p. 254, *et. seq*):

> "June 1st (1816). This day has brought to me the treaty of alliance by which Nagpur in fact ranges itself as a feudatory State under our protection. A singular contention of personal interests at the court of that country, resulting from the unexpected death of Raghoji Bhonsle, the late Raja, has enabled me to effect that which has been fruitlessly laboured at for the last 12 years. Though dexterity has been requisite, and money has removed obstructions, I can affirm that the principles of my engagement are of the purest nature."

Mills' comments on the treaty read:

> "The conditions of the treaty were somewhat severe and the amount of the subsidy exceeded a due proportion of the revenues of the country. The charge of the contingent was an addition to the burden already too weighty for the State and the Raja had some grounds for complaining of the costliness of his new friends." (Mill, Vol. VIII, p. 186)

Two Groups at Bhonsle's Court

Hastings has referred to "contention of interests" at the Nagpur court. It appears from letters written at the time by Englishmen that the court was split up into two groups. One supported Bala Sahib, the Raja, and was making ceaseless efforts to effect a genuine and strong re-union of Bhonsle, Sindhia and the Peshwa. The other was on the side of the English, in the forefront of whose intrigues was Appa Sahib. The terms of the treaty signed by Appa Sahib considerably strengthened the first group, and Jenkins began to fear that so long as Bala Sahib was on the *gadi,* there was a real danger of his being prevailed upon to disown a treaty which he had not signed.

Sudden Death of Bala Sahib—Appa Sahib Occupies the Gadi

Bala Sahib was found dead in his bed on the morning of 1st February, 1817. The state of his body indicated that he had been murdered. There were widespread rumours throughout Nagpur that Jenkins had him murdered. Appa Sahib, who had been out of Nagpur, now returned and occupied the *gadi*.

Tension Between Jenkins and Appa Sahib

Appa Sahib soon realised that the burden of the treaty which he had signed was too heavy for the State. He also came to know that two of his ministers Nagu Pandit and Narayan Pandit had been bought over by the English. He dismissed both of them and this deprived Jenkins of two of his important secret agents and spies. Jenkins retaliated by becoming progressively rude and insolent in his behaviour towards Appa Sahib. An instance might be given.

It was customary for the Peshwa as the suzerain to present to his feudatory Bhonsle a *Khillat* (ceremonial dress) whenever a new Raja succeeded to the *gadi*. The Raja used to put it on publicly at a *Durbar* as a token of his acknowledgement of the Peshwa's suzerainty. Accordingly, Appa Sahib received the *Khillat* and arranged to hold a *Durbar,* but he refused to attend it on the ground that the acceptance of the *Khillat* by Bhonsle was an overt act of hostility against the English. It may be noted that the war against the Peshwa was not on then and the Peshwa had sent the *Khillat* with the knowledge and concurrence of Elphinstone, the English Resident at Poona.

Appa Sahib Complains to Governor-General

Appa Sahib approached the Governor-General with his complaints against Jenkins and the Company. He stated that the contingent of the Subsidiary Army stationed at Nagpur was much larger than that contemplated in the treaty and that the Company refused to pay any octroi to the State on provisions and other supplies brought into Nagpur for such a large force. He appealed for a revision of the treaty and for reduction in the amount of the subsidy payable by him in view of the State's administration. Sir John Malcom met Appa Sahib in this connection and was given a very warm and hospitable reception. After meeting Appa Sahib, Sir John Malcolm wrote to the Governor-General that Appa Sahib was quite sincere in his desire to maintain his friendship with the English. But on 26th November, 1817, Jenkins asserted in his letter to the Governor-General that the fact of Appa Sahib's daring to make such complaints was by itself an incontrovertible proof of his disloyalty to the English!

Company's Army in Front of Bhonsle's Capital

As a matter of fact Jenkins had been making his preparations for a long time, and, early on the morning on 26th November, 1817, had drawn up in battle array a very large force on the Sitabaldi Hills facing Nagpur. The force consisted of most of the Company's Subsidiary Army of Berar, two battalions of Madras sepoys, one of white soldiers, one of Indian horse-battery, three regiments of VI Bengal lancers, two heavy guns, two companies of Bengal infantry, some Madras cavalry and about 400 other soldiers. All these had assembled under Jenkins' orders in the Nagpur Residency maidan by the night before the 26th.

The First Clash—Suspension of Hostilities

The English manoeuvre threw the Nagpur statesmen into a panic and were, therefore, divided about the line of action to be taken. Appa Sahib and some of his companions wanted to avoid a conflict, if at all possible. Others saw that war was inevitable and counselled an immediate attack on the Company's army at Sitabaldi. The matter was still under discussion when a detachment of Appa Sahib's army, without any reference to him, attacked the Company's army on the evening of the 26th. They were repulsed. Appa Sahib then sent a message to Jenkins, expressing his deep regret at his army's attacking the Company's troops against his orders and offered to accept any terms imposed on him to stop further fighting. Jenkins replied that he could do nothing as the matter was now in the hands of the Governor-General, but, pending the latter's decision, he was prepared temporarily to suspend hostilities, if Appa Sahib immediately withdrew his army beyond certain specified limits. During the night of the 27th Appa Sahib withdrew his army as desired by Jenkins.

It appears from a letter of Hastings that Jenkins' object in suspending hostilities was to give his tired troops some rest and to gain time for the arrival of reinforcements, which arrived on the morning of the 29th. That very evening Appa Sahib wrote to Jenkins offering to disband most of his army and appealed for the continuation of the subsidiary alliance and the redress of his grievances. Jenkins' answer was the same, that the matter was no longer in his hands. Thereafter, more battalions of the Company's army continued to arrive at Nagpur.

Jenkins' Ultimatum to Appa Sahib

On 14th December, Jenkins had an ultimatum delivered to Appa Sahib that he should by 4 a.m. on the 16th

(i) acknowledge that as a penalty for the attack on the Company's army, the entire State of Nagpur would be *ipso facto* handed over to the English Government,

(ii) hand over to the Company his entire store of munitions, arms, guns, etc.,

(iii) send his entire army including the Arab contingent to any place to be specified by the English and to disband it later in co-operation with the Resident,

(iv) vacate the city of Nagpur for occupation by the English force, and

(v) deliver himself up at the Company's Cantonment and remain there till the dispute was finally decided and peace restored.

Humiliating as the demands were, Appa Sahib was willing to comply with them. Some of his army, particularly the Arab contingent, however, stoutly opposed his committing political suicide that way and would not let him go to the English Cantonment.

At 6 a.m. on 16th December, Jenkins received a message from Appa Sahib saying that the Arabs on guard at the palace would not allow him to go out, that compliance with the other demands including the surrender of arms and munitions, would take some more time, and that everything would be done in two or three days. Jenkins' reply was that if Appa Sahib surrendered himself at the Cantonment within three hours, he would be given more time to comply with the other demands, otherwise an attack on his army would be launched from all sides. Appa Sahib arrived at the Cantonment and surrendered himself a little before 9 a.m.

Resistance by Arab Soldiers

There were hundreds of Arab soldiers in the Nagpur army, who formed a compact body under Arab N.C.O.'s. They were noted for their loyalty and were entrusted with the duty of guarding the palace. Led by them, the Nagpur army refused to carry out Appa Sahib's orders to hand over arms and ammunition to the Company's army and on 16th December started shooting when a detachment of the Company's army arrived to capture them. The detachment was unable to overcome the loyal Nagpur soldiers and had to return empty-handed. During the next two days Jenkins made repeated efforts to persuade the Arabs to vacate the palace and the city but the Arabs refused pointblank to do so. It was then decided to eject them forcibly, and, after obtaining some heavy guns from Akola, General Doveton led an attack on the Arabs on 24th December, but was repulsed with heavy losses. Another five days were spent in parleys with the Arab officers who were pressed by Appa Sahib to leave the palace. Eventually on the morning of 30th December the Arab troops left. An English officer escorted them and their families to Malkapur and the Company's army occupied the undefended city and the palace.

Terms Dictated by the English Accepted by Appa Sahib

Appa Sahib, still in English hands at the Cantonment, was told that he could regain the Nagpur *gadi* only by accepting and complying with the following terms:

(i) That his entire territory in the north of the Narmada and some of it to its south must be ceded to the Company, which should further be vested with all his rights relating to Berar, Gawilgarh, Surguja and Jashpur.

(ii) That the ministers appointed for the administration of the rest of his territory should be such as enjoyed the confidence of the Company and should follow the Resident's advice in all matters.

(iii) That Appa Sahib and his family should reside in the palace under the watch and ward of the Company's troops.

(iv) That the arrears of the subsidy stipulated in the midnight Treaty of 24th April, 1816, should be paid up by the State and the subsidy should be continued to be paid till the above-mentioned territories were actually handed over.

(v) That whichever forts in the State the English wanted should be handed over to them.

(vi) That the State subjects named by the English should be arrested and handed over to them.

(vii) That both the hills at Sitabaldi, its adjoining Bazar and all the area around it wanted by the English for constructing their fortifications should be given to them.

Appa Sahib was barely 22 years old then and could see no other course open to him which could bring him freedom from incarceration in the Cantonment. He accepted the terms and was allowed to return to his palace on 9th January, 1818.

Rejection of Appa Sahib's Prayer

Appa Sahib found it utterly impossible to meet the expenditure of administration and the demands of the Company with the revenues of the territory which the English had left with him. He therefore, prayed that this territory too might be taken over by the English and he might be given an annual maintenance allowance. Hastings turned down the request, because, as he reported to the Company's Directors, it meant a financial loss to the Company. He did covet the rest of the State but hated to spend any money for it. He and Jenkins, therefore, looked for an excuse for grabbing it without having to pay anything. Jenkins soon found one.

Arrest and Deportation of Appa Sahib

Jenkins, aware of what Hastings wanted, lost no time in accusing Appa Sahib and two of his ministers of hatching a plot against the English with the Commandants of Bag Chowragarh and Mandla Forts, the Subedar of Ratanpur and the Peshwa Bajirao. But the "proofs" collected by Jenkins to bolster up this charge were considered too flimsy even by Hastings. Thereupon Jenkins dug up and came forward with a new charge, that Appa Sahib, had, a year ago, ordered the murder of Bala Sahib which had been duly carried out. In his "Essay on Warren Hastings", Macaulay observes that the English Government in India of those days had "only to let it be understood that it wishes a particular man to be ruined and in twenty-four hours it will be furnished with grave charges, supported by depositions so full and circumstantial, that any person, unaccustomed to Asiatic mendacity, would regard them as decisive." Hastings in his "Despatch to the Secret Committee of the Court of Directors", said that whilst the evidence in support of the former charge could not satisfy anybody, "... we could not go on stronger grounds in deposing him than those of a murder. The proofs for conviction were easily producible ..." On the basis of these proofs Appa Sahib was on 15th March, 1818, taken in custody from the palace. He was never faced with the "proofs" or given a chance to defend himself but was held to be guilty and sentenced to imprisonment and deportation to the Company's fort at Allahabad.

On the vacant Nagpur *gadi* was put an infant grandson of Raghoji Bhonsle as the nominal Raja, and it was proclaimed that during his minority the entire administration of Nagpur State would be carried on by the English Resident.

Annexation of Half the State of Nagpur and Occupation of its Forts

Under cover of the treaty which Appa Sahib had been forced to sign, about half of his territory, comprising the most fertile and prosperous regions of the State, were brought under the Company's rule and permanently annexed to its possessions. The annexations increased the Company's income, according to the Governor-General, by twenty-two-and-a-half lacs per year.

The English, thereafter, proceeded to take possession of Forts in the State. The site and the strength of some of them had elicited the administration of more than one English General. According to an English writer,

> "She (Nature) seems to have marked them out as a theatre, on which the battles of freedom and independence might be successfully fought." (*Journal of the Sieges of the Madras Army*" by Lieut. Lake, p. 107)

The Commanders and the garrisons of some of the forts ignored the proclamation issued by the Company in the name of the infant Raja and flatly refused to surrender the forts. They bravely fought against their occupation by the English. But the English soon overcame this resistance either by armed strength or by intrigues and bribery, and eventually succeeded in occupying some 30 big and small forts of the State. The longest and stiffest resistance was offered by the Arab garrison of Assergarh Fort, but it was of no avail and the Fort fell to the English on 7th April, 1819. With its fall the Company completed the acquisition of every inch of the Bhonsle territory and every fort mentioned in the latest treaty made with Appa Sahib.

Last Days of Appa Sahib

Whilst being taken to Allahabad, Appa Sahib made good his escape from the custody of the armed guard which was escorting him. The English offered huge rewards for information leading to his apprehension but it proved useless. Appa Sahib reached the Mahadeva Hill where the Gonds readily helped him. With their armed help he took and occupied Chowragarh Fort. It has been stated that his partisans in Nagpur also helped him with money and in other ways. The English, failing in their efforts to rearrest him, then announced that if Appa Sahib surrendered himself to them, he would be given a pension of a lac of rupees a year and permitted to reside anywhere he liked within the Company's territory. But Appa Sahib would not surrender. He preferred to wander from one *Durbar* to another requesting help. He did not receive any. At last disguised as a Fakir, he sought refuge in the Mahamandir Temple at Jodhpur. The English pressed Raja Mansingh of Jodhpur to hand over Appa Sahib to them, but the Raja declined to do so and Appa Sahib lived there till the end of his days. Thus ended the lineage of the Bhonsle Rajas.

Unprovoked and Undeclared War Against Holkar

It will be recalled that some ten years earlier, circumstances had forced the English into a treaty with Jaswantrao Holkar which had, by no means, added to their prestige. After that, Jaswantrao Holkar died insane and the administration of the State passed into the hands of Amir Khan. The latter's intrigues with the English, which have been mentioned before, resulted in internal dissensions and misrule, so that virtual anarchy prevailed throughout the State, Hastings took advantage of this confusion and without any reason, or, even an excuse, attacked the State.

Battle of Mahidpur—Treaty of Mandeshwar

On 20th December, 1817, the Company's army engaged Holkar's army in battle at Mahidpur. Holkar's Muslim Captain-General of Artillery, Roshan Beg, was in over-all command and put up such a stiff fight with his artillery that at one time the Company's force wavered and was on the brink of disaster when treason in Holkar's camp once again retrieved the situation for the English. Nawab Abdul Ghafoor Khan, the son-in-law of the treacherous Amir Khan, was one of the Commanders under Roshan Beg and he

> "played the part of a traitor to his master and deserted the field of battle with the force under his command, just at the moment when the English were on the point of losing the battle through the loyal and gallant exertions of Roshan Beg". (*The Autobiography of Lutufullah*, pp. 103–04)

The Battle of Mahidpur was in this way "won" by the Company, and was followed by the Treaty of Mandeshwar, whereby a very large part of Holkar's territory was annexed by the Company and the minor Maharaja Holkar purported to enter into the Subsidiary Alliance with the Company.

As the price of his treason, Nawab Abdul Ghafoor Khan received from the Company what is now (1929) known as Jaora State in Malwa which has been ruled ever since by his descendants.

Holkar was the last of the independent Maratha rulers to be subdued by Hastings and his subjugation marked the end of the Third Maratha War.

We would now summarise the gains to the English which resulted from it.

English Gains Resulting from the War

The gains were territorial, financial, and political. Territorially they gained more than 50,000 square miles. The additions comprised the areas covered by the present (1929) Central India and Central Provinces and the Peshwa's entire territory with the exception of the little bit given to Satara, and some of the most fertile provinces of Sindhia, Holkar and Bhonsle. Other gains were the considerable areas of land and large amounts of money exacted from the Rajputana princes in return for the Company's protection during the war. Politically, the principal feudatories of Sindhia, including the rulers in Rajasthan, had been prevailed upon to break away from him and to establish direct political relations with the Company, under whose protection they placed themselves. Holkar became a feudatory of the Company and the latter's Subsidiary Army was permanently stationed in Nagpur. But the most important gain was that the Peshwa, the central figure and head of the Maratha Confederacy, had been finished once and for all and Maratha power was destroyed for ever. Hastings had achieved complete success in his plans for the establishment of the English political paramountcy, the goal which he had set before himself as recorded in his "Private Journal", quoted earlier. Another entry in the same journal throws a good deal of light upon the Company's political relations with the Indian rulers and the role of the English Residents deputed to the Indian *Durbars*. It reads:

> "In our treaties with them we recognise them as independent sovereigns. Then we send a Resident to their courts. Instead of acting in the character of ambassador, he assumes the functions of a dictator; interferes in all their private concerns; countenances refractory subjects against them; and makes the most ostentatious exhibition of the exercise of authority ... and the Government identifies itself with the Resident ... on the whole tenor of his conduct."

Hastings' Personal Gain

The grateful Directors of the Company rewarded Hastings for the English "victory" in the Third Maratha War by presenting him with £60,000 with which to acquire for himself an estate in England.

Edmund Burke's Description of Company's Unscrupulousness

The treatment meted out by the Company to the Peshwa Bajirao and Appa Sahib Bhonsle was quite in accordance with the pattern drawn by Edmund Burke in his speech on the India Bill delivered some 35 years earlier in the British Parliament from which we quote the following extract:

> "First, I say, that from Mount Imaus (Himalayas) ... to Cape Comorin ... there is not a single prince, state or potentate,

great or small, in India with whom they have come into contact, whom they have not sold, I say sold, though sometimes they have not been able to deliver according to their bargain. Secondly, I say that there is not a single treaty they have ever made, which they have not broken. Thirdly, I say that there is not a single prince or state who ever put any trust in the Company who is not utterly ruined; and that none are in any degree secure or flourishing but in the exact proportion to their settled distrust and irreconcilable enmity to this nation. These assertions are universal, I say, in the full sense universal."

7

LORD AMHERST (1823–1828)

Adams

After Hastings, Adams was the Governor-General *protem*. His short regime of about seven months is notable for the first, and perhaps the only, deportation of an Englishman from India. The victim was J. S. Buckingham, the Editor of "the Calcutta Journal". Adams disapproved of the publication in the Journal of something about a Scotch clergyman and ordered that Buckingham be packed off to England. The order was carried out.

Lord Amherst

Lord Amherst arrived at Calcutta on 1st August, 1823, relieved Adams and took over as Governor-General. Within a few months he started the Burmese War.

English Relations with Burma

The English had long had their eyes on Burma which then was a sovereign and prosperous State. The Burmese provinces of Assam and Arakan bordered Beanal and Arakan's boundary touched that of the Chattgram (Chittagong) district in Bengal. The Raja of Arakan was a feudatory of the King of Burma. English relations with Burma had begun to deteriorate in the later nineties of the eighteenth century, when the English began countenancing Kingbaring, a refractory and powerful *Sardar* of the Arakan *Durbar,* and ultimately won him over.

Arakanese Migrate to Chattgram District

During 1797–98 some 30 to 40 thousand Arkanese led by Kingbaring left their country and migrated to and settled in Chattgram district. According to the English writer, Wilson:

"The Government of Bengal had resolved to admit the emigrants to the advantages of permanent colonisation and assigned them unoccupied lands in the southern portion of the district." (Mill, Vol. IX, p. 11)

An English officer, Capt. Cox, was appointed to look after and administer the emigrants' settlement, which later came to be known as Cox Bazar.

Raids by the Emigrants

From the security of their settlement in the Company's territory, the emigrants began to sally forth in raids on the Arakan territory. The raids were encouraged, if not instigated and aided, by the Company's representatives. In his letter dated 23rd January, 1812, Lord Minto has fully described to the Directors a major raid into Burmese territory led by Kingbaring in May, 1811. He has clearly stated in this letter that Kingbaring had been making preparations for this raid since 1797 and had collected a strong band of raiders in Chattgram. He has also stated that after the raid, Kingbaring returned to the Company's territory with considerable booty. Mention has also been made in the letter of Kingbaring's hostility towards the King of Burma.

Burmese Requests and Their Results

The King of Burma wrote to the Company's government requesting the latter either to hand over Kingbaring and his gang to the Burmese Government or to permit the latter's troops to enter the Company's territory to arrest them. The English promised to hand over Kingbaring but did not do so. Kingbaring continued his raids for some years and, whenever he was pressed hard by the Burmese troops pursuing him, invariably sought refuge in the Company's territory and each time the Company barred the entry of the pursuers into their territory. Kingbaring's death in 1815 did not end the troubles of the Burmese subjects, as other leaders of raids were soon found to take his place. Lord Minto has admitted in his letters to the Directors that very heavy losses were suffered by the people of Arakan in consequence of these raids and that Burmese requests were fair and reasonable, but the acceptance of either of them militated against the principles of the English Government, whose subjects the raiders were. So the raiders were neither surrendered to the Burmese Government, nor were the latter's troops permitted to enter the Company's territory.

In sharp contrast to this partiality for the raiders may be recalled the fact that the Company had attacked Kutch State because, it was alleged, some raiders from the State had raided the Peshwa's feudatory, Kathiawar, and the Peshwa was a friend of the English. Later, the English had invaded the Peshwa's territory under the pretext of suppressing the Pindari "robbers".

Efforts to Pacify the Government of Burma

Capt. Canning was sent to Ava, the capital of Burma, to counteract the annoyance which the English attitude was bound to cause at the Burmese Court. He tried to convince the King of Burma that the Company's government was a real and true friend of his and had nothing whatsoever to do with the raids into Arakan. At the same time, Capt. Canning functioned as the spy and secret agent of the Company at Ava to collect information and to create and promote Burmese ill-will and disaffection towards their Government. He also made vigorous attempts to entice the Burmese Government to enter into the subsidiary alliance with the Company. In one of his letters to Lord Minto, he wrote:

> "... should it enter into the views of Government to obtain a preponderating influence in the Burmese dominions, the present was certainly the most favourable moment, as the weakness of the Government and general discontent of the people would put the whole country at the disposal of a very small British force". (Minto's "Despatch" to the Court of Directors, 4th March, 1812)

Lord Minto Recommends War Against Burma

On 1st August, 1812, Lord Minto wrote to the Directors:

(i) That Capt. Canning's statement about the benefits which the English Government could derive from a war with Burma was undoubtedly reasonable;

(ii) That the sea-board of that country was unfortified and was open to attack;

(iii) That there was only one part of the Company's territory which was at all approachable by the Burmese troops and it could be easily successfully defended; and

(iv) That there was no doubt about a complete and quick English victory in a war against Burma.

Other Disputes with Burma

In addition to the raids there were other matters, too, which were in dispute with Burma, such as intrusions into the Ramoo Hills of Burma by the Company's men for catching elephants, the questioning of Burma's riparian rights in the Naaf river which flowed through Burma, the Burmese ownership of the Shahpuri islet, etc. The Company's boats used the Naaf river for the transport of goods and merchandise, but refused to pay any duty to Burma. In January, 1823, a boat of the Company carrying rice was alleged to have been fired upon by the Burmese officials, because it had refused to pay the duty demanded by the officials on the ground that only one bank of the river was owned by Burma, the other being owned by the Company. In the firing, the Company's boatman was killed. Thereupon the Company's troops occupied the islet of Shahpuri, in spite of Burmese protests. The Burmese troops then dislodged the Company's troops from the islet and reoccupied it. But reinforcements were sent from Calcutta. These arrived at Shahpuri on 21st November, 1823, took possession of it without any opposition by the Burmese and issued a tempting proclamation to win over the people there.

Infructuous Joint Commission

A joint commission of two representatives of the Company and four of the Raja of Arakan was appointed to adjudicate upon the issue of Shahpuri's ownership. Arakan's representatives naturally asked that before the commission began its work, both sides should vacate the islet. This was not agreed to by the Company and so the Arakan representative returned home without doing anything.

War with Burma Decided Upon

Thereafter, the Burmese Government arrested Captain Chew and some of the crew of the Company's vessel *"Sofia"* which had arrived at Shahpuri and offered to release the arrested persons if the Company's Government arrested and handed over to them the leaders of the raids on Burmese territory which had been going on for years. The English, whose preparations for war were by then completed, ignored the offer and decided upon an immediate war with Burma.

The People of Burma

The Burmese were not divided, like Indians, by different religious faiths, and caste, or geographical sectarianism. They were a united and completely integrated nation–brave, spirited and ambitious. In several aspects of culture, they were more advanced than the Europeans and in no European country was education so widespread as in Burma. We quote below the historian Wilson about the Government and the people of Burma:

> "The vigorous despotism of the Government and the confident courage of the people crowned every enterprise with success and for above half a century the Burman arms were invariably victorious, whether wielded for attack or defence. Shortly after their insurrection against Pegu, the Burmans became masters of that Kingdom. They next wrested valuable districts of the Tenasserim coast from Siam.

They repelled with great gallantry a formidable invasion from China, and by the final annexation of Arakan, Manipur and Assam to the Empire, they established themselves through the whole of the narrow, but extensive tracts of the country, which separated the Western provinces of China along the Eastern boundaries of Hindustan." (*Narrative of the Burmese War* by H. H. Wilson, pp. 1–2)

Burmese Rule in Assam

The King of Burma had taken military action to end disorder and misrule in Assam and to establish law and order. He had appointed a *Sardar* of his, Menji Mahasilve, as the provincial governor of Assam. Menji Mahasilve's relations with the English were very friendly, as admitted by the Governor-General in his despatch to the Court of Directors dated 12th September, 1823; "yet", the Governor-General added, "the substitution of a warlike and comparatively speaking powerful Government in the place of the feeble administration that formerly ruled Assam" could not but be harmful to English interests. Wilson has gone a step further and stated that such a powerful and ambitious neighbour (Burma) was dangerous to the English. Efforts were, therefore, made to incite the people of Assam against their Burmese Government.

Plans and Preparations for Invasion of Burma

The attack on Burma was planned to be launched from two directions simultaneously. One at the border of the Assamese territory of Burma and the other at Rangoon. Forces for the former were to be sent by land and for the latter by sea from Madras and Calcutta.

To harass the Burmese Government still further, efforts were made to persuade the people of Siam to invade Burma from the south. But the Siamese declined to oblige the English.

In Rangoon, propaganda was started to convince the people there that they were not Burmese at all, but "Rangoonese", and as such owed no allegiance or loyalty to their "foreign" Burmese rulers. It was, however, as ineffective as the proverbial water on a duck's back because the way in which the Government of Burma ruled its subjects was most considerate, liberal and beneficial.

The force detailed for invading the Assam border was dispatched about the end of 1823, that is, months before the declaration of war. Lord Amherst has mentioned in one of his letters (dated 2nd April, 1824) that those in charge of this force made vigorous efforts to tempt the people of Assam to revolt against the Government of Burma. Wilson has confirmed this and has added that as soon as the force neared Assam, it issued a proclamation to the Assamese and the neighbouring tribes making specious promises of good things if they sided with the invaders.

War Declared–Cachar Won Over

On the allegation that the King of Burma was plotting against the English in conjunction with the Marathas and some other Indian rulers, Lord Amherst formally declared war against Burma on 5th March, 1824. The next day, the Raja of Cachar, a small independent state between Sylhet and Manipur, capitulated to the English and sold his independence to them by a treaty. The war had started.

The Company's Force at Rangoon

On 10th May, 1824, the ships carrying the Company's troops anchored off Rangoon harbour, which as mentioned before, was unfortified. After some shelling of Rangoon, the force landed and occupied the town without meeting with any resistance worth the name. They found the town completely deserted by its inhabitants who had left it with their families, goods and chattels, cattle, carts and boats, and taken refuge in the distant shrubberied country. The English were sorely disappointed in their expectations of getting supplies and transport at Rangoon for their march up the Irrawady river to Ava, the capital of Burma. Snodgrass, in his *Narative of the Burmese War* (pp. 17–18), writes:

> "In boats, especially, Rangoon was known to be well supplied; and it was by many anticipated that ... that city would afford the means of pushing up the river a force sufficient to subdue the capital and bring the war at once to a conclusion.
>
> But in these calculations, the well considered power and judicious policy of the Government towards its conquered provinces were overlooked and the warlike and haughty character of the nation was so imperfectly known, that no correct judgement could be formed of our probable reception."

The invaders were in a fix. They could not proceed up the river because of utter lack of boats or transport of any kind. They could not stay on where they were, because not only were they unable to procure any stores or provisions whatsoever in the deserted town, but also had to suffer helplessly the harassment of being the victims every night of raids carried out by groups of Burmese soldiers who were experts in night fighting.

The Rout of the Company's Force on Assam Border

The King of Burma sent a force some 12,000 strong commanded by his famous General, Maha Menji Bandoola, to oppose the Company's force nearing the border of Assam. In early May, 1824, Bandoola's force crossed the Neaf river and went into camp at Ratnapullang, some 14 miles south of the Ramoo Hill. Later, they fought a fierce battle with the advancing force of the Company, in which the latter were severely beaten and had to retreat in disorder, leaving behind several officers and numerous men dead on the battle-field.

Panic in Calcutta

The crushing defeat drove the English Government circles in Calcutta into a panic. According to Major Archer:

> "The Supreme Government was actually afraid of a Burmese invasion in Calcutta by way of the Sunderbans."

Sir Charles Metcalfe on the Company's Defeat

In Sir Charles Metcalfe's papers to the Governor-General, 8th June, 1824, we read as follows:

> "The Burmans have commenced the war with us in a manner which perhaps was little expected. They have the advantage of first success and we have the disadvantage of disaster, which is likely ... to be of worse consequence to us than it would be to any other power in the world ... The progress of the enemy has carried alarm to Dacca and even to Calcutta, where alarm has not been felt from an external enemy since the time of Sirajudaula and the Black Hole ... Our enemies appear not to be deficient in either spirit or numbers; ... there is real danger to our whole Empire in India ... All India is at all times looking out for our downfall. The people would everywhere rejoice ... at our destruction; and numbers are not wanting who would promote it by all means in their power. Our ruin ... will probably be rapid and sudden ... From the pinnacle to the abyss might be but one step. The fidelity of our native army, on which our existence depends, depends itself on our continued success ..."

Burmans Miss the Opportunity

The Company's troops did not stop in their head-long flight from the battlefield, till they reached Bhadarpur behind the Ramoo Hill and there they stayed put for months.

Wilson has expressed the opinion that had General Maha Bandoola been free to follow up his victory by pressing on further at this juncture, very probably he would have had no great difficulty in conquering most of English-occupied Bengal including Calcutta. But, fortunately for the English, he was ordered by the King of Burma to return to Rangoon which he had to do with the bulk of his army.

The Company's government had plenty of money exacted from the princes and people of India and had a large number of Indian troops at its disposal. The respite was utilised by it in heavily reinforcing its forces at the Burmese front.

The Pillars of British Empire

We have to digress here to narrate a horrifying event which took place on 1st November, 1824, namely, the deliberate shelling of the Company's 47th Indian Infantry by the Company's artillery. Metcalfe has referred to it in the following words:

> "It is an awful thing to mow down our own troops with our own artillery, specially those troops on whose fidelity the existence of our Empire depends." (Kaye's *Selections from the Papers of Lord Metcalfe*, p. 153)

Metcalfe might have added with equal truth that the foundations of the Empire were raised mainly on the Indians' "bones and blood". As the historian Lecky puts it, "a people who are submissive, gentle and loyal fall by reason of these very qualities under a despotic Government". More than one English writer and administrator has freely eulogised these qualities of the Indian sepoy. Yet the latter was never treated fairly *vis-a-vis* the white soldier. The following instances will give one an idea of the undisguised discrimination. On enlistment, the white recruit received a bounty in cash, the sepoy got nothing. The former was provided with quarters in barracks built and reserved for the white personnel of the Company's army, whereas the Indian personnel had to put up their own thatched huts for their quarters. The highest military rank was attainable by the white soldier, whilst not one of the three lacs of Indian sepoys was ever permitted to rise above the humble rank of Subedar-Major. The sepoy had to carry a gun heavier than that of the "Tommy", and had to carry his own heavy knapsack which, in the words of Sir Mark Cubban, K.C.B., was "the curse of the Native Army". The white soldier had to carry nothing. There was a world of difference in the pay, furlough, pension and allowances to which the white soldier and the Indian sepoy could become entitled. On transfer, the Indian personnel had to arrange for their quarters at the new station and at their own cost. The Company provided the white soldier with everything. Next to nil was the consideration paid to the religious feelings and social customs of the Indian sepoy and he was called upon to perform duties which were, as a rule, more arduous than those of his white counterpart.

The Barrackpur Massacre

The 47th Native Infantry was serving at Barrackpur under the above conditions, when it was ordered to proceed to Burma. According to the historian Thornton, the Indian sepoys were unable to get bullock-carts for the transport of their personal luggage and appealed for help to their English officers who told them that they had to make their own arrangements for transport to Calcutta, from where they would be taken to Burma by sea. All the sepoys were high-caste Hindus and were bound by their rigid social customs which forbade travelling by sea. They sent a long but respectfully-worded petition to the Commander-in-Chief setting forth their grievances and the fear of being outcast if they travelled by sea. They also submitted that they had been recruited for service on land exclusively and were willing and ready to go anywhere on land. The petition was ignored and on 30th October, 1824, the Regiment was ordered on parade. The sepoys, assembled in parade formation, again made their submission to the Officer Commanding the parade, but no reply was vouchsafed to them. The Commander-in-Chief in Calcutta was informed of the situation and he immediately dispatched to nearby Barrackpur two battalions of white soldiers, a detachment of artillery and another of the Governor-General's Bodyguard.

On 1st November, 1824, the 47th was again ordered on parade. When the sepoys arrived in formation, they were encircled by formations of the white soldiers and behind the latter the Company's artillery had taken up positions—a fact which the sepoys did not notice. They were ordered to lay down their arms immediately if they were unwilling to go wherever they were ordered. The "arms" were unloaded guns on their shoulders weighted down by their bulky knapsacks. Sir John Kaye states that the artillery stationed behind their backs started firing on them without any warning. The sepoys were thus mowed down by gun-fire. Some ran towards the river and jumped into it to escape the bullets. Those that were not drowned were caught and later hanged. The name of the 47th was struck from the rolls of the Company's "Native" Regiments. It may be that Herbert Spencer had this massacre in mind when some years later he wrote:

"Down to our own day continues the cunning despotism which uses native soldiers to maintain and extend native subjection—a despotism under which, not many years since a regiment of sepoys was deliberately massacred for refusing to march ..."

We have only to add that the news of the horror perpetrated by the Company demoralised the Indian troops already in Burma.

English Intrigues in Burma

Coming back to events in Burma, the retreat of the Company's army in the north and the stalemate at Rangoon apparently brought home to the English the realisation of their inability to subjugate Burma by fair fight alone. So they had recourse to their weapon of intrigues and spent money freely in their efforts to corrupt and win over the officials and the people of certain Burmese regions accessible to them. Wilson states that on 8th August, 1824, an English agent, Col. Kelly, was sent to the Burmese district of Dalla to incite the people there against the Burmese Government. The same writer also states that the Company's army at Rangoon finding it impossible to advance towards Ava, started to take by intrigue some districts along the seacoast of Burma. A beginning was made with the Tennasserim district. On 20th August, 1824, a detachment of the Company's army turned up at the fort of Tennasserim and, it is stated, a subordinate officer of the garrison treacherously got hold of the garrison Commander and handed him over to the English enemy, who occupied the undefended city without firing a shot. The English intrigues also achieved for them a certain amount of success in most of the minor engagements that followed.

Maha Bandoola's Death

At this stage the Burmese cause sustained a severe blow. Maha Bandoola was killed on 1st April, 1825, by the accidental explosion of a shell in the Tunueu fort which he was defending against the

Company's army besieging it. Burma lost a military Commander whose patriotism, loyalty, courage and ability as an expert in warfare evoked the unstinted admiration of many Englishmen and writers. Major Snodgrass has testified that Maha Bandoola had declared at Tunueu his resolve to "win or die".

English Efforts for Peace on Their Terms

Apparently, the English had had enough of war, and, as Wilson puts it, expressed their readiness to stop fighting if the Burmese Government undertook to make good all their losses up-to-date "There were rumours current which gave us hope that our efforts for peace would succeed." It was extensively declared that people were up in arms in many parts of the Burmese Empire. There were also widespread rumours that the King of Burma had been deposed. All these rumours were false and proved to be so. The Burmese Government refused to consider the English terms and the war continued. The English later made a second attempt, and the English Commander in Rangoon sent a letter to the King of Burma through a priest, called Raj Guru, through whose efforts fighting was suspended, and, on 30th December, 1825, the representatives of the parties met to discuss terms. By 2nd January, 1826, a draft treaty was drawn up and it was settled that the war should remain suspended at least till the 18th idem. The King of Burma rejected the terms of the proposed treaty and war was resumed.

Thereafter an event in Northern India helped the English cause in Burma. The event was as follows.

The Siege and Fall of Bharatpur

Metcalfe wrote in 1814 that four successive attacks on Bharatpur and the greatest possible efforts of the combined armies from Bengal and Bombay had failed and "most of our military glory found its grave in Bharatpur". Since then, the English had been continuously looking for a favourable opportunity to wipe off that disgrace, and to resuscitate their military reputation in the Doab and Northern India. Not only did their utter discomfiture at Bharatpur continue to rankle in the English hearts, but their failure at Burma, too, made it all the more necessary for them to achieve something spectacular which could retrieve their well-nigh lost reputation as invincible fighters. The death of the Maharaja of Bharatpur in 1825 provided them with the long sought opportunity. There was some conflict with regard to succession. Two cousins claimed the right to occupy the vacant *gadi*. The English promptly espoused the cause of one of the claimants, Balwant Singh, and on 10th December, 1825, a detachment of the Company's army 25,000 strong and equipped with heavy guns laid siege to the Bharatpur Fort under the personal command of the Commander-in-Chief himself. The Bharatpur *Durbar* was then a house divided against itself. Nearly half of it were supporters of Balwant Singh and co-operated with the English besiegers to the limit. Even so it was more than five weeks before the fort fell to the English on 18th January, 1826. The English losses have been put by Col. Maleson at 1,050 killed and wounded, including 48 officers of whom seven were killed in action. Col. Skinner states that the English had learnt from the Marathas the technique of laying mines. The English had also acquired from the Hathras Fort a general outline of the Bharatpur Fort which was constructed on the same lines. "Even after the Bharatpur Fort was taken, no native would believe it was captured by storm; and to the last hour of my residence in India, they persisted in asserting that it was bought, not conquered" (Welsh's *Military Reminiscences,* Vol. II, pp. 240–41). We need hardly point out that the succession to the Bharatpur *gadi* was purely and simply an internal affair of the State and Metcalfe agrees that the English did not have even the shadow of a justification for interfering or taking sides in it. Metcalfe comments as follows:

> "It is ... acknowledged as a general principle, that we ought not to interfere in the internal affairs of other states; ... the capture of Bharatpur ... would do us more honour throughout India, by the removal of the hitherto unfaded impressions caused by our former failure, than any other event that can be conceived." (Kaye's *Selections from the Papers of Lord Metcalfe,* pp. 122–31)

The conquest of Bharatpur did not add an inch to the Company's territory but it did go a long way in rehabilitating its military reputation.

"Loans" Exacted by Lord Amherst

To defray the expenditure of the Burmese War and the siege of Bharatpur, Lord Amherst resorted to ways and means which John Malcolm Ludlow has described as follows:

> "The time for openly plundering native princes was gone with Warren Hastings. One observes, however, at this time, the extreme prevalence of the practice of obtaining loans from them. At the end of 1825, the King of Oudh lends £10,00,000 sterling; 15,00,000 for two years the next year. Baiza Bai, after Scindhia's demise, lent 18,00,000. In the general loans which were contracted, we find smaller chiefs contributing their quota, the Raja of Nagpur 15,00,000, the Raja of Benares 120,000; even the unfortunate Baji Rao, the ex-Peshwa, refunding a very considerable sum for the purpose, out of the savings from his pension." (*British India,* Vol. II, p. 65)

Subjugation of Alwar

It was about this time that Lord Amherst brought the State of Alwar under the Company's control by the traditional English "secret methods".

Treaty with Burma

The fall of Bharatpur weakened Burmese resistance. Another factor weakening it was that the English had by then won over several feudatories of the Burma *Durbar* and ultimately the latter executed a treaty with the English at Yendabu. According to Wilson, both sides had suffered very heavy losses in men and money. In addition, Burma lost forever several feudatory princes who had been paying tributes to the Burma *Durbar* and had formed part of the Burmese Empire.

Delhi Emperor Deliberately Affronted

The English had been acknowledging the Delhi Emperor as the *de jure* Emperor of Hindustan and themselves as his subjects, at least in name. Lord Amherst set about doing away with both the fictions and, with the intention of demoting the Emperor's status, visited Delhi on 15th February, 1827, for a pre-arranged audience with Akbar Shah. The latter had been assured that if he dispensed with the customary ceremonial etiquette which those who were received in audience had to observe, and received Lord Amherst in the way in which Lord Amherst described, then all the promises made to him by Lord Lake would be forthwith fulfilled by the Company. At the audience given to Lord Amherst "the Emperor sat on the Peacock Throne, whilst Lord Amherst occupied a royal chair in front of the Emperor on the latter's right and turned his face sideways to the Emperor's left" (Punjab Government Records, Delhi Residency and Agency, 1807–57, Vol. I, p. 338). Akbar Shah put before Lord Amherst all his grievances and the promises made by Lord Lake. Lord Amherst resorted to a new and offensive way of addressing the Emperor, paid scant attention to what the Emperor was saying, and cavalierly brushed it all aside by indicating that the undertakings given were nothing but political moves. This rude and impudent attitude was deliberately adopted by Lord Amherst with the intention of lowering the Emperor's status *vis-a-vis* the English in the eyes of the courtiers and others present at this audience. Thereafter, the customary ceremonial phraseology of the letters addressed to the Emperor was abandoned too. The Emperor then sent a representative, Raja Ram Mohan Roy, to England armed with the original agreement signed by Lord Lake for obtaining a redress of his grievances. But no one in England paid any attention to the representations made by Raja Ram Mohan Roy, who returned empty-handed.

The incident rankled in the hearts of not only the members of the Emperor's family but of Delhi citizens too. That all of them meekly pocketed the insult publicly offered to their Emperor goes to prove that Indians then sadly lacked self-respect and a sense of knowing and doing what the honour of the nation demanded.

Lord Amherst's Departure

After his achievement at Delhi, Lord Amherst spent the summer at Simla and sailed for England in March, 1827.

8

LORD WILLIAM BENTINCK (1828–1835)

The Company's Rule—Its Settled Policy

Lord William Bentinck, who succeeded Lord Amherst as Governor-General, has himself compared the Company's rule in India with that of the Mughals in the following words:

> "In many respects the Mohammedans surpassed our rule; they settled in the countries which they conquered; intermixed and intermarried with the natives; they admitted them to all privileges; the interests and the sympathies of the conquerors and the conquered became identified. Our policy, on the contrary, has been the reverse of this—cold, selfish and unfeeling."

Lord William Bentinck had previously been Governor of Madras and, during that time a prominent Member of his Council, William Thackeray, enunciated the policy which the English Company had to follow. In a Minute, Thackeray wrote:

> "... but in India, that haughty spirit, independence, and deep thought, which the possession of great wealth sometimes gives, ought to be suppressed. They are directly adverse to our power and interest ... We do not want generals, statesmen, and legislators; we want industrious husbandmen".

It will be readily understood, therefore, that Lord William Bentinck had to carry out the policy outlined by Thackeray, which had become the settled policy of the Company's rule in India. Inevitably, Lord William Bentinck's regime was marked by an administration which continued to be as "cold, selfish and unfeeling" as that of his predecessors. Frederick Shore has summed it up thus:

> "... his (Lord William Bentinck's) good intentions were never to interfere with the main principle of the British Indian Government, profit to themselves and their masters at the expense of the people of India ... The abominable system

of purveyance and forced labour is still in full force. The commerce and manufactures of the country are daily deteriorated by the vexatious system of internal duties which is still preserved ... the people are neither happier nor richer than they were before—indeed, their impoverishment has been progressive—for while the evils enumerated have continued in full force, the revenue screw has scarcely been relaxed half-a-thread of the many hundreds of which it is composed ..." (*Notes on, Indian Affairs* by Frederick Shore, Vol. II, pp. 223-24)

Coorg

Coorg was a small hill state near Mysore. Its scenic beauty and salubrious climate was almost matchless in India and, unfortunately for its independence, it had drawn the attention of the English as eminently suitable for colonisation by them.

In 1790, when the English were preparing for war against Tipu, a treaty had been entered into by them with the Raja of Coorg, whereby both parties agreed to treat Tipu as their common enemy and the Raja undertook to harass Tipu to the limit of his power. He also granted to the English the monopoly of purchasing all the products of the state and further agreed to have no relations whatsoever with any other European power. The Company, in return, promised to preserve and protect the independence of Coorg if and when a peace treaty with Tipu materialised, to safeguard the rights and interests of the Raja. The Raja faithfully fulfilled all his promises and co-operated with the English in their war on Tipu. He and his people had, however, to pay the penalty for having been false to their country and for backing the English against the gallant and patriotic Tipu.

Interference in Coorg's Internal Affairs

Veer Rajendra, the Raja of Coorg, had died when Lord Amherst was Governor-General. The English Government had, during his lifetime, undertaken to support the claim of the Raja's daughter, Devammaji, to succeed to the *gadi* in accordance with the Coorg tradition. But on Veer Rajendra's death, a brother of Devammaji was installed on the *gadi*. The English had broken their promise and acknowledged the brother as the rightful Raja.

Lord William Bentinck now took a hand in the matter. It was given out that the Raja was an inhuman monster who, for entertainment, killed his relatives and other people. To save Devammaji and her husband from a similar fate, the English gave them asylum in their Residency at Mysore.

War Declared

War was then formally declared against the Raja and a detachment of the Company's army was sent under English officers for the conquest of Coorg. The Raja, who was totally unprepared for war, was nonplussed. Rev. Dr. Moegling writes:

> "The Raja, incited partly by the ... hope that a reconciliation was yet possible, partly by the fear, that he might lose all if matters went to extremities, sent orders prohibiting the Coorgs from encountering the troops of the Company. To this vacillation of the Raja, the several divisions of the British expedition, then marching into Coorg, were more indebted for their success and even safety than to the skill and talents of their commanders." ("History of Coorg" published in "The Calcutta Review" for September, 1856, p. 199)

Annexation of Coorg

The English deposed the Raja and deported him under custody to Benares. Devammaji was totally ignored by the English, who openly annexed the entire Coorg territory, on the ground alleged in the preamble to their proclamation which read: "Whereas the entire population of Coorg wants that the English take them under their protection, etc. etc." The proclamation assured the Coorg people:

(i) That the English will never allow any Indian Government to rule Coorg,

(ii) That animal-slaughter will be prohibited, and
(iii) That rents of agricultural lands would continue to be realised in kind.

Within a short time, however, the Company started realising rents in cash exclusively. The distressed people rose up in arms against this practice of their foreign rulers. The revolt was ruthlessly crushed.

All the English writers unanimously declared that Coorg was never "conquered". The deported Raja, finding the treatment meted out to him unbearable, went to England with his family to seek redress. Nobody paid any attention to his grievances. There his daughter was induced to embrace Christianity and later she married an Englishman.

Division of Loot

The extent to which Coorg was looted is indicated by the following amounts of money which were openly given to the English officers as their share:

> (Lindsay, the Commanding Officer was given one-sixteenth of the total amount looted.)
> (Each Colonel received ... Rs. 25,000/-)
> (Each Lt.-Col. received ... Rs. 15,000/-)
> (Each Major received ... Rs. 10,000/-)
> (Each Captain received ... Rs. 5,000/-) and
> (Each Subaltern received ... Rs. 2,500/-).

Thereafter the object of the annexation was very soon achieved. The land was most suitable for growing coffee. A number of Englishmen were given extensive lands free for coffee plantations, which by 1904, covered about 50,000 acres, and the number of English settlers ran into thousands.

Annexation of Cachar and Part of Jaintia

It has been mentioned in the preceding chapter that Lord Amherst in 1824 entered into a treaty with the Raja of Cachar as a part of his preparations for the invasion of Burma. The Raja was killed by some unknown person (?). He had no son, and on the ground that the deceased Raja had no successor, Cachar State was annexed by Lord William Bentinck to the Company's territory.

Shortly before he left India, Lord William Bentinck also annexed a part of the Raja of Jaintia's state as an indemnity for the alleged breach by him of some provisions of the treaty with the Company.

No other Indian State was directly annexed by Lord William Bentinck, but Mysore was indirectly brought by him under the immediate control of the English.

English Commission for Ruling Mysore

It will be recalled that after Tipu's death in 1799, a part of the extensive dominion of Mysore was given, on hard terms, to a member of the family of the Hindu ex-Raja of Mysore, who had entered into the subsidiary alliance with the Company. All the succeeding Rajas had been observing the terms imposed by the treaty of the alliance and had been punctually paying the stipulated subsidy to the Company.

Besides the utter lack of an excuse or a plausible justification for the annexation of Mysore State, there was another serious problem. If it was annexed, half of it would have to be given to The Nizam in accordance with the undertaking given by the Company to him when Mysore was first dismembered after Tipu's death. Lord William Bentinck could not comply with that undertaking as it would augment the Nizam's strength, and, non-compliance would mar the friendly relations with him which had to be maintained intact. Lord William Bentinck solved the problem by artifice. On 7th September, 1831, the Raja received a letter from the Governor-General informing him that because of some alleged grave defects in his administration of the State, an English Commission composed of the English officers named therein would be in charge of the entire administration of Mysore. It was a bolt from the blue for the hopeless and helpless Raja, who was never given a chance to controvert the charges, as the Commission arrived simultaneously with the letter and took over the administration from the Raja. Major Evans Bell, in his book, *The Mysore Reversion,* writes:

"... the grounds alleged for the ... attachment of the country are not only unsustainable by the terms of the treaty, but are found to be even more opposed to truth ..." (pp. 21, 24)

For the next 50 years, Mysore State was ruled by the Commission and it was restored to the Raja's descendants in 1881 on terms which were harsher than those of 1799–1800.

Jaipur and Jodhpur

Lord William Bentinck planted one of his proteges, Jootha Ram, at the Jaipur *Durbar* and forced the Maharaja to appoint him as his Minister. This was a clear breach of the Company's treaty with the Maharaja. It has been stated that whilst Jootha Ram was the Minister, there was extensive maladministration of the State, which was either inevitable or intentional.

A part of the subsidy payable by the Maharaja of Jodhpur to the Company had fallen into arrears and as a security for the payment of the same, the Sambhar district and a part of the Sambhar Lake region were attached by the Company, and its troops moved in. Incidentally, parts of the district and the lake region belonged to Jaipur but these too were occupied. The Maharaja and the people of Jaipur were, according to Ludlow, very much agitated by this high-handed act and the exasperated people rose up in arms. On 4th June, 1835 they attacked the English Resident and killed his assistant, Mr. Black.

Interference in Oudh

Lord William Bentinck visited Oudh in 1831. The Nawab Wazir of Oudh was then designated by the English as the "King of Oudh". Every department of the State was subjected to interference and wholesale changes dictated by the Governor-General to such an extent, that some newspapers in Calcutta asserted that the English had decided to annex Oudh. The "King" was confounded and sent a Frenchman, Dubois, to England as a special envoy to appeal to the British Parliament. Dubois was soon on his way to Europe, when, overawed by Lord William Bentinck's threats, the "King" had to withdraw Dubois' credentials. A full description of the incident was published in the periodical, "The Indian Examiner and Universal Review" dated 24th April, 1847, over the pen-name of "Veritas".

Pressure on Delhi Emperor

Lord William Bentinck also pressed the Delhi Emperor, Akbar Shah, to recall his representative, Raja Ram Mohan Roy, from England. Akbar Shah declined to do so, but as stated before, Raja Ram Mohan Roy failed in England to interest anyone in the Delhi Emperor's grievances. Lord William Bentinck continued the grossly discourteous behaviour towards the Emperor which had been initiated by Lord Amherst.

Gwalior

Young Junkojirao Sindhia was then on the Gwalior *gadi*. Widespread disturbances not unconnected with English intrigues posed a constant threat to his rule:

> "But if these dangers surrounded him in his capital, he was threatened with no less danger from the Council of Calcutta. Secret deliberations were being held with a view to discover what profit could be made out of the troubles of this weak but faithful young prince ... A demi-official letter was written to the Resident by the Chief Secretary of the Foreign Department, desiring him to learn, at a private interview, by way of a feeler, if the Maharaja, encircled as he was by serious troubles—troubles mainly caused by our Government—would like to resign, assigning over the country to the British Government, and receiving a handsome pension, which would be paid out of his own revenues ..." (*The House of Scindia, a Sketch* by John Hope, published in 1863 by Messrs. Longman, Green, Longman, Roberts and Green)

Lord William Bentinck's hopes that Junkojirao Sindhia would be so unnerved by the troubles which hemmed him in that he would voluntarily abdicate, and that Gwalior State would fall into the English lap like a ripe plum, did not, however, materialise:

> "Presently another demi-official letter arrived ... strongly expostulating with Mr. Cavendish upon his proceedings and concluding with the significant remark: 'You have thus allowed a favourable chance of connecting Agra to the Bombay Presidency, to escape.'" (ibid.)

An Interesting Incident

John Hope in his book has related an amusing anecdote as follows:

> "Lest it be thought by anyone ... that, in this little sketch of his (Lord William Bentinck's) foreign policy, we have given even the slightest touch of colouring, we will relate, by way of illustration, an amusing anecdote, which is known to three or four persons now living, and which sufficiently confirms our statement that, in respect of the rights of native states, His Lordship entirely overlooked the tenth commandment. It happened that Major Sutherland was selected to fill the office vacated by Mr. Cavendish ... He, therefore, waited on the Governor-General in Calcutta to learn what the policy was to be at Gwalior; was it to be intervention? Lord Bentinck who loved a joke quickly replied: "Look here Major", and His Lordship threw back his head, opened wide his mouth, and placed his thumb and finger together like a boy about to swallow a sugar-plum. Then, turning to the astonished Major, he said: 'If the Gwalior State should fall down your throat, you are not to shut your mouth as Mr. Cavendish did, but swallow it: that is my policy ...'" (ibid.)

Indore

Maharaja Malharrao Holkar of Indore died in 1834, leaving behind an adopted son who was his rightful heir. But two other claimants to the *gadi* sprang up. The dispute gave the English a chance to intervene and to support, for a consideration, one of the two. Unfortunately for them, however, no bargain could be struck with either of them. The adopted son succeeded to the *gadi,* and, in umbrage, Lord William Bentinck forbade the English Resident at Indore from attending the installation *Durbar.*

Jhansi

A similar dispute regarding succession to the *gadi* arose in Jhansi, when the Raja died in 1835 leaving behind an adopted son. Lord William Bentinck espoused the cause of another claimant, Raghunathrao, an uncle of the deceased Raja, and got him installed on the *gadi,* clearly violating the adopted son's indisputable right to succeed.

Survey of the River Indus

Sir John Malcolm, aware that the English coveted Sindh, Punjab and even Afghanistan, had drawn the attention of the Directors of the Company and the English Government of India to the vital importance of possessing Hyderabad (Sindh) and the river Indus. The latter, he had pointed out, was an easier route for the transport of English troops for the invasion of Sindh and later of Punjab. It thus became important to survey the whole river in order to find out if it was navigable by ships. At the same time, it was realised that an entry into Sindh, which was an independent state, to survey the Indus might arouse suspicions and would very likely be forbidden by the Amirs of Sindh. So artifice had to be resorted to "for obtaining information in regard to the Indus, and the probable facilities it might offer to navigation". The scheme was to tell the Amirs that King William IV of England had sent an English coach as a present for Maharaja Ranjit Singh of Punjab and it could reach the latter only by the river-route. The transmission of the present would thus serve, it was expected, as a cloak for the survey of the Indus. In October, 1830, Sir Charles Metcalfe, then a Member of the Governor-General's Council, expressed his disagreement in a Minute from which we quote:

> "The scheme of surveying the Indus, under the pretence of sending a present to Raja Ranjit Singh, seems to me highly objectionable."

"It is a trick, in my opinion, unworthy of our Government, which cannot fail when detected, as most probably it will be, to excite the jealousy and indignation of the powers on whom we play it. If the information wanted is indispensable, and cannot be obtained by fair and open means, it ought, I conceive, to be sought by the usual mode of sending unacknowledged emissaries, and not by a deceitful application for a passage under the fictitious pretence of one purpose when the real object is another, which we know would not be sanctioned." (Kaye's *Selections from the Writings of Lord Metcalfe*, pp. 211–17)

The idea of stationing in Kabul a 'commercial agent' of the Company was also under consideration at the time. In the opinion of Kaye, the Indus survey and the stationing of the commercial agent could be regarded as the prologues of the future Afghan War. As a matter of fact, both the proposals were nothing but the beginning of the preparations by Lord William Bentinck for the invasion of Sindh, Punjab and Afghanistan, which have been very fully described by Masson in his *Travels* (Vol. III, p. 432).

According to Victor Jackmond, the Amirs of Sindh were threatened with serious displeasure of the Company and of Maharaja Ranjit Singh, if permission for the English ships' passage along the Indus was refused. They were further told that the refusal would inevitably compel the English to help the Maharaja to conquer Sindh. On the other hand, if the permission was given by the Amirs then, so the latter were assured, it would consolidate the friendly relations between the Amirs and the Company. Thus by an astute combination of threats and guile, the Amirs were prevailed upon not only to give the required permission but also to provide all facilities for the passage of the Company's ships along the Indus. According to Masson, the Company, under the pretence of sending the presents to Maharaja Ranjit Singh, dispatched its troops to the bank of the Indus near its mouth, where some half-a-dozen men-of-war had already arrived.

The nautical survey of the Indus was thus undertaken and completed. It was one of the most important achievements to the credit of Lord William Bentinck as it facilitated the execution of the English designs against Afghanistan, Punjab and Sindh.

Double Threat to Sindh

In the treaty of 1809 between the Company and Maharaja Ranjit Singh, it had been clearly stipulated that the latter would be free to expand his dominion, as much as he wanted, on the side of the Indus nearest to his territory, and that there would be no hindrance on the part of the English. Ranjit Singh then conquered, one after the other, Kashmir, Multan and Peshawar and annexed them to his dominion. His vast army was then counted amongst the bravest and best equipped armies of the Indian rulers. His dominion was far-flung, fertile and prosperous. After he had annexed Peshawar, he decided to invade Sindh and began preparing for it. But the English Company too wanted Sindh, and so regardless of the 1809 treaty, efforts were made to check him or to dissuade him from invading Sindh. The presents said to have been sent for him by King William IV were a part of these efforts. Lord William Bentinck also requested a personal interview with him and Maharaja Ranjit Singh feeling happy over the presents readily acceded to the request.

At the Interview

About the end of 1831, Lord William Bentinck met Maharaja Ranjit at Rupar, with the pomp and show considered appropriate in the East and for which he had taken with him a considerable body of troops. There was, however, an irreconcilable difference of opinion over Sindh, which according to Capt. Cunningham, later turned out to be one of the causes of the Sikh War. But there was an agreement about the invasion of Afghanistan, and according to J. M. Ludlow, it was decided that Shah Shuja, the ex-King of Kabul, who was living at Ludhiana, as a refugee under English surveillance, was to be used as a stalking-horse for the invasion. With an army 30,000 strong which was furnished to him, Shah Shuja advanced towards Kandahar, but Dost Mohammad Khan, the reigning King of Kabul, routed him and he returned to his refuge at Ludhiana.

About Sindh, Lord William Bentinck represented to Maharaja Ranjit Singh that the Company wanted to control the lower reaches of the Indus for the expansion of its trade in that direction and so it would be quite essential for them to establish their military posts along the river bank which should be agreed to by Ranjit Singh. The latter at first declined, as the demand was contrary to the 1809 treaty. But later, Lord William Bentinck somehow succeeded in securing his acceptance, and so in stopping him, *ipso facto*, from attacking Sindh. Perhaps Ranjit Singh did not have the guts to go against the express wishes of the English, but the pressure to which the latter subjected him did make him quite suspicions about the English.

Resumption of Lakhiraj Lands

For hundreds of years before the advent of Lord William Bentinck, the Mughal Emperors, as also other Hindu and Mussalman rulers and princes in India, had been making grants of rent-free lands and estates to old aristocratic but needy families, charitable, religious, educational and other public institutions for their maintenance. The grants were called "Lakhiraj lands" and the beneficiaries numbered many thousands. The English Government too had not in any way interfered with the grants till Lord William Bentinck took over. But shortly after his arrival in India, every District Collector was given the authority to resume in the Company's name, and at his discretion, any or all "Lakhiraj lands" in his district. It was a death-blow to the beneficial activities of thousands of ancient public institutions that had served the people for centuries. It also rendered homeless and destitute thousands of old and respected families constituting part of the country's landed gentry and aristocracy. This would appear to have been deliberately intended as Lord Bentinck was very keen on the extinction of the old and influential families owning lands or estates. The right of an adopted son, a brother or other blood-relation to inherit the estate of a deceased *jagirdar*, or estate-holder, was denied, and Lord Bentinck considered it just and lawful for the Company to usurp the *jagir* or the estate. In Bombay Presidency alone, a very large number of *jagirs* and estates were thus acquired for the Company.

Extinction of Indian Nationalism

Lord William Bentinck believed that the nationalism and patriotism of the Indians could be neutralised and that they could be made more useful tools of the foreign rulers, if their language, dress and ways of living and thinking could be anglicised. He, therefore, initiated the replacement of Persian and other Indian languages by English in the Company's courts and offices. He was a strong opponent of the freedom of the Press, and did his very best to establish English colonies in the country.

To sum up, Lord William Bentinck did everything possible to strengthen still further the British Empire in India and to rivet, more firmly than ever, the irons of slavery on the people of India.

CHARTER ACT OF 1833

The Reforms Act 1832—Its Effect on India

The Act was passed by the British Parliament in response to the demand of the British people for more political rights.

During the preceding twenty years the wealth and prosperity of England had increased by leaps and bounds in the wake of the phenomenal progress of her industries and the expansion of her overseas trade, thanks mainly to her Indian Empire. Much of this had been achieved at the cost of Indian industries and export trade, which had been deliberately ruined for England's benefit. The increase in England's population, too, had been keeping pace with material prosperity, and the ambitions of the English had gone up considerably. All these factors naturally led to the English people's demand for a greater share in the Government of their country, and the British Parliament had to accede to it.

It would, however, appear that any increase in or extension of the political rights and privileges of the English people had always been concomitant with a proportionate loss of the Indians' human rights and with the tightening of their political bondage. In other words, the political and commercial gains of the English had been the measure of the Indians' loss in these fields. It had to be so. The interests of the English rulers of India were naturally incompatible with and even diametrically opposed to those of their Indian subjects. As Lord Macaulay has very aptly put it: "Of all forms of tyranny ... the worst is that of a nation." And according to Abraham Lincoln, the American President: "There is no nation good enough to govern another nation."

In the light of the foregoing circumstances and observations, our readers can well imagine the Indian people's plight at the time of the enactment of the Charter Act of 1833. It was intended to replace the old Charter Act of 1813, which was due to expire after twenty years. It was the British Parliament's practice to pass a new Charter Act every 20 years for the continuation, under its authority, of the Company's rule over India.

The New Act of 1833

It added to the heavy burden which British rule had already imposed on the people of India. The sphere of the 1813 Act was expanded and the number of ways and means by which the English could drain the wealth of India was considerably increased. Doubtless to hoodwink the Indian people some isolated expressions were used here and there in the Act to show the English regard for India's welfare and interests. These, however, did not in any way affect the basic principles on which the Act was founded. After the Act, the English Government of India continued with an added zest their efforts to amalgamate the Indian States with the British Empire.

We propose to present our readers, at the end of this chapter, with passages culled from a comprehensive evaluation of British rule in India for the twenty years that followed the passing of the 1833 Act. It was published in a tract of the Indian Reform Society of England, 1853, under the heading, "The Government of India since 1834". It will give a fuller picture drawn by Englishmen of the effects of the Act on India and its people.

Lord Macaulay—The First Law Member

The 1833 Act had added a Law Member to the Governor-General's Council. The post carried a salary of £ 10,000 a year, and Lord Macaulay was appointed the first Law Member. The historian, Wilson, has expressly stated that there was nothing special about the work for which the incumbent of the post had to be imported from England at such a heavy cost.

Lord Macaulay, then about 34, was a learned man, but was not well-off, as in England he could earn barely £ 200 a year. His main object in coming out to India was the same as that of all Englishmen who came out here, namely, to earn more money. He hoped, as he wrote to his sister (17th August, 1833), whilst still in England, to save at least half of his munificent salary, and to return to England at the end of his five years' tenure of office, in the prime of his life, with his savings, which, with interest, would have, by then, amounted to £ 30,000. As he said in the letter he had never wished for anything better or more. As a matter of fact, he was paid in addition to the yearly £ 10,000, another £ 5,000 a year for working as Law Commissioner. What his work as Law Commissioner was is by no means clear. Incidentally, the Law Member-cum-Law Commissioner of the English Government in India cost the poor Indian peasants something like 36 lacs of rupees during the 20 years that followed the passing of the Charter Act of 1833.

Lord Macaulay's Work, Policy and Aims

His main duty was to frame laws for the Indian people. But unfortunately, he, although talented, was ill-equipped for its proper performance. He did not know any of the Indian languages' and was equally ignorant of the Indian people's history, their way of life, and their customary codes of moral, social and religious conduct. In addition, he disliked India and its religious and social institutions, in short, everything Indian. His guiding principle, as stated by himself, was: "We know that India cannot have a free government. But she may have the next best thing—a firm and impartial despotism."

He strongly advocated the education of suitable Indians in English and through the English language. Not, be it noted, for their benefit, but to meet the growing need of the English Government in India for English-knowing, loyal, competent and cheap *Babus* to fill the numerous minor posts in the administrative offices of their extensive "Indian Empire". Another of his objectives was to perpetuate British rule in India by the extinction of its people's nationalism which would result from their instruction in English. He succeeded in accomplishing both. In addition, "Lord Macaulay's triumph ... was really the triumph of a deliberate intention to undermine the religious and social life of India" (*The Indian Daily News,* 29th March, 1909).

As a bye-product of his educational policy, Lord Macaulay had also expected the spread of Christianity in India. Within two years of his arrival in India, he had written to his father that he was convinced that if his educational policy and plans were duly carried out, after 30 years not a single idol-worshipper would be left amongst the respectable Hindus of Bengal.

The Indian Penal Code

By far the most notable of Lord Macaulay's achievements was the drawing up of the Indian Penal Code, which has stood the test of time and remained practically unchanged for a much longer period than any other law enacted by the English up till now (1929).

Indian patriots have, however, likened it to the Irish Penal Code which has thus been described by Edmund Burke:

> "Well digested and well disposed in all its parts; a machine of wise and elaborate contrivance, and as well fitted for the oppression, impoverishment and degradation of a people, and the debasement in them of human nature itself, as ever proceeded from perverted ingenuity of man."

The Marquis of Hastings had in 1819 described, in a letter to the Company's Directors, similar evil effects on the Indian people of the laws enacted for them by the English from 1780 onwards. A number of Indian thinkers are of opinion that the evil effects described by Hastings were very much worsened by Macaulay's Indian Penal Code and by the ways in which its provisions were exploited to strengthen the English hold on India and to increase its people's subservience to the English. In the penal code of no other civilized country were such drastic and severe penalties and punishments laid down as found a place in the Indian Penal Code. This is quite understandable, because Macaulay considered the Indians ruled by the English as nothing but "dumb-driven cattle" owned by the English!

The Indian Reform Society of England, 1853, undertook an "enquiry" regarding the effects over India of some twenty years of British rule. The Society published its findings in a tract under the heading, "The Government of India Since 1833." We append some excerpts from it.

"The enquiry in hand and the issue now raised by the fluxion of the Charter Act cannot be better stated than in the language used by the late King. It denotes in the simplest terms the purpose of the Statute"—the improvement and happiness of the natives of India, and by doing so it enables the country and the legislature to apply to its success or failure tests of the most infallible description. For there is nothing in this world so patent and certain and easily ascertainable as good government ...The first step in the enquiry is, therefore, to apply some of the tests of good government to the Government of India, as it has been administered under the system established in 1833.

I. *Peace*

"Perhaps the most important of these tests is peace ... Now since 1834, the Government of India, as established in the preceding year, has, out of the nineteen years that have passed, been in a state of war for fifteen years ..."

"These wars were not necessary for the safety,—they have retarded the improvement, and diminished the happiness of the natives of India, whilst they have exhausted the resources of the Government: but they were the natural result of the system established in 1833; for it wanted the responsibility and the 'correctives' which alone keep human rulers at peace."

"Applying, then, the test of peace to the last twenty years, what opportunity, what means, what chances can a Government occupied more or less with war for fifteen of those years have had of working out the improvement and happiness of the natives? ..."

II. *Finances*

"... Pecuniary prosperity being the second great test of good Government everywhere."

"In England a deficit in the Treasury is the most heinous of all Government offences ... Turn to India, and what, during the last fourteen years, do we find? Deficit—deficit—deficit."

"When the present system of Government was framed in 1833, the military charges of India were about eight million sterling, or 49 per cent of its net revenue. Twenty years of anticipated "improvement and happiness" have now almost elapsed and the military charges now exceed twelve million sterling and eat up 56 per cent of the net revenue ... These are the first results of the legislation of 1833 which arrest our path in clearing the way for legislation in 1853."

III. Material Improvements

"Of course, a system of Government which in the last twenty years has gone on increasing its military expenditure from eight to twelve million sterling, and thus adding to its debt, has had little to spend on what are, in such a country as India, the next evidence of good Government—Public Works ... So out of a revenue exceeding twenty-one million sterling, the rate of Government expenditure on public works has, according to Mr. Campbell, been two and a quarter per cent, or less than £ 500,000 a year, spread over a country as large as Europe ... And of these sums so debited against public works, some portion is, it must be borne in mind, spent on barracks and purely military undertakings." The figures, too, include the cost of superintendence, which has sometimes wasted 70 per cent of the outlay.

IV. Condition of the People

"But, in spite of war, deficit and want of roads, bridges, harbours and public works, has the condition of the people improved during the last twenty years? Try the Act of 1833, then, by this test. There can be none better or surer."

The writer then goes on to show from official accounts the miserable condition of the Bengal *ryot* under the *Zemin-dary* system—the Madras *ryot* under the *Ryotwari* and the Bombay *ryot* under the composite system. Then he concludes as follows:

"... It is on India as a whole that attention must be fixed; and how sad the condition of the cultivator is in Bengal, with a population of 40 million, how far worse it is in Madras with its 22 million and how bad it is in Bombay with its 10 million, the evidence thus briefly produced ... will give some general idea of it. It is not merely cultivation that is depressed; it is society itself that is being gradually destroyed. The race of native gentry has already almost everywhere disappeared; and a new danger has arisen—that in another generation or two, the cultivators will not be worth having as subjects. For moral debasement is the inevitable consequence of physical depression … This prospect may be deemed 'satisfactory' by the persons responsible for it. But to India it is ruin and destruction; to England it is danger and disgrace."

V. *Law and Justice*

"The state of the law, the forms of legal procedure, and the administration of justice—these form another test by which to try the legislation of 1833. And these, in the case of that Act, are a special and peculiar test. For law reform was not only declared to be one of its most prominent objects, but it contained large and costly provisions to advance that priceless object."

"Then, as to the actual state and administration of civil law. In the Regulation Provinces there is nothing worthy of the name of law; but to a system unworthy of that sacred name are appended cumbrous legal forms and legal tax. To enter into the courts of what is called justice, it is not only necessary that you should have a plaint, but money to pay (not lawyers but also) the Government. So that to all the Company's subjects who cannot commence the search of justice by paying a tax to the Government the doors of the courts are closed; for them there is neither law nor justice. And having money, what, when admitted, do they find? Judges, as Mr. Campbell confesses, a scandal to the British name."

"For fifteen years has the criminal law, as administered by the Company's courts, been condemned by Government itself. It is just as fit for the Christian people of this realm as for the Hindu subjects of the Queen in India …"

VI. *Police*

"If there be little or no criminal law, there is, however, a police. But it has, we quote the declaration of 1252, 'not only failed to effect the prevention of crimes, the apprehension of offenders, and the protection of life and property; but it has become the engine of oppression and a great cause of the corruption of the people'."

"... Tried then by the tests of law, justice, and crime, the legislation of 1833 has not resulted in the improvement and happiness of the natives of India."

VII. *Education*

"Measure the system of 1833 by the wand of education, short as we may choose to make it, and the result is worse still. So paltry an item of expenditure is Native Education that it does not even constitute an item in the yearly Finance Accounts laid before Parliament. It is, therefore, impossible to say what percentage of a net revenue of twenty-one million sterling is spent on this means of promoting the improvement and happiness of the natives. But this is well known, that, whereas in Hindoo times every village community had its school, our destruction of village societies or municipalities has deprived the natives of their schools, such as they were and had substituted nothing in their place. In short, out of these 22 million people the Indian Government yearly educates 160. And when in Bengal the richer natives do send their sons to England for education, the young men, returning duly qualified, are refused Government employment on the same terms and on the same rank as Europeans. Within the last five years a Hindoo young gentleman carried off several medical prizes at University College, and received the Diploma of M. D. The Court of Directors, and individual Directors were applied to by some of the most eminent of the retired public servants of India to give Dr. Chuckerbutty a commission as Surgeon in a native regiment, but the request was refused. And by gentlemen, too, who, it stands in evidence, have at home spent out of Indian taxation during the last twenty years the enormous sum of £ 53,000 in public banquets and more select house dinners. It is not by such educational expenditure, or by such treatment when native gentlemen do educate themselves, that 'the improvement and happiness of the natives of India' can be promoted.

VIII. *Public Employment of the Natives*

"And the insufficiency of this test of education naturally brings us to another, *viz.*, the employment of natives. In our earlier Indian career, natives were employed in the most important and confidential posts of our Government. Our regiments were officered by natives; in many places we had native agents and representatives; everywhere we were then obliged to make use of native talent. But in those days Indian salaries were at least moderate. But gradually this use of native ability was displaced, and every post of profit, of trust, of value transferred, at enormous addition to the cost of Government, to Englishmen, until at last it become part and parcel of our established policy. The legislation of 1833, however, attempted to remedy this monstrous injustice by enacting that none should be excluded from any office by reasons of religion, place of birth, descent or colour. But so far from the enactment having remedied the wrong, 'this provision' was, according to Mr. Campbell, 'a mere flourish of trumpets and of no practical effect whatever as far as the natives are concerned'. Indeed, according to him, it has been prejudicial rather than advantageous to native employment; 'for,' he adds, 'the only effect has been to open to Europeans offices originally intended for natives'."

"The division between the covenanted and uncovenanted services is still kept up; though the covenant itself is absurd and ridiculous now that the East India Company has nothing to do with trade. And the purpose for which it is maintained is to draw an artificial line by means of which the natives may continue, however educated, able, and competent, to be excluded from all high and lucrative employment. The Act of 1833 declares that religion, birth, and colour shall not exclude any man from any office. But the Government of India refuses to allow any native, Hindoo, Mahomedan, or Parsee, admission into its covenanted service. Thus it defeats, by a rule of its own, the provision of the legislature of 1833, which particularly aimed at promoting 'the improvement and happiness' of the natives of India by employing them in the public service; and by their employment reducing the cost of Government. Some few thousands—3,000 or 4,000 out of 150 million—do indeed get small posts, worth on an average £ 30 a year. But any real share in Government administration, trust and responsibility is denied the people of India. Yet, in Lord Grey's work on the *Colonial Administration of Lord John Russell's Government*, he is found boasting, how on the Gold Coast of Africa the Governor summoned its Chiefs into council; and how, out of this rude Negro Parliament England is creating an African nation."

"But in India, a people 'learned in all the arts of polished life, when we were yet in the woods, less favoured than the Fantees of Cape Coast Castle, are proscribed as a race of incompetent, helpless incapables, and condemned to everlasting inferiority in lands which their forefathers made famous."

IX. *Popular Contentment*

"Are then the people of India content with the working of the legislation of 1833? It would be strange if they were; and they are not. They do not rebel; they do not resist; they do not rise against the Indian Government …; for, under the British rule the power of the Government is too strong and well organised for a successful resort to these violent modes of manifesting public opinion. But now that the opportunity has arisen—now that there is a chance of improvement, they petition Parliament. And what say their petitions? That they are happy and prosperous? That they are satisfied with the results of the Act of 1833? That they regard its renewal with contentment and hope? Nothing of the sort. The very reverse …"

"The people of Madras complain that the whole framework of society has been overthrown, to their injury, and almost to their ruin."

"They complain that salt, the only condiment for their tasteless rice, and without which neither they nor their cattle can live, is a Government monopoly."

"They complain that not only are they taxed for their shops in towns, and for stalls and sheds on roadsides but for each tool and implement of the trades; nay, for their very knives, 'the cost of which', they tell Parliament, is frequently exceeded six times over by the Moturpha (Tax) under which the use of them is permitted."

"They complain, that in order to raise revenue from ardent spirits, the Government is forcing drunkenness on them; 'a vice', they add, 'forbidden by Hindu and Mohammedan law.'"

"If contentment, therefore, be a test of good Government, the Act of 1833 has signally failed."

X. Home Control

"Another test yet remains. The Act of 1833 was proposed as a substitute for a constitution. If we cannot, it was then argued by Mr. Macaulay, on behalf of Lord Grey's Government, safely entrust the people of India with popular rights and privileges, we will at least have a constituency at home bound by their own interests to watch over and protect them; a constituency which, to use his exact words, *shall feel any disorder in the finances of India in the disorder of their own household affairs.* Has this anticipation been realized—has this intention been fulfilled? No; disorders there have been for fifteen years in the finances of India: but those disorders have not been felt in the 'household affairs' of the proprietors of East India stock. Despite Indian deficits, English dividends of ten and a half per cent have been regularly maintained and 'well and truly paid'. And thus India has lost that English security for good Government which Mr. Macaulay announced it was a design of the Act of 1833 to establish."

"But it is unnecessary ... to pursue the enquiry further. Enough has been sketched ... to make rational, benevolent, and patriotic men hesitate when asked to consent to a renewal of the Act of 1833; enough has been stated to make them doubt whether the present system of Government is even capable of improvement; enough, we believe, to convince all impartial men that a new plan of Indian administration must be cast."

NATIONAL EDUCATION UNDER BRITISH RULE

Education in India Before the English Arrived

At the end of the 18th century and for sometime afterwards, the percentage of literates in the population of India was higher than that in the population of any European country.

There were four kinds of institutions which imparted education to the people; namely,

(i) Lacs of Brahmin families who took in resident students,

(ii) *Tols* or *Vidya-peeths* for imparting education in Sanskrit existed in all the principal towns,

(iii) Hundreds of thousands of Hindoos and Mussalmans were educated in Urdu and Persian in the *Maktabs* and *Madrassas* which covered the whole country, and

(iv) The village schools or *Pathshalas*, of which even the smallest village had at least one, to impart education to all the children of the village. The maintenance of the village *Pathshala* was considered by the village *Panchayat* to be its bounden duty, which it never failed to discharge. The advent of the East India Company's rule over India ended the ancient institution of the village *Panchayat*, which inevitably led to the extinction of the village *Pathshala* too.

Keir Herdie, the well-known Member of the British Parliament, has stated in his book *India*:

> "Max Mueller, on the strength of official documents and a missionary report concerning education in Bengal prior to the British occupation, asserts that there were then 80,000 native schools in Bengal, or one for every 400 of the population. Ludlow, in his *History of British India*, says that 'in

every Hindoo village which has retained its old form,' I am assured that the children generally are able to read, write, and cipher, but where we have swept away the village system as in Bengal, there the village school has also disappeared."

It will be noted that, according to Ludlow, what Max Mueller said about Bengal was equally true of the other regions of India too.

About the rural population, we quote from the "Report of the Select Committee on the affairs of the East India Company":

"... the peasantry of few other countries would bear a comparison as to their state of education with those of many parts of India". (Vol. I, p. 409, published 1832)

Indian System of Education

The Western countries learned from India what is now termed "mutual tuition" in the Western educational systems. This is borne out by the following quotations:

(i) From the Letter from the Court of Directors to the Governor-General-in-Council of Bengal, dated 3rd June, 1814:

"The mode of instruction that from time immemorial has been practised under these masters has received the highest tribute of praise by its adoption in this country, under the direction of the Reverend Dr. Bell, formerly chaplain in Madras; and it is now become the mode by which education is conducted in our national establishments, from a conviction of the facility it affords in the acquisition of language by simplifying the process of instruction."

"This venerable and benevolent institution of the Hindoos is represented to have withstood the shock of revolutions ..."

(ii) From "The Report of A. D. Campbell, Collector of Bellary, dated 17th August 1823", as quoted in the above-mentioned "Report of the Select Committee", Vol. I:

> "The economy with which children are taught to write in the native schools and the system by which the more advanced scholars are caused to teach the less advanced, and at the same time to confirm their own knowledge, is certainly admirable, and well deserves the imitation it has received in England ..."

But even so it could not long survive the economic calamity which overtook the people and eventually there were "multitudes who could not even avail themselves of the advantages of the system" (A. D. Campbell, ibid.).

Economic Causes of the Extinction of the Indian People's Educational System

The process of extinction in each Indian Province set in with the establishment of the Company's rule over it. A. D. Campbell describes it as follows:

> "I am sorry to state, this is ascribable to the gradual but general impoverishment of the country. The means of the manufacturing classes have been of late years greatly diminished by the introduction of our own English manufactures in lieu of the Indian cotton fabrics. The removal of many of our troops from our own territories to the distant frontiers of our newly-subsidized allies has also of late years affected the demand for grain; the transfer of the capital of the country from the native government and their officers, who liberally expended it in India, to Europeans, *restricted by law from employing it even temporarily in India, and the daily draining it from the land*, has likewise tended to this effect, which has not been alleviated by a less rigid enforcement of the revenue due to the State. The greater of the middling and lower classes of the people are now unable to defray the expenses incident upon the education of their offspring, while their necessities require the assistance of their children as soon as their tender limbs are capable of the smallest labour ... Of nearly a million of souls in this district, not 7,000 are now

at school, a proportion which exhibits but too strongly the result above stated. In many villages where formerly there were large schools, there are now none, and in many others where there were any schools, now only a few children of the most opulent are taught, others being unable from poverty to attend ... Such is the state in this district of the various schools in which reading, writing and arithmetic are taught in various dialects of the country, as has been always usual in India ... Learning ... has never flourished in any country except under the encouragement of the ruling power, and the countenance and support once given to science in this part of India has long been withheld. Of the 533 institutions for education ... in this district, I am ashamed to say, not one now derives any support from the State ..."

"There is no doubt, that in former times, especially under the Hindoo Governments, very large grants, both in money and in land, were issued for the support of learning ..."

"Considerable alienations of revenue, which formerly did honour to the State by upholding and encouraging learning, have deteriorated under our rule into the means of supporting ignorance; whilst science, deserted by the powerful aid she formerly received from Government, has often been reduced to beg her scanty and uncertain meal from the chance benevolence of charitable individuals; and it would be difficult to point out any period in the history of India when she stood more in need ..." (ibid.).

Causes of Extinction of Ancient Educational Institutions

Four principal causes can be enumerated, namely:

(i) The ruin of the country's industries and handicrafts added to the drain of its wealth by the Company,

(ii) The disappearance of the ancient village *Panchayats*, with which lacs of village *Pathshalas* also became extinct,

(iii) The resumption by the Company of the *Jagirs*, lands, etc., which the old Hindu and Mussalman rulers had granted to educational institutions as financial help, and

(iv) The systematic opposition by the new English rulers to any effort to make the people knowledgeable.

It appears necessary to deal more fully with the last-mentioned cause. The controversy about the benefit or the contrary, resulting from the education of Indians, lasted for about a century from 1757 onwards. In the beginning almost all the Englishmen ruling the country opposed their education. J. C. Marshman, in his evidence before the Select Committee of the House of Lords appointed to enquire into the affairs of the East India Company, has stated (15th June, 1853):

> "For a considerable time after the British Government had been established in India, there was great opposition to any system of instruction for the natives."

Marshman also stated that when the Charter Act of 1792 was under discussion in the Parliament, a Member, Wilberforce, moved the addition of a new clause which purported to provide for the education of a small number of Indians but the other Members and the Company's shareholders strongly opposed the addition and Wilberforce had to withdraw his motion.

> "On that occasion, one of the Directors stated that we had just lost America from our folly, in having allowed the establishment of schools and colleges, and that it would not do for us to repeat the same act of folly in regard to India; … For twenty years after that period down to the year 1813, the same feeling of opposition to the education of the natives continued to prevail among the ruling authorities of this country." (Marshman, ibid.)

Perpetuation of Caste and Tribe Divisions

Sir John Malcolm was one of those experienced English statesmen who had specialised in and contributed very largely to the expansion of the British Empire in India in the beginning of the 19th century. We quote from his evidence before the Parliamentary Committee (1813):

> "... In the present extended state of our Empire, our security for preserving a power of so extraordinary a nature as that we have established rests upon the general divisions of the great communities under the Government, and their sub-division into castes and tribes; while they continue divided in this manner, no insurrection is likely to shake the stability of our power ..."

> "... we shall always find it difficult to rule in proportion as it (the Indian community) obtains union and possesses the power of throwing off that subjection in which it is now placed to the British Government."

> "... I do not think that the communication of any knowledge, which tended gradually to do away the subsisting distinctions among our native subjects or to diminish that respect which they entertain for Europeans, could be said to add to the political strength of the English Government ..."

One Lac of Rupees for Literary Development

The Charter Act of 1813 contained a clause to the effect that the Governor-General was to spend every year, out of the savings in the income of British India, any amount up to a lac of rupees for the revival and development of literature and the encouragement of Indian scholars. The letter of instructions dated 3rd June, 1814, which the Directors sent to the Governor-General, however, makes it quite clear that no part of the grant was to be used for the establishment of any public college. It directs that it was to be used exclusively for

(i) consolidating the existing political relationship between England and India,

(ii) promoting closer contacts between the English in India and the Indian leaders of thought in order to maintain the existence of the English Empire in India,

(iii) helping such Englishmen as wished to learn Sanskrit,
(iv) translating ancient Sanskrit literature into English,
(v) investigation of such old educational institutions of India as had escaped extinction,
(vi) investigation of the sentiments of the Indians towards the English, and
(vii) subsidising the *Pandits* at Banaras and elsewhere. (*Vide Affairs of the East India Company*, published 1832, Vol. I, pp. 446–47).

Lionel Smith's Fears

During the enquiry of 1831, Major-General Sir Lionel Smith, K.C.B., confirmed the views expressed by Sir John Malcolm in 1813. He said:

> "The effect of education will be to do away with all the prejudices of sects and religions by which we have hitherto kept the country—the Mussalmans against Hindoos, and so on; the effect of education will be to expand their minds and show them their vast power."

English-educated Indians Needed for the Company's Offices and Courts in India

By the end of the 18th century, however, the English rulers' ideas had undergone a change for two reasons. One was that they had come to realise how extremely difficult, if not impossible, it would be to man the Company's offices and courts without English-knowing Hindus and Mussalmans, whose number was steadily declining. The other was that they felt the pressing need of a body of English-educated Indians who could keep them posted about the prevalent inner feelings of the Indian people towards them, and could influence the Indian people's ideas and opinions in favour of the English. These needs have been repeatedly mentioned in the 1830 Report of the Parliamentary Committee which also makes it quite clear that the "Mussalman Madrassa" of Calcutta and the "Hindu Sanskrit College" of Banaras were established to meet these requirements, which were intended to be further met by the establishment of the Deccan College at Poona in 1821, of the Medical College at Calcutta in 1835, and of the Engineering College at Roorkee in 1847.

The Directors had written to the Governor-General on 5th September, 1827, that the educational grant was to be used for the "education" of

> "... the superior and middle classes of the natives, from whom the native agents whom you have occasion to employ in the functions of Government are most fitly drawn, and whose influence on the rest of their countrymen is the most extensive".

Increase in Educational Grant

The education in English of at least some Indians had thus become unavoidable for the English rulers. So the (1813) one-lac grant was, in 1833, increased tenfold to 10 lacs. Another reason for the increase was that during the previous 20 years a very large part of India had been added to the territory under the rule of the foreign Company.

It may be mentioned that from 1757 to 1857, the main question before the English rulers was whether any education of Indians would be beneficial or harmful to the existence of their empire in India.

Propagation of Christianity

A number of English statesmen at that time favoured the propagation of Christianity in India, and felt that it was necessary to translate Christian religious literature into Indian languages to assist English missionaries coming out to India and to provide Government help for mission schools. This was also one of the reasons why many Englishmen supported the policy of educating Indians. One comes across it again and again in the course of the controversy that followed 1813.

Fear of Educated Indians

The last Charter Act was passed in 1853. Before it was passed, a Parliamentary Committee collected evidence on the issue of the education of Indians. Amongst the witnesses examined was Major Ronaldson who had been for 17 years the Persian interpreter attached to the Commander-in-Chief at Madras, and had also been the Secretary of the Education Committee of that Presidency's Government. He was asked (on 4th August, 1853) by the Parliamentary Committee:

> "Question—You have expressed your opinion that the education of Indians results in making them hostile to the English Government. Will you explain why? What sort of hostility is it? What is its nature?"
>
> "Answer—It is my experience that their knowledge of the core of the British Indian history added to their general knowledge of European history brings home to them the enormity of a vast country like India lying under the heels of a handful of foreigners. This realisation naturally leads to a eagerness in their hearts to help in the liberation of their country from foreign rule. The absence of anything to counteract the effects of this eagerness, and of any deeply-rooted loyalty to the English, helps to make them hostile to the British Government ... I have noticed this hostility in Hindus and Mussalmans—to a greater degree in the latter—particularly when these people come to know the secret of the basis of the English rule over them, do they become discontented and hope is awakened ..." (*Sixth Report from the Select Committee on Indian Territories*, 1853, pp. 155–57.)

Different Views

Most Englishmen agreed with Major Ronaldson, but quite a good few held the opposite view. They considered the uneducated Indians more dangerous for the foreign rule than the educated. They thought that the only way to extinguish the patriotism of the Indians and to turn them into useful tools of the foreign rule was to impart western education to them. Amongst the notable English statesmen and politicians holding this view may be mentioned Marshman and Sir Frederick Halliday, the first Lieutenant-Governor of Bengal. Both attested accordingly before the Parliamentary Committee.

Controversy Between Orientalists and Occidentalists

In the first quarter of the 19th century another important question faced such of the English rulers as advocated the education of Indians. It divided them into what were later known as the Orientalists and the Occidentalists. The former were in favour of educating the Indians in the latter's own ancient literature and sciences and in Sanskrit, Persian, Arabic and the Indian languages, whilst the latter considered it to be more in English interests to educate the Indians in English and in Western literature and sciences.

The controversy had been going on for 12 years, when in 1834, Lord Macaulay arrived in India and decided the issue in favour of the Occidentalists. His chief aim was to prevent the rebirth of Indian nationalism amongst the superior classes and to turn them into useful tools of the English administration in India. We quote from Macaulay's famous Minute of 1835:

> "We must do our best to form a class who may be interpreters between us and the millions whom we govern; a class of persons Indian in blood and colour, but English in taste, in opinion, words and intellect."

The Governor-General's Decision

Lord William Bentinck, who was a great friend of Lord Macaulay, and who whole-heartedly agreed with his views, passed on 7th March, 1835 the following resolution:

> "... all the funds appropriated for the purpose of education would be best employed on English education alone".

Thus it was that Macaulay's views as expressed in his report prevailed. The well-known historian, Prof. H. H. Wilson, has characterised the achievements of the Macaulay-Bentinck policy thus:

"... We created a separate caste of English scholars, who had no longer any sympathy, or very little sympathy with their countrymen." (Before the Select Committee of the House of Lords, 5th July, 1864)

Suppression of Indian Languages

Another aspect of the policy pursued by Macaulay and Bentinck was the suppression of the Indian languages, as far as possible, simultaneously with the education of Indians in English. Dr. Duff the historian, whilst commending this policy, has compared it with the policy of the ancient Romans who invariably suppressed the language and the literature of the people conquered by them and educated the latter in Roman language, literature, ideas and ways of life. He adds:

> "... 1 venture to hazard the opinion, that Lord William Bentinck's double act for the encouragement and diffusion of the English language and English literature in the East ... is the grandest master-stroke of sound policy that has yet characterized ... the administration of the British Government in India" (Dr. Duff, in "The Lords' Committee's Second Report on Indian Territories", 1853, p. 409)

Dr. Duff also confirmed the views of another English scholar about the tremendous influence which the language used by a people has on the ideas entertained by them. He stated that the Indians' loyalty and devotion to the Emperor at Delhi would persist so long as Persian continued to be the medium of all communication between the English and the rulers. Lord William Bentinck apparently agreed and banned the use of Persian. He was the first Governor-General who made it a rule to correspond with the Indian rulers in English and English alone.

Incidentally, the English followed a similar policy in Ireland, and where they promulgated peculiar laws "for the purpose of changing Irishmen into Englishmen, if that were possible" (Prof. H. Holman in his *English National Education*, p. 50).

Political Tendency of Different Systems of Education in India

Sir Charles E. Trevelyan, a powerful advocate of the instruction of Indians in English, presented to the Parliamentary Committee of 1853, a paper under the above title. It is a very clear picture of the English educational policy followed in India and of its aims and implications. We give below some extracts. The instruction of Indians in Arabic and Sanskrit, and of keeping alive their age-old national literature, ideas and opinions would, in his view

> "... be perpetually reminding the Mohammadans that we are infidel usurpers of some of the fairest realms of the faithful, and the Hindoos, that we are unclean beasts, with whom it is a sin and a shame to have any friendly intercourse. Our bitterest enemies could not desire more than that we should propagate systems of learning which excite the strongest feelings of human nature against ourselves.
>
> "The spirit of English literature, on the other hand, cannot but be favourable to the English connection. Familiarly acquainted with us by means of our literature, the Indian youth almost cease to regard us as foreigners. They speak of our great men with the same enthusiasm as we do. Educated in the same way, interested in the same objects, engaged in the same pursuits with ourselves, they become more English than Hindoo ... they cease to think as violent opponents, or sullen conformists, they are converted into zealous and intelligent co-operators with us ... they cease to think of violent remedies ..."
>
> "... As long as the natives are left to brood over their former independence, their sole specific for improving their condition is the immediate and total expulsion of the English. A native patriot of the old school has no notion of anything beyond this ... It is only by the infusion of European ideas that a new direction can be given to the national views. The young men, brought up at our seminaries, turn with contempt from the barbarous despotism under which their ancestors groaned

to the prospect of improving their national institution on the English model ... So far from having the idea of driving the English into the sea uppermost in their minds, they have no notion of any improvement but such as rivets their connection with the English, and makes them dependent on English protection and instruction ..."

"The only means at our disposal ... is to set the natives on a process of European improvement, to which they are already sufficiently inclined. They will then cease to desire and aim at independence on the old Indian footing. A sudden change will then be impossible; and a long continuance of our present connection with India will even be assured to us ... The natives will not rise against us ... The national activity will be fully and harmlessly employed in acquiring and diffusing European knowledge, and naturalising European institutions. The educated classes ... will naturally cling to us ... There is no class of our subjects to whom we are so thoroughly necessary as those whose opinions have been cast in the English mould; they are spoiled for a purely native regime; they have everything to fear from the premature establishment of a native Government ..."

"The Indians will, I hope, soon stand in the same position towards us in which we once stood towards the Romans. Tacitus informs us that it was the policy of Julius Agricola to instruct the sons of the leading men among the Britons in the literature and science of Rome and to give them a taste for the refinements of Roman civilization. We all know how well this plan answered. From being obstinate enemies, the Britons soon became attached and confiding friends; and they made more strenuous efforts to retain the Romans than their ancestors had done to resist their invasion. It will be a shame to us if, with our greatly superior advantages, we also do not make our premature departure be dreaded as a calamity ..."

"These views were not worked out by reflection, but were forced on me by actual observation and experience. I passed some years in parts of India, where owing to the comparative novelty of our rule and to the absence of any attempt to alter the current of native feeling, the national habits of thinking remained unchanged. There high and low, rich and poor, had only one idea of improving their political condition. The upper classes lived upon the prospect of regaining their former pre-eminence; and the lower, upon that of having the avenues to wealth and distinction reopened to them by the re-establishment of a native government. Even sensible and comparatively well affected natives had no notion that there was any remedy for the existing depressed state of their nation except the sudden and absolute expulsion of the English. After that, I resided for some years in Bengal, and there I found quite another set of ideas prevalent among the educated natives. Instead of thinking of cutting the throats of the English, they were aspiring to sit with them on the grand jury or on the bench of magistrates …"

Plain Speaking by Trevelyan

On the basis of his above-mentioned paper, Sir Charles E. Trevelyan was closely examined for some days by the Parliamentary Committee. On 23rd June, 1853, he stated:

> "According to the unmitigated native system the Mohammedans regard us as *Kafirs*, as infidel usurpers of some of the finest realms of Islam … According to the same original native views, the Hindoos regard us as *Mlechhas*, that is, impure outcasts with whom no communion ought to be held, and they all of them, both Hindoo and Mohammedan, regard us as usurping foreigners, who have taken their country from them, and excluded them from the avenues to wealth and distinction. The effect of a training in European learning is to give an entirely new turn to the native mind. The young men educated in this may cease to strive after Independence."

> "They cease to regard us as enemies and usurpers, and they look upon us as friends and patrons, and powerful beneficent persons, under whose protection all they have most at heart for the regeneration of their country will gradually be worked out. According to the original native view of political change,

we might be swept off the face of India in a day, and, as a matter of fact, those who look for the improvement of India according to this model are continually meditating on plots and conspiracies with that object; whereas, according to the new and improved system, the object must be worked out by very gradual steps, and ages may elapse before the ultimate end will be attained."

Lord Monteagle, the Chairman of the Committee, then plainly asked Sir Charles to state whether the ultimate aim of the latter's proposition was to end the political connexion of England with India or to perpetuate it for ever. Sir Charles replied:

"... Now my belief is, that *the ultimate result of the policy of improving and educating India will be to postpone the separation for a long indefinite period*, ... whereas I conceive that the result of the opposite policy ... may lead to a separation at any time, leading to it at a much earlier period and under much more disadvantageous circumstances. I am recommending the course which, according to my most deliberate view which I have held for a great many years, founded, I believe, on a full knowledge of the subject, will be most conducive to the continuance of our dominion ... I may mention, as a familiar illustration, that I was 12 years in India, and that the first six years were spent in the country, with Delhi for my headquarters, and the other six at Calcutta. The first six years represent the old regime of pure native ideas, and there were continual wars and rumours of wars. The only form which native patriotism assumed in the country was plotting against us, and meditating combinations against us and so forth. Then I came to Calcutta: and there I found quite a new state of things. The object there was to have a free press, to have municipal institutions, to promote English education and the employment of the Natives, and various things of that sort."

Lord Monteagle of Brandon: "Then supposing one of two courses to be taken, either the abandonment of the education and employment of the Natives, or an extension of education, or an extension with due precaution of the employment of the Natives, which of those two courses, in your judgement, will lead to the longest possible continuation of the connexion of India with England?"

"Decidedly the extension of education and the employment of the Natives; I entertain no doubt whatever upon the question."

It will be noted that what Lord Monteagle termed "the connexion of India with England" was in reality nothing but the English "dominion" over India, for "the longest possible continuance" of which. Trevelyan was asked to point the way. The latter recommended the "course" which, in his view would be "most conducive to the continuance of our (English) dominion for a long indefinite period." Needless to say, both Macaulay and Bentinck held identical views. Indeed, there was at that time hardly any Englishman who seriously questioned the fact that the sole aim and object of imparting English education to the "natives" was to perpetuate their political subjugation to the English domination. The only difference of opinion was about the best way of achieving it. The course recommended by Sir Charles Trevelyan was ultimately adopted by the Directors of the Company, who on 19th July 1854, sent to Lord Dalhousie, the then Governor-General of India, the famous "Education Despatch".

Incidentally, Sir Charles Trevelyan was not wrong in warning his countrymen that "the only form which native patriotism assumed in the country was plotting against us", and that the people in the north and around Delhi, who were either uneducated or had not been imparted English education, were "continually meditating on plots and conspiracies" and that the English "might be swept off the face of India". His fears were not unfounded as only a few years later, the foundations of the British Empire in India were very badly shaken by the people's revolt of 1857.

The Education Despatch of 1854

The "Despatch" has ever been the fountain-head of the English educational policy in India which is even now (1929) followed by the present Education Department of the Government of India. We quote some of its significant passages which clearly express two of its important objectives. One was to enable the Governor-General

> "to obtain the services of intelligent and trustworthy persons in every department of Government." (Para 2)

and the other was

> "to secure to us (in England) a larger and more certain supply of many articles necessary for our manufactures and extensively consumed by all classes of our population as well as an almost inexhaustible demand for the produce of British labour." (Para 4)

The English in India were, by then, quite convinced that the policy of Trevelyan, Macaulay and others like them was sound and far-sighted and they started to carry it out.

Official Universities

In pursuance of the said policy official universities at Calcutta, Bombay and Madras were constituted by an Act passed in 1857. Lord Canning was then the Governor-General. In 1859, the "Despatch" was confirmed by the British Prime Minister.

Consequences of the English Educational Policy in India

A Kashmiri Brahmin, Pandit Mohanlal, who, in connection with the First Afghan War, rendered very valuable help to the English as their secret agent, spy and "traitor-maker", was one of the first students of the College established by the English at Delhi. He was a typical product of the "education" advocated and aimed at by Sir Charles V. Trevelyan. The life and character of a large majority of Indians educated under the system dictated by that policy, as also their ways of living, demonstrated the farsightedness not only of Macaulay and Trevelyan but also of those Englishmen who adopted and carried out the policy. The inevitable result was that an independent country which was considered, from the point of view of the education of its people, to be one of the foremost countries in the world, sank, after 150 years of foreign rule, to the lowest position amongst the civilized nations. In a country in which almost everyone had known the three R's, as many as 94 out of every 100 are quite illiterate now (1929). Most of the few Indians who have been educated in English have become utterly indifferent to the weal and woe of their compatriots. Poles apart from all sense of genuine patriotism, they constitute the backbone of the foreign rule. The English objective has been achieved even more fully than the English had hoped.

11

THE FIRST AFGHAN WAR

Lord Auckland

After Lord Bentinck, Sir Charles Metcalfe was the Governor-General *pro tempore* from March 1835 to March 1836. The British Government wanted to appoint the well-known politician, Elphinstone, as successor to Lord Bentinck. Elphinstone had been the Governor of Bombay and his successes at the Nagpur and Poona *Durbars* as also his prominent share in ending the Peshwa Raj have been described in an earlier chapter. It is said that for reasons of health he could not accept the Governor-Generalship and so, in consultation with Lord Bentinck, Lord Auckland was appointed as the Governor-General and arrived in India in 1836.

Lord Auckland's regime was a milestone in the history of British India, as it was marked by the war against Afghanistan. For the prosecution of the war, the fruits of the Indus survey were handy and proved extremely useful. It will be recalled that the survey had been carried out under the pretext of conveying by the river-route the English King's presents to Maharaja Ranjit Singh. Also it was during the Auckland regime that the idea of acquiring a "scientific frontier" for British India was first conceived. As a result of the English efforts to secure the "scientific frontier", Sindh, Punjab, Chitral and parts of Afghanistan lost their independence, one after another.

Dost Mohammad Khan was then the King of Afghanistan. His predecessor, ex-King Shah Shuja, was a political refugee living at Ludhiana as a "guest" of the English Government, who gave him a pension.

A shrewd Englishman, Lt. Burnes, had been deputed to take the above-mentioned presents to Maharaja Ranjit Singh. After he had done that, he was sent to Central Asia with a party in 1832. His declared mission was to win over to the Company's side the various powers ruling the territory between India and Central Asia as a precautionary measure against the threat of an invasion of India by Russia. The party included another Englishman, Dr. Gerard, the Kashmiri Pandit Munshi Mohanlal (mentioned in the preceding chapter) and a Mussalman surveyor, Mohammad Ali. The first country visited by them was Afghanistan, where they were received and treated very hospitably by the Afghan King, Dost Mohammad Khan. The party toured Central Asia for about a year, and returned to India in 1833 with a sheaf of letters, maps and plans. Burnes' work was very much appreciated in India and in England and when he arrived in England (shortly after his return to India) "he was lionised" and was received in audience by King William IV himself.

The English had long coveted the expansion of their Indian Empire up to Afghanistan. The bogey of a Russian invasion trotted out by them was more of a pretence than otherwise. After Lord Auckland had taken over, Burnes was once again sent to Afghanistan, this time on a "commercial mission". The historian, Sir John Kaye, has described it thus: "Commerce in the vocabulary of the East," he writes, "is only another name for conquest... and this commercial mission became the cloak of grave political designs" (*Lives of Indian Officers,* Vol. II, p. 36).

The "mission" arrived at Kabul on 20th September, 1837, and was very cordially received by the Afghan King and the people. The real object of the mission was to induce the Afghan King to side with the English and help them in case Russia attacked them, but the mission did not succeed and returned to India.

Dost Mohammad Khan's Terms

The Afghan King wanted a *quid pro quo* for the help which the English mission requested. He told the latter that if they wanted his help against Russia, then they should, in return, help him to recover from Maharaja Ranjit Singh the eastern territory of Afghanistan, including Peshawar, which the Sikh monarch had annexed. But the English would not agree for two reasons. Firstly, they did not want to add to the strength of Dost Mohammad Khan, who was already a powerful and capable ruler. Secondly, they fully expected to be able to annex the territory themselves after Ranjit Singh's death. So the mission failed.

The Decision for War Against Afghanistan

Whilst Burnes was at Kabul, trying to win over Dost Mohammad Khan, "other counsels were prevailing at Simla—the great hot-bed on the Himalayan hills ... They conceived the idea of reinstating the old deposed dynasty of Shah Shuja, and they picked him out of the dust of Ludhiana to make him a tool and a puppet" (Kaye's *Lives of Indian Officers,* Vol. II, p. 36). So the English were probably happy at the failure of the Burnes mission as it gave them an excuse for invading Afghanistan. But the English Government in India alone were not responsible for the decision to go to war against the unoffending Afghans. The historian Keene has expressly stated that the British Ministers in England had, much earlier, decided upon the invasion of Afghanistan, and that requisite instructions had been sent by the British Prime Minister, Lord Palmerston, in confidential letters addressed to the Governor-General in India. The latter was also advised by the Chairman of the Board of Directors of the Company to conquer Punjab first and then to invade Afghanistan through Punjab.

Falsification of Parliamentary Papers

Burnes' letters from Kabul were on official record. In them, he had expressed his unstinted admiration for Dost Mohammad Khan's character. This did not suit the English who desired to degrade him in public estimation and so to justify his deposition by military action. Consequently, the letters in the Parliamentary Reports were mutilated and altered so as to contain nothing but a revilement of Dost Mohammad Khan supposed to have been expressed by Burnes. The lie was exposed when, after Burnes' death, his father petitioned the King of England, accusing the British Ministers of an attempt to calumniate his dead son. Kaye's characterisation of the sordid episode is as follows:

> "I cannot indeed suppress the utterance of my abhorrence of this system of garbling the official correspondence of public

men … the dishonesty by which lie upon lie is palmed upon the world has not one redeeming feature … In the case before us … the character of Dost Mohammad Khan has been lied away; the character of Burnes has been lied away; both by the mutilation of the correspondence of the latter have been fearfully misrepresented—both have been set forth as doing what they did not, and omitting to do what they did …" (Kaye's *Lives of Indian Officers,* Vol. II)

Before war was declared, a treaty was concluded between the Company, Maharaja Ranjit Singh and Shah Shuja, the deposed King of Afghanistan. Under it the English undertook to reinstate Shah Shuja, and the latter, in return, promised to let the English have a free hand in Sindh. The treaty thus doomed the existence of Sindh as an independent sovereign country. Ranjit Singh did not derive any particular benefit from the treaty. He was in fact unwilling, it has been stated, to be a party to it. But he was somehow prevailed upon to append his signature. He died shortly after, leaving a free field for the Company to carry out its designs against Punjab.

The Declaration of War

The Company then issued a proclamation declaring war against Afghanistan.

The Company's North-Indian army marched to the Afghan frontier through Punjab and the Khyber Pass. Its army from Bombay came by sea and went towards Afghanistan through Sindh and Baluchistan.

How the passage was secured is best described in the words of the historian Kaye. He writes:

> "It was determined by the Simla Council that Shah Sooja and the Army of the Indus should be sent through the country of the Ameers. To accomplish this, it was necessary that, in the first instance, an existing treaty should be set aside. When the Ameers consented to open the navigation of the Indus, it was expressly stipulated that no military stores should be conveyed along the river. But as soon as ever Lord Auckland had resolved to erect a friendly power in Afghanistan and to

march a British army across the Indus, it became necessary to tear this prohibitory treaty to shreds, and to trample down the scruples of the Ameers ..."

"... The Ameers were known to be weak; and they were believed to be wealthy. Their money was to be taken; their country to be occupied; their treaties to be set aside at the point of the bayonet but amidst a shower of hypocritical expressions of friendship and good will" (Kaye's *History of the War in Afghanistan,* Vol. I).

A new treaty was drawn up for the Ameers to sign. It contained the following undertakings by the Ameers:

(i) that they will acknowledge Shah Shuja as their suzerain and themselves be his vassals,
(ii) that they will provide the English with funds for the latter's war for reinstating Shah Shuja, and
(iii) that the funds will consist of an annual tribute of three lacs of rupees payable by them in addition to the cash down payment of Rs. 21 lacs.

Captn. Eastwick was deputed to present the treaty to the Ameers and to get them to put their signatures on the dotted line. He sought an interview with the Ameers "to administer the black dose of his mission to his hosts" and had the treaty read out to the assembled Ameers of Sindh. The latter listened composedly ... When the reading was over, the Baluchis showed great excitement. At this time a slight signal from their Highnesses would have been sufficient to terminate the lives of all our party under the swords of the barbarian and remorseless Baluchis ... Mr. Nur Mohammed first observed, in Baluchi, to his two colleagues, "Cursed be he who puts reliance upon the promises of the *Feringees*;" and then, addressing himself seriously to the British representative, he spoke thus in Persian : "Your treaties, I believe, are changeable at your pleasure and convenience; is this the way to treat your friends and benefactors? You asked our permission to allow your armies a free passage through our territories. We granted it without hesitation ... Had we know that, after the entrance of your army into our lands, you would threaten our safety, and enforce another treaty upon us, demanding an annual tribute of Rs. 3,00,000 and a ready payment of Rs. 21 lacs for the immediate expense of the army, we would, in such case, have adopted measures for the security of our country and persons … "

Captain Eastwick heard all this with calmness, and gave brief replies in Persian and Arabic proverbs … Mr. Nur Mohammed smiled, and spoke to his cousins in Baluchi, … and then, with asigh, he said to Captain Eastwick, "I wish I could comprehend the meaning of the word 'friend' which you use. We cannot give a decisive reply to your present demands at once …" (*Autobiography of Lutfullah,* pp. 277–79, 294–96).

Pressure Tactics

The English then proceeded to overawe the Ameers by demonstrating to them that they (the English) could and would get by force whatever, their army needed, if the Ameers did not part with the same amicably. The Company's troops pillaged the Ameers' subjects living along the line of their march. Numerous atrocities including extortions, tortures and deliberate shootings were perpetrated on the hapless people. Quite a number of these gruesome incidents have been narrated by some of the English officers of the Company's army and are recorded in the *Narrative of the Campaign of the Army of Indus in Sindh and Cabul in 1838–39* by P. H. Kennedy. The Ameers found themselves powerless to protect their subjects and, unable to bear the latter's calamities, they signed the Treaty in July 1839. Thereafter, the Company's army marched on to Afghanistan with Rs. 21 lacs handed over under the Treaty by the Ameers and laden with considerable booty to which it had helped itself.

Occupation of Kabul

The Company's army marched into Afghanistan, apparently unopposed, and, entirely through the English intrigues, lavish promises and expenditure of money in bribery and corruption of several Afghan chieftains, succeeded within a short time in occupying Kabul and in deposing Dost Mohammad Khan, who was taken prisoner and deported. Shah Shuja was installed on the Afghan throne and the declared object of the English military expedition was achieved. It did not however mean the end of hostilities.

Those who had been won over by the English promises were soon disillusioned as there were no signs of the promises being fulfilled. The disappointed elements made common cause with such of their compatriots as had throughout been hostile to Shah Shuja and his allies, the English. They found a leader, namely, Dost Mohammad Khan's son, Akbar Khan, and continued to rise in revolts here and there for the next two years.

The English Handling of the Situation Created by them in Afghanistan

Our readers will recall the Kashmiri Pandit Mohanlal, who was in the Company's employ as a *Munshi*. He had been taken to Afghanistan along with the expeditionary force, presumably because he was supposed to be "... endowed with a genius for traitor-making". We quote from his book, *Life of Dost Mohammad Khan:*

> "... we were certainly very wrong in not keeping our adherence, even for a short time, to those engagements and promises which we had so solemnly and faithfully made to the various chiefs in return for their taking up our cause and abandoning their long-known and established masters... As soon as we found that... there was no necessity for wearing any longer the airy garb of political civilities and promises, we commenced to fail in fulfilling them. There are, in fact, such numerous instances of violating our engagements and deceiving the people in our political proceedings, within what I am acquainted with, that it would be hard to assemble them in one series." (pp. 208–09)

About the administrative set-up inaugurated and maintained by the English in Afghanistan during the Shah Shuja regime, Munshi Mohanlal has this to say:

> "We neither took the reins of Government in our own hands, nor did we give them in full powers into the hands of the

Shah. Inwardly or secretly we interfered in all transactions, contrary to the terms of our own engagement with the Shah, and outwardly we wore the mask of neutrality. In this manner we gave annoyance to the King, on the one hand, and disappointment to the people, on the other." (ibid. p. 313)

Mohanlal's Assignments

"Traitor-making" was not the only work entrusted to Mohanlal. He was also assigned the tasks of sowing dissensions amongst the Afghans by playing off the Shias against the Sunnis. We quote from Kaye's *History of the Afghan War* (Vol. I, p. 202):

> "This Mohan Lai had other work entrusted to him ... he was not directed merely to appeal to the cupidity of the chiefs by offering them large sums of money to exert their influence in our favour. He was directed also to offer rewards for the heads of the principal insurgents. As early as the 5th of November (1841), Lieutenant John Conolly, who was in attendance upon Shah Soojah in the Balla Hissar (fort), wrote to Mohan Lal:"
>
> "Tell the Kuzzil Bash chiefs, Shereen Khan, Nayab Sheriff, in fact, all the chiefs of Shiya persuasion, to join against the rebels. You can promise one lakh of rupees to Khan Shereen on the condition of his killing and seizing the rebels and arming all the Shiyas, and immediately attacking all rebels. This is the time for the Shiyas to do good service. Tell the chiefs who are well-disposed to send respectable agents to the Envoy. Try and spread 'Nifak' among the rebels. In everything you do consult me and write very often 'I promise ten thousand rupees for the head of each of the principal rebel chiefs.'"

Mohanlal had no scruples, but he was a shrewd man, and wanted to get the above instructions confirmed by the English envoy, Sir William MacNaghten. So he wrote to the envoy that he could not find out from Conolly's letter how the assassinations were to be carried out "but the men now employed promise to go into their (the rebels') houses and cut off their heads when they may be without attendants".

> "The victims said to have been first marked for the assassin's knife were Abdoolah Khan and Meer Musjedjee". (ibid., pp. 218–19)

Misdeeds of English Agents and Officers

Sir John Kaye, in his *History of the Afghan War,* writes:

> "The temptations which are most difficult to withstand were not withstood by our English officers. The attractions of the women of Kabul they did not know how to resist. The Afghans are very jealous of the honour of their women; and there were things done in Kabul which covered them with shame and roused them to revenge…"

> "For two long years … had this same been burning itself into the hearts of the Kabulies; and there were some men of note and influence among them who knew themselves to be thus wronged; complaints were made, but they were made in vain. The scandal was open, undisguised, notorious. Redress was not to be obtained. The evil was not in course of suppression. It went on till it became intolerable and the injured then began to see that the only remedy was in their own hands." (Vol. I, pp. 143–44)

The Afghans' Reaction—Shah Shuja Shot Dead

The Afghans were a fearless, self-respecting people and utterly without guile. Naturally they did not suspect the foreigners, and were furious when they discovered that the English had deceived them by promises which were never intended to be kept. They also saw that all that they got from the English was brutal treatment like pillage, murder and the desecration of everything they held sacred. On top of all that, they saw their women dishonoured. Their eyes were at last opened to the political and social immorality of the English character. They were not a people divided amongst themselves, like Indians, by casteism, sectarianism and communalism. On the contrary, they were a united and organised nation. They made up their minds to drive the English from their land. Much as they hated The English, they hated Shah Shuja even more, as they regarded him as the root cause of all their calamities. It was to restore the Afghan throne to him that the English had invaded their country. Shah Shuja came to know of the strength of his subjects' intense bitterness against himself, and realised that his very life was in danger. He tried to save himself by running away, but failed, as he was shot dead by a patriotic Afghan on 5th April, 1842, whilst attempting to escape.

Assassination of Sir Alexander Burnes

Another victim of the Afghan fury was Sir Alexander Burnes, C. B., then on the English political staff in Afghanistan. As mentioned before, he had first visited Kabul as Lieutenant Burnes and had repeated his visits and received every time lavish hospitality from the Afghan King (Dost Mohammad Khan) and his people. The latter now saw in Burnes an unscrupulous spy who had abused their friendly trust and repaid their hospitality by treachery. They meted out to Burnes the treatment which under International Law is proper for spies, and cut him down in broad daylight in the main street of Kabul.

English Ambassador Sir William Macnaghten

It would appear that MacNaghten had the ambition to emulate Clive and strove to achieve in Afghanistan what Clive had some 80 years before accomplished in Bengal. But he had overlooked the all-important fact that Afghanistan was *not* Bengal. When the situation deteriorated and got out of control, he, with the approval of the then Governor-General (Lord Ellenborough), entered into an engagement with Dost Mohammad Khan's son, Akbar Khan, whereby the English undertook to bring back Dost Mohammad Khan and re-instal him on the throne at Kabul. Even though MacNaghten signed the agreement, he did not refrain from his machiavellian tactics designed to sow dissensions between Akbar Khan and the chiefs friendly to him. He wrote to Akbar Khan assuring him of his friendship and expressing a desire to meet him. In the same letter he also mentioned some Afghan chiefs by name, and hinted that as they were plotting against him (Akbar Khan), he had better "liquidate" them. At the same time he wrote severally to the chiefs he had accused, and tried to incite them against Akbar Khan. As soon as the latter received MacNaghten's letter, he called a meeting of all the Afghan chiefs, including those named by MacNaghten. At the meeting, Akbar Khan produced MacNaghten's letter whereupon the accused chiefs produced the letters which MacNaghten had written to them. The trickery was exposed and it filled the assembled chiefs with indignant rage. Akbar Khan, however, bided his time and invited MacNaghten for the interview sought by the latter.

Some time earlier, Lord Ellenborough had stated in his letter to Queen Victoria, dated 5th October, 1842, that he had issued a proclamation offering a huge reward for the head of Akbar Khan. MacNaghten had been informed of the proclamation when it was issued. (*Nairang-i-Afghanistan* by Syed Feda Hussain, reviewed in "The Modern Review," for February, 1907, p. 224).

> "When MacNaghten went to meet Akbar Khan, he ordered a portion of his troops to lie in ambush, instructing their commander to rush forward at a given signal. When the interview took placc, Akbar Khan began to reproach MacNaghten for his treachery and asked him to explain the meaning of those letters, written to himself and his Sirdars. When MacNaghten was trying to explain his conduct, an Afghan came running to Akbar Khan and, speaking in Pushtu, informed him of the movement of the English troops, which had been deputed to lie in ambush. On this both Akbar Khan and MacNaghten stood up and an altercation ensued. The first shot was fired by Mac-Naghten, and he was killed by Akbar Khan."

In face of the facts narrated above, some English writers would still have it that Akbar Khan treacherously murdered MacNaghten.

Annihilation of the Company's Expeditionary Force

The three leading actors in the drama of the attempted conquest of Afghanistan, Shah Shuja, Burnes and MacNaghten had met their end. Thereafter numberless Englishmen were put to the sword, one by one, by the Afghans. The survivors of the expeditionary force requested Akbar Khan to permit them to return to India and promised to return Dost Mohammad Khan safe and sound, as soon as they reached India. Akbar Khan granted their request and allowed them to depart, but held back some English officers as hostages. It will be recalled that on their march to Afghanistan, the expeditionary force had, for two years, subjected the Baluchis of Sindh and the Afghans living along their line of march to wholesale pillage and extortions. Their retreat back to India provided their former victims with the opportunity of avenging those atrocities and the latter took their revenge fully. The severe winter added its quota to the miseries and misfortunes of the retreating force, and the retreat was far more disastrous than any rout oil a battle-field. All dropped on the way, dead, wounded or taken prisoner. Of the 16,000 strong force that had two years earlier set out from India to conquer Afghanistan, only one, Dr. Brydon, succeeded in staggering into Jelalabad on the outskirts of the Company's territory.

Lord Ellenborough—His Political Views

In February 1842, Lord Ellenborough had succeeded Lord Auckland as Governor-General. It was during the former's regime that Shah Shuja, Burnes and MacNaghten had met their end.

Lord Ellenborough's preceptors in politics were the Wellesley brothers, famous in British history as the Marquess of Wellesley and the Duke of Wellington, respectively. We would pause here for a moment and digress from our narrative of the Afghan War to describe the political views and convictions of Lord Ellenborough. Some nine years before he took over as Governor-General, he had, on 5th July 1833, spoken thus in the House of Lords:

"No man in his senses would propose to place the political and military power in India in the hands of the natives... Our very existence in India depended upon the exclusion of the natives from military and political power in that country... We had won the Empire of India by the sword, and me must preserve it by the same means."

Before he left England for India, Ellenborough had written to the Duke of Wellington a letter on 15th October, 1841, which clearly indicates that he had his eye on Punjab and Nepal and was keen on annexing both to the British Empire anyhow. His other letters also go to show that he considered it as much justifiable as any of the previous Governors-General to violate, whenever necessary or expedient, any of the treaties solemnly entered into by the English with the Indian rulers or princes.

False Proclamations

The disaster and the resulting disgrace of British arms in Afghanistan had an effect on the Indian people and princes which was none too favourable to the English. Ellenborough has admitted in his letter to the Duke of Wellington, dated 15th May, 1842, that to counteract the harmful effect, "I have not hesitated to publish all over India garbled accounts through proclamations." The proclamations were widely distributed, particularly in Hyderabad (Deccan). Sindh, Nepal, Saugor district and Bundelkhand.

Ellenborough believed that the Mussalmans were particularly inimical to the English and would never side with them. His policy, therefore, was to keep the Hindus as happy as possible and on the English side. The Afghan War was exploited by him to gratify the Hindus. The beautifully jewelled gates of the Somnath Temple had reportedly been taken away to Ghazni by Mahmud Ghazni in the 11th century, and were stated to be still adorning Mahmud's mausoleum. Ellenborough ordered that the famous gates be brought back from Ghazni paraded throughout India and then installed in their original position at the Somnath Temple. The orders were carried out and the gates, supposed to have been brought back by the English from Afghanistan, were paraded with great pomp and show throughout Punjab and up to Agra. On 16th November, 1842, Ellenborough issued a proclamation to the Hindu Maharajas, Rajas, chiefs and people of India assuring them of the English Government's support of the Hindus and their religion and informing them that the gates would be duly re-installed at the Somnath Temple. But in spite of all this fanfare, the gates did not go farther than Agra.

Before the gates had reached Agra, some Englishmen, led by Lord Macaulay, vociferously opposed Ellenborough's move, as they did not consider it to be in the interests of the British rule to antagonise the Mussalmans of India. In March, 1843, Lord Macaulay declared in the British Parliament:

> "The Mohammedans are in a minority, but their importance is much more than proportioned to their number; for they are a united, zealous, ambitious and a war-like class... Nobody who knows anything of the Mohammedans of India can doubt that this affront to their faith will excite their fiercest indignation."

Ellenborough was even charged with the disparagement of Christianity by his symbolic support of the Hindu's idolatry.

Other Englishmen, however, favoured Ellenborough's disregard of the Mussalman feelings, and commended his efforts to strengthen the Hindus' alliance with the English by doing something special which would stir up their religious sentiments in favour of the English. Lord Ellenborough had himself written to the Duke of Wellington on 18th January, 1843:

> "I have every reason to think that the restoration (recovery?) of the gates of the temple of Somnath has conciliated and gratified the great mass of the Hindoo population. I have no reason to suppose that it has offended the Mussalmans, but I cannot close my eyes to the belief that that race is fundamentally hostile to us, and therefore our true policy is to conciliate the Hindoos..."

The controversy seems to have led to the abandonment by Ellenborough of his pet "political measure" and the Somnath gates stayed at Agra.

It may be pointed out, however, that neither he nor Macaulay had any real liking for the Hindoos or the Mussalmans, respectively. But to keep the two communities at loggerheads, it was considered expedient to make a show of favouritism alternately for Hindus and the Mussalmans. This was even at that period considered essential under the policy followed by the English rulers of India.

But were the paraded "Somnath gates" genuine? Our readers must have been wondering by whom, how and when they were brought from Ghazni in Afghanistan to India. The expeditionary force which,' presumably, had been ordered to bring them had perished to a man during its retreat from Kabul. The sole survivor, Dr. Brydon, who had staggered into Jelalabad, more dead than alive, could hardly have lugged the gates along. The version that they were fashioned out of sandalwood at Jelalabad under Ellenborough's orders would appear to be true. If it is so then the whole episode is an illustration of the political chicanery resorted to by the Company's representatives in India, including the Governor-General himself. We quote an illuminating extract from his letter to the Duke of Wellington dated 22nd March, 1843:

> "You know better than anyone the difficulties I found on my arrival. I have only been able to meet those difficulties by *acts and language which even in India, I should not myself have adopted under ordinary circumstances.*"

Financial Consequences of the War

We now resume the thread of our narrative of the war. Its cost in terms of money can be estimated from the following figures given by Lord Ellenborough in his letter to Queen Victoria:

> "… the political and military charges … incurred beyond the Indus amounted to £1,250,000 a year; … the estimates of the expense of the additions made to the army in India since April 1838 was £1,131,750 a year; … the deficit of Indian revenue in 1839-40 having been £2,425,625, a further deficit of £1,987,000 was expected …"

The financial burden having become unbearable, the war had to be ended anyhow and as soon as possible.

The End of the War

But matters could not be left at the unsettled stage at which they were when Dr. Brydon reached Jelalabad. Also the disgrace of the military disaster had to be white-washed and the English prestige had to be rehabilitated. Some sort of settlement with the Afghans had to be made whereby the English hostages in Afghanistan could be liberated. All this could not be achieved without a resumption of hostilities, even though it would be only a fight for terms.

So General Pollock was sent with a large force to Afghanistan. He met with some initial success. He blew up the main Bazar at Kabul and razed to the ground some prominent buildings including two principal mosques. The city was looted too. Ultimately, however, the Afghans, led by Akbar Khan, defeated Pollock and made peace with the English. Dost Mohammad Khan returned and re-occupied the Afghan throne. The English hostages were released and Pollock was allowed to leave Afghanistan peacefully with his force. Thus failed the first English attempt to rob the Afghans of their independence. Kaye in his *History of the Afghan War* thus concludes the story:

> "... the wisdom of our statesmen is but foolishness, and the might of our armies is but weakness, when the curse of God is sitting heavily upon an unholy cause ..."

Bengal and Afghanistan

We would like to add that the English had, apparently, planned a repeat-performance in Afghanistan of their exploits in Bengal after the Battle of Plassey, with MacNaghten, Dost Mohammad Khan and Shah Shuja cast for the parts of Clive, Sirajudaula, and Mir Jafar, respectively. But it was a flop, not only because the Afghans were radically different from the people of Bengal but mainly because the star actors on the Afghan stage, MacNaghten, Dost Mohammad Khan and Shah Shuja, particularly the last-mentioned, were as, different from Clive, Sirajudaula and Mir Jafar, as cheese is from chalk. So the Machiavellian tactics of the English failed, for the first time, to secure for them a "victory" in a clash of arms.

12

ANNEXATION OF SINDH

Sindh's First Contacts with the English

Sindh had been a province of the Mughal Empire for many years and had been paying tribute to the Mughal Emperors till 1749, when the Amirs of Sindh acknowledged the King of Afghanistan as their suzerain and began to pay tribute to him. In other respects they continued to be independent rulers of their country.

In 1758, Amir Ghulamshah Kalhor gave the East India Company permission to establish their factories and commercial houses at Thatta and Aurangbandar. Thatta was then an important centre of the textile industry. Sir Henry Pottinger has stated that 40,000 weavers of fine cloth and 20,000 other crafts-men lived in Thatta at that time. The commercial community, traders, bankers and grain merchants numbered 60,000. In 1809, that is, within 50 years of the East India Company's advent, the population of Thatta had shrunk to 20,000 souls in all (*Sind Gazetteer*, Vol. A, p. 116).

Amir Ghulamshah had also granted to the Company many commercial concessions and facilities. These were, however, abused by the Company's agents to such an extent that, in 1775, Ghulamshah's son, Sarfaraz, closed down the Company's factories and commercial houses.

In 1799, a new agent of the Company, Nathan Crow, arrived at Hyderabad (Sindh) and at his request, the then Amir, Fateh Ali Khan, permitted the English to carry on business in Sindh. Crow was also given permission to build a house for himself at Karachi. But his conduct again became intolerable, and in 1802 he was ordered to leave Sindh, bag and baggage, within 10 days.

In 1807, the English Governor of Bombay sent an envoy to Sindh to establish political relations with the then Amirs, Ghulam Ali, Karam Ali and Murad Ali. There was an unusual but ancient tradition in Sindh, according to which brothers became joint-Amirs sometimes and ruled the country in all amity.

The English envoy succeeded in persuading the Amirs to enter into a treaty of friendship with the English Company in 1807; it recited that it would last "from generation to generation till the Day of Judgment". Also, the English thereby assured the Amirs that they would never covet "even a foot" of the Amirs' territory. Nevertheless, the treaty remained in force for less than two years.

Second Treaty of 1809

But the Governor-General did not approve of a clause in the treaty of 1807; which provided that the parties would help each other against an enemy of either of them. So another English envoy, Smith, was sent to Sindh to get the treaty re-placed by a fresh treaty, which was signed on 22nd August 1809. It contained four articles, namely:

(i) There shall be eternal friendship between the British Government and the Government of Sindh.
(ii) Enmity shall never grow between the two States.
(iii) The mutual despatch of the Vakeels of both Governments, namely, the British Government and the Sindh Government, shall continue.
(iv) The Government of Sindh will not allow the French to settle in Sindh.

Capt. Eastwick, who was later appointed Assistant English Resident in Sindh, describes the circumstances under which the treaty was being negotiated. He writes:

> "... At the very moment we sent an ambassador to the court of Sindh with expressions of friendship and good will, our envoy at Kabul was proposing to the Governor-General to subjugate the country ... and incorporate the territory with the British possessions in India." (*Dry Leaves from Young Egypt* by W. J. Eastwiek, M. P., p. 334)

But the proposition was not acceptable to Lord Minto, the then Governor-General, as he did not consider the time ripe for the annexation of Sindh.

Third Treaty with the Amirs of Sindh

In 1816, the English invaded the State of Kutch. It took them three years to subjugate it. The borders of Kutch and Sindh being contiguous, it was considered necessary to conclude a fresh treaty with the Amirs. So the third treaty was signed in 1820. How far the English considered these treaties to be binding and inviolable is thus described by Capt. Eastwick:

> "... we swore perpetual amity until a convenient opportunity for appropriating the country, and the destruction and imprisonment of our allies." (ibid., p. 244)

Derryana's Warnings to the Amirs

We have now come to the beginning of 1831, when Sir Alexander Burnes, then Lieutenant Burnes, arrived in Sindh with presents for Maharaja Ranjit Singh. As related in an earlier chapter, the conveyance of the presents was only a pretence under which the nautical survey of the Indus was intended to be carried out. Derryana, a Hindu merchant of Sindh, had been for years warning the Amirs against the English and repeatedly told them, according to Sir James Mackintosh, "*This tribe never began as friends without ending as enemies, by seizing the country which they entered with the most amicable professions.*" Sir James, in his journal has stated that Derryana was "a shrewd dog".

In *Burnes Travels* (Vol. III) an interesting incident is recorded by him. As he entered the river Indus, a Sindhi standing on the water's edge told his companion:

> "Alas! Sindh is now lost, since the English have seen the river which is the road to conquest."

The English not only found the river Indus navigable but also that the Amirs were fabulously rich. They judged it from the costly presents and the lavish hospitality they received from the Amirs. Two more treaties were concluded with the Amirs in 1832 and 1834, whereby the English acquired the right to go up the river Indus. Ironically enough:

> "The two contracting powers bound themselves from generation to generation never to look with the eye of covetousness on the possessions of each other." (*Dry Leaves from Young Egypt*, p. 249)

Tripartite Treaty and Amirs of Sindh

We have in the preceding chapter described the Tripartite Treaty, concluded on 26th June, 1838, between the English, Shah Shuja and Maharaja Ranjit Singh. The Amirs were totally ignored in the negotiations preceding the treaty which sealed their fate. Sir John Kaye writes:

> "From that hour of the 26th day of June 1838, the Ameers may date their ruin. From that hour they virtually ceased to exist as independent rulers". (ibid.)

English Demands on Amirs

We have mentioned above that the Amirs of Sindh were at one time paying tribute to the King of Afghanistan, thereby acknowledging the latter to be their suzerain. In the 1809 Treaty with the Amirs, the Governor-General had admitted that the King of Afghanistan had no right to exact tribute from the Amirs. But in spite of this admission and in contravention of all the treaties which they had till then concluded with the Amirs, the English called upon the latter to shoulder almost all the financial burden of the English expedition undertaken for the restoration of the Afghan throne to the rightful king, Shah Shuja, who was stated to be the Amirs' suzerain. It was demanded that the Amirs must:

(i) allow the expedition to pass through Sindh on its march to Afghanistan,

(ii) provide all the stores and provisions needed by the expedition throughout Sindh,

(iii) hand over to the English troops for occupation and use some specified fortresses,

(iv) pay immediately to the Company Rs. 21 lacs in adjustment of the tributes till then payable by them to the King of Afghanistan, and

(v) pay in future Rs. 3 less every year to the Company on account of the tribute payable by them to the King of Afghanistan.

With regard to the last two items, the Amirs produced two agreements signed and sealed by the Afghan King himself, in which it was expressly declared that in future, no tribute of any kind whatsoever would be payable by the Amirs to the King. The English, however, would not pay the slightest attention to the protests of the Amirs, who were plainly told that the English friendship for them could last only if they gave the demanded help.

The impropriety of the English attitude is thus brought out by Sir John Kaye:

> "And this is British justice … The British were the first to perpetrate a breach of good faith. They taught the Amirs of Sindh that treaties were to be regarded, only so long as it was convenient to regard them … The wolf in the fable did not show greater cleverness in the discovery of a pretext for devouring the lamb than the British Government has shown in all its dealings with the Amirs". (Kaye, "The Calcutta Review", Vol. 1, pp. 220–23)

Mir Rustam Khan of Khairpur

We must explain here that Sindh was divided into Upper and Lower Sindh, each having its own set of Amirs. The capital of Upper Sindh was Khairpur and that of Lower Sindh was Hyderabad. Of the two sets of Amirs, the Hyderabad Amirs enjoyed a higher status than the Khairpur Amirs. But instead of being rivals, the two sets lived amicably and treated each other as equals. Captain Eastwick's interview described in the preceding chapter was with the Hyderabad Amirs led by one of them, Mir Nur Mohammed. The next to be tackled were the Khairpur Amirs led by Mir Rustam Khan. The latter was an old man of about eighty, and an uncle of the Hyderabad Amirs who genuinely venerated him. When Burnes had visited Khairpur, Rustam Khan had sent his old Wazir, Fateh Mohammed Khan Ghori, with palanquins, horses and presents some 80 miles out of Khairpur to give Burnes a warm welcome. Rustam Khan kept Burnes as his guest at Khairpur for three weeks, during which there were receptions and sumptuous dinners given in honour of the guest. Burnes has in his *Travels* (Vol. VIII) described Mir Rustam Khan as a broad-minded, courteous and soft-spoken gentleman who trusted everybody.

In an earlier treaty, the English had agreed never to desire possession of any fortress or place on the right or left bank of the Indus. When planning the invasion of Afghanistan the English had felt that it was essential for its success that they should acquire the citadel at Sukkur, an island in the Indus, and asked Mir Rustam Khan to hand it over. When the latter reminded the English of the earlier treaty, the Governor-General assured Rustam Khan in writing that only temporary use of the citadel was required for the duration of the war, and that its possession would be restored to him after the war was over. According to Eastwick, Mir Rustam Khan trusted the express and solemn promise and handed over possession of the Sukkur citadel to the English, whereupon the Governor-General profusely thanked Rustam Khan in very complimentary terms. However the citadel was never restored to him.

New Treaty with Mir Rustam Khan

Embodying the above-mentioned assurances given by the Governor-General, a new treaty was concluded by the English with Mir Rustam Khan on 24th December, 1838. Its other principal stipulations were:

(i) there shall be eternal friendship between the English and the Khairpur *Durbar*,

(ii) the English shall defend the Khairpur State and the Khairpur *Durbar* shall help the English in all their undertakings.

(iii) the Khairpur Amirs will never enter into any engagement or any correspondence with any foreign power without prior consultation with the Company.

(iv) the English shall not take any cognizance of any complaint against Mir Rustam Khan made by any relative, family-member or subject of his, nor shall the English interfere in any internal affair of the Khairpur State, and

(v) the parties shall exchange envoys to be stationed at each other's courts. (*Dry Leaves from Young Egypt* by Eastwick, pp. 252–53).

Another Treaty with Hyderabad Amirs

The Hyderabad Amirs, too, were prevailed upon to execute a fresh treaty on 11th March, 1839. When the treaty was presented on behalf of the Company for the signatures of the Amirs, one of them produced the bundle of the earlier treaties and asked "What will happen to these now?" The Amirs went on to say "From the day that we signed the first treaty, we have been continually asked to enter into a fresh engagement, one after the other. We do want to maintain friendly relations with you (English) but refuse to be pestered like this. We allowed your troops to pass through, and now you want to station your army permanently in our territory ..." (*Empire in Asia*, p. 295). Notwithstanding the Amir's outburst, the treaty was signed.

After the Khairpur Treaty

The Company's army occupied the Sukkur citadel and established its camps at a number of places. Therefore, the attitude of the English towards the old Amir Rustam Khan became more and more aggressive and his ministers were openly insulted. Eastwick writes:

> "Every step, *i.e.*, every encroachment, that could be made without hazard was made; and the more violent aggressions, which obviously could not be inflicted without risking an inopportune war, were suspended until our own influence should be substituted in Sindh; in other words, until Sindh was reduced to a British dependency. And this is what we call making an alliance." (*Dry Leaves from Young Egypt*, pp. 253–54)

Intrigues

The English in Sindh then resorted to intrigues and machinations, for which tried and expert intriguers were imported from India. Mir Ali Murad, a younger brother of Mir Rustam Khan, was won over and used to create disaffection against the latter. Quarrels were started between the two, in all of which the English sided with Mir Ali Murad.

Accusations Founded on Forgery

Accusations were made against the Amirs. Mir Naseer Khan, one of the Hyderabad Amirs, was accused of having written a letter to Diwan Sawan Mal of Multan, inciting the latter against the English. Mir Rustam Khan was accused of having written a similar letter to Sher Singh. Eastwick, who had personal knowledge of the English political intrigues of this kind, writes:

> "Why the whole matter is clearer than the sun at noon: Mir Ali Murad forged these letters." (*Dry Leaves from Young Egypt* by Eastwick, M.P., p. 259)

Real Reasons for Annexation of Sindh

Five principal reasons why the English were bent upon annexing Sindh may now be briefly stated.

(i) English avarice, which has thus been described by Sir Charles Dilke in his book *Greater Britain*:

> "It is in India ... we begin to remember our descent from Scandinavian sea-king robbers. Centuries of education have not purified the blood; our men in India can hardly set eyes on a native prince or a Hindoo palace before they cry, 'What a place to break up!' 'What a fellow to loot!'"

(ii) The English had discovered that the Amirs' treasuries were full to the brim with gold, silver and jewels.

(iii) The facilities offered by the Indus river-route for the transport of the Company's troops, wherever necessary, to the north-western frontier of India. This reason has been stated by Lord Ellenborough in one of his letters to the Duke of Wellington.

(iv) The English feared an invasion of their Indian Empire by the Russians or a Central Asian power through Sindh, and so wanted to have the whole of Sindh under their control.

(v) The fourth reason has been stated by Sir John Kaye as follows:

> "But the real cause of this chastisement of the Amirs consisted in the chastisement which the British had received from the Afghans. It was deemed expedient at this stage of the great political journey to show that the British could beat someone, and so it was determined to beat the Amirs of Sindh ... the Governor-General resolved that the Amirs who a few months before had spared our army, when they might have annihilated it, should be the victims of this generous policy." ("The Calcutta Review," Vol. I, p. 232)

The Duke of Wellington had, on 30th March, 1842, written to Lord Ellenborough saying that it was essential to rehabilitate British prestige, which had been sunk so low by the defeat in Afghanistan, and suggesting that to white-wash that disgrace, some Indian ruler's territory might be invaded and annexed.

(vi) The fifth reason, which had its origin in the fact that the Amirs were Mussalmans, was Ellenborough's antipathy towards Mussalmans whom he thoroughly distrusted.

It must be mentioned that in his letter dated 22nd March, 1843, Ellenborough did state to the Duke of Wellington that the accusations against the Amirs which were based on letters alleged to have been written by them were without any foundation at all. Some time later, the letters were proved to be forgeries before the British Parliament.

Having resolved to subjugate Sindh, Lord Ellenborough entrusted the task to Gen. Sir Charles Napier, who started for Sindh with a considerable force on 26th August, 1842. Entering Sindh on 9th September, he went through Hyderabad to Sukkur, which he made his headquarters. He was joined there by Ali Murad (the younger brother of Mir Rustam Khan) who had already been won over, as stated earlier. As his first step, Napier decided to depose Mir Rustam Khan, the Amir of Khairpur, and to seize his territory.

> "Neither the venerable prince ... nor any of his brethren had ever injured a hair of the head of any British subject; but they had, in the hour of our greatest need, placed their country and its resources at our disposal" (*Conquest of Sindh, a Commentary* by Col. Outram, Vol. II, p. 90).

Napier's progress to Sukkur had been unimpeded as it was made "amidst a shower of hypocritical expressions of friendship and goodwill" for Sindh and its Amirs. Arriving at Sukkur, Napier started a campaign of intrigues against the Amirs with the wholehearted co-operation of Ali Murad. Capt. Eastwick writes:

> "The General openly avowed his anxiety to obtain a pretext for coercing them; and can we wonder that there were found—amongst the basest and lowest of the people—some to complain of ill-treatment at the hands of their rulers, or that the agents of Ali Murad should have taken advantage of such general encouragement for their fabrications?" (*Dry Leaves from Young Egypt*, p. 267)

On the basis of the above-mentioned forged letters and fabrications, General Napier issued a proclamation in Sindh, announcing that a part of Mir Rustam Khan's territory, from Robri to Sabzai-Garh, had been confiscated because of his misrule and disloyalty to the English. Needless to say, the latter had not faced Mir Rustam Khan with any charges, much less had they given him any chance to defend himself. In addition, a charge-sheet of 24 accusations, founded on fabrications, was drawn up against the Amirs of Hyderabad also. Eastwick characterises them as "frivolous accusations, which were concocted for the simple purpose of making out a case" (ibid., p. 269).

Without making any reference to the Amirs at all, Gen. Napier, on 7th December, 1842, started his preparations for the occupation of the "confiscated" territory. By then, another accusation had been added to the charges against Mir Rustam Khan. It was stated that the latter had had the Company's mail looted. Eastwick states clearly that the "looting" was staged through Ali Murad, and goes on to comment:

> "One feels sick with shame and disgust that such barbarous and malignant falsehoods could be winked at by men calling themselves Englishmen." (ibid., p. 27)
>
> A week later, on 14th December, 1842, Mir Rustam Khan wrote to Gen. Napier, asserting that all the charges against him were false, and that he was still as anxious as ever to maintain friendly relations with the English.

Mir Rustam Khan Ordered to Leave Khairpur

Mir Rustam Khan was then 85. He made repeated but fruitless efforts for a peaceful settlement and requested interviews with Gen. Napier. The interviews were not granted. Then without any rhyme or reason Napier marched his infantry and artillery into Khairpur, and sent a message to the aged Amir, that if the latter valued his life he could save it only by leaving Khairpur immediately for Hyderabad, where he (Napier) would later meet him along with the other Amirs. Mir Rustam Khan complied with the order and left for Hyderabad with the members of his family. Napier's troops then looted the town of Khairpur.

Thereafter, Gen. Napier attacked the fort at Imamgarh, demolished it and ransacked Imamgarh town. He then proceeded to Hyderabad.

Sometime earlier, Gen. Napier had sent Col. Stanley to the Hyderabad Amirs with a new treaty, which the Amirs were to be asked to sign. Its terms being humiliating to the Amirs, they had sent their emissaries to Gen. Napier for a further discussion of the terms, but the latter had refused to see them.

When the Amirs got the news about the fate of Khairpur and Imamgarh and about Napier's advance towards Hyderabad, they sent their emissaries to Gen. Napier once again and offered to sign the new treaty which Col. Stanley had taken to them earlier. The emissaries met Gen. Napier at Nowshera (between Khairpur and Hyderabad) who gave them a letter for the Amirs. The letter stated that Major Outram was being sent with the new treaty to obtain their signatures, and that Major Outram would also settle all matters relating to Mir Rustam Khan, who was expected to be in Hyderabad by then. The letter also contained a definite assurance to the Amirs that Napier would not advance any farther for the time being.

Major Outram reached Hyderabad on 8th February, 1843, and desired the Amirs to hand over their respective seals to him for affixation to the treaty. The Amirs delivered the seals.

On account of Napier's advance towards Hyderabad, the Baluchis living in and near the town were greatly agitated. So the Amirs requested Major Outram, that in order to quieten the Baluchis' increasing agitation, it was essential that Napier should give up his march, as they (the Amirs) had already given their seals to Major Outram. The latter agreed and immediately wrote to Napier accordingly. He sent the letter through an English messenger. The letter was duly delivered to Napier within a couple of days as reported to Major Outram by the English messenger. Outram saw Mir Nasir Khan, one of the Amirs, that very afternoon, and assured him on oath that Napier had no intention whatsoever of seizing and annexing the Amirs' territory. He pressed the Amirs to sign the treaty which, he said, would be enclosed by him with a second letter to General Napier, and the Amirs could send it by their own special messenger. The Amirs signed the treaty and Major Outram enclosed it with his promised letter and handed both to Mir Nasir Khan for transmission to General Napier. It was sent by a very fast camel-rider who, after delivering the treaty and the letter to Napier, returned with the disquieting news that even after receiving the letter and the signed treaty, General Napier continued as before to advance towards Hyderabad. Thus ended the assurance given by Colonel Outram that on receipt of the signed treaty, Napier would finally give up his march on Hyderabad and return towards the north.

The Amirs' Endeavours to Avoid Bloodshed

Mir Rustam Khan had, by then, reached Hyderabad and his tale of woe further infuriated the Baluchis. Then an unoffending old Baluchi Sirdar, Hayat Khan, was taken into custody by General Napier. This added fuel to the fire, but Mir Nasir Khan somehow managed to calm down his Baluchis. The Amirs then wrote directly to Gen. Napier asking him why he was persisting in his march on Hyderabad, in spite of their having signed, sealed and delivered the treaty. No reply was vouchsafed and the advance continued. Then on 15th February 1843, some 5,000 Baluchis of Hyderabad collected outside the town to defend it. Mir Nasir Khan came out of his palace and tried to persuade them to disperse by giving an undertaking that he would send a *Vakeel* of his the very next day to General Napier in a last attempt to avoid useless bloodshed and to arrive at a settlement peacefully.

On that very day, there was a brawl in the streets of Khairpur between the Baluchis and the Company's soldiers, in which two Baluchis and one Company's soldier were killed. The Baluchis took two English soldiers into their custody, but they were treated well and fed by Mir Nasir Khan and Mir Mohammad Khan, and were later released. Major Outram fearing more trouble sought refuge in an English boat.

The Battle at Miami

The Baluchis had not dispersed and Sir Charles Napier was a high-handed officer who did not want a peaceful settlement and therefore a clash of arms was inevitable. According to Mir Nasir Khan, the first shot was fired by Napier's force at about 4 a.m. on 17th February, 1843. The Baluchis were out-numbered and did not have an over-all commander to lead them. Even so they would not give in. They fought fiercely and the battle lasted the whole day till late in the evening. The Baluchis discarded their muskets, drew their swords and fought the invaders hand-to-hand. They repulsed every onslaught by

Napier's soldiers. Major Badington, who was present at the battle, states that at one stage, General Napier himself became extremely doubtful about his success. Some of the surviving English officers later expressed their unstinted admiration for the unflinching tenacity and gallantry of the Baluchis.

Whilst the battle was raging at Miami, Mir Nasir Khan and the other Amirs sat unconcerned in their palace in the Hyderabad Fort, either because they were too cowardly, or because they still cherished hopes of retaining their territory, if they kept away from the battle. Apparently, they still relied on the assurances given to that effect by Major Outram. So much so that Mir Nasir Khan did go out to Miami, not to encourage the Baluchis who were fighting for his independence, but to persuade them to give up fighting!

Men were falling dead on every side. According to Major Badington, 400 corpses were counted within 50 paces, at one place. But the Baluchis had died in vain. We quote from *Life of Sir Richard Burton* by Lady Burton (p. 141):

> "Neither of our authorities tells us, nor can we expect a public document to do so, how the mulatto who had charge of the Amirs' guns had been persuaded to fire high and how the Talpur traitor who commanded the cavalry openly drew off his men and showed the shameless example of flight."

Thus it was that the battle of Miami was "won" and during the night before 18th February, 1843, Napier's force marched, literally on the dead bodies of the Baluchis strewn on the Miami plain, and entered Hyderabad the next morning (Torrens' *Empire in Asia*).

Doubtless to create the impression that the battle at Miami had been won against heavy odds by the small force under him, General Sir Charles Napier stated that he had only 1700 men. On the other hand, Major Badington has given reasons for stating that their number was not less than 3,000. But the official report puts the figure of the survivors, who received the prize-money, at 4,856!

On entering Hyderabad, Gen. Napier assured Mir Nasir Khan, in the presence of Major Outram, that the Sindh Amirs' conquered territory would be restored to them, if their Baluchi army was disbanded forthwith, and the men sent away from Hyderabad immediately. Mir Nasir Khan trusted Napier's word and complied with the demand. But no sooner had the last dismissed Baluchi soldier left Hyderabad than Napier put under arrest the three Amirs, Mir Nasir Khan, Mir Shahdad Khan and Mir Rustam Khan. Three days later, Napier occupied the Hyderabad Fort and palaces with a battalion of infantry, a regiment of cavalry, two pieces of artillery and some English officers.

Looting of the Palaces

Then followed a veritable "reign of terror" for the inmates of the Amirs' palaces and harems. We would spare our readers' humanitarian feeling and so abstain from giving details of the horrific outrages perpetrated on the men, particularly women, for days and nights on end. These have been given in an authenticated statement made by an eye-witness, which has been translated and published by Eastwick (*Dry Leaves from Young Egypt*, pp. 342–44). The statement has been fully supported by the historian, J. P. Ferrier (*History of the Afghans* translated by Captain Jesse, London, John Murray, 1858, p. 287). *The harem ladies were not only plundered of their ornaments they had on their person, but their noses and ears were horribly mutilated* ("The Tribune" of Lahore, September 1893). Some of the unfortunate ladies sought refuge in flight, barefooted and with nothing but the barest of clothes to cover their shame and lacerated bodies. Eastwick gives a word-picture of their plight thus:

> "Women of England! Think of the mothers and sisters of princes, stripped of their ornaments, torn from their homes, driven to wander houseless and friendless in the wild jungles and poisonous swamps." (*Dry Leaves from Young Egypt*, p. 238)

Not only were jewellery, gold and silver articles and ornaments looted, but the palaces and the men and women therein were stripped bare of every single thing that had any value, including gold and silver embroidered silks and clothes. Mir Nasir Khan has stated that the value of the wholesale plunder was about Rs. 18 crores. The rich booty was secured and sealed in huge packages which were shipped to Bombay.

Barring that part of Mir Rustam Khan's dominion which was granted to the traitor Ali Murad, the rest of the entire territory of Sindh was annexed by the English. Round about 1849–50, Ali Murad was deprived of half of the territory granted to him on the charge that he had committed forgery seven years earlier! His descendants have since then ruled the small State of Khairpur up till 1929.

With the exception of Ali Murad, all the other Amirs of Sindh and their sons were transported in fetters. They were lodged in jail at Poona, Calcutta, Hazaribagh, Surat, etc., care being taken to keep the fathers and sons separate from each other in different jails. Mir Nasir Khan and old Mir Rustam Khan died in prison at Calcutta and Poona, respectively. The other Amirs of the Talpur dynasty similarly rotted in prison till death released them. Moved no doubt by the fate which the English meted out to the Amirs, Eastwick writes that they were

> "... our own allies ... victims, round whom was woven a web of cunning villainy, and who were trapped with falsehoods which now make day hideous by their revelation! Men of England! Think of your boasted freedom, and let your pulse beat quick for those who died by your sword in defence of their liberties and homes, and for that smaller but far more wretched band, once your friends, once aye! your benefactors, now lingering out a miserable exile in a distant land, whose jailers you now pay, whose hospitalities, whose alliance, you once sought." (*Dry Leaves from Young Egypt*, p. 238)

About such members of Mir Rustam Khan's family and his dependants, mostly old women and boys who were not exiled, Eastwick writes that they wandered homeless. *Hunger and thirst and cold nakedness and have been their portion* (ibid., p. 291).

Apparently to provide some sort of justification for the deeds of Sir Charles Napier and his myrmidons in Sindh, the Amirs and their people have been painted black, "*... it is a custom among us ...,*" writes Sir John Kaye, "*to take a native ruler's kingdom and then to revile* the deposed ruler ..." (*History of the Sepoy War,* Vol. III, p. 361). It has been declared that the Amirs were quite illiterate and drink and drug addicts. Even the 85-year-old Mir Rustam Khan has been stated to be a lustful weakling given to heavy drinking.

Capt. Gordon, an English officer, who had long lived with the Amirs at Hyderabad, was asked by Col. Outram to state what he knew about the Amirs' personal habits. We quote Capt. Gordon's view:

> "I observe, therefore, in reply to your query, that the Amirs are the most temperate of men, rigidly abstaining from wine and every kind of liquor, while to smoking also, they have a strong aversion and cannot even endure the smell of tobacco. In regard, therefore, to smoking and drinking, the Amirs are examples to most of us, who boast a higher civilization, and a more self-denying morality." (*Dry Leaves from Young Egypt*, p. 286)

Dr. James Burnes, F.R.C.S., the brother of Sir Alexander Burnes, has, after months of full personal investigation, confirmed Capt. Gordon's statement about the Amirs' temperate habits and has stated it as an established fact that none of the Amirs ever took any intoxicating drink or drug. "The *Hukka* is never seen in their *Durbars* and neither they nor any members of their family smoke or take opium." He also states that Mir Nasir Khan wrote poetry under the pen-name of "Jaffir" and mentions a collection of his verses published under the title of *Diwan-i-Jaffir* (*Amirs of Sindh* by Dr. James Burnes, p. 67).

Eastwick affirms that not only the men in the Amirs' families, but all the women too knew how to read and write Persian and Arabic.

The English Civil Surgeon at Poona, under whose observation Mir Rustam Khan passed the last years of his life, has testified that there was not the slightest indication of the old man's intemperance or licentiousness then or ever before. "He performs his religious rituals regularly, lives abstemiously, takes only one meal a day, and never drinks anything but water or milk" (*The Conquest of Sindh, a Commentary* by Col. Outram, Part II, p. 514).

It is unnecessary to give more evidence to show that the revilement of the Amirs was nothing but a tissue of lies resorted to for the obvious purpose of minimising the enormity of what the English had done in Sindh.

We would however quote from Eastwick's book one instance of Mir Rustam Khan's strict and impartial justice in dealing with the misdemeanour of a member of his own family, a young man named Mohammed Khan. A lady teacher was employed in the Amir's zenana, and used to visit the harem to give lessons to the ladies. Mohammed Khan made improper overtures to her, which led to a savage assault by her father on the young man. The latter recovered, only to be banished for life from Khairpur by Mir Rustam Khan who declared: "We will have no connexion in future with one who is guilty of such a grave sin." Further, he refrained from taking any action against the assailant of Mohammed Khan (*Dry Leaves from Young Egypt,* p. 68).

Dr. James Burnes has referred to an official report submitted to the Bombay Government which was to the effect that trades people and the commercial community generally were so well looked after and encouraged by the Amirs, that many a businessman from other provinces and countries migrated to Sindh and settled there.

Trade and commerce in Sindh, particularly the profitable pearl trade in Karachi, were controlled almost entirely by Hindus. Eastwick states that under the Amirs the city of Hyderabad became well-populated and very prosperous, and that whilst plunder and bloodshed were rampant in the English-ruled regions of India, peace and prosperity reigned in Sindh due to the beneficent administration of the Amirs (*Dry Leaves from Young Egypt,* p. 242). "In the administration of justice the Amirs erred on the side of clemency. They were most averse to the shedding of blood" (ibid., p. 68).

The agriculturists, constituting a very large majority of the population of Sindh, were happy and flourishing. They paid rents mostly in kind and the proportion of the Government's share of what they produced was fixed for all time. The countryside was covered by cultivated fields and growing crops. For providing greater irrigation facilities to the peasantry, the Amirs dug a long canal called Phuleli. It was a model canal and, unlike its counterparts in British India, did not need desilting or cleaning every now and then.

The humblest of the people could approach their ruler directly for redress. Although the Mussalmans constituted a vast majority of the people, there was not the slightest discrimination against or intolerance of Hindus. Many well-to-do Hindu families from Kutch, Gujarat and Rajputana, belonging to the business community were settled in Hyderabad where they were very well treated. On the occasion of the Hindu festival of Diwali, the whole town on both sides of the Indus, including mosques and mausoleums, was profusely illuminated and the Sukkur Fort presented a huge picture of brilliant lights. The river was crowded with wooden floats on which the images of the goddess Lakshmi were installed (ibid., p. 89).

The advent of the East India Company's rule changed the scene entirely very much for the worse. Military rule was imposed on the country, with General (Sir Charles) Napier as the first Governor of Sindh. All the high-ranking Sindhi officials were replaced by Englishmen. "Then began a system of universal fraud and speculation" (ibid., p. 306). Security of life and property became a thing of the past. The system of assessing and collecting land revenue was drastically changed and it increased the peasants' burden enormously. The total land revenue in 1843 was no more than Rs. 9,38,000. For the year 1844 it was assessed at over Rs. 27,40,000! The result was that agricultural produce declined rapidly as cultivation of land no longer provided the cultivator with even the barest livelihood. It was abandoned in one place after another all over the country. Discontent, produced by want, became widespread amongst all classes of people (ibid., p. 71). The Amirs collected their moderate rents almost effortlessly. The new administration could not collect is exorbitant demands without resorting to wholesale oppression of the peasantry.

While enumerating the reasons which were responsible for the invasion of Sindh by the English, we gave the first place to "English avarice" and, in support of our view, we quoted that expressed by Sir Charles Dilke. We would now quote General Sir Charles Napier himself:

> "Our object ..., the object of all our cruelties, was money, lucre; a thousand millions sterling are said to have been squeezed out of India in the last sixty years. Every shilling of this has been picked out of blood, wiped, and put into the murderers' pockets; but, wipe and wash the money as

you will, the 'damned spot' will not 'out'. There it sticks for ever, and we shall yet suffer for the crime, as sure as there is a God in heaven, where the 'commercial interests of the nation' find no place ... justice and religion are mockeries in the eyes of 'a great manufacturing country', for the true God of such a nation is Mammon. I may be singular, but in truth, I prefer the despotic Napoleon to the despots of the East India Company." (*Lights and Shades of Military Life,* edited by Sir Charles Napier, pp. 297, 298)

Eastwick wonders whether our readers would believe that the man who penned the above words had himself waded through rivers of blood to the "treasures of Sindh"!

The end of Sindh's independence secured to England another market for the goods produced and exported by her, and a fresh field for her "boys" to earn their livelihood in.

The British Parliament, on behalf of the British nation, passed a vote of thanks to Lord Ellenborough, General Sir Charles Napier and the officers and men of the British army for their achievements in Sindh, for which the British nation had more than one reason to be grateful. But:

"*No reasoning can, in my opinion, remove the foul stain it has left on our faith and honour.*" (Sir Henry Pottinger's letter to *The Morning Chronicle,* 8th January, 1844)

No Englishman had greater first-hand knowledge of the English dealings with the Amirs than Sir Henry Pottinger, who was later appointed Governor of Madras.

13

ELLENBOROUGH'S ACTION AGAINST INDIAN RULERS

Sindhia

Of all the Maratha States constituting the Maratha Confederacy, Gwalior, ruled by the Sindhias, was the most powerful. In earlier chapters we have narrated the futile attempts made by the English to cripple Maharaja Doulatrao Sindhia of Gwalior. Later, Lord William Bentinck tried, without success, to deprive Gwalior of its independence by engineering intrigues inside the State: As stated in the Report of the Select Committee of the House of Commons, 1832,

> "Within the Peninsula, Scindhia is the only Prince who preserves the semblance of independence."

In reply to the question "What is the relation in which Scindhia stood to the Company?", Major Close replied, "He is independent." There were several treaties, Major Close said in reply to another question, "but they are not such as to abrogate his independence". This position continued till the death of Maharaja Jankojirao Sindhia on 7th February, 1843, whereupon Ellenborough started to deprive the State of its independence, bit by bit.

Like some other Indian States, the chief administrative and executive powers of the State were exercised by the *Durbar*, which was the name of a council of Ministers headed by the Maharaja. Jankojirao had died childless, and his widow, with the unanimous assent of the *Durbar*, adopted as her son, Bhagirathrao, a boy of eight, a relation of the ruling family of Gwalior. The adopted son occupied the Gwalior *Gadi* as Jayajirao Sindhia. The administration of the State continued to be carried on by the *Durbar* with the widowed Maharani as Regent for the minor Maharaja. Ellenborough has admitted in his letters that the *Durbar* was a capable and successful administrator.

The widowed Maharani was young and this fact gave Ellenborough the excuse to interfere and try to get her replaced as

Regent by a nominee of his. We quote from the *Sketch of the House of Scindhia* by John Hope (p. 42):

> "As Lord Ellenborough had firmly resolved, though his resolution was not then made known, first to disregard the rights of this state, and afterwards deprive it of its independence, the preliminary step would necessarily be to set aside the Maharanee on the ground of her infancy and to put up in her place as Regent a person who would cheerfully do the bidding of the British Government. The election was in the hands of the *Durbar*. Now there was only one individual in that council who would lend himself to carry out an antinational policy, and he was called the Mama Saheb. Accordingly, the Resident laid aside the principle of nonintervention which hitherto had guided his conduct and strained every nerve to effect this man's election."

The *Durbar*, however, had other plans. They wanted to appoint Dada Khasgiwale as the Prime Minister for heading the administration, on behalf of the young Regent the Maharani and the minor Maharaja. Dada Khasgiwale was competent, honest and patriotic, and so his appointment could not suit Ellenborough. Just before the election, a letter from Ellenborough was delivered to the *Durbar*, in which it was stated:

> "The Governor-General would gladly see the Regency conferred upon the Mama Saheb."

Ellenborough had backed the above expression of his wishes by a show of force, by himself marching to Agra and stationing a contingent of the Company's army on the border of Gwalior State near Agra. He stayed on at Agra and from there directed his campaign of intrigues inside the State.

Thus the Gwalior *Durbar* was stampeded into appointing Mama Saheb. It did not, however, elect him as Regent but appointed him as the Prime Minister. Mama Saheb proved to be incompetent, unreliable and unpopular. It was soon discovered that he was only a willing tool of the English. Then he tried to get the boy Maharaja married to a niece of his, who was only six. This was the last straw. The

Durbar unanimously resolved to dismiss Mama Saheb and he was relieved of his office on 20th May, 1843, with the concurrence of the Regent Maharani. Four days later, he was expelled from the State. The Regent Maharani then instructed the *Durbar* to appoint Dada Khasgiwale as the Prime Minister, which was done by a unanimous vote.

Col. Spiers the English Resident at Gwalior was apparently not a man after Ellenborough's heart, and so was replaced by Col. Sleeman, who later became notorious for his Machiavellian tactics and exploits in Oudh.

Ellenborough thought up a new ground for interference in the State's administration. "It is a matter." he wrote in a despatch, "of paramount importance that there should exist in Gwalior a Government willing and able to preserve tranquillity along that extended line (meaning the frontier), for the British Government cannot permit the growing up of a lax system of rule, generating habits of plunder along its frontier."

This was obviously intended to serve as an excuse for sending the Company's troops into the State. But the utter hollowness of the excuse is exposed by the following facts:

(i) It was the Gwalior Maharani's army which had been requisitioned to save "from destruction" the Balabehut town in the English territory. The Gwalior contingent under Col. Salvadore was even then engaged in saving the town.

(ii) Another wealthy town, Khimlasa, belonging to the English, and only a hundred miles from Gwalior, the capital, was being guarded on the very day that Ellenborough was penning the despatch by a contingent of 2,000 men from the Gwalior army.

(iii) The province of Bundelkhand, which was under English control, and the two rich provinces of Saugor and Nerbudda, which were absolutely British territory (the frontiers of which bordered on the frontiers of Scindhia's dominions) were at this time, and had been for two years, in a state of open insurrection. (*Vide Sketch of the House of Scindhia* by John Hope, p. 52)

If the Government of any territory has the right to send its troops into an adjoining territory because of violent disorder and open insurrection in the latter, then the Gwalior State had unquestionably acquired the right to send its troops into British territory, and not *vice versa*. But then, any excuse, howsoever absurd, was good enough for Lord Ellenborough, whose preparations for the invasion of Gwalior were very nearly complete by then.

The new Prime Minister of the Gwalior *Durbar* was a definite acquisition. He strengthened the administration of the State. He immediately cleared the arrears into which the pay due to the troops had fallen, and made arrangements for punctual payments in future. He weeded out of the army some European and "half-blood" officers who had been inciting the men under them against the *Durbar*. Some senior and competent officers, who had been dismissed at the instance of the English Resident, were reinstated by him. As a capable and honest administrator, he won the people's respect. Above all, he was the one man in the Gwalior *Durbar* who had the influence, the strength and the will to thwart Ellenborough's designs against the independence of Gwalior. Ellenborough realised the danger, and proceeded to get Dada Khasgiwale removed not only from office but from the State also.

On the frivolous charge that Dada Khasgiwale had intercepted a letter sent to the Regent Maharani by Lord Ellenborough, the latter based his preposterous demand that Dada Khasgiwale be arrested forthwith and handed over to the English. The *Durbar* and the Regent Maharani protested and requested Ellenborough to consider the demand, but the latter was adamant and insisted that what he had demanded must be done immediately.

Some time earlier, "the members of the Indian Government" had "unanimously decided upon the formation of an army at Agra of about 12,000 men besides artillery" and other measures had been taken "for the purpose of enabling the Government to concentrate a much larger force" (Ellenborough's letter to Queen Victoria dated 13th August, 1843). The concentration of the "much larger force" at Agra had been accomplished when Ellenborough pressed his demand.

The Gwalior *Durbar* tried to appease Ellenborough by removing Dada Khasgiwale from office, and by putting him under arrest. They also appointed Ramrao Phalke as the Prime Minister in place of Dada Khasgiwale. But Ellenborough did not desire appeasement, and threatened immediate war unless Dada Khasgiwale was handed over to him without any further delay. Under his orders, a strong detachment of the Company's troops was stationed on the northern border and another on the eastern border of the State. The *Durbar* and the Regent Maharani feared that war may be started any moment, and they did not want it, whatever the cost of avoiding it. So they submitted and handed over Dada Khasgiwale to Ellenborough, who immediately made him a prisoner in the English camp, and later sent him to the English prison at Benares, where the honest and loyal Prime Minister of Gwalior was confined till his death, 10 years later.

The Gwalior *Durbar* was, however, soon to be disappointed in its hope that Dada Khasgiwale's surrender would avert the danger of an invasion by the English.

The demand for Dada Khasgiwale's custoday having been met, Ellenborough had to cast about for another excuse for the entry of his troops into the State.

The fact of the matter was that after his "conquest" of Sindh, Ellenborough had made up his mind to annex Punjab. But before taking any steps in that direction, he had considered it prudent to muzzle Gwalior, for accomplishing which the death of Jankojirao Scindhia without a male issue had given him a splendid opportunity. The strength of the Gwalior Army added to the State's independence would be, according to Ellenborough, a potential danger in his rear, which had to be got rid of before he invaded Punjab. On 22nd April, 1843, he had written from Agra to the Duke of Wellington:

> "Depend upon it, I will never, if I can avoid it, have two things on my hands at a time."

Consequently, he decided to settle Gwalior's hash first. But even after Dada Khasgiwale had been surrendered to him, he saw "no appearance of a settlement without authoritative intervention of the British Government" (Letter to the Queen, dated 20th November, 1843), backed by the presence of the Company's army inside the State. For the "authoritative intervention", which was his euphemism for aggression, Ellenborough discovered a reason which was nothing but a bare-faced sham.

The new Prime Minister of Gwalior, Ramrao Phalke, was sent by the Gwalior *Durbar* to Agra to wait on Lord Ellenborough.

> "'I have found,' said his Lordship to Ramrao Phalke, a clause in a treaty made with Dowlatrao Scindhia at Burhan poor, which obliges the British Government, if at any time Scindhia should be unable to cope with his enemies, to afford him military assistance. It is true, indeed, that the clause carefully guards against the danger of a great military power forcing its unsolicited assistance on a very weak one by the insertion of the words *on the requisition of the Maharajah*, but it is impossible, on account of his tender years for Gyajee Scindhia to make the requisition, and, as I am the only judge of his necessities, I shall march my army to Gwalior... Ramrao Phalke was astounded and replied '... As nothing whatever had been mooted on the Burhanpoor treaty, I have brought with me no copy of if to refer to ... the invasion of a friendly State on such a pretext was quite a strange anomaly in the conduct of the Honourable Company.'... But all his arguments, all protestations failed, as would those of a goose who with equal pertinacity declined the proffered aid of a hungry fox" (John Hope in his *Sketch of the House of Sindhia*, pp. 66–67).

> "Respecting the clause in the Burhanpoor treaty on which the Governor-General pretended to justify that invasion, it cannot be controverted that there was no such treaty in existence. That which had been made in 1804, containing a stipulation of the kind alleged ... was abrogated the following year to serve our own (English) interests." (ibid., p. 72)

Nothing, however, could or did deter Ellenborough from invading the dominion of Sindhia, and he did so before the *Durbar* could be ready for war. On 29th December, 1843, two battles were fought at Maharajpur and Punniar, in both of which, according to Torrens, heavy losses were sustained by the invaders. Ultimately, Sindhia's forces were defeated, and a treaty was forced on the Gwalior *Durbar*. As stated by Lord Ellenborough in his letter of 16th February, 1844, he did not attempt to annex the entire dominion of Sindhia as it would have strongly agitated the other ruling princes of India. He therefore contented himself with a treaty whereby the entire administration of the State was secured to the English for at least ten years. The main clauses of the treaty executed by the *Durbar* provided:

(i) That the size of Gwalior's subsidiary army was to be substantially increased and that certain districts of the State were to be ceded to the English to meet the additional expenditure.

(ii) That the widowed Maharani was to be deprived of all authority and powers as Regent and was to be given, in return, an annual pension of Rs. 3 lacs.

(iii) That during the minority of the Maharaja, a Council was to carry on the entire administration of the State.

Another clause made it incumbent on the Council to carry out the behests of the English Resident posted at Gwalior.

Kaithal was a Cis-Sutlej Sikh State, some 30 miles beyond Karnal. Ellenborough annexed it on the ground that the Raja having died without a male issue, the State had lapsed to the British Government. But the latter were *not* the 'grantors' of the State and so it could not, in law, "lapse" to or be "resumed" by them. Kaithal was an independent State which had in 1809 entered into a treaty of friendship with the English. The widow of the late Raja had the right to adopt a son and heir to her husband, but Ellenborough denied that right and sent a military detachment of 300 men to take possession of the "lapsed" State and occupy its capital. It was opposed by the passive resistance of the deceased Raja's family and his *Durbar* and later by the armed resistance of the people of the State who flocked to the capital. The detachment was repulsed on 10th April, 1843, and had to retreat to Karnal. On 14th idem, however, 1800 troops were assembled at Thaneshwar and

> "on their arrival on the 16th within eight miles of Kaithal, it was found that the town and the fort were evacuated by the armed retainers on the 15th. The ministers and the merchants of the place had come into the British camp on the 14th". (Ellenborough's letter to the Queen dated 20-4-1843) Thus it was that the State was annexed and its capital occupied.

Punjab

After Maharaja Ranjit Singh's death in 1839, virtual anarchy reigned in Punjab. Revolts, disturbances, murders and plunderings were occurring everywhere. That the English were not unconnected with this state of affairs was indicated by the London periodical *The British Friend of India*, from the December, 1843 issue of which we give the following excerpt:

> "... We strongly suspect the Company's influence has been employed in framing and fomenting these plots ... a ... mercenary Company, wielding a hireling army, cannot live but by plunder ... we see too clearly, that backed as it necessarily now is, by all the resources of Britain, Lahore will be sacked, the kingdom rent in pieces." (pp. 247–8)

It is quite evident from the letters which at that time passed between Lord Ellenborough and the Duke of Wellington that the English intentionally coveted Punjab and that the former created and fomented disaffection against the Sikh Raj amongst the Sardars, officials and the retinue of Ranjit Singh's successor, and bought over quite a number of influential men at the Lahore *Durbar*. He also succeeded in inciting the Sikhs and the Afghans to fight each other. Ellenborough has admitted in one of his letters that he had allowed and even encouraged the Sikhs to occupy Jellalabad, so that the bulk of the Sikh army may leave Lahore and Amritsar to go to Jellalabad, thus leaving the capital undefended and at the mercy of his planned attack on Lahore. On 20th October, 1843, Ellenborough wrote to the Duke of Wellington, expressing the hope that Punjab would be in English hands within a year or two. In Lahore itself disaffection against Raja Hira Singh, the Prime Minister, was created and promoted amongst the Sikh soldiery. Efforts were made to incite and win over Raja Gulab Singh of Jammu against the Lahore *Durbar*.

In May 1844, the English got hold of three Sikh leaders, Bhai Bheem Singh, Atar Singh and Kashmira Singh, the last of whom was falsely stated to be the adopted son of the late Maharaja Ranjit Singh. Atar Singh was promised the Prime Ministership at Lahore in place of the then Prime Minister, Hira Singh. The three were equipped with an army at Thaneshwar, from where they were made to march towards Lahore. The boy Dulip Singh, son of Maharaja Ranjit Singh, was then on the Lahore *gadi*. On 7th May, 1844, a battle was fought near Ferozepore between the rebels and the troops of the Lahore *Durbar*. In the battle all the three rebel leaders were killed. Lord Ellenborough's letters bear mute but clear evidence of his share in the above-mentioned happenings. It goes without saying that all these activities and plottings of Lord Ellenborough were in patent contravention of the treaties which the English had made with the late Maharaja Ranjit Singh.

The Nizam

Ellenborough adopted a different policy for dealing with Hyderabad (Deccan), the biggest of the Indian States. He began by advancing loans to the Nizam, ostensibly to help the latter out of the financial morass into which he had been led. The real intention, however, was to acquire, in return for the loans, a firm political footing for the English in the Hyderabad Administration, as a preliminary to the gradual absorption of the State into the Company's territory. He wrote to Queen Victoria on 13th August, 1843:

> "The financial difficulties of the Nizam's Government have led to the resignation of the old Minister, and their tendency is to place the whole of His Highness's dominions for a series of years, if not permanently, under the British Administration, in consideration of a loan of a million, which must be advanced for the payment of the troops and of debts to bankers and others. The decision of the Nizam upon the several propositions submitted to His Highness will be known in a few days."

It may be mentioned that nearly half the number of the Hyderabad Forts were garrisoned by Arabs, whose loyalty to the Nizam was proverbial, and who could not be easily subverted into traitors. This might have been the reason why Ellenborough preferred "peaceful penetration" to strong-arm tactics. Anyway he was too busy in the north to follow up his policy and his subsequent recall saved the State the fate which he had in store for it.

Another victim of Lord Ellenborough's principle that "might is right" was Jetpur, a small state in the Bundelkhand region. It had only two fortresses. Ellenborough seized both on 27th November, 1842, and "confiscated" the state for its Raja's alleged hostility to the English. The dispossessed Raja escaped with only ten followers and his Raj was given to another Bundelkhand Raja who was subservient to the English.

The Nawab, or as he was called by the English, the 'King', of Oudh had ever been the milch-cow of the Governors-General of India. Lord Ellenborough too had been milking it from time to time. On 16th September, 1842, he wrote to the Duke of Wellington; "I have *got* the King of Oudh to lend ten lacs *more*."

The English had been well aware for some time that the Mughal Emperor was the only personage whose standard could be the rallying-point for the Hindus and the Mussalmans, if they ever combined in a struggle to throw off the foreign yoke. So from Lord Amherst onwards, every Governor-General had done something to lower the prestige of the "Emperor of India", as he was even then acknowledged to be.

> "Up to 1842, the Governors-General who visited Delhi presented a Nazir of 101 gold mohurs to the Emperor as a mark of fealty and acknowledgment of holding the British territories in India subject to his authority." (Edwards in his *Reminiscences of a Bengal Civilian*, p. 307)

Every Englishman in India, too, used to present offering as a token of homage to the Emperor. The latters' prestige was thus maintained at its pristine level in the eyes of the Indian people. Lord Ellenborough "immediately issued instructions, forbidding the presentation in future to the King of any offerings by British subjects", including of course the Governor-General himself (ibid., p. 57).

Ellenborough was very keen on getting possession of Delhi and the Red Fort and on establishing there the capital of British India. But the Duke of Wellington had warned him of the danger to the British Empire involved in such a move. Ellenborough's reaction to the warning is thus expressed in his reply (dated 18th December, 1842) to the Duke:

"...I had already come to your conclusion that it would be an unadvisable step to do anything having the appearance of violence towards the old King. With his successor, my successor may be able to make some arrangement for the transfer to us of the citadel. To have in our hands the ancient seat of Empire, and to administer the Government from it, has ever seemed to me to be a very great object."

Nor were the poverty-stricken people of British India spared. Ellenborough increased their burden by an enhancement of the duty payable on salt, a commodity which even the poorest of the poor could not do without.

Recall of Lord Ellenborough

Lord Ellenborough handed over charge to Lord Hardinge (then Sir Henry Hardinge) on 1st August, 1844. Various reasons have been stated for his recall after only 2½ years of office. One of them is that he had incurred the displeasure of the Court of Directors by lavish expenditure of huge sums of money, "without previously taking the pleasure of the Court", on new cantonments, stations and barracks for the army. A number of Directors, apparently of Lord Macaulay's way of thinking, charged Ellenborough with having antagonised the important Mussalman community by his persistent partiality for Hindus and their sentiments. A third reason mentioned by the Duke of Wellington in his letter to Ellenborough (dated 5th July, 1843) was that the Opposition in the British Parliament had drawn the conclusion that he (Ellenborough) had been *acting with views of conquest inconsistent with the declarations and principles of the law.*

14

THE FIRST SIKH WAR

Sir Henry Hardinge (Later Lord Hardinge)

We have ended the preceding chapter by quoting the conclusion drawn by the Opposition in the British Parliament about Ellenborough's annexations to "the overgrown Empire of India" (as it was called by Sir Robert Peel). The conclusion, however, did not in any way weaken the resolution of the authorities in England to annex Punjab, which had been coveted by them even during the life-time of Maharaja Ranjit Singh. This is indicated by the selection of Sir Henry Hardinge, a distinguished soldier-statesman of a British cabinet minister's status, as Governor-General in place of Ellenborough. The latter himself wrote to his protege, Major Broadfoot, on 17th June, 1844:

> "You will have heard that the Court of Directors have thought fit to recall me. My successor will carry out all my views."

We have briefly related in the preceding chapter Ellenborough's Machiavellian schemes and what he had accomplished in accordance with his "views" about the annexation of Punjab. By the time of his recall, he had gone forward with his preparations and plans for war against the Sikhs. Ellenborough's two-pronged activities were continued by Hardinge with such zeal that the preparations were completed weeks before Ellenborough had expected them to be.

Hardinge's Warlike Preparations

Broadly speaking, the river Sutlej separated the Company's possessions on its left from the dominion of Maharaja Ranjit Singh's infant son and successor, Dulip Singh, on its right. The Company's troops were stationed in Cantonments at Ludhiana and Ferozepur, near the Sutlej, and in two other Cantonments at Ambala and Meerut. When Ellenborough left, the total strength at the four Cantonments was 17,612 men and 66 guns, which Hardinge increased to 49,523 men and 94 guns. At Ferozepur and Ludhiana, he more than doubled the number of men. He doubled the number of guns to 24 at Ferozepur, which was nearest the Sutlej and later served as the base. At Ambala, which was made his headquarters at the start of the war, the strength of the men was increased from a little over four thousand to nearly 13 thousand, and an artillery of 32 guns was massed. Another 4,000 men and eight guns were added to the contingent at Meerut. For the projected invasion of Punjab, the crossing of the Sutlej was a "must", and the plan was to cross it between Ferozepur and Ludhiana by a bridge of boats. So in September 1844, the flotilla of 56 boats of five tons each, exactly similar, and each containing everything necessary for its equipment as a pontoon, which Ellenborough had ordered to be built on the Indus, was brought near Ferozepur, and their crews were regularly exercised in the formation of boat-bridges.

Maharaja Dulip Singh being a minor, the administration of the State was carried on by his mother, Rani Jhinda Kaur, as Regent with Raja Lal Singh, her reputed favourite, as the Prime Minister of the *Durbar,* at which he wielded great influence.

> "It was sufficiently certain and notorious at the time that Lal Singh was in communication with Captain Nicholson, the British Agent at Ferozepur, but... the details of the overtures made and expectations held out cannot now be satisfactorily known." (*History of the Sikhs* by Cunningham, p. 305)

Subsequent events, however, leave no doubt whatsoever, that Lal Singh had betrayed into English hands his boy-Maharaja, his countrymen and Rani Jhinda Kaur whose favours he was enjoying.

Another prominent figure at the *Durbar* was Tej Singh, the Commander-in-Chief of its Army. The English bought him over too.

The third traitor, and one who gained the most by his treason, was the Dogra Rajput Raja of Jammu, Gulab Singh. He asked for and got Kashmir as his price.

Deterioration of Indians' Character

The awful depths to which the character of Indians had sunk is shown in Punjab's history more vividly than in the history of any other province or region of India. Over a hundred years ago, an English officer wrote:

> "... We must at once admit that our conquest of India was, through every struggle, more owing to the weakness of the Asiatic character than to the bare effect of our own brilliant achievement ... On the same principle we may set down as certain, that whenever one-twentieth part of the population of India becomes as provident and as scheming as ourselves, we shall run back again in the same ratio of velocity ..."
> (*Carnoticus*, in the *Asiatic Journal*, 1821)

Major Broadfoot

Major Broadfoot was the Governor-General's Agent for the then North-Western Frontier Province, and was stationed at Ludhiana, an important town on the border between Punjab and the English possessions. He was known as "Ellenborough's man", and Hardinge had appointed him to the strategical post at the instance of Ellenborough. He was entrusted with the twofold task of fomenting internal quarrels and disorders in Punjab and of exasperating and provoking the Sikhs into providing the English with a *casus belli*. Broadfoot was successful in accomplishing both.

There were some Cis-Sutlej States, like Patiala, which were under British protection. In addition to these, there was some territory owned and ruled by the Lahore *Durbar*, with which the English had undertaken never to interfere, as provided in the treaty which they had made with Maharaja Ranjit Singh. But according to Cunningham:

> "One of Major Broadfoot's first acts was to declare the Cis-Sutlej possessions of Lahore to be under British protection equally with Putteeala and other chief-ships, and also to be liable to escheat on the death or deposition of Maharaja

Dulip Singh. This view was not formally announced to the Sikh Government, but it was notorious and Major Broadfoot acted on it." (*History of the Sikhs*, pp. 297 *et seq*)

Incidentally, Ellenborough, although he was no more the Governor-General and had left India, was still guiding Broadfoot from London in all the latter's activities calculated to perpetuate and intensify the quarrels and dissensions amongst the different factions in Punjab. In one of his letters to Broadfoot (dated 7th May, 1845), Ellenborough expressed his satisfaction that "our friends on the other side of the Sutlej" (meaning the traitors in the Lahore *Durbar*)

> "have been doing apparently all we could desire, or nearly so; but still, I fear, they will be alarmed by the close neighbourhood of so many of our troops and make up their quarrels, if they can."

Ellenborough therefore pressed Broadfoot to see to it that the "quarrels" were not made up.

Two very significant letters from Hardinge to Ellenborough are on record.

One of them was written on 23rd January, 1845, some six months after Hardinge had taken over as Governor-General, when the Lahore *Durbar's* administration was in very serious difficulties. We quote from it:

> "Even if we had a case for devouring our ally in his adversity, we are not ready and could not be ready until the hot winds set in and the Sutlej becomes a torrent ... but *on what plea could we attack the Punjab* if this were the month of October, and we had our army in readiness? Self-preservation may require the dispersion of this Sikh army; ... but ... *who are we to justify the seizure of our friend's territory who in our adversity assisted us to retrieve our affairs?*"

The phrase "who in our adversity assisted us" refers to the very essential and valuable help rendered by Maharaja Ranjit Singh to the English, which has been narrated in earlier chapters. Had Maharaja Ranjit Singh made common cause with Jaswantrao Holkar, then, very probably, nay, almost certainly, the English would have been uprooted from the soil of India.

The other letter was written by Hardinge on 23rd October, 1845, after his preparations for war were completed. "The Punjab," he wrote, "must however be Sikh or British ... The delay is merely a postponement of the settlement of the question; at the same time we must bear in mind that *as yet no cause of war has been given*."

The date of Hardinge's last quoted letter is important, as it gives the lie direct to Broadfoot's allegation about the "serious violation" of the English frontier by the Sikhs in March 1845, which, if true, would have been a sufficient *casus belli*.

The trivial incident on which the allegation was founded may be related. Amongst the Lahore *Durbar's* Cis-Sutlej possessions was a town called Kot Kapoora at which a small posse of mounted police was maintained by the *Durbar* for watch and ward. It was periodically relieved by a fresh posse from Lahore, which crossed the river near Ferozepur in order to reach Kot Kapoora. The relieved posse similarly crossed the river on its way back. In March 1845, the relieving posse from Lahore crossed the Sutlej as usual, and was on its way to Kot Kapoora, when Broadfoot with an armed escort caught up with it and ordered it to turn back and re-cross the river. The posse turned back but Broadfoot "considered them dilatory in their obedience, he followed them with his escort, and overtook them as they were about to ford the river. A shot was fired by the English party, and the extreme desire of the Sikh commandant to avoid doing anything which might be held to compromise his government alone prevented a collision" (Cunningham's *History of the Sikhs*, p. 296).

This "serious violation" of the English frontier was unacceptable even to Hardinge as a *casus belli*.

The Lahore *Durbar* protested against Broadfoot's highhandedness in firing upon its unoffending patrol in violation of the treaty of amity into which the *Durbar* had entered with the British Government. It also complained that the English had increased their military strength at Ferozepur by 150 to 200 per cent in violation of the terms under which they had been permitted by the *Durbar* to occupy Ferozepur. One of the terms was that the Company's troops there would not be increased beyond a specified limit without the *Durbar's* permission. These and other breaches of the treaty were persistently committed and high-ranking officials of the *Durbar* were deliberately treated with indignity to provoke the Sikhs to hostilities. But the *Durbar* bore it all patiently and would not be provoked.

Hastings Takes a Hand

It was now October, 1845, and the most favourable time of the year for launching the attack on the Sikhs had arrived. But Hardinge was still without any plausible pretext for "devouring" Punjab. So he decided to take matters in his own hands and left Calcutta for the frontier.

Both Lal Singh and Tej Singh had by now burnt their boats and thrown in their lot with the English. The latter pressed them somehow to get the Sikh soldiery to invade the "British territories" across the Sutlej. Agents provocateurs were profusely employed and infiltrated into the Sikh army. They incited the soldiers with the imminent danger of the invasion of the Sikh homeland by the English which was portended by the massing of the Company's armed might on the opposite bank of the Sutlej. Lal Singh and Tej Singh helped with their own exhortations. Cunningham writes:

> "Had the shrewd committees of the armies observed no military preparations on the part of the English, They would not have heeded the insidious exhortations of such mercenary men as Lal Singh and Tej Singh… But the views of the government functionaries coincided with the belief of the impulsive soldiery, and when the men were tauntingly asked whether they would quietly look on while the limits of the Khalsa dominion were being reduced, and the plains of Lahore occupied by the remote strangers of Europe, they answered that they would defend with their lives all belonging to the commonwealth of Govind, and they would march and give battle to the invaders on their own ground."
> (*History of the Sikhs*, p. 299)

Thus it was that the Sikh army led by Lal Singh in person, marched from Lahore about the middle of November and in due course crossed the Sutlej.

At last, Hardinge was furnished with a *casus belli* and he promptly issued a proclamation on 13th December, 1845, declaring war against the Sikhs and also declaring "the possessions of Maharaja Dulip Singh, on the left or the British bank of the Sutlej confiscated and annexed to the British territories."

Lal Singh, after crossing the Sutlej, led his army up the river towards Mudki, instead of forthwith attacking the Company's troops near Ferozepur. On 18th December, 1845, according to English writers, the Sikhs fought the Company's troops fiercely at Mudki and inflicted heavy losses on them. But they were betrayed by traitors in their own camp, who had been bought over by the English through the arch-traitors, Lal Singh and Tej Singh. Inevitably, therefore, the English won the day.

The Sikh army retired to Ferozeshahr from Mudki. At the fierce battle which was fought at Ferozeshahr, the Governor-General himself served as Second-in-Command under Sir Hugh Gough, the Commander-in-Chief. The losses inflicted on the English were the heaviest till then sustained by them on any battlefield in India. Many senior English officers, including Major Broadfoot, and a very large number of men of the European regiments were killed in action. Hardinge lost his nerve completely, and planned to "retreat to Firozpur" that very night.

Surprisingly enough, the Sikhs did not follow up their advantage. The desperate plight of the English and the reason for the Sikh inactivity have thus been related by William Edwards:

> "Had they (the Sikhs) advanced during the night, the result must have been very disastrous for us, as our European regiments were much reduced in number, and our ammunition both for artillery and small arms almost expended ... It was inexplicable at the time to us why this ... army had failed to advance ... Subsequently at Lahore, however, I was informed that their leaders had restrained the men on the pretext that the day was inauspicious for a battle, it by no means being the intention of the regency that their troops should be successful, but, on the contrary, be destroyed by the British, so as to get rid of them for ever."
> (*Reminiscences of a Bengal Civilian*, p. 97)

Thus it was that the battle at Ferozeshahr, was, in effect, lost by the Sikhs even at the very moment when complete victory was within their grasp.

The raising of traitors like Lal Singh and Tej Singh did not produce results satisfactory to Governor-General Hardinge.

> "Perhaps neither the incapacity nor the treason of Lal Singh and Tej Singh was fully perceived ... and hence the anxiety of the Governor-General may be ... inferred from his proclamation encouraging desertion from the Sikh ranks, with the assurance of present rewards and future pensions, and the immediate decision of any law-suits in which the deserters might be engaged in the British provinces."
> (Cunningham's *History of the Sikhs*, p. 311)

Rewards Promised to Patiala

We cull the story from the account in the *Reminiscences of a Bengal Civilian* (pp. 84,87,92-93) by its author, W. M. Edwards, who was sent to Patiala by the Governor-General, on the mission of securing the continued faithfulness of the State to the English, which was in danger of being discontinued.

The battle of Ferozeshahr had given rise to widespread reports that both the Governor-General and the Commander-in-Chief had been killed in the battle, that the English Army had been annihilated and that the victorious Sikhs were in full march on Delhi.

The Maharaja, who had been a staunch friend of the English, had suddenly died under suspicious circumstances, and the Governor-General feared that the disorder and disorganisation in the State which were bound to follow the Maharaja's death, added to the above-mentioned reports, might lead to an alliance between the State and the Khalsa soldiery against the English. He therefore instructed W. Edwards.

> "to proceed instantly to Puttialah to install the young Maharaja on the throne, in place of his father, who had suddenly and mysteriously died, it was feared by poison, on account of his steady adherence to British interest. The

> Principality of Puttialah was in consequence of this Chief's death in a very excited and disturbed state, and it was considered of the greatest importance to secure the fidelity of his son and successor, as should the state become hostile to us, the main army's communication with its rear, which passed chiefly through Puttialah territory, would be cut off, and the results might be very disastrous. I was instructed, therefore, to use my best endeavours to induce the young Chief, to continue to follow his father's example and, with his subjects, remain faithful to British interests."

W. Edwards told the young Maharaja that if the latter remained steadfast to the British interests, then he would be "rewarded" by the bestowal upon him of some lands which would become British territory on the successful termination of the war.

> "Finally, I said," writes W. Edwards, "… that if the Maharaja aided us by forwarding supplies, and keeping open our communications with the rear," the Government "would not only raise his rank above all other Cis-Sutlej States, his former compeers, but place him at once on a level with the great and ancient Rajas of Hindustan."

W. Edwards succeeded in his mission.

The third "battle" is supposed to have been "fought" at Aliwal, and the official reports have magnified it into a "grand combat" won by the English. But candid witnesses tell a far different story. Andrew Leith Adams, M.D., Surgeon, 22nd Regiment, writes:

> "I wandered over the field with one who had been present at the engagement; he assured me, and his testimony has been corroborated by many others, that *a fruitful imagination was at work when the official account was drawn up.* His words were 'Aliwal was *the battle of the dispatch*,' for none of us knew we had fought a battle until the particulars appeared in a document … "

What would appear to have happened *in fact* was that the baggage of the English army had been seized by the Sikh army at Budiwal. Shortly afterwards, a patrol of the Sikh army, passing through Aliwal, was fired at by some men of the English army. Some desultory shooting on both sides followed, but there was no clash and no damage was done to either side. The "Battle of Aliwal" was thus "lost" by the Sikhs and "won" by the English, without having ever been "fought"!

Having failed to achieve any success at Mudki or Ferozeshahr, the Sikh soldiery lost faith in Lai Singh, Tej Singh and their other military leaders, all of whom

> "they accused of conspiring with the British Government for their destruction, and invited Gulab Singh to place himself at their head. The Raja (Gulab Singh) promised compliance, and arrived in due time at Lahore with a large body of his own hill troops, in whom he could place implicit reliance. He persuaded the *Durbar* to allow him to garrison the fortress at Lahore with these men, while the Sikhs then occupying it were ordered to proceed to join their brethren on the Sutlej (at Subraon) … Gulab urged the (Sikh) army not to attempt attacking the British until he joined them, and this he evaded doing on one pretext or another, knowing full well that in due time the British would attack and capture the position at Subraon." (W. Edwards in his *Reminiscences of a Bengal Civilian*, p. 104)

Gulab Singh, Lal Singh and Tej Singh thus formed a triumvirate of traitors with the common object of the annihilation of the Sikh army by the British. The understanding arrived at with the latter was that the Sikhs would be attacked-by the English, and that when attacked they would be abandoned by their own leaders. Lal Singh's emissaries gave valuable information respecting the position held by the Sikhs and the plans for the attack were drawn up and were later duly carried out:

> "The Sikhs made a gallant and desperate resistance, but were driven towards the river and their bridge of boats, which, as soon as the action had become general, their leaders, Lal Singh and Tej Singh, had by previous consent, broken down, taking the precaution first to retire across it themselves." (W. Edwards, ibid., pp. 99–100)

Their leaders urged the troops and their artillery almost into the waters of the unfordable Sutlej, and looked on unconcernedly, whilst their own men, the trapped Sikhs, were being slaughtered.

> "... Yet, although assailed on either side by squadrons of horse and battalions of foot, no Sikh offered to submit ... or asked for quarter ..." (Cunningham's *History of the Sikhs*, p. 283)

The current of the river Sutlej was choked and crimsoned with the bodies and blood of those who had preferred death to dishonour.

A memorable example amongst those who died fighting was set by the old Sardar Sham Singh of Atari, who

> "... remembered his vow: he clothed himself in simple white attire, as one devoted to death, and calling on all around him to fight ... repeatedly rallied shattered ranks, and at last fell, a martyr, on the heap of his slain countrymen." (Cunningham, ibid., p. 327)

Two hundred and twenty pieces of Sikh artillery fell into the hands of the English

> "of which 80 pieces exceed in calibre anything known in European warfare. The weight of the Sikh gun in proportion to its calibre is much heavier than ours, and the range of the six-pounder is longer. The recoil on the carriage is less and their guns do not heat so rapidly after firing." (*vide* the Governor-General's report)

On the battle-field of Subraon the independence of the Punjab and its gallant Sikh people was buried by treason. It was the beginning of the end of the empire built up by Maharaja Ranjit Singh.

The battle was completely over at 1 p.m. on 10th February, 1846, when not a single Sikh soldier remained alive on the English side of the Sutlej at Surbraon. The Governor-General returned to his camp at Ferozepur, and began preparations for his march to Lahore. In reply to some earnest remonstrances against the crossing of the English army into the Punjab, he at once replied:

> "Depend upon it I am right, for the safest and the wisest course, when you have knocked the wind out of your enemy,

is to go right at the heart at once before he has time to recover." (*Reminiscences of a Bengal Civilian,* p. 101)

Within the next two days the entire English army had crossed the Sutlej and on 12th February, 1846, the Governor-General himself with his staff crossed the bridge of boats. Thanks to Gulab Singh, who had stayed on in Lahore with the entire body of his own troops, and made all the *necessary arrangements,* Hardinge's progress to Lahore was absolutely unmolested. Hardinge could have annexed the whole of the Punjab straightaway, but

> "Annexation of the country was, with the force at our disposal, perfectly out of the question, had it been in other respects politic or desirable. This, in Lord Hardinge's opinion, it could not be, as the Punjab would never, he fell assured, repay the cost of its administration, and that of the large force which would be required to garrison it, and which being no longer available for the protection of our old territory, would have to be replaced by fresh masses of troops." (ibid., pp. 105, 106)

So the First Treaty of Lahore was executed in March 1846, whereby some valuable portions of the child-Maharaja Dulip Singh's territory were declared annexed to the English possessions, and Lal Singh was appointed Administrator of the rest in his capacity as *Wazir* of the Lahore *Durbar.* The treaty also contained a clause by which Kashmir was to be transferred to Gulab Singh.

Soon after the treaty of March, 1846, Hardinge considered it very necessary to abrogate it and to replace it by another. One of the reasons was that Raja Lal Singh, now the *de facto* head of the State, was very much disgruntled because what he had been led to expect as the price of his treason was not forthcoming. As a matter of fact, he had been given next to nothing. On the other hand, Gulab Singh had been rewarded by the formal transfer to him of the vast Kashmir territory for the nominal price of Rs. 1,000,000,000. The treatment meted out to him (Lal Singh) rankled in his heart and he became hostile to the English. The latter suspected Lal Singh of inciting Sheikh Imamuddeen, the Governor of Kashmir, into a refusal to give possession of Kashmir to Gulab Singh. Later, Sheikh Imamuddeen yielded to English threats, and Gulab Singh got its possession. But Hardinge saw that from a faithful friend Lal Singh had turned into a dangerous foe, and must be removed from the position which the earlier treaty had put him in. So the latter was abrogated and Hardinge forced the Treaty of Bhaironwal on the Lahore *Durbar*. According to it, Rani Jhinda Kaur was "excluded from all power, receiving a pension of £ 15,000 a year." A Council of Regency, consisting of eight Sardars, including Tej Singh, "was appointed during the minority of Dulip Singh; and it was stipulated that they should act under the control and guidance of the British resident" (Charles Viscount Hardinge in the biographical sketch of his father, p. 147). Lal Singh was dismissed and later deported to Dehra Dun as a political prisoner. The new treaty also provided for the payment by the Lahore *Durbar* of a huge war penalty to the English. Under its provisions most of the *Durbar's* army was disbanded and replaced at Lahore by the Company's troops, for whom the *Durbar* had to pay.

Punjab was not "annexed" but Hardinge had delivered a mortal blow to its independence. For this achievement, Hardinge was raised to the peerage by the British Government and the grateful Company granted him a life-pension of £ 3,000 a year, to be disbursed of course out of the taxes exacted from the helpless Indians.

Some Notable Incidents of the Hardinge Regime

The innocent but deposed Raja Pratap Singh of Satara—the lineal descendant of Shivaji—was a prisoner at Benares. Major Carpenter, his jailor, wrote to Hardinge that Pratap Singh was not only innocent but was in a position to prove it too. But Carpenter's intercession earned for him a sharp reprimand from Haidinge, and Pratap Singh, whose wife had already succumbed to the rigours of life in jail, and whose own health was fast deteriorating, was left to rot to death in prison. He died in 1847. "With this evil deed, Lord Hardinge's name is inseparably connected" *(British India* by Ludlow, Vol. II, p. 154).

Ever since the British resident had been posted in Nepal, domestic feuds, intrigues and disorders became as rampant there as they had been in the Punjab before the war. The Nepalese have a significant proverb to the effect that with the merchant comes the musket and with the Bible the bayonet" (Wright's *History of Nepal,* pp. 54, 68).

Hardinge went to Lucknow to "warn" the King of Oudh, as a preliminary, we suppose, to the absorption of his kingdom, but apparently found that the time was not till then ripe for it.

In October, 1846, Hardinge issued a notification making it obligatory on *everyone* to observe the Sabbath and to do or take no work on Sundays. This was the first step taken to impose Christianity on Indians.

Hardinge's Resignation and Return to England

On the change of Ministry in England (1847), Hardinge resigned his office and left India for England on 18th January, 1848. Lord Dalhousie succeeded him as Governor-General.

15

THE SECOND SIKH WAR

The British Empire in India was expanded almost to its fullest dimension during the Dalhousie regime. The doctrine of "lapse" was used by him for the absorption of the territories of seven Indian States. He also annexed Oudh and forced the Nizam of Hyderabad to "lease" to the Company the fertile province of Berar, which constituted nearly one-third of his dominion. All this was in addition to the annexation of the Punjab as the result of the Second Sikh War and of the Pegu Province of Burma as the result of the Second Burmese War.

These acquisitions however can hardly be attributed to his personal or free action. The policy which he had to give effect to had been settled years earlier by the authorities in England.

> "... Long before the appointment of Lord Dalhousie, there was a conclave of Whig Ministers and magnates at Lord Lansdowne's place, Bowood, to discuss the policy of upholding or of absorbing the Native States, and it was decided that we should avail ourselves of all opportunities for adding to our territories and revenues at the expense of our allies and of stipendiary Princes like the Rajah of Tanjore and the Nawabs of Carnatic and Bengal. In this direction the Bombay Government set the example by annexing the inconsiderable principality of Colaba, under the pretext that an adopted heir had no right of succession. This led the way to the more important and more impolitic cases, under Lord Dalhousie, of Jhausi and Nagpore. Dalhousie only acted on the policy prescribed by the Ministers of England." (*Memoirs of General John Briggs*, p. 277)

In this connection, it is interesting to recall that the 1793 Charter Act had solemnly declared:

> "To pursue schemes of conquest and extension of *dominion in India is a measure repugnant to the wish, honour and policy of the British nation*" (Italics ours).

But much water flowed under the Westminster Bridge since then.

Creation of Disaffection in the Punjab

Sir Henry Lawrence was the resident at Lahore when Hardinge resigned. Both left India by the same boat. Sir Frederick Currie was appointed the resident when Dalhousie took over. Sir Frederick's letters written about that time show that he was an inveterate enemy of the Sikh *Raj* and of the minor Maharaja Dulip Singh, and was bent upon destroying both. So he did everything possible to provoke the Sikhs into doing something which could serve as an excuse for another war against them. Under the Bhaironwal Treaty, the resident had become the virtual ruler of the Punjab, and Sir Frederick used his powers to replace all the high and responsible Indian officers in every department by Englishmen. It was one of the steps he took to promote disaffection amongst the people of the Punjab, who began to suspect the English intentions about the restoration of the Punjab to Dulip Singh on his attaining majority, as stipulated in the Bhaironwal Treaty. Sir Frederick then deliberately adopted a behaviour which lent support to these suspicions and doubts, which, in his view, could not but result in the people's open and active hostility to the English.

Events in Multan have been stated to have led to the Second Sikh War and might be related here in some detail.

Maharaja Ranjit Singh had in 1818 annexed the province of Multan, which was thereafter administered on behalf of the Lahore *Durbar* by Diwan Sawan Mull. The latter had to pay to the *Durbar* annually half the total annual revenue of the province but in all other respects he enjoyed the status and exercised the authority of an independent ruler. The Company's official reports testify that under Sawan Mull, Multan's material and economic progress was excellent. He dug a number of canals which turned barren lands into fertile fields. He developed trade, industries and crafts People from the regions adjoining the province were attracted to migrate to it in number to share the prosperity of the people of Multan.

After Sawan Mull's death, his son Mool Raj was entitled to succeed him as the Diwan of Multan. But Lal Singh, who was then the virtual head of the Lahore *Durbar*, demanded from Mool Raj the sum of 18 lacs of rupees as *Nazrana* to the *Durbar* before the latter recognised him as his father's successor. Mool Raj consented to pay it, although it amounted to more than the yearly amount of 17 lacs which till then was paid to the *Durbar* by the Diwan of Multan. It soon became doubtful, however, as to who held the reins of the Government at Lahore—Lal Singh or the British resident. Mool Raj, therefore, thought it wiser to postpone payment. After the First Treaty of Lahore, Lal Singh sent an expedition to Multan under his brother, Bhagwan Singh, to subjugate Mool Raj and enforce payment. The English too wanted to break Mool Raj and to replace him by Bhagwan Singh. The latter was repulsed by Mool Raj who, however, appears to have afterwards purchased peace by ceding to Bhagwan Singh a portion of his territory with an annual income of Rs. 8 lacs.

> "Dewan Moolraj was subsequently summoned to Lahore personally to settle his accounts, and came to the capital on the guarantee of the British officers, having good reasons to believe himself the object of a scheme to take his life. During his visit to Lahore a settlement ... was made and he was again confirmed in the government of Multan." (*Annals of India,* 1848, p. 5.)

Multan after the Bhaironwal Treaty

Only a few months after the Bhaironwal Treaty, the English desired to replace Mool Raj by a creature of their own and began to worry the life out of Mool Raj in order to force him to resign. The annual tribute payable by him was increased from Rs. 17.50 lacs to Rs. 19.75 lacs, subject, nevertheless, to the proviso that it would be increased to Rs. 25 lacs after two years and to Rs. 30 lacs three years thereafter. It was also proposed to saddle him with two commissioners, nine collectors and seven judges—all Englishmen of course—for the purpose of "guiding" and "helping" him in the administration. The guidance and the help was not at all necessary because, according to English writers, Mool Raj's administration was "excellent", Mool Raj's self-respect and his love for his country and his people revolted against the proposed handing over of both these virtues to the rule of foreigners, and he repaired to Lahore where he tendered his resignation. It was not accepted because the English were not yet ready for its acceptance.

At this stage, Sir Frederick Currie took over as the British resident at Lahore. He was determined to pick a quarrel with Mool Raj and harassed the latter endlessly. He was backed by Dalhousie and Mool Raj was pressed to renew his resignation, which he did. The resignation was accepted and one Kahan Singh Mann was appointed to replace Mool Raj on a salary of Rs. 30,000/- a year. Two Englishmen, Agnew and Anderson, were appointed to go to Multan with Mann who was directed to carry on the administration under their control. The trio left Lahore with a detachment of troops and reached Multan on 18th April, 1848. The next day Mool Raj quietly handed over charge and left the city. Agnew immediately posted English guards on all the gates of the city. Then, on that very day, practically all the Multani soldiers in the city were dismissed and replaced by English soldiers. The people saw at once that thenceforward they were going to be ruled not by the Lahore *Durbar,* but by the latter's masters, the English. The discontent was intense and widespread. Within a few hours, Agnew, who was riding by, was set upon by two Multani horsemen who had been dismissed earlier in the day. Agnew was severely wounded, but Mann rushed to his rescue and saved his life.

The Open Revolt

The next day, on April 20, 1848, the dismissed Multani soldiery surrounded the Idga outside the city, where Agnew, Anderson and their troops were quartered. The Indian soldiers in the English detachment went over to the Multani soldiery, but most of their officers stayed with the English and Mann. Both Agnew and Anderson were killed in the armed clash that ensued. Kahan Singh Mann was wounded and taken prisoner.

We would now leave the Multan scene for the moment and narrate the happenings at Lahore.

Arrest of Maharani Jhinda Kaur

The armed revolt at Multan served as an excuse for the arrest and deportation of Maharani Jhinda Kaur, who was accused of having had a hand in the revolt. No inquiry was held, nor was she given a chance to defend herself. Also no Hindu or Sikh member of the Council of Regency was consulted. On 16th May, 1848, the resident, Sir Frederick Currie, wrote in a despatch:

> "Maharanee Jhinda Khore, the mother of Maharajah Duleep Singh, was removed from the fort at Sheikhopoor, by my orders yesterday afternoon and is now on her way under charge of an escort to Ferozepore.
>
> Her summary banishment from the Punjab, and residence at Benares, under the surveillance of the Governor-General's Agent, subject to such custody as will prevent all intrigues and correspondence for the future, seems to me the best course which we could adopt.
>
> At Benares she should be subject to such surveillance and custody as will prevent her having intercourse with parties beyond her own domestic establishment, and holding correspondence with any person except through the Governor-General's Agent." (*Punjab Papers, 1849*, p. 168)

Real Motive Behind the Arrest

We have already referred to Sir Frederick Currie's deliberate adoption of the role of an *agent provocateur* for exasperating the Sikhs to such an extent that they would be provoked into overt hostility against the English and so provide the latter with a plausible excuse for renewing the war against them, which was necessary for "devouring" the Punjab. The whole of the Punjab, particularly the Sikhs, revered the Maharani as their mother. Her arrest and deportation did have the intended result. With evident glee, Sir Frederick wrote to the Governor-General on 25th May, 1848:

> "The reports ... are that the Khalsa soldiery, on hearing of the removal of the Maharanee, were much disturbed; they

said that she was the mother of the Khalsa, and that as she was gone and the young Duleep Singh in our hands, they had no longer anyone to fight for and uphold, that they had no inducement to oppose Mulraj and if he came to attack them, would seize the Sardars and their officers and go over to him." (*Punjab Papers, 1849*, p. 179)

Raja Sher Singh, a prominent and important member of the Council of Regency at Lahore, issued a manifesto to the people of the Punjab, beginning:

"It is well known to all the inhabitants of the Punjab, to the whole of the Sikhs, and in fact to the world at large, with what oppression, tyranny and undue violence the Feringhees have treated the widow of the great Maharajah Runjeet Singh, now in bliss.

They have broken the treaty by imprisoning and sending away to Hindustan, the Maharanee, the mother of her people". (*Punjab Papers, 1849*, p. 362)

Not only were the Sikhs and the people of the Punjab agitated over the incident but, the Amir of Afghanistan, Dost Mohammad, was also moved. He sounded a note of warning (in his letter to Capt. Abbott, one of the resident's assistants) as follows:

"There can be no doubt that the Sikhs are daily becoming more and more discontented. Some have been dismissed from service, while others have been banished to Hindustan, in particular the mother of Maharajah Duleep Singh, who has been imprisoned and ill-treated. Such treatment is considered objectionable by all creeds, and both high and low prefer death." (*Punjab Papers, 1849*, p. 512)

Sardar Chatar Singh Atariwala

The only other "tall poppy" in the Punjab which had to be 'beheaded' was the old Sardar Chatar Singh, father of Raja Sher Singh. Chatar Singh wielded a tremendous amount of influence as he commanded respect throughout the Punjab. When the Lahore *Durbar* acquired the Province of Hazara from Gulab Singh, in exchange for some of the *Durbar's* territory, Chatar Singh was appointed its Governor, or *Nazim,* by the *Durbar.* The above-mentioned Capt. Abbott was deputed by the English to go with Chatar Singh "to aid and advise" the latter "in the execution of his duties". Abbott took his cue from what the resident, Sir Frederick Currie, had been doing with Mool Raj of Multan, and began to annoy Chatar Singh persistently by rude and even contemptuous behaviour, which no self-respecting man could put up with and which elicited a mild remonstrance even from the resident himself.

Chatar Singh Accused of "Cold-blooded Murder"

Most of the population of the Hazara Province consisted of simple but spirited and warlike armed Mussalmans. Abbott acquired influence over them by a lavish expenditure of money and then proceeded to incite them against the Sikhs by telling them that the Sikhs had always been the enemies of Mussalmans, and they could now avenge themselves if they joined the English in destroying the Sikhs. Chatar Singh was then living in Haripur, where a contingent of the Sikh army, commanded by Col. Canora, was stationed for security purposes. On 6th August, 1843, a violent mob of Mussalmans incited by Abbott surrounded Haripur. Chatar Singh ordered Col. Canora to lead out his men and disperse the mob. Not only did Col. Canora refuse to obey the order, but loaded two of his guns and "standing between them with a lighted port fire in his hand said he would fire on the first man who came near" (*Punjab Papers, 1849*, p. 280). Later, he ordered a Havildar under him to fire on some soldiers sent by Chatar Singh to seize the guns. On the Havildar's refusal to fire at the approaching soldiers, Col. Canora cut him down Then he himself was shot by two of the soldiers.

In his report to the resident, Abbott accused Chatar Singh of the "cold-blooded murder" of Col. Canora. The resident, Sir Frederick Currie, did not, however, agree. We give below some extracts from his letter to Abbott in this connection:

> "Sirdar Chuttur Singh was the Governor of the province, military and civil, and the officers of the Sikh army were bound to obey him … Taking the worst possible view of the case, I know not how you can characterise it as 'a cold-blooded murder'. None of the accounts that have yet been made justifies you in calling the death of Commandant Canora a murder, nor in asserting that it was premeditated by Sirdar Chuttur Singh." (*Punjab Papers,* 1849, pp. 313–316)

But the rebuff did not, in the least, deter Abbott from carrying on his intrigues against the Sikhs.

Incitement of Mussalman Chiefs of Hazara

We would now let Capt. Abbott himself tell the story. He wrote in one of his despatches:

> "I assembled the Chiefs of Hazara; explained what had happened, and called upon them by the memory of their murdered parents, friends and relatives to rise, and aid me in destroying the Sikh forces in detail. I issued *purwannahs* to this effect throughout the land…" (*Punjab Papers*, 1849, p. 311)

Sardar Chatar Singh repeatedly complained about Abbott's nefarious activities to the Lahore *Durbar* and to the resident, but neither of them paid any heed to his complaints. In despair of getting any help from either, the old Sardar had to fall back on his own resources to defend his country, his faith and the Khalsa Raj.

On the Multan Front

Sir Frederick Currie pressed the Lahore *Durbar* to send a punitive expedition to Multan and punish Mool Raj for the revolt there. But most of the *Durbar's* army had been disbanded under the Treaty of Bhaironwal and replaced by the Company's troops stationed at Lahore, Jullundur and Ferozepur. It had been declared in the Treaty that these troops were to be maintained for the preservation of peace in the Punjab and for putting down disorders and revolts against the *Durbar,* and, so the latter was to pay for them. Naturally, therefore, the Durbar asked that the Company's troops be sent to Multan to quell the "rebellion". The resident, in violation of the treaty, refused to send a single soldier. He went a step further and held out the threat that if the Durbar did not or could not put down the Multan revolt with its own troops, then the *Durbar's* entire territory would be annexed by the British Government. Thus the real reason of the refusal to give the requested military help to the *Durbar* stands out clearly. It also becomes clear that the Company's troops, maintained at the cost of the *Durbar,* were never intended to help it, but were meant to be used for its destruction.

Under the above threat, the *Durbar* was forced to send the expedition to Multan from its own depleted army. It was commanded by Raja Sher Singh, the Member of the Regency Council and son of Sardar Chatar Singh, the Governor of Hazara. Curiously enough, the resident ordered one of his assistants on the Frontier, Lieut. Edwardes, too, to proceed to Multan with a military detachment. Edwardes' subsequent activities go to show that he was entrusted with the mission of seeing to it that the *Durbar* did not succeed in reducing Mool Raj. Edwardes incited the Frontier Mussalmans against the Sikhs and helped to get together an armed force of Mussalmans, which was later joined, thanks to his efforts, by the troops of the Nawab of Bahawalpur. Another Mussalman chief won over by Edwardes whilst on his way to Multan was Sardar Fateh Khan Tiwana, whose relations with Mool Raj had been strained for some time. Edwardes, apparently without any authority, appointed Fateh Khan the "Governor" of Dera Ghazi Khan and Bannu, and instigated him to plunder and murder the Sikhs in these places. But before Fateh Khan could do that, he himself met his death at the hands of the Sikhs.

There were several engagements between the troops of Mool Raj and Edwardes, in two of which Edwardes was victorious. He then advanced to the Multan Fort and intended to besiege it. But the guns and reinforcements which he had asked for did not arrive, and he had to stay put where he was. In the meantime, thousands of Mussalmans and Sikhs had mustered under the flag of Mool Raj. Even the Sikh soldiers under Raja Sher Singh had gone over to Mool Raj, and Edwardes apparently feared that Raja Sher Singh himself might follow suit, so he got "… busy writing false letters from General (Raja) Sher Singh to fall into the hands of Mool Raj to create suspicion, in which he partially succeeded and prevented Mool Raj from attacking him" (*Life of Sir Charles Napier,* Vol. IV, p. 129).

Abortive Siege of Multan Fort

Anyway, the Multan Fort was besieged, but the English appear to have depended for success more on treason in Mool Raj's camp than on their own military prowess. In August, 1848, Sir Charles Napier wrote to his brother:

> "If he (Lt. H.B. Edwardes) beats Mool Raj, he will be safe; but if Mool Raj gets an advantage, Edwardes' position will be dangerous … If Mool Raj's men are true, Edwardes cannot take Multan. If they are false, the town will open its gates." (ibid., p. 106)

The siege was raised in September, 1848.

Aftermath of English Failure at Multan

The Punjab was, by then, seething with anger and hostility against the English. Mool Raj's successful defence of Multan heartened the people and the Sikh Sardars immeasurably, and they began to rally under the flag of Raja Sher Singh for the defence of the Khalsa Raj and for the preservation of their independence which was very nearly in the clutches of the foreigners. It was now

> "… many more times more difficult to subdue Punjab than in 1846 … then … the Sardars accepted promises, nay took bribes too, but now they will not take bribes, and animated with great hatred for the way they were treated … the Sikhs will turn out to a man, unless something extraordinary may happen to prevent it, which I cannot vouch for at present." (ibid., p. 125)

In spite of these difficulties, the English did not swerve from their determination to conquer and annex the Punjab. They intensified their efforts to incite the Mussalmans all over the Frontier and the Punjab against the Sikhs by specious and often spurious accounts of the latter's past and persistent tyrannical maltreatment of the followers of Islam, and the English efforts did succeed to some extent.

Notable Events of Second Sikh War

The English having assembled their forces now made an all-out effort to conquer the Punjab. The British Commander-in-Chief, Lord Gough, himself took the field. The Sikhs were led by Raja Sher Singh. The siege of Multan had been raised in September, 1848. In October, 1848, Multan was invested again. Notable amongst the battles of the war were those fought at Chilianwala and Gujrat.

At Chilianwala, the Sikhs, though out-numbered by the force under Lord Gough, inflicted a crushing defeat on the latter. The losses on the English side were more than 23,000 killed and wounded, including 26 English officers killed and 66 wounded. In addition, several infantry regiments were crippled. It was the most complete victory, as it was the last, won by the Sikhs on Indian soil against the English.

Then the old story of Sikh inactivity and failure to follow up their advantage was repeated. For some inexplicable reason, differences arose amongst the Sikh Commanders. The consequence was that Raja Sher Singh instead of following up the victory and wiping out Lord Gough's army, had to march to Lahore, and on his way, met his Waterloo at Gujrat, where his force was practically routed by the English.

At Multan too, Mool Raj had to surrender. He had gallantly resisted the siege for nine months, but could do so no longer, as he had completely run out of provisions and his store of ammunition had been destroyed by fire.

Mention must also be made of the way in which the Govindgarh Fort was delivered into English hands. "Fakir Shamsuddin, second son of Nuruddin, was Thanadar of the Gobindgarh Fort during the Second Sikh War. In this position he behaved with great fidelity, and made over the fort to European troops at a time when any hesitation on his part might have produced very serious results" (Sir Lepel Griffin in *The Punjab Chiefs,* New (1890) Edn.,Vol. I, p. 1109). Nuruddin, mentioned in the quotation, was a Member of the Council of Regency at Lahore and according to Sir Lepel Griffin, "he at all times was ready to facilitate matters for the British resident." It has been stated that it was under Nuruddin's advice that Maharani Jhinda Kaur was ordered to be arrested and banished by the resident and that Nuruddin "personally saw to the order being carried out" (*Punjab Papers, 1849,* p. 228). Ironically enough, it was Maharaja Ranjit Singh, the husband of Maharani Jhinda Kaur, who had lifted Nuruddin's family from obscurity and raised Nuruddin's brother Fakir Azizuddin to the position of one of his trusted Ministers.

Annexation of Punjab—Its Political Morality

On 29th March, 1849, Governor-General Lord Dalhousie issued a proclamation whereby the Punjab was annexed to and became a Province of the British Indian Empire.

Major Evans Bell has very closely examined the various allegations made in the Proclamation in support of the annexation and has demonstrated them to be without any force or substance. He sums up thus:

> "Lord Dalhousie's procedure in settling the future relations of the Punjab with British India after the campaign of 1849, just amounts to this: a guardian, having undertaken for valuable consideration, a troublesome and dangerous trust, declares, on the first occurrence of those troubles and dangers, of which he had full knowledge and forewarning, that as a compensation for his exertions and a protection for the future, he shall appropriate his Ward's estate and personal property to his own purposes." (*Retrospects and Prospects of Indian Policy,* p. 142)

It may be added that the Lahore *Durbar* had not committed a single breach of any of the terms of its treaty with the English nor was the *Durbar* in any way responsible for the various disorders or revolts in its territory.

And so the minor Maharaja Dulip Singh was deprived of his territories by his self-appointed guardians, the English.

What Two Sikh Wars Demonstrated

A handful of shrewd foreigners from across the seas, noted rather for their commercial acumen than for their military process or ability or for their valour on the battle-field, had conquered a spirited people who had proved their mettle in numerous battles, as also their efficiency in the arts of war and peace. That the people of the Punjab excelled the English in all these qualities and were happy and prosperous under their own administration has been freely admitted by many English writers and high civil and military officials. Yet they lost their country and their independence. The reason is not far to seek. Peace and prosperity had led to wealth which, as often happens, bred vice and corruption amongst the upper and the middle classes, who were then the natural leaders of the rest of the people. The character of these classes in the Punjab, particularly of those who were at the helm of affairs, had sunk very low, dragging down with it, almost to vanishing point, the sentiments of national pride and of love of freedom and country. These were utterly lacking amongst the leaders of the Punjab and that was the one and only reason which inevitably led to the "conquest" of a proud and gallant people.

Cotton

Besides the expansion of the British Empire, the annexations of Sindh and the Punjab, one after the other, resulted in another and very substantial gain to the English textile manufacturers. Both Sindh and the Punjab grew cotton abundantly. The English textile manufacturers needed it badly but naturally wanted to pay as little as possible for it. The political domination of these regions by their countrymen made available to the textile manufacturers of Lancashire and Manchester all the cotton they wanted and *at their own price.*

16

THE SECOND BURMESE WAR

Creation of *Casus Belli*

As in the case of the Punjab, no *casus belli* existed in connection with Burma. So one had to be created. Lord Dalhousie entrusted the task to the "too combustible" Commodore Lambert, who with two English gunboats, the *Fox* and the *Serpent*, left Calcutta for Rangoon to demand and exact payment, by the Government of Burma, of £ 910, which the Governor-General had decreed to be due as reparations to Capt. Shepperd (£ 350) and to Capt. Lews (£ 560). The claim was founded on the following facts:

> "In June, 1851, the British barque *Monarch* of 250 tons, last from Moulmein, reached Rangoon, the principal port of the Burmese Empire. On the second day after their arrival, Captain Shepperd, the master and owner, was taken before the police to answer the charge of having, during the voyage, thrown overboard the pilot Esoph, preferred by a man named Hajim, a native of Chittagong, who stated that he was the brother of the said pilot ..." (presented to Parliament, June, 1852, p. 5)

A second charge against Capt. Shepperd was:

> "A charge was brought by a man named Dewan Ali (a British subject, employed in one of the Moulmein gunboats), calling himself a brother of the pilot, bringing forward a claim for a sum of 500 rupees, which he stated his brother had taken with him ..." (ibid.)

A Burmese court tried Shepperd for murder and robbery. After recording the evidence of some eye-witnesses from the gunboat, the court found Shepperd guilty on both counts. Shepperd was sentenced to pay a fine of £ 46 for having committed murder, and was further ordered to pay £ 55 to Dewan Ali on the robbery charge.

In August, 1851, another English vessel *Champion* with Capt Lewis as master, reached Rangoon from Mauritius. Lewis was charged with murder and other serious offences by two Bengali labourers and was tried and convicted by a Burmese court and sentenced to pay a fine of £ 70.

Shepperd and Lewis, on their return to India, approached the Government of Lord Dalhousie with a claim for £ 1,920, against the Government of Burma. It will be noted that both had to pay in fines only £ 171 in all. It must be mentioned, too, that the Government of Burma was fully as sovereign and independent as the British Government and could not be ordered about or over-ruled by the latter. The complainants in both cases were British subjects, and so there could not be the slightest suspicion about the Burmese court's partiality for them. Finally, the Governor-General of India did not have even the shadow of any legal authority under the International Law to review, much less rescind, the judgments of the Burmese courts of law at the instance of two non-official Englishmen engaged in their own private business.

Yet in spite of all these considerations, Lord Dalhousie not only awarded £ 910 (against £ 1,920 claimed) to Capt. Shepperd and Capt. Lewis but also proceeded to coerce the Government of Burma into paying the amount by a show of force.

Dalhousie's Instructions to Lambert

A letter addressed to the King of Burma was given to Lambert who was instructed to forward it to the King, if the Burmese Governor of Rangoon did not meet the demand for £ 910 decreed by Lord Dalhousie. The Parliamentary Papers mentioned above indicate clearly that some secret instructions also were given to Lambert. It is significant that instead of claiming the amount through the usual channel of communication with the Government of Burma or of sending it through a special civilian officer as an emissary, the claim was made and payment demanded through a military officer backed by two gunboats. John Lawrence, in his letter to Country, the Private Secretary to the Governor-General, asked:

> "Why did you send a Commodore to Burma if you wanted peace?" (*Life of Lord Dalhousie* by Lee-Warner, Vol. I, p. 417)

Commodore Lambert's Activities at Rangoon

On arriving at Rangoon, Lambert sent a haughty letter of demand to the Burmese Governor of Rangoon on 27th November, 1851. Next day he sent, through the Governor, the Company Government's letter addressed to the King of Burma (which Lord Dalhousie had given him) and demanded that a reply should reach him within five weeks.

Whilst waiting for the reply, Lambert got busy with the collection of complaints against the Government of Burma and/or the Governor of Rangoon from Englishmen residing in Rangoon, most of whom were traders. He collected as many as 38 complaints. Most of them bore no date and all of them were unsigned. The famous English writer-statesman, Cobden, has characterised the complaints as "absurd". Even Lord Ellenborough stated in Parliament on 6th February, 1852, that the class of people who were supposed to be the complainants could not be called reliable.

Lambert, however, forwarded the complaints to the Government of Burma and demanded redress. He had obviously banked on the rejection of his demands by the Government of Burma for providing Lord Dalhousie with the much sought-after *casus belli*.

Acceptance of Demands by Government of Burma

But what Lambert had anticipated did not happen. The reply of the King of Burma was received within the time-limit of five weeks set by Lambert on 1st January, 1852. The King accepted all the complaints, promised redress and reparation, and also agreed to pay the sum of £ 910 to Shepperd and Lewis as demanded by Lord

Dalhousie. As an earnest of his good faith, the King also dismissed the Governor of Rangoon and appointed another Governor in his place. That very day Lambert wrote to the Government of India:

> "... The Burmese Government have dismissed the Governor of Rangoon, and promised to settle the demand made on them by the Government of India. I am of opinion that the King is sincere and that his Government will fully act up to what he has promised." (Parliamentary (Burmah) Papers, 1852, p. 43)

The new Governor of Rangoon arrived on 4th January, 1852. On the 5th Lambert sent one of his men, Edwards, to him to inquire whether the new Governor would receive from Commodore Lambert a letter stating the nature of the claims which the Government of British India had made on that of Burma. The Governor replied that the Commodore could send the letter the very next day or whenever convenient to him. Edwards also mentioned orally some minor grievance which the new Governor removed immediately.

On 6th January, 1852, Lambert sent to the Governor, not a letter but a deputation of five English military officers. On their arrival they had to wait for a few minutes before they were received as the Governor had not expected a deputation and was not ready to meet them immediately in the usual ceremonial way. The Commodore later wrote to Lord Dalhousie about the deputation "having been kept waiting for a full quarter of an hour in the sun". Lambert had evidently considered it enough reason for going to war with Burma, which he immediately did almost within the hour.

Commodore Lambert's Notification

Without any reference to the Government of India or to that of Burma or even to the Governor of Rangoon, Lambert immediately issued a notification of blockade, in which he declared:

> "In virtue of authority from the Governor-General of India, 1 do hereby declare the rivers of Rangoon, the Bassein and the Salween above Moulmein, to be in a state of blockade; and, with a view to the strict enforcement thereof, a competent force will be stationed in or near the entrance of the said rivers immediately." (*Parliamentary Papers, 1852*, p. 46)

Simultaneously he issued a warning to the English residents of Rangoon and desired them to leave the town immediately with their women and children and take refuge in the English ships anchored in the river.

Lambert's Stratagem and its Success

Lambert then resorted to a stratagem calculated to force the Burmese to fire the first shot. A ship—usually called the *Yellow Ship*—belonging to the King of Burma was anchored a little above Lambert's fleet.

> "On the 6th, at night, Commodore Lambert seized the King's ship, which he held in his possession at anchor opposite the town for three days, during which time the Burmese made no attempt to retake it, but on the contrary, conciliatory visits were paid to the Commodore by the authorities of the highest rank in the neighbourhood." (*How Wars are Got up in India* by Cobden, p. 66)

But the Commodore paid no heed to the requests of the Burmese officials for the ship's release. In despair, the officials had to make it plain that if any attempt was made to take the King's ship out of the harbour, then it would become the officials' bounden duty to resist the attempt, even by force if it became necessary. The use of force by the Burmese was exactly what Lambert wanted, and so on 10th January, 1852, he started towing away the *Yellow Ship*. What happened thereafter was thus reported by Commodore Lambert himself:

> "Her Majesty's steam-sloop *Hermes* with the King of Ava's ship in tow, passed us at half past nine, when the stockade opened a sharp cannonade on Her Majesty's ship *Fox* which was instantly returned with shot and shell, and the Burmese battery was in a short time silenced. On the smoke clearing away, not a person was to be seen on the shore or in the boats."

> "Our fire, I have no doubt, must have done great execution, for I have reason to believe that at least 3,000 men were opposed to us." (*Parliamentary Papers*)

Commodore Lambert's stratagem had succeeded. The Burmese did fire the first shot. Why they had to do so is thus related by Cobden:

> "There is no reason to suppose that any act of hostility would have been committed had the King's ship been merely kept at anchor in the power of the British. But to have allowed a Burmese ship of war to be towed out of the river by foreigners passing under the great stockade or battery without molestation would have involved the disgrace and destruction of those who were responsible to the King of Ava for the protection of his property." (*How Wars are Got up in India* by Cobden, pp. 66–69)

Conciliatory Attempt by Governor of Rangoon

On 2nd February, 1852, the Governor of Rangoon wrote to Lord Dalhousie, through the latter's Secretary, Halliday, a letter which concluded thus:

> "Therefore, as soon as the officer which the Government of India is prepared to appoint, in conformity with existing treaties, shall arrive, a satisfactory and amicable arrangement can be made of the payment of the 9,000 rupees extorted from captains Lewis and Shepperd; also with reference to the re-delivery of the King of Ava's ship, seized by Commodore Lambert." (ibid., p. 77)

But the Governor-General wanted, not peace, but war, and so, even after receiving the above letter from the Governor of Rangoon, he issued orders for preparing an armed expedition against Burma. He also wrote to the Burmese Governor stating that the Burmese Government would have to pay a sum of one hundred thousand pounds as the price of peace.

> So the "war" was vigorously proceeded with, writes Cobden: "A war it can hardly be called. A rout, a massacre, or a visitation would be a more appropriate term. A fleet of war-steamers and other vessels took up their position in the river, and on

the 11th April, 1852, *being Easter Sunday,* they commenced operations by bombarding both the Rangoon and Dallah shores. Everything yielded like toywork beneath the terrible broadsides of our ships." (ibid., p. 98)

War Ends with the Annexation of Pegu

The "massacre" of the Burmese people continued for six or seven months and was stopped only after the annexation of Pegu in December, 1852. Pegu was the biggest, wealthiest and most fertile province of the Burmese Empire. It had long been famous for its reputed rich gold mines and constituted the chief financial resource of the Empire.

Cobden's Comments on the War

"These wars are carried on at the expense of the people of India ... What exclusive interest had the half-naked peasant of Bengal in the settlement of the claims of Captains Shepperd and Lewis, that he should alone be made to bear the expense of the war which grew out them?

Lord Dalhousie begins with a claim on the Burmese for less than a thousand pounds; which is followed by the additional demand of an apology from the Governor of Rangoon for the insult offered to our officers; next his terms are raised to one hundred thousand pounds, and an apology from the king's ministers; then follows the invasion of the Burmese territory; when, suddenly, all demands for pecuniary compensation and apologies cease, and His Lordship is willing to accept the cession of Pegu as a 'compensation' and 'reparation' for the past." (ibid., pp. 101–04)

General Cass on the War

The war had repercussions in America too. In December, 1852, Senator General Cass delivered a speech in the Senate of the United States of America, in the course of which he said:

"Another of the native Powers of Hindostan has fallen before the march of a great commercial corporation and its 8,000,000 or 10,000,000 of people have gone to swell the immense congregation of British subjects in India. And what do you think was the cause of the war which has just ended in the swallowing up of the Kingdom of Burma? ... Had we not the most irrefutable evidence we might well refuse credence to this story of real rapacity. But the fact is indisputable that England went to war with Burmah, and annihilated its political existence for the non-payment of the disputed demand of £ 910 ... Well does it become such a people to preach homilies to other nations upon disinterestedness and moderation?"

Resistance of Burmese People

The people of Burma, however, continued to resist the English, in every way open to them, including the use of armed force. The resistance continued till April, 1855, when a "revolution" was somehow staged in Ava, the capital of Burma, and a new king was installed on the throne. Thereafter, the province of Pegu became secure in English hands forever. As our readers must have noticed, we have founded our narrative of the Second Burmese War on Cobden's book, *How Wars are Got up in India,* from which we have quoted copiously. Cobden has, in writing his book, relied *almost entirely* upon the Parliamentary Papers. So the authenticity of the events related above is beyond question.

17

USURPATIONS

"Lapse"—Paramountcy

By the year 1834, the Directors of the East India Company had made up their minds to exercise openly the right of suzerainty over such of the Indian States and their rulers as had concluded friendly alliances and/or treaties with the Company's Government of India. A beginning was made with the arrogation by the said Government of the authority and the option to recognise or not an adoption of son and heir by an Indian ruler who had no son of his own. The instructions given by the Court of Directors of the East India Company in 1834 to their Government in India were:

> "Whenever it is optional with you to give or to withhold your consent to adoptions, the indulgence should be the exception and not the rule, and should never be granted but as a special mark of approbation."

Accordingly, the States of Colaba, Mandvi and Ambala had been seized some time before Lord Dalhousie took over. He too had been instructed by the Secretary of State for India that on the death "of a prince without a son", "no adoption should be permitted" and his State "should be merged in the British Empire".

Lord Dalhousie carried out these instructions vigorously and usurped state after state sometimes two within a year and attempted in each case to give the usurpation a legal colour by a fantastic interpretation and application of the English legal doctrine of "lapse". This was later exposed and condemned by the "highest legal authority in England, the Judicial Committee of the Privy Council", whose observations are quoted by us in a subsequent paragraph, "Tanjore and Karnatic" (p. 251). Where the existence of a son and heir rendered the application of "lapse" utterly impossible, as in the case of Oudh, Lord Dalhousie's Government simply walked in and brazenly seized the State even when the ruler was alive, on flimsy pretexts. Where flagrant seizure of the entire State was considered impolitic or unmanageable, as in the case of Hyderabad, Lord Dalhousie personally used threats to coerce the ruler to give possession of a big slice of his territory to the Company's Government under some fictitious legal formula.

Apparently, Lord Dalhousie himself realised that the doctrine of "lapse" was a broken reed and could not be relied upon to justify the usurpations made under its cloak because:

(i) None of the "lapsed" States had ever been held as a grant made by the British Crown or the East India Company and so could not revert or lapse to either of them, and

(ii) The denial of the right of a ruler, in treaty with the Company's Government, to adopt a son and heir in accordance with his personal law, not only nullified his personal law but also violated the treaty and engagement made with him.

So Lord Dalhousie had recourse to "paramountcy", and, when annexing Nagpur declared that the State had lapsed to the "paramount power in India". Since then, up till now (1929), every act or omission, indefensible under a law or treaty, has been defended by the Governments of India and England under the dictum "Paramountcy is Paramount". We might add that when Lord Dalhousie left India, his acquisitions had expanded the British Empire in India very nearly to its present (1929) boundaries and the limits beyond which far-sighted people glimpsed the great calamity which was to overwhelm the English Company ruling the country, and which dealt a death blow to the policy of annexation under "lapse". In other words, having "sown the wind", Lord Dalhousie left his successor to "reap the whirlwind" of 1857.

We now proceed to give seriatim the story of each unlawful acquisition of the Dalhousie regime.

Annexation of Satara

The first victim of usurpation under the distorted doctrine of "lapse" was the State of Satara, The Rajas of Satara were the descendants of Shivaji and in 1818 the Company had issued a proclamation assuring all the rulers and *Jagirdars* who constituted the Maratha Confederacy at the time that their and their successors' rights of rule, ownership and possession of their respective States and holdings would never be questioned or interfered with by the Company. Further in order to enlist the support of the Satara State against the Peshwa Bajirao, a clear, specific and definite undertaking had been given to the Raja of Satara, that if the latter helped the English to crush the Peshwa, then the Raja would be re-instated and installed as the head of the Maratha Empire in place of the Peshwa Bajirao and that the Empire's capital would be shifted from Poona to Satara. The Raja of Satara, relying upon this solemn promise given by the English, had forthwith issued a proclamation isolating the Peshwa Bajirao who was ultimately destroyed.

Raja Partapsinh of Satara had proved himself a shrewd and capable ruler and so soon became a sore in English eyes. Sir Robert Grant, the Governor of Bombay, decided that he should be crushed. A plot was successfully engineered and Raja Pratapsinh was taken in to custody and deported to Benares. His brother was installed on the Satara *Gadi*. Raja Pratapsinh died in prison at Benares and on his death, Hobhouse, the Secretary of State for India, wrote to Lord Dalhousie:

> "The death of the ex-Raja of Satara certainly comes at a very opportune moment. The reigning Raja is, I hear, in very bad health, and it is not at all impossible we may soon have to decide upon the fate of his territory. I have a very strong opinion that on the death of the present prince without a son, *no adoption should be permitted, this petty principality should be merged in the British Empire*; and if the question is decided in my 'day of sexton- ship', I shall leave no stone unturned to bring about that result" (italics ours). (Letter from Hobhouse to Lord Dalhousie, 24th December, 1847)

Raja Pratapsinh's brother too died shortly after. Both the brothers had adopted sons which they were definitely allowed under their personal (Hindu) law. Lord Dalhousie carried out the above-quoted instructions of his superior. He refused to recognise either of the adoptions and, distorting the English doctrine of "lapse", declared the Satara State to have lapsed to the English Company's Government. The State was seized and annexed to the Company's possessions in 1848, in flagrant violation of the terms of the proclamation of the Company's Government, and the assurances and pledges specifically given to the Raja of Satara.

Sambalpur and Jaitpur

The independent but weak State of Sambalpur and the small Jaitpur State were the next victims of the Dalhousie regime's version of the doctrine of "lapse".

In 1849, the year following the annexation of Satara, Sambalpur was annexed and absorbed in the then Central Provinces, and is now (1929) part of the Bihar and Orissa Province of British India.

In the same year Jaitpur State in Bundelkhand was similarly seized and annexed because it was held to have "lapsed".

Neither of the Rajas of these States had ever held from, or had been granted by, the East India Company or the British Crown their respective territories. Therefore the same could not "lapse" under law to either of them.

The Nizam Coerced to Part with Berar

At the end of the Second Maratha War, Berar, as stated earlier, became part of the dominion of Hyderabad.

Berar's misfortune was that it grew the best cotton in India, and so it had to be possessed by the Company for the benefit of their countrymen, the textile manufacturers of England. But according to Robert Knight ("The Statesman", July 1, 1880, p. 162), "the process ... was only delayed by the wars in the Punjab and Burma". When these were over, Lord Dalhousie turned his attention to Hyderabad. In due course, riots between the Hindus and the Mussalmans and other disturbances became widespread throughout Berar. For putting them down, the Nizam requested but was refused the help of the Company's Subsidiary Army, which was maintained by him at an enormous cost. Instead, the Nizam was pressed to employ and maintain an additional contingent in Berar officered by Englishmen. The Nizam yielded once again, and it led to a further increase in his already heavy indebtedness to the several English banking concerns which had established themselves in Hyderabad and had readily advanced as loans to the Nizam all the money that was needed to meet his "forced" commitments to the Company. He was thus "pushed on the road to ruin". When he was on the brink or bankruptcy, the Company demanded from him the repayment of these loans, as though they had been advanced by the Company and *not* by the said private English banking concerns.

On 6th November, 1851, Lord Dalhousie wrote to the Nizam personally a very rude and threatening letter. Some small fortresses in the Nizam's dominion manned by the latter's faithful Arab soldiery were still holding out and would not capitulate to the English. In the letter Lord Dalhousie advised the Nizam not "to provoke the resentment of the British Government ... whose power can crush you at will", and further told him that he stood in "imminent danger" and must disband his Arab soldiers, and see to the "early liquidation of the accumulated debt" which, as stated above, the Nizam was *not owing to the Company*, but to others. Finally, Lord Dalhousie demanded that the Nizam must "forthwith make over" to the Company Berar, his richest province which constituted nearly one-third of his territory. The contingent employed by the Nizam, but officered by Englishmen, was stationed in Berar and in virtual occupation of the province, So the Nizam had to yield, and handed over Berar. It was then solemnly declared by the English that Berar would be held by them only till the "accumulated debt" had been liquidated, and would, thereafter, be restored to the Nizam. It would, however, appear that, according to the English, the "debt" had not been liquidated even after 50 years, and Lord Curzon made the Nizam "lease" Berar *and his sovereignty over it permanently* to the Government of India.

Annexation of Nagpur State

Writes Ludlow:

> "It is clear ... that the Nizam's cessions ... led to the annexation of Nagpur in 1854. For, as Lord Dalhousie phrased it, the 'essential interests of England' required that the territory of Nagpur should pass under the British Government. The great field of the best and cheapest cotton grown in India lies in the valley of Berar ... and in 'the districts adjacent to it'. Those

'districts adjacent' were in Nagpur. During the past year, the Government had obtained ... not the sovereignty indeed, but the ... possession and administration of the valley of Berar. The cottonfields were, however, 'inaccessible for want of railroads'; the possession of Nagpur would enable us to make them. We took both ..." (*Thoughts on the policy of the Crown towards India*, Allahabad reprint)

In the 1826 treaty of "perpetual friendship and alliance" entered into by the Company and the Nagpur State, the latter had been described as "one of the substantive powers of India". General Low, a Member of the Governor-General's Council, has been quoted by the historian Kaye as having recorded in a Minute book that the Treaty "did not limit the succession" to the Nagpur *Gadi* to "heirs of the body" of a deceased Raja. According to Major Evans Bell:

"In the year 1844 the Governor-General-in-Council, in reply to the Resident Colonel Spiers' request for instructions in the event of the Raja dying without issue, made a distinct recognition of the right of adoption by the Raja, and by members of the family in case of his death without having made an adoption." (*The Empire in Asia*)

The above was the legal position when the last Raja of Nagpur, Raghoji Bhonsle III died on 11th December, 1833. He had no son and hence a near relation, a youth named Yeshwantrao, was duly adopted. The adopted son performed the funeral rites of his adopted father, whom he was clearly entitled to succeed. Yet barely six weeks after the death of Raghoji Bhonsle III, Lord Dalhousie, on 28th January, 1834, declared that "the sovereignty of Nagpur had lapsed to the paramount power, for there was no heir or representative of the Bhonsle family or even a claimant to the throne of Nagpur". Lord Dalhousie has also recorded a specious reason for his refusal to recognise the adoption of Yeshwantrao. To quote Major Evans Bell again:

"Lord Dalhousie protested that the Ranees' natural jealousies, their feelings and interest *must* make them averse to the continuance of the Raj in the person of an adopted son, and it would really be inhuman ..." (ibid.)

As a matter of fact, the Ranees

> "... were never invited to express an opinion on the subject of the succession ... they were abruptly told that there was no heir to the *musnud* and that the Rajah's dominions had *'reverted to the British Government'*" (italics ours) (ibid.)

How could the dominion "revert" to a government which was *not* the original grantor? Another English writer (presumably Sir Richard Temple) has stated:

> "The policy of the Government of Lord Dalhousie has secured to us a province not much inferior to Oudh or the Punjab."

The same writer also describes the difficulties which faced the Government in acquiring Nagpur in any other way. He writes:

> "A kingdom constituted like that of Nagpur might have been difficult to conquer but when once annexed ... was easy of retention. The officers of the King ... were *not easily seduced*, and the opposition they might make would be considerable."

We leave it to our readers to draw their own conclusions about the real reasons for Nagpur's annexation and for the way in which it was accomplished.

Loot of Nagpur Palace

The historian Kaye observes:

> "... The spoliation of the palace ... followed closely upon the extinction of the Raj ... the venerable Bankha Baee ... was so stung by a sense of the indignity offered to her, that she threatened to fire the palace if the furniture was removed. But the furniture was removed, and the jewels of the Bhonsle family, with a few propitiatory exceptions were sent to the Calcutta market ... Between five and six hundred elephants, camels, horses and bullocks were sold for £1,300 ... a pair of hackery bullocks, valued at 100 rupees were sold in the above sale for 5 rupees."

"Sins of Fathers Visited upon Children"

The Bhonsle Rajas were Shivaji's descendants. Yet when patriots Nana Fadnavis and Haider Ali were struggling to preserve the independence of India from the English Company's rapacity, the then Bhonsle Raja of Nagpur had sided with the English and had materially helped them to make a beginning with the establishment of the British Empire in India. His last descendant had to pay for this betrayal of his country.

Annexation of Jhansi

The region of Jhansi, situated in Bundelkhand, was, in the times of the early Peshwas, administered by a Subedar appointed by them. With the passage of time the office of the Subedar became hereditary. In 1817, a treaty had been concluded between the Company and the then Subedar, Ramchandrarao, whereby the Governor-General agreed to acknowledge "Row Ram Chand, his heirs and successors, hereditary rulers of the territory enjoyed by the late Row Sheo Bhow at the period of the commencement of the British Government". During the regime of Lord William Bentinck the title of Subedar was changed to that of "Raja" in 1832.

Gangadharrao, the young Raja of Jhansi, died on 21st November, 1853. Sometime before his death, he had adopted as his son a boy named Damodarrao, who was a near relation of his. As stated by Major Evans Bell, the adoption ceremony was duly performed in accordance with the Hindu *Shastras* and law. Several English officers attended the ceremony, and the Company's Government was officially informed of the adoption.

All the same, Lord Dalhousie proclaimed the annexation of Jhansi and it was annexed on 13th March, 1854. In his Minutes dated 27th February, 1854, he had written:

"There is no heir of the body of the late Raja—there is no heir whatever of any Raja or Subedar of Jhansi with whom the British Government has at any time had relations."

There was no stipulation in the 1817 Treaty that the "heirs and successors" of Ramchandrarao had to be "male heirs of the body" of the deceased Subedar. Moreover, as pointed out by Major Evans Bell, the Subedar Ramchandrarao did not "hold his Principality as a grant ... because Ramchandrarao was already in possession" of it at the time of the 1817 Treaty, as clearly stated therein. At that time "there was no pretension", writes Major Evans Bell, "to the relations of sovereign and subject, for there already existed relations of amity and defensive alliance; there was no grant made, no *sunnud* issued, but a new treaty was concluded between two States."

> " ...... By the treaty of 1817," proceeds Major Bell, "it was certainly not contemplated by either party to the treaty that the heir of a Subedar of Jhansi could under any circumstances fail to be his successor. No other law was intended or thought of except the Hindu law of inheritance, in which adoption is an ordinary and essential incident. No article or stipulation in the treaty gave us the right to interfere with the operation of the Hindu law, to mutilate it or to substitute any other law of the descent." (*The Empire in India*, pp. 202-209)

The gross illegality and rank injustice of the usurpation of Jhansi brought its own nemesis some four years later, when the famous Rani Lakshmibai of Jhansi personally took the field against the English in 1857-58.

Tanjore and Karnatic

About the end of the eighteenth century, Sarboji, the Raja of Tanjore, had lost his sovereignty and Azamuddaula, the Nawab of Karnatic, had also lost his.

The former was forced by the then Governor-General to cede to the English the principality of Tanjore, with the exception of a tiny bit, and to become a sort of hereditary pensioner of theirs. Lord Dalhousie, undercover of the doctrine of "lapse", annexed the tiny bit too in 1855 and stopped the pension, as the Raja had died without a "male heir of the body". Major Evans Bell has stated that "the highest legal authority in England, the Judicial Committee of the Privy Council, emphatically denounced the Tanjore spoliation". We quote him below:

"Kamachi Bai, the senior widow of the Rajah of Tanjore, filed a bill in the Supreme Court of Madras, to recover possession of her deceased husband's private property, which has been sequestered by the local Government. The Court decided in her favour. The Government of Madras carried the case in appeal before the Judicial Committee of the Privy Council. The decree of the Supreme Court of Madras was reversed, because the Lords of the Privy Council held that the seizure was 'an act of State' and therefore not questionable in any municipal court. But Lord Kingsdown, who delivered the judgment, made use of the following emphatic language:"

"It is extremely difficult *to discover* in these papers *any ground of legal right on the part of the East India Company, or of the Crown of Great Britain to the possession of this Raj*, or of any part of the property of the Rajah on his death ... The Rajah was an independent sovereign of territories undoubtedly minute, and bound by treaties to a powerful neighbour, which left him practically little power of free action; *but he did not hold his territory, such as it was, as a fief of the British Crown, or of the East India Company; nor does there appear to have been any pretence for claiming ... it by any legal title*, either as an escheat or as *bona vacantia*." (italics ours)

The portions italicised by us are as much applicable to the other States annexed under the doctrine of "lapse" as they were to Tanjore, whose annexation was characterised "as a most violent and unjustifiable measure" by the Attorney-General, who appeared before the Privy Council *not* for the Government of Madras (the Appellant) but for the Respondent, Rani Kamachi Bai.

Lord Wellesly had installed Azamuddaula on the Karnatic *Gadi* and the latter had obediently signed the treaty dictated by the Governor-General whereby the entire Karnatic territory was ceded by him to the Company and Azamuddaula's Nawabdom was limited to the capital town of Arcot and his residence to the Chipok palace. Mohammad Ghaus, the last Nawab of Karnatic, died in October, 1855, also without an heir. About the time of his death, Lord Harris, the Governor of Madras, wrote in one of his Minutes to the Governor-General:

"The semblance of royalty, without any of the power, is a mockery of authority which must be pernicious … it is impolitic and unwise to allow a pageant to continue, which, though it has been politically harmless, may at any time become a nucleus for sedition and agitation."

Apparently, Lord Dalhousie was of the same view for he refused to recognize Azam Jah—the deceased Nawab's heir as the Nawab of Karnatic. Once again the doctrine of "lapse" was resorted to and even the remnants of the Karnatic territory left to the Nawabs were annexed.

Nawab Wazirs of Oudh

Let us briefly recapitulate the story of Oudh up to the Dalhousie regime in order to provide a background for what follows.

Oudh was originally a part of the vast Mughal Empire, and the Nawabs of Oudh were the hereditary Wazirs of the Mughal Emperor, and were designated "Nawab Wazirs". With the decay of the Mughal Empire the Nawab Wazirs became progressively independent rulers. In 1764, the Company established contact with the reigning Nawab Wazir, and advised him to make use of its troops for the security of his territory. He consented and the Company's troops were stationed in Oudh. For their maintenance the Nawab Wazir agreed to pay Rs. 16 lacs per year to the Company. Later, it proved to be the thin end of the wedge as the troops rapidly swelled into the Subsidiary Army, for the maintenance of which the Nawab Wazir had to cede to the Company his Rohilkhand and Doaba regions. The annual net revenue from these was not less than Rs. two crores.

In 1801 a fresh treaty was concluded between the Nawab Wazir and the Company, whereby it was agreed by the latter that the remaining territory of Oudh would forever remain under the rule of the Nawab Wazirs, generation after generation, and that the English would never interfere with the Nawab Wazirs' administration of the same. But the clause which sounded the death-knell of the Nawab Wazirs' independence and proved to be the root-cause of all their future troubles, was the one whereby the English were vested with the sole responsibility for the security of Oudh "against all foreign and domestic enemies".

Thereafter, Oudh became the milch-cow of the Company, which the succeeding Governors-General and representatives of the Company milked at will, and to the extent of tens of crores of rupees, either as loans, which were never repaid, or as outright gifts to help not only the Company but also a number of Englishmen individually. All that the Nawab Wazirs got in return was the empty title of "His Majesty the King of Oudh", which the Marquess of Hastings bestowed upon the then Nawab Wazir in 1819, not so much in appreciation of the Nawab Wazirs munificence as in order to achieve the complete break-off of the latter from the Mughal Emperor and to make him entirely dependent on the English for his very existence. Whenever the English needed money, the Nawab Wazir, himself in sore financial straits, had to exact it from his people. As time passed, the English demands became heavier and more frequent, and the Nawab Wazirs as well as their people grew poorer day by day.

A British Resident was posted at Lucknow, the capital of Oudh, and English interference in the Nawab Wazir's administration was extensively resorted to English officers were put in charge of the administration of a number of regions. All this brought in its wake the obviously intended maladministration of the entire State. Sir Henry Lawrence wrote in "The Calcutta Review" (1845):

> "If ever there was a device for insuring mal-government, it is that of a Native Ruler and Minister, both relying on foreign bayonets and directed by a British Resident."

The English, however, held the Nawab Wazir responsible for all the evils which his people suffered from, and roundly accused him of inefficiency as a ruler, which they stated, led to widespread discontent of the people of Oudh. Charles Ball in his *History of the Indian Mutiny* (Vol. I, p. 152) gives the lie direct lo these allegations. He writes:

> "As a matter of fact, the true and effectual way of introduction of an administration which would render the people happy would have been to recall the British Residents back and to give the Nabob a free hand in the administration of his

dominion. *Thus the whole guilt of unrest in his territory rests on the head of the Company."* (italics ours)

But the "King of Oudh", as he was designated by the English, was rendered even more helpless and bound hand and foot to the English will by the treaty of 1837.

Wajid Ali Shah, the Last "King of Oudh"

Such was the state of affairs in Oudh when in 1847, the year preceding Lord Dalhousie's taking over, Wajid Ali Shah ascended the throne. He was a sensible and energetic young man, who saw clearly what had been basically wrong with the Oudh administration, and immediately set about effecting some much-needed reforms. He gave top priority to the reorganisation and strengthening of such troops as were still under his control. With that aim, he not only made new rules but saw to it that they were strictly observed by everyone, including himself. All the troops of the Lucknow *Durbar* had to assemble at the Parade ground every morning at a certain appointed hour, to be drilled under his personal supervision. He was meticulously punctual in reaching the parade ground in uniform and on horse-back. According to Metcalfe, if anything delayed him, which was extremely rare, he would fine himself publicly and pay the fine fixed by him for unpunctuality on the part of anyone else.

The Company's representatives did not like it at all, and forced him to give up his attendance at the drilling of his troops. Wajid Ali Shah was the first "King of Oudh" who thought of and worked for getting rid of the pernicious English interference in his administration. This was a grave offence in English eyes and inevitably led to his downfall. Naturally enough, the English decided that with such a "King" at the head of its administration, the annexation of Oudh could no longer be delayed.

Lure of Oudh

Lord Dalhousie, who had taken over in 1848, saw that Wajid Ali Shah was working to save his country from English rapacity, and there was a risk of the much-coveted Oudh slipping out of the English grasp. He too could not resist the lure of Oudh, not only because it was a most fertile and prosperous region or because "no climate could be finer than that of Oudh", but chiefly because its wealth was considered practically inexhaustible as it had served, for half-a-century continuously, "as a wet nurse to relieve the difficulties of the East India Company's finances".

Lord Dalhousie's Difficulty and Decision

Oudh could not be annexed under even Lord Dalhousie's version of "lapse". Wajid Ali Shah was already on the throne and had been acknowledged as the King of Oudh by the English when Lord Dalhousie took over. Even if Wajid Ali Shah died as some other Indian rulers had done during the Dalhousie regime, he had more than one legitimate son and heir living, who were "heirs, male of the body" and entitled to succeed. There was no *casus belli* either, as all the treaties had been scrupulously observed by Wajid Ali Shah. Neither could one be created. Lord Dalhousie cut the Gordian knot by claiming that Wajid Ali Shah was not suitably reforming his administration and was, in fact, incapable of doing so. On that ground Lord Dalhousie, a little before he left India, proclaimed his decision to annex Oudh. In 1856 he sent Outram the Resident at Lucknow to Wajid Ali Shah, with instructions to get the latter's signatures on a letter of voluntary abdication. Wajid Ali Shah refused to sign it, in spite of the bribes and threats held out to him by Outram. After three days of futile efforts to get Wajid Ali Shah to sign the letter of abdication, Lord Dalhousie took the bull by the horns, trampled into dust all the treaties till then made with the Nawab Wazirs, 'Kings' of Oudh, and ordered the soldiers of the Subsidiary Army to march into the Lucknow Palace of Wajid Ali Shah, who was taken into custody and sent to Calcutta as a captive. The Company's soldiers plundered the palace and its inmates, and dishonoured the Begums in the manner which had become traditional in the armies employed by the Company or officered by Englishmen. The annexation of Oudh became an accomplished fact.

Vilification of Wajid Ali Shah

We have earlier quoted the historian Kaye to the effect that it had become customary with the Company's representatives in India, first to grab an Indian ruler's territory, and then to degrade him in public estimation by besmirching his personal and moral character. The custom was duly observed in the case of the unfortunate Wajid Ali Shah too. Sir Edwin Arnold was pressed into service for writing a book in which Wajid Ali Shah has been depicted as a hopelessly depraved and dissolute man addicted to women and wine, who had no time for anything except the pleasures of the flesh. It is hardly possible to contradict the lies in the book after about 75 years, but we would point to one fact. If a monarch is as black a devil as Wajid Ali Shah has been alleged to be, then his subjects hate him like poison and welcome his downfall. Did the subjects of Wajid Ali Shah do so? The very next year provided the answer. So great was their anger and indignation at the treatment meted out by the English to Wajid Ali Shah, that Hindus as well as Mussalmans of Lucknow and Oudh fought the English relentlessly in the upheaval of 1857.

Oppression of Oudh Estate-holders

The "cruel wrong" done to the *Taluqdars* and *Zamindars*, big and small, of Oudh, who had held grants for generations from successive Nawab Wazirs of Oudh has been described in detail by Sir John Kaye. Lord Dalhousie appointed what was called "The Inam Commission" to investigate the titles of all the estate-holders, and even of small land-holders in the country. The Commission investigated some 35,000 holdings and *Jagirs*, and declared confiscated to the Company as many as 21,000 of them, big and small.

Departure of Lord Dalhousie

Almost immediately after the annexation of Oudh, Lord Dalhousie left India. Sir Edwin Arnold in his book on Lord Dalhousie's administration writes:

"The administration of British India, under the Marquis of Dalhousie, consummated a policy and closed a period ... Beneath his rule the territory of 'the British merchants trading in the East' received its latest extension; and at his departure, the sun of their power verged to a stormy setting."

BEFORE THE 1857 REVOLUTION

Lord Canning

In 1856 Lord Canning succeeded Lord Dalhousie as Governor-General of India. His regime was marked by the countrywide conflagration of 1857 which, at one time, appeared likely to reduce to ashes the edifice of the British "Empire" in India, built up by the English over a period of a hundred years by the use of every artifice they could lay their hands on.

Plassey

As a matter of fact, the fire had been lighted on the battlefield of Plassey. "We will avenge Plassey" was one of the war-cries most frequently used by the 1857 revolutionaries. Some Delhi newspapers prominently published a prophecy in May/June 1857 to the effect that 23rd of June, 1857, the centenary-day of the Battle of Plassey, would see the end of the English domination of India.

From Plassey to Vellore

We have already narrated at some length the story of the British rule in India from Clive to Dalhousie. Throughout this period the discontent and the indignation of the suffering people of India, from prince to pauper, had kept the fire smouldering underground. There were some sporadic outbursts, like the bitter and unrelenting fight for freedom put up by Nana Fadnavis and Haider Ali, and the attempts made by both to win the help of the Mughal Emperor and other Indian rulers for their cause. The 1806 Mutiny at Vellore, by the Indian troops of the East India Company, was an indication that the cauldron of revolt was still simmering, although it took another 50 years to boil over and result in the most devastating catastrophe that ever befell the British Empire in India.

Fuel to Fire

But for the events in the Dalhousie regime, the fire would have possibly died out. The East India Company's Empire-hunger dictated the policy followed by Lord Dalhousie. The policy initiated by the Company had the backing of the British Secretary of State for India too. Neither, apparently, realised that they were blowing the dying embers into a conflagration which did consume the East India Company.

In the preceding chapters we have narrated how some of the Indian States' territories were usurped or acquired by force and coercion, how tens of thousands of the landed aristocracy and gentry were reduced to penury. Earlier, we have also described the deliberate, planned and systematic ruination of India's external and internal trade and commerce, its industries, and handicrafts, and even its national system of education.

Added to all these was the recently-developed haughty behaviour of Englishmen generally towards Indians, high or low. Any Indian riding within sight of an Englishman was forced to get down and walk. The English officials of the Company made it a rule publicly to ride rough-shod over the religious susceptibilities of the "natives" and their religious or social customs. A beginning was also made with the extinction of the Indian system of medicine by the promulgation of an order (in Saharanpur) prohibiting the practice of medicine by *Ayurvedic* or *Unani* physicians. Even a *pardanashin* woman had to go to the public hospital set up by the Company.

Immediate Causes of the 1857 Upheaval

At least five causes can be enumerated whose cumulative effect was the rising-up in arms of the people of India under the flag of Bahadur Shah, the last Mughal Emperor.

(i) The humiliating treatment to which the Mughal Emperor was subjected by the English, 'and progressive usurpation by them of all his authority even to the extent of nominating his heir-apparent, without the slightest previous reference to him.

(ii) The unlawful deposition and deportation in captivity of the Nawab Wazir of Oudh followed by the annexation of Oudh and the confiscation of thousands of *Jagirs* and Estates in Oudh and elsewhere.

(iii) The usurpation by legal chicanery of a number of Indian States.

(iv) The rancour against the English which rankled in the heart of Nana Dhundopant, the adopted son of the last deposed Peshwa Bajirao, and,

(v) English objective of wholesale conversion of the "natives" to Christianity, and their persistent efforts to propagate it, by fair means and foul, particularly in the Indian army employed by them.

We shall now proceed to deal with each of these causes in some detail.

Mughal Emperor and the English

The turning-point in English relations with the Mughal Emperor was reached during the reign of the Emperor Shah Alam, who had in 1765 granted to Clive the *Diwani* of the Bengal and Bihar Provinces, and had later, granted *Jagirs* to the Company to set up its factories and commercial houses in Calcutta, Madras, Surat, etc., for which the Company paid to the Emperor the usual money tributes. It was also during Shah Alam's reign that the struggle between the Marathas and the English for the control over the Mughal Emperor, his Court and capital, started and was continued. The Marathas and Mahadji Sindhia succeeded, and took all the three under their wing together with some territory adjoining Delhi. Then General Lake, presented to Shah Alam a signed Memorandum of Agreement containing the promises and undertakings given by the Company. This was done to lead the Emperor up the garden path, and to secure his assent and help for the expulsion of the Marathas from Delhi. Arrangements were also made to pay to the Emperor Rs. 12 lacs per year for his personal use and an increment at a later date was also promised in the Memorandum. The old Emperor succumbed and, countenanced by him, the English drove the Marathas out of Delhi. The English then took over the responsibility of the security of the Emperor, his capital and his territory adjoining Delhi. For some time the English kept up the outward show of deference and subservience. The Company's coinage was inscribed with the Emperor's name and title, and the seal over which the Governor-General affixed his signatures on all communications addressed to the Emperor read *Badshah-La-Fidwi-i-Khas* (the Emperor's own faithful servant). But after expelling the Marathas from Delhi in 1804, the English threw off the mask, and Lord Wellesley suggested that the Emperor and his Court should leave the Red Fort and Delhi and shift to the Company's Fort at Monghyr. The Emperor, his Court and the people of Delhi became so furious at the suggestion that Wellesley thought it prudent to drop the proposal. But the seeds of suspicion and distrust of the English and of their real intentions were irretrievably sown in the minds of all the three and bore fruit in 1856–57. Shah Alam died in 1806 a disillusioned old man.

Shah Alam was succeeded by Emperor Akbar Shah. It was during his reign that Sir Charles Metcalfe, the Company's Resident at the Delhi Court, changed, in obedience to instructions, the customary ceremonial respects till then paid by his predecessors to the Emperor, and adopted an overbearing attitude highly derogatory to the dignity of the Emperor.

Akbar Shah desired to nominate one of his sons, Mirza Saleem, as his heir-apparent. It was, however, said that Mirza Saleem was hostile to the English, and so the latter found an excuse for sending him to Allahabad and kept him there under strict surveillance. As none of the promises and undertakings contained in General Lake's Memorandum had till then been honoured, Akbar Shah sent Raja Ram Mohan Roy as his Envoy Extraordinary to London to obtain the implementation of the Agreement. But the authorities there treated the Company's signed and sealed Memorandum of Agreement as no better than a mere scrap of paper. When the news reached Delhi, the Emperor's well-wishers and the people of Delhi generally became very gravely suspicious about the honesty and good faith of the

English, and were greatly perturbed about the future of the Royal Family and Delhi, if the English continued to be the arbiters of the destiny of both. Their hostility to the English grew in intensity and bitterness proportionately. Akbar Shah died in 1837 to be succeeded by Bahadur Shah, the last of the Mughal Emperors, who was fated to die an English prisoner.

Bahadur Shah tried to get an implementation of one of the terms of the Memorandum of Agreement which provided an increment in the annual payment of Rs. 12 lacs and asked for the increment. He was told that an increment could be given if he formally surrendered to the Company all of his own remaining rights, as also those of his family members and descendants. Bahadur Shah did not agree. Some years later, Ellenborough, immediately after taking over, forbade the presentation of *Nazars,* which according to the Delhi Court etiquette, had all along been presented to the Emperor either personally by the Governor-General and the Company's Commander-in-Chief or through the Resident, on the Emperor's birthday, and on the festivals of Id and Nowroz. In 1839 the heir-apparent to the Mughal throne died, and Bahadur Shah wanted to declare another son of his, Prince Jawan Bakht, as the heir-apparent. Jawan Bakht was a very promising and self-respecting young man, the son of his gifted mother Zeenat Mahal. She later proved to be an uncommonly capable organiser in the 1857 Revolution. The English did not approve of Bahadur Shah's choice, and so the Governor-General entered into a secret pact with another son of Bahadur Shah, Mirza Farukh. The latter agreed in writing that immediately after ascending the throne, he would leave the Red Fort and Delhi, and go to live wherever the English directed him. Lord Dalhousie then had Mirza Farukh formally proclaimed in Delhi as the heir-apparent against the express wishes of Bahadur Shah. Then Mirza Farukh too died in 1854. Bahadur Shah had nine sons then living and he still wanted Jawan Bakht, the most promising amongst them, to be the heir-apparent. All the other eight sons agreed with their father's choice and supported it in a written declaration signed by all of them. The declaration was personally handed over to the Resident by Bahadur Shah himself. But the English had other plans, as they had decided to abolish the title of Emperor and to do away with every single symbol or token pertaining to the status of an

Emperor of India. They made overtures to Mirza Quoyash, one of the nine sons of Bahadur Shah, and when he (Quoyash) agreed to their terms in writing, the English publicly recognised him as the heir-apparent. No prior reference at all was made to Bahadur Shah, who was officially informed in 1856 that Mirza Quoyash had agreed to the following terms and had been nominated heir-apparent by them. The terms as communicated to Bahadur Shah were:

(i) That after succeeding to the throne, Mirza Quoyash will not bear the title of "Emperor" and will be called "Prince",

(ii) That Mirza Quoyash will have to vacate the Red Fort at Delhi, and

(iii) That instead of a lac of rupees per month which are being paid to Bahadur Shah, Mirza Quoyash will receive only Rs. 15,000/-

This was the last straw and the smouldering fires of revolt burst into furious flames shortly afterwards, when the Emperor, his Court and capital became the rallying-point of the revolutionaries of 1857 who fought under his flag.

Oudh

The rape of Oudh has been described by us in the preceding chapter. It has been recorded in more than one book of history that hundreds of thousands of people of thousands of villages in Oudh were deeply moved by the calamities that had overtaken their ruler, their *Tahludars* and *Zamindars,* who were reduced to pitiful straits by the forcible annexation. The villagers suffered too under the Company's administration, which closely followed the pattern described by J. S. Sullivan, a Member of the Madras Council, as follows:

> "Upon the extermination of a native state, an Englishman takes the place of the sovereign under the name of Commissioner; three or four of his associates displace as many dozens of the native official aristocracy, while some hundreds of our troops take the place of the many thousands that every native chief

supports. The little court disappears, trade languishes, the capital decays, *the people are impoverished, the Englishman flourishes, and acts like a sponge drawing up riches from the banks of the Ganges, and squeezing them down upon the banks of the Thames.*" (Italics ours) *(A Plea for the Princes of India* p. 67)

The reason why the people of Oudh were amongst the leading and most active revolutionaries was the fact that most of those who had enlisted in the Company's army hailed from Oudh, and the atrocities committed on the sepoys' kith and kin in the villages under the Company's rule had become unbearable, inflaming the sepoys to an open revolt against the Company.

Usurpations and Fraudulent Acquisitions

The annexations and acquisitions, one after another, of Satara, the Punjab, Sambalpur, Jetpur, Pegu, Sikkim, Nagpur, Jhansi, etc., have already been narrated. Their effects on the people of India have thus been characterised by the historian Ludlow:

> "Surely, the natives of India must be less than human if their feelings could not be moved under such circumstances in favour of the victims of annexation, and against the annexer. Surely there was not a woman whom such annexation did not tend to make our enemy, not a child whom they did not tend to train up in hatred to the *Firangee* rule." (*Thoughts on the Policy of the Crown*, pp. 35, 36)

Denial of Nana Dhundopant's Just Claim

In 1818, the Company's Government had agreed to give to the last Peshwa, Bajirao, an annual pension of Rs. 8 lacs for his own maintenance, and "the support and maintenance of his family-members and dependants". He was also granted the Bithoor *Jagir* (near Kanpur), to which he was externed from his capital. He lived at Bithoor thereafter with some 8,000 souls, who had accompanied him in his exile, and who were supported by Bajirao out of the pension. In 1827, Bajirao had adopted Nana Dhundopant, then a child of three, as his son. Bajirao died when Nana was about 27. He was, in the words of Sir John Kaye, a

> "... quiet, unostentatious young man, not at all addicted to any extravagant habits, and invariably showing a ready disposition to attend to the advice of the British Commissioner". (*History of the Sepoy War*, Vol. I, p. 101)

On the death of Bajirao, the pension was stopped and even the payment of its arrears was refused. When Nana protested he was told that in addition to the stoppage of the pension, the Bithoor *Jagir* too was liable to be retaken by the Company if it so desired. Nana submitted a memorial to Lord Dalhousie founding his claim on previous treaties and engagements by the Company, and prayed that the pension be continued. The prayer was rejected. Nana then sent to England a competent representative of his, Azeemullah Khan, to appeal to the British Government. The latter too turned a deaf ear to the appeal. Sir John Kaye, Sir G. O. Trevelyan, Charles Bowle and R. M. Martin, the noted historians, have all of them declared that Nana's claim was just and fair. Its rejection embittered Nana and from then onwards he devoted himself to plans for delivering himself and his countrymen from the English clutches. Ultimately he became one of the top leaders of the 1857 Revolution.

Propagation of Christianity

Some sixty years before 1857, the front-rank politicians in England had arrived at the conclusion that the only way to secure the permanence of English rule over India was the wholesale conversion to Christianity of all Indians, civil as well as military. Thereafter, steps had been continuously taken to reach that goal. As related earlier, a beginning was made in Madras which offered the most promising field for the propagation of Christianity. But when efforts were made and various ways and means adopted to convert the Indian soldiers in the Company's army too, the result was the Vellore Mutiny described in Chapter XXVII.

Not only political exigency but also religious fanaticism inspired the English ambition to proselytise the whole of India. Rev. Kennedy, the English divine wrote:

> "Whatever misfortunes come on us, as long as our Empire in India continues, so long let us not forget that our chief work is the propagation of Christianity in the land until Hindustan, from Cape Comorin to the Himalayas, embraces the religion of Christ and *until it condemns the Hindoo and the Moslem religions,* our efforts must continue persistently. For this work, we must make all efforts we can and *use all power and all the authority in our hands* ..." (Italics ours) Even so responsible a person as Mr. Mangles, the Chairman of the Directors of the East India Company, said in the House of Commons:

> "Providence has entrusted the extensive Empire of Hindustan to England in order that the banner of Christ should wave triumphant from one end of India to the other. Everyone must exert all his strength that there may be no dilatoriness on any account in continuing in the country the grand work of making all India Christian."

Similar ideas were expressed by Lord Macaulay in his writings and, to a certain extent, shaped the educational policy and the system of education followed by the English rulers of India.

The enthusiasm for the conversion of the Indian military personnel cooled down considerably after the Vellore Mutiny. Other ways were, however, adopted to intensify the propagation of Christianity amongst the people generally and to facilitate their conversion.

Under the Hindu Law, a convert from Hinduism, *ipso facto* lost all his rights to property vested in him by the mandatory provisions of Hindu Law. In 1832, a law was enacted to abrogate this provision in cases of Hindus converted to Christianity. Soon after the establishment of the Company's rule over India, the ancient rent-free *Jagirs* granted to thousands of temples and mosques were forfeited to the Company. It was made impossible for the prisoners in jails to observe their religious rites of prayers, etc. As mentioned before, the Hindu Law relating to adoption was nullified. Lord Canning supplemented these ways and means by spending lakhs of rupees from the Indian Exchequer in paying munificent salaries to archbishops, bishops and clergymen. In the Company's offices, its officers started pressure-tactics to convert their Indian employees. The missionaries and other preachers of Christianity took to public revilement of Hindu and Muslim faiths and to the use of abusive language in their references to the revered religious leaders of both. Captain T. Macan, in his evidence before the Commons Committee (22nd March, 1832), testified on his personal knowledge that a clergyman speaking at a street corner gathering told his Muslim audience that Mohammed, through whom they hoped that their sins would be forgiven, "was himself in hell", and that they too would be there, if they followed his teachings and principles.

Christian Missionary Zeal in The Punjab

The Punjab was annexed in 1849, and thereafter, vigorous and special efforts were made by Sir Henry Lawrence, Sir John Lawrence, Sir Robert Montgomery, Donald McLeod, Col. Edwardes and others to convert the Punjab into a model Christian Province. Several of them advocated the handing over of the educational department and its entire work to the missionaries and the giving of all financial help to the mission schools, as also the closing down of all other schools run by the Government. The Company's Directors held similar views with which Lord Dalhousie had to agree. Some Englishmen in authority went even further and wanted that:

(i) The Bible be taught and instruction in the Christian faith be made a "must" in all Government schools and colleges,

(ii) The Hindu and Muslim religious beliefs should in no way be encouraged or even tolerated by the Government,

(iii) No holidays for Hindu or Muslim festivals be observed in any Government department or office.

(iv) The Hindu and Muslim religious and secular laws should find no place in the Company's courts of law, and

(v) The celebration of Hindu and Muslim religious festivals be banned (*The Memorandum on the Elimination of all un-Christian Principles from the Government of British India* by Sir Herbert Edwards).

The programme in implementation of the above policy could not openly be carried out in its entirety in view of the then peculiar conditions prevailing in the country.

Propagation of Christianity in the Indian Army

The propagation had never been allowed to be at a complete standstill. According to the historian Nolan, the Company's Government progressively ignored and even ran counter to the religious sentiments, beliefs and prejudices of the Indian soldiery. English officers took to proselytising the sepoys as part of their work. An English Commander of the Bengal Infantry has written in his official report that for 28 years he has been continuously putting into practice the policy of converting the sepoys to Christianity, and that the saving of the un-Christian souls from the Devil has been an important part of his military duties. More informative light on this aspect of the Christian missionary propaganda is thrown by "A Hindoo of Bengal" in his contribution to the Journal *Causes of the Indian Revolt* (Published from London, by Edward Stanford, 6 Charing Cross) dated Calcutta, 18th August, 1858, from which we quote some extracts below:

> "At the beginning of the present year (1857) a great many colonels in the Indian army were detected in a task not less monstrous and arduous than that of Christianising it. It has afterwards transpired that some of these earnest ... worthies ... entered the army ... solely and wholly for the purpose of conversion. The army was specially selected, as in times of peace it affords the utmost leisure to both soldiers and commanders. And as there the heathens may be found in great abundance...without the trouble and expense and ... scampering from village to village ... They began preaching and distributing tracts and translations among the Hindoo and Mohammedan officers and soldiers. In the beginning these were tolerated, sometimes with disgust, and sometimes with indifference. When, however, the thing continued, when the evangelizing endeavours became more serious and troublesome, the sepoys of either persuasion felt

alarmed ... The 'Missionary Colonels' and 'Padre Lieutenants' as these curious militaries were called, emboldened by the toleration of the sepoys ... grew more violent ... and louder in their denunciation of Hinduism and Islam ... Mohammed and Rama, hitherto mere so-so beings turned sublime impostors and unmitigated blackguards ... By and by the proselytising Colonels tempted the sepoys to Christianity with bribes and offered promotions and other rewards to converts. The sepoys protested, and their European officers promised to make every sepoy that forsook his religion a Havildar, every Havildar a Subedar Major, and so on! Great discontent was the consequence."

It is over 72 years today (1929) since the above was published; during all these years the truth of the above statements has not been challenged by any writer English or European. On the contrary, the English editor of the journal, Malcolm Lewin, who had been at one time a judge of the Madras Supreme Court and later a Member of the Madras Council, contributed a preface to the *Causes of Indian Revolt* in which he made comments, based on his own experience, which we quote below:

"We are ignorant of each other, as members of society; the bond of union has been that of Spartan and Helot... we have insulted their caste; we have abrogated their laws of inheritance; we have changed their marriage institutions; we have ignored the most sacred rites of their religion; we delivered up their pagoda-property to confiscation; we have branded them in official records as 'heathens'; we have seized the possessions of their native princes, and confiscated the estates of their nobles; we have unsettled the country by our exactions, and collected the revenue by means of torture; we have sought to uproot the most ancient aristocracy of the world, and to degrade it to the condition of pariahs...if a tree be known by its fruits, if the morals of England and India are to be held as tests of their respective creeds, India would not lose by comparison."

Another factor which contributed to the sum-total of the Indian soldiers' deep discontent was the persistent indifference with which their real grievances about pay, living conditions and want of ordinary necessary amenities of human life were treated by their English officers.

Explosive Material

The five causes enumerated above had the cumulative effect of filling their cup of woe to the brim; the hearts of the entire Indian people in all walks of life were filled with distrust, anger and hatred of the English. The explosive material had been piling up during the hundred years of English rule. All that was needed was the emergence of a leader capable of igniting it into a country-wide conflagration, regardless of consequences.

True Picture of Revolution

Very probably because the Indian soldiers took the lead in it, the revolution has been called the "Sepoy Mutiny" or the "Sepoy War". In reality, it was much more than that. It was a war desperately waged by the princes and people of India, Hindus and Muslims, civil and military, for the emancipation of their country from foreign rule. In the words of Sir William Howard Russell:

> "......We had a war of religion, a war of race, and a war of revenge, of hope, of national determination to shake off the yoke of a stranger and to re-establish the full power of native Chiefs and the full sway of native religions." *(My Diary in India in the year 1858-59)*

Envoys of Nana Dhundopant and the ex-Raja of Satara in London

Nana Sahib's envoy, Azimullah Khan, and Rango Bapooji, whom the deposed Raja of Satara had sent to England as his envoy at about the same time, got together in London. Both had been sent by their respective masters on the mission of appealing to the British

Government against the injustice done to them by the Government of India. The rejection of their appeals by the British Government embittered both and brought them very close to each other. They discussed and evolved the outline of the next desperate step of armed rebellion. Thereafter, Rango Bapooji returned to India for securing the co-operation of the South Indian rulers in the projected rebellion. Azimullah Khan went on a tour of Europe for an assessment of England's status and influence on the continent and for securing the sympathy and, if possible, active help of at least some of the European powers for India's contemplated fight for freedom.

Azimullah Khan's European Tour

Azimullah Khan, who later became the second most prominent leader of the revolution, was a very able politician and spoke both English and French fluently. He invariably put on the Indian dress, and was a presentable man of attractive manners readily welcomed in the high social circles of London. Russell, the famous correspondent of the London *Times,* who met Azimullah Khan in Russia, relates an incident indicative of the latter's high personal courage. Russia was at war with England at that time and Azimullah Khan had gone to Russia to explore the possibility of an alliance between Nana Sahib and Russia against the English. One day when he and Russell were interestedly watching an artillery duel between the English and the Russians, a shell fell end exploded almost at Azimullah Khan's feet. Azimullah Khan did not move an inch according to Russell.

Azimullah Khan went to Italy, Turkey and Egypt too, but he does not appear to have met with much success in his mission. Lord Roberts has mentioned in his *Forty Years in India* that he had come across some letters written by Azimullah Khan to the Sultan of Turkey and to Omar Pasha about the English atrocities in India. Whilst the revolution was on, there were two reports widely current in the revolutionary circles. One was to the effect that some understanding had been arrived at between the Czar of Russia and Nana Sahib. The other was that the famous Italian patriot Garibaldi was about to sail from Italy with a contingent for the help of the Indian revolutionaries. It is said that he could not do so in time, on account of his own preoccupations with disturbances in Italy, and that later when he was on the point of sailing for India, he heard that the revolution in India was over.

Finalisation of Plans at Bithoor

Whilst Rango Bapooji was secretly carrying on from Satara an intensive propaganda for the revolution amongst the rulers and the people of Southern India, Azimullah Khan, on his return from Europe, got busy, in consultation with Nana Sahib, with the finalization of their plans for the revolution.

The main objective of the planners was first to rally the Hindus and the Muslims under Bahadur Shah's flag and fight the English till they were driven out of India, and then to establish afresh a proper Government under the Emperor for the administration of the country.

It was rightly realised that the revolution could succeed only if it caught the English napping and suddenly broke out on the same day all over the country. To ensure this a far-flung, secret and efficient organisation was the prime necessity and the planners set about it.

Propaganda and Secret Organisation

Bithoor was the centre from where the agents of the underground movement spread out into the country. It was so well-planned and comprehensive and progressed so secretly that even the ever-alert Englishmen had no inkling of what was a-foot. The competence and the capacity of those who inspired and led the movement and later led the revolution itself have elicited the unstinted admiration of several English writers. We quote from one of them:

> "But it is difficult to describe the wonderful secrecy with which the whole conspiracy was conducted and the forethought supplying the schemes, and the caution with which each group of conspirators worked apart, concealing the connecting links, and instructing them with just sufficient information for the purpose in view. And all was equalled only by the fidelity with which they adhered to each other."
> (*Western India* by Sir George Le Grand Jacob, K.C.S.I.)

Sometime before 1856, Nana Sahib had sent out from Bithoor his special emissaries to the *durbars* of all the Indian rulers from Delhi to Mysore and his secret agents went out in all directions to win over the Indian soldiers in the Company's armies and the people generally, and to secure the active cooperation and help of both in the projected revolution. In his letters to the rulers, Nana Sahib drew pointed attention to the way in which the English had swallowed up one Indian State after another for the achievement of their ambition to rule over the whole of India. "From one native court to another, from one extremity to another of the great continent of India, the agents of Nana Sahib had passed with overtures and invitations discreetly, perhaps mysteriously, worded to princes and chiefs of different races and religions."

The Delhi Emperor's Court at the Red Fort, Delhi, proved to be the most fertile soil for the seeds of the armed revolution to grow and flourish. The reasons for it have been mentioned already. Bahadur Shah, his capable wife Begum Zeenat Mahal and his counsellors unanimously decided to espouse the cause for which Nana Sahib and his followers were going to risk everything, namely, the country's freedom from foreign rule. The people of Delhi too did not lag behind and enthusiastically held secret meetings to form plans for joining the revolutionaries.

Oudh and the Revolution

According to Sir John Kaye, the last annexation (of Oudh) by the English had the most disquieting effect on the people, who began to ask themselves and each other, "Who can be safe and secure now?" and "What is the use of loyalty to the English who have unlawfully seized the State of a loyal friend and a faithful ally like the Nawab, who had invariably helped them when they most needed help?" He (Kaye) also states that the other Rajas and Nawabs who had been hesitating till then made up their minds and responded to Nana Sahib's appeals with promises of full co-operation and help.

Not only Wajid Ali Shah, the deposed and exiled Nawab and his shrewd Minister Alinaqi Khan, but all the *Taluqdars, Zamindars* and the whole population of Oudh were now ready for all the sacrifices which the success of the revolution was likely to demand. Begum

Hazrat Mahal, Wajid Ali Shah's talented wife, and Alinaqi Khan were amongst the prominent moving spirits of the revolution. The latter, in exile at Calcutta with Wajid Ali Shah, sent out (from Calcutta) his emissaries disguised as Muslim *Faqirs* or Hindu *sadhus*, to wherever the Indian soldiers of the Company were stationed, and carried out secret correspondence with their Indian officers. Begum Hazrat Mahal did propaganda work amongst the aristocracy and the civil population by correspondence carried on under cover. Kaye has stated that inspired by the efforts and the messages of Alinaqi Khan, thousands of Indian soldiers and their officers, Hindus and Muslims, took the most sacred oaths—the Hindus with water from the Ganges and the Muslims with the Holy Quran in their hands—to join the fight to drive the English out of the country.

Scope and Effects of Propaganda

There were five principal centres which organised and directed the propaganda throughout the country from Barrackpur to Peshawar and from Lucknow to Satara. These were located at Delhi, Bithoor, Lucknow, Calcutta and Satara. Later, more centres were established at other places too. All of them kept in touch and corresponded secretly with one another in code language and script. Religious preachers, *Maulvis* and *Pandits*, *Faqirs* and *sadhus* also carried on the propaganda enthusiastically and prayers for the extinction of the English domination over India were openly offered. At sacred places like Kashi (Banaras), Prayag (Allahabad) and Hardwar, the pilgrims joined in the prayers and expressed their resolve to take part in the coming revolution. Thousands of nationalist *Faqirs* and *sannyasis* went about from village to village and from battalion to battalion exhorting the people and the soldiers to make common cause with those who were aiming at a revolution.

In most of the stations under the Company's rule, the police, many Indian officials and even the Indian domestic servants of the English joined in the propaganda and carried it on.

The "political" *Faqirs* and *sadhus* carrying on the good work were provided with transport—sometimes an elephant—and a disguised armed guard for their personal protection.

The organisers of the propaganda and later the revolutionaries got all the money that was needed from the rich, the bankers and others, who placed heavy purses at the disposal of the protagonists of the national uprising.

The propaganda was by no means carried on only by the civilian population. The soldiers on their own carried it on amongst themselves. The regiments corresponded with each other to co-ordinate their efforts. One of the letters seized by the English contained an appeal which, translated into English, read:

> "Brothers, the dagger is no doubt English, but no other hand except our own is stabbing us with it. If we rise then success is certain, and we are bound to be victorious from Calcutta to Peshawar."

In a number of places the country's determination to rise against the English in a revolution was announced by posters which appealed to every Indian to sacrifice everything, even life, for country and religion. One such poster was found in Madras early in 1857. Secret meetings attended by thousands of people were held everywhere. Even puppet-shows, open-air theatricals and folk-songs were used as the medium of propaganda.

Emblems of the Projected Revolution

The red "lotus" flower and the *Chapati* (bread) were the emblems which the revolution's organisers adopted for circulation amongst the military and the civilian population, respectively.

The soldiers of a regiment circulated the lotus amongst themselves from hand to hand and the last recipient took it to another regiment in token of his own regiment's readiness and determination to fight in the revolution. Thousands of "lotus" flowers were thus circulated in the various Indian regiments from Peshawar to Barrackpore.

The *Chapati* (bread) was circulated in a different way. The *Chowkidar* of a village received a *Chapati* from the *Chowkidar* of a nearby village. He broke off and ate a piece himself, and mixed the rest of it with some flour to make more "*Chapatis*" which the villagers also ate in token of their willingness to join the revolutionaries. The last *Chapati* was taken over to the *Chowkidar* of the next village to be used similarly. Miraculous as it might appear, yet within a few months the *Chapatis* had been circulated in hundreds of thousands of villages.

Nana Sahib goes on a 'Pilgrimage'

The time was now ripe for unifying the scattered propaganda organisations into a single organisation for starting and carrying on the revolution according to plan. An agreed date had also to be fixed for the simultaneous outbreak all over the country. A simultaneous outbreak was of course essential for the success of the revolution.

Nana Sahib undertook both the tasks and early in March, 1857, he left Bithoor on what was called a "pilgrimage". Azimulla Khan accompanied him. They went to Delhi first and held secret consultations with Bahadur Shah, Begum Zeenat Mahal and other prominent leaders of Delhi. Then they went to Ambala and after visiting many other places reached Lucknow on 18th April. At Lucknow Nana Sahib was very enthusiastically received by the people who took him out in a grand procession. They returned to Bithoor, *via* Kaipi, at the end of April, 1857. According to the author Russell, they made it a point, throughout their tour, of visiting all the Company's cantonments that lay along their route. Wherever Nana Sahib went, he invariably visited the local English officials and did his best to disarm any suspicions that might have arisen in their minds about his activities.

'D-Day' for Revolution

Before Nana Sahib returned to Bithoor, he appears to have fixed, in consultation with the other leaders, 31st of May, 1857, as the day on which the revolution was to break out all over the country. "From the available evidence I am quite convinced that the 31st of May, 1857, had been decided on as the date for simultaneous rising" (J. C. Wilson's *Official Narrative*). The decision was conveyed only to the principal leaders and organisers of the revolution in each locality, and to no more than three Indian officers of each regiment.

19

GREASED CARTRIDGES– 'FAT IN THE FIRE'

Greased Cartridges

Were the cartridges, in fact, lubricated with cow's fat and lard? If so, were they the sole or even the main cause of the 1857 Revolution? To what extent, if any, did the greased cartridges reduce the chances of the success of the Revolution? These are the questions which we now proceed to deal with.

Nearly all writers, English and Indian, who have compiled history books prescribed for students in Indian Government schools, have stated that the cartridges were *not* lubricated, that the report about the said lubrication was false and that the sepoys were crazy enough to believe it. During the revolution, every English officer in India, from Lord Canning downwards, solemnly declared and tried to convince the sepoys that the story of the lubrication was utterly false and had been concocted by mischief-mongers to undermine the Indian Army's loyalty to the Company and so to ruin the Army.

On the other hand, Sir John Kaye, who is acknowledged to be the most authentic chronicler of the 1857 upheaval, has stated:

> "There is no question that beef fat was used in the composition of this tallow." (*Indian Mutiny*, Vol. I, p. 581)

Kaye has stated, too, that Col. Tucker had in 1853 expressly written that the new cartridges were lubricated with cow's fat and lard. The agreement with the contractor for supplies to the Dum Dum Cartridge Factory, which manufactured the new cartridges, contained a clause whereby the contractor undertook to supply "cow's fat at four annas a seer". Lord Roberts, who was in India during the revolution, has stated:

> "The recent researches of Mr. Forrest in the records of the Government of India prove that the lubricating mixture used in preparing the cartridges was actually composed of the objectionable ingredients, cow's fat and lard, and that

read: incredible disregard of the soldiers' religious prejudices was displayed in the manufacture of these cartridges." (*Forty-one Years in India* by Lord Roberts, p. 421)

The comments of the well-known historian, W. E. H. Lecky, read:

> "It is a shameful and terrible truth that as far as the fact was concerned, the sepoys were perfectly right in their belief ... but in looking back upon it, English writers must acknowledge with humiliation that, if *mutiny is ever justifiable, no stronger justification could be given than that of the sepoy troops.*" (italics ours) (*The Map of Life*, pp. 103, 104)

Lecky, too, like some other English historians, appears to have held the greased cartridges to be the sole or the chief cause of what he has called the "Sepoy Mutiny" (*vide* the italicised portion in the preceding quotation). A different view is expressed by Justin McCarthy:

> "The fact was that throughout the greater part of the northern and north-western provinces of the Indian peninsula, there was a rebellion of the native races against the English power ... The quarrel about the greased cartridges was but *the chance spark flung in among all the combustible material ... a national and religious war*" (italics ours) (*History of Our Own Times*, Vol. III)

Medley has stated:

> "But, in fact, the greased cartridge was merely the match that exploded the mine which had, owing to a variety of causes, been for a long time preparing." (*A Year's Campaigning in India, from March 1857 to March 1858*)

Charles Ball, in his narrative of 1857, relates the fact that Disraeli, who later became the British Prime Minister, used to assert that no one believed the greased cartridges to have been the real cause of the Indian revolution of 1857.

A significant fact, vouched for by another English writer, would appear to be that the very same cartridges were unhesitatingly used by the Indian sepoys when fighting the English during the revolution.

It is an undisputed fact that the cartridges did infuriate the sepoys and led to a *premature* outburst at places as far apart as Barrackpore and Meerut. Consequently, the plan for the sudden and simultaneous outbreak of the revolution all over India on 31st May, 1857, miscarried, and so reduced to a minimum the chances of its success. Three historians, Malleson, White and Wilson, are unanimous in declaring that the premature outbreak was as much a piece of good luck for the English as it proved to be disastrous for the revolutionaries. Malleson asserts, in plain words, that had the revolution started simultaneously all over India on the appointed date and according to plan, English rule over India would have collapsed forever.

We now proceed to relate briefly the incidents at Barrackpore and Meerut which stemmed from the greased cartridges.

Introduction of Greased Cartridges

Prior to 1853, the ends of the cartridges were broken off by hand by the soldiers immediately before use. In that year, however, new cartridges, whose ends had to be *bitten off*, were issued to the sepoys. Factories for their manufacture had been set up at a number of places. At first the new cartridges were issued to only two battalions. The sepoys did not know, for a considerable time, that the cartridges were lubricated with cow's fat and lard, and so unquestioningly bit off their ends before using them. Gradually, the supply of similar cartridges was extended to other battalions.

Barrackpore—Mangal Pandey

A trifling incident near the Dum Dum sepoy barracks disclosed the nature of the components of the lubricating mixture. A sweeper of the untouchable caste asked a passing Brahmin sepoy for the latter's water-filled *lota* (goblet) to drink some water from. The sepoy treated the request with contempt. "Do not be so proud of your Hindu high caste," retorted the sweeper, "now that you bite off the end of your cow-fat-smeared cartridges". "Do you know," went on the irate sweeper, "that fat-smeared cartridges are made at the factory near Barrackpore?" The Brahmin sepoy was taken aback, and carried the news to his battalion. The sepoys of the battalion were enraged at what they thought to be a surreptitious English attempt to defile them religiously. The sepoys had been unswervingly loyal to the English even against their own countrymen, and the English, so the sepoys thought, had repaid the loyalty by the utterly contemptuous disregard of the Hindu and Mussalman sepoys' religious sentiments and prejudices. They asked their English officers and were told that the report was quite false. Not quite satisfied, the sepoys made searching inquiries at the nearby factory itself, and discovered it for a fact that cow-fat and lard were being used as lubricants in the manufacture of cartridges. The sepoys were furious at the English deception practised on the entire Indian Army and broadcast it all over India. Within a couple of months, thousands of letters about the foul attempt to defile the Hindu and Mussalman sepoys reached all the English cantonments in the country, from Barrackpore to Peshawar and Maharashtra. The infuriated sepoys were keen on immediate reprisals, but their leaders managed to restrain them, at least for the time being.

Shortly after the beginning of this unrest amongst the sepoys, the Company's Government issued a mendacious proclamation, declaring that not a single cartridge of that kind had been issued to any army unit anywhere in India. The fact, however, was that only a short while earlier, 22,500 cartridges from the Ambala depot, and 14,000 cartridges from the Sialkot depot had been dispatched to the Indian Army units. That was not all. The English officers had attempted to enforce the use, by the sepoys, of the new cartridges. At one or two places, the sepoys had persisted in their refusal to use them, and the entire regiment had been severely punished.

In February, 1857, the XIX Indian Infantry sepoys at Barrackpore were given the new cartridges. The sepoys refused to use them. At that time, there was not a single white soldier anywhere in Bengal. So the English officers did not press the matter for the moment. They asked, however, that a contingent of white soldiers be immediately sent to Barrackpore. When the contingent arrived from Burma, the officers decided to disarm and disband the XIX Indian Infantry. The latter was ordered out on parade on 29th March, 1857. It had hardly fallen in, when a youthful sepoy, Mangal Pandey, broke the ranks and rushed to the front with his loaded gun to the shoulder and shouted to the men to join him in starting the religious war against the *Feringhees*. Serjeant-Major Hewson ordered the arrest of Mangal Pandey; but no one came forward to carry out the order. Mangal Pandey fired and shot Hewson dead. Lt. Waugh then rode out to the front. Mangal Pandey fired again and Lt. Waugh's horse rolled on the ground with its rider. Before Mangal Pandey could fire again, Lt. Waugh got up and fired his pistol at Mangal Pandey. The latter was unscathed, drew his sword and cut Lt. Waugh down. Then Colonel Wheeler came up and ordered the men to take Mangal Pandey into custody; but they refused point-blank. Col. Wheeler lost his nerve and rushed; to the General's residence. The General then went to the scene with some white soldiers who advanced towards Mangal Pandey. To avoid arrest Pandey shot himself but he did not die. He lay wounded on the ground as the white soldiers came forward to arrest him. He was court-martialled and sentenced to death. The execution was fixed for 8th April, 1857. No executioner willing to hang Mangal Pandey could be found locally, and so four men had to be brought from Calcutta and Mangal Pandey was duly hanged.

The unrest that followed Mangal Pandey's execution was not confined to the XIX Indian Infantry. It spread to the XXXIV also. Secret meetings were held by the sepoys of both to formulate plans for a revolution against the English. The latter got scent of this state of affairs and took some steps. They hanged a Subedar of the XXXIV on the charge that secret meetings to engineer a revolt were being held in his quarters. Ultimately, both the infantries were disarmed and disbanded. The news soon spread throughout northern India.

Northern India

Numerous bungalows of Englishmen and the barracks of white soldiers at Lucknow, Meerut and Ambala were set on fire and burnt down during the month of April, 1857, according to the revolutionaries' plans. The English did their best to trace the incendiaries but could not, as their investigating Indian police had already made common cause with the revolutionaries.

Meerut

On 6th May, 1857, a Company of Indian Cavalry posted at Meerut was summoned to a parade. The men were handed the new cartridges and were ordered to bite off their ends. This was done as an experiment to test the strength of the English office's hold on the men. Eighty-five of the ninety men composing the Company refused to obey the order. They were court-martialled for disobeying orders and convicted; but sentence was not pronounced. On 9th May, all the Indian troops in Meerut, including the 85 cavalrymen were summoned to a parade, at which a detachment of white soldiers and an artillery corps manned by Englishmen were stationed facing the Indian troops. A sentence of 10 years' rigorous imprisonment for each of the 85 cavalrymen was announced. The uniforms in which they had attended the parade were stripped off. They were hand-cuffed and fettered and marched off to the jail direct from the parade. The thousands of sepoys who had been summoned to the parade only because the English wanted them to watch this demonstration of the English might were infuriated. But they had orders from their leaders to do nothing for another three weeks—till 31st of May—and so they controlled their feelings and marched back to their barracks.

All this happened in the morning. Towards evening some sepoys went to the city. They were jeered at wherever they went. Women hurled opprobriums at them. "Fie on you," some women called out, "your brethren are in jail and you are idling about in the bazars … your existence is a disgrace to manhood," etc. The barbed taunts went home. That very night the sepoys held secret meetings and decided to wait no longer for 31st of May. There and then they sent word to the revolutionary leaders at Delhi, apprising the latter of their intention to start for Delhi the very next day. J.C. Wilson has declared in his *Official Narrative* that as a matter of fact, the real saviours of the English Raj in India were the women of Meerut, who had incited the sepoys to a premature revolt.

The rest of the night of 9th of May was spent by the sepoys in hectic preparations for the morrow, which was a Sunday. During that day, thousands of armed men from the adjoining villages kept pouring into Meerut. The outbreak started in the cantonment. Some cavalrymen went to the jails. The jailors had already been won over. The walls of the jails were demolished and the fetters of all the prisoners were cut away. Then pandemonium ensued. Hindus and Mussalmans, infantry sepoys and cavalrymen, as also the Indian personnel of the artillery rushed out to wipe out all the English in Meerut. Many Englishmen were killed. The bungalows, offices and hotels were set on fire. The battle cries of "*Deen-Deen*", "*Har-Har Mahadeva*" and "Kill the *Feringhees*" filled the air. Telegraph wires were cut and the railway line was taken under their control by the revolutionaries, according to plan. Some of the Englishmen escaped death by taking refuge in hospitals, in drains and in the homes of their Indian servants. As disorder spread in the town and the cantonment, the small body of English soldiers was demoralised and they did not know what to do. Many Englishwomen and children perished in the flames of their houses. As night fell the sepoys started for Delhi.

Delhi

Some 2,000 fully armed horsemen from Meerut reached the outskirts of Delhi on 11th May. The English at Delhi were completely taken by surprise when they got the news. Col. Ripley, an officer of the Company's army at Delhi, was directed to take necessary action. He immediately called to arms the LIV Indian Infantry and led it out to check the advance of the force from Meerut. When the two Indian forces faced each other, the one from Meerut raised the slogans, "Down with the English Raj", "Victory for the Emperor Bahadur Shah". The sepoys of the LIV heard the slogans and immediately went over and hugged their brethren from Meerut. Col. Ripley and all the English officers of the LIV were killed. The combined forces then entered Delhi through the Kashmir Gate, set fire to the English bungalows in Daryaganj and took possession of the Red Fort. The Emperor, Bahadur Shah, and Begum Zeenat Mahal both thought it imprudent to wait till 31st of May. By then, the infantry and the artillery from Meerut had also arrived. The artillery, on entering the Red Fort, fired a salute of 21 guns for the Emperor. Charles Ball relates that a deputation of the Indian military officers, Hindus and Mussalmans, waited on the Emperor Bahadur Shah, tendered their homage and begged for his leadership of the revolution. According to Metcalf, the Emperor told them that he had no money and so could not pay the salaries of the deputationists and their men. The deputationists' reply was that they would get hold of all the money that would be needed from the English treasuries in India and would "pour it at the Emperor's feet". The old Emperor Bahadur Shah accepted the leadership of the revolution and the Red Fort echoed with the repeated acclamations raised in his honour. The gold and green flag of the emperor was hoisted on the Red Fort and it was under this flag that the revolutionaries later fought all over the country. The citizens of Delhi very warmly and hospitably welcomed the revolutionaries, and co-operated with them to the fullest possible extent.

The English bank at Delhi was taken into possession by the revolutionaries and English buildings were demolished. No white troops were then stationed in Delhi, but there was a big magazine stored with huge stocks of gunpowder, shots and shells, besides some 10,000 muskets and 900,000 cartridges. The guard on the magazine was composed of only nine men—Lt. Willoughby and eight English soldiers. The revolutionaries called upon Lt. Willoughby, in the name of the Emperor Bahadur Shah, to surrender the magazine. Lt. Willoughby refused, and, hopelessly outnumbered though they were, the nine Englishmen fought every inch of the ground, and, when further resistance became useless, they deliberately blew themselves up along with the magazine. All honour to them for preferring death to surrender.

The explosion sounded like the simultaneous firing of a thousand guns, and shook houses all over Delhi. Some 300 Indians in nearby streets were blown to pieces. All the English officers in the Delhi Cantonment were killed. The general massacre of the English by the revolutionaries in Delhi lasted from 11th to 15th May. Some hundreds of the English in Delhi did succeed in getting away through one ruse or another. Quite a number painted their faces black or disguised themselves as *Faqirs*. But most of them died of heat or fatigue, or were killed by the villagers. A few were given asylum by some kind-hearted villagers, who hid them in their homes at no small risk to themselves. When passions are roused in men, the lust to kill very often dominates them and they are turned into ferocious beasts; the revolutionaries hunted down and killed every Englishman they could find in and around Meerut and Delhi. But no Englishwoman appears to have met with any violence at the hands of the revolutionaries.

> "However much of cruelty and bloodshed there was, the tales which gained currency, of dishonour to ladies, so far as my observation and inquiries went were devoid of any satisfactory proof"—Hon. Sir William Muir, K.C.S.I, Head of the Intelligence Deptt.

On 16th May, 1857, Delhi, the ancient capital of India, again became free under the proclaimed rule of the Mughal Emperor. The event electrified the whole country. Nana Sahib and other leaders of the revolution could now legitimately, in the Emperor's name, call upon the princes and the people of India to rally under the Emperor's flag, and fight the English till the latter were driven into the sea. The call was issued immediately, and was responded to by risings in a number of places *before* 31st May.

Aligarh, Etawah and Mainpuri

The IX Indian Infantry of the Company's Army had its headquarters at Aligarh with three contingents stationed at Bulandshahr, Etawah and Mainpuri.

About the middle of May, 1857, a Brahmin revolutionary preacher arrived at the Bulandshahr lines to do propaganda amongst the sepoys. He was informed against, arrested, sentenced to death and brought to Aligarh for execution. On 20th May, the sepoys at Aligarh were drawn up in a parade and the Brahmin was hanged in front of them. The sight of a Brahmin swinging from the gallows inflamed the sepoys, one of whom rushed out and, pointing his drawn sword at the dead body, shouted: "Brethren, this martyr is having a bath in his own blood for the sake of us all." The infuriated sepoys could not restrain themselves and wait till 31st May. The IX Infantry immediately rose up in arms to a man. The English officers were, however, allowed to go away in peace with their women and children and by midnight the green flag was fluttering over Aligarh. The sepoys marched to Delhi with the money and arms taken from the Company's treasury and armoury.

The news reached Mainpuri on 22nd May, and the sepoys there revolted too, and acted like the sepoys at Aligarh. They gave the English a chance to go away peacefully, took the money, the arms and ammunition from the Company's treasury and armoury, and loading the same on camels started for Delhi on 23rd May. The green flag flew over Mainpuri.

At Etawah, the English tried to offer some resistance and Mr. Hume, the Collector, appealed to the armed police and to some other people for help, but they all sided with the revolutionaries. Some fighting ensued in which the Assistant Magistrate Daniels was killed. On 23rd May, the revolutionaries took possession of the Company's treasury and demolished the jail. But they too allowed the English, men, women and children, to depart unmolested. Mr. Hume, it has been said, thought it more prudent to disguise himself as an Indian woman (*The Red Pamphlet* by G. B. Malleson, Part II, p. 70). The liberation of the town was proclaimed by beat of drum and the green flag was hoisted.

The administration of all the three towns liberated by the IX Infantry was entrusted to the inhabitants of each of them and the liberators, having spared the lives of non-combatant Englishmen, marched, as stated above, to Delhi, equipped with arms, ammunition, money and provisions taken from the Company's possession.

Nasirabad

Nasirabad was an important English cantonment near Ajmer. A battalion of Indian infantry, a company of English soldiers and an artillery corps were stationed there. The sepoys of Meerut had spread out far and wide, and some of them reached Nasirabad. On 28th May, the Indian infantry at Nasirabad revolted. The English soldiers fought them, lost some lives and then ran away. The leaders of the sepoys took over the administration of the town in the name of the Emperor and then left for Delhi with thousands of Indian soldiers, the money in the Company's treasury and the arms and ammunition seized from the Company's armoury.

Rohilkhand (Bareilly, Shahjehanpur, Moradabad, Budaun)

The Rohilkhand province had been, at one time, under the independent rule of the Rohila Pathans, who had established their capital at Bareilly. The English had ousted them and were ruling the Province. In 1857, Khan Bahadur Khan, a descendant of the last Rohila Nawab, was the incumbent of the judge's office under the Company. Later, he became the chief revolutionary leader of Rohilkhand.

The Company's troops stationed at Bareilly were commanded by General Sibbald and consisted of the VIII Indian Cavalry, the XVIII Indian Infantry and the LXVIII Indian Infantry and some Artillery.

Immediately after the revolt at Meerut, the Company's Commander-in-Chief in India had issued a proclamation to all the Company's military units in the country. It announced that the use of the new cartridges had been given up, and that, in future, only the old-type cartridge would be issued to the sepoys. It could not, however, influence the course of the revolution in any way.

The Indian officers of the troops at Bareilly and Moradabad were pressed by the commander of the revolutionary troops at Delhi to march to Delhi immediately. Khan Bahadur Khan, however, decided to take no overt action till 31st May, the date fixed for the outbreak. In the meantime he saw to it that his own behaviour and that of the Indian troops did not give rise to any doubts about their loyalty to the English.

Exactly at 11 a.m., on 31st May, a gun was fired. It was the signal for the starting of the revolution. The sepoys had been well organised by the revolutionary leaders, and the LXVIII Indian Infantry began by killing the English and burning their bungalows. Capt. Brownlow's home was the first to be burnt down. General Sibbald and numerous

English officers were killed and only 32 Englishmen succeeded in escaping to Naini Tal. Within six hours the Union Jack was hauled down and the green flag went up in its place. Subedar Bakht Khan of the Company's artillery took over his supreme command of the revolution sepoys. He enjoined the men under the command to be just and peaceful in all their dealings after full independence had been achieved. The people acclaimed Khan Bahadur Khan as the Emperor's Subedar of Rohilkhand. By sunset a messenger was sent by the Subedar to Delhi to apprise the Emperor of Rohilkhand's liberation from English rule.

Some 47 miles away from Bareilly, the XXVIII Indian Infantry was stationed at Shahjehanpur. On 31st of May, it rose up in arms and liberated Shahjehanpur.

On the other side of Bareilly, the Indian Infantry was stationed at Moradabad. On 18th May, its English officers came to know that some revolutionary sepoys from Delhi had arrived near Moradabad. They ordered the Infantry to attack and drive away the Delhi sepoys. A fight was faked and it was reported to the English officers that the Delhi sepoys, all except one, had run away. It was later discovered that they all had, in fact, stayed the night in the Infantry barracks as guests. On the morning of 31st May the sepoys of the Infantry assembled on the parade ground and notified their English officers: "The Company's rule is at an end. If you want to save your lives, leave Moradabad within twenty-four hours." The police and the people of Moradabad sided with the revolutionaries. Some Englishmen, including the Collector, the Judge and the Civil Surgeon left the town with their families. Mr. Powell, the Commissioner of Moradabad, and some other Englishmen became converts to Islam. Their lives were spared. The Company's treasury was seized by the sepoys as well as all its property. Before sunset the green flag was up at Moradabad too.

At Budaun, the fourth important town of Rohilkhand, the revolution started on the morning of 1st June. The sepoys, the police and the prominent citizens of the town proclaimed the end of English rule, by beat of drum, and its replacement by the administration of the Emperor's Subedar, Khan Bahadur Khan. The English in Budaun fled to the jungles where many of them perished.

Thus it was that within two days the whole of the Rohilkhand province was freed from the Company's rule. Khan Bahadur Khan recruited and organised a fresh army and established law and order throughout the province. Most of the Indian employees in the Company's administration were retained. The land revenue was, thereafter, collected in the name of Emperor Bahadur Shah, to whom Khan Bahadur Khan submitted a report written in his own hand about the recent events in Rohilkhand.

Khan Bahadur Khan's Proclamation

It was addressed to the "People of India" and its copies were distributed throughout Rohilkhand. We give below a close English rendering of some extracts from it:

> "The auspicious day of our freedom has dawned ... Will you, Hindus and Mussalmans of Hindostan, seize this glorious opportunity for your and your country's benefit or will you let it slip through your fingers? ... If the English continue in Hindostan, it would mean the end not only of the religious faith of us all, but also of our existence as free and self-respecting human beings ... Up till now the people of Hindostan have been taken in and deceived by the English, and have been cutting, in the latter's carefully concealed interests, their own throats. We sold our country and have expiated the sin. The English will again resort to deceit. They will try their hardest to incite the Hindus against the Mussalmans and vice versa. Hindu brethren beware of the machinations in which the English are experts. Is it necessary to point out to you that the English never perform what they promise? Have they not forcibly deprived adopted children of their lawful rights? Have they not swallowed up the territories of our Rajas? Who usurped the Nagpur Raja and the Kingdom of Lucknow? Who has trampled under foot both the Hindus and Mussalmans? Mussalmans, if you revere the Holy Quran, and Hindus, if you venerate the cow-mother, sink your petty differences and join hands in this holy war. Rush to the battle-field, fight under one flag and with the free flow of your blood wash away the stigma

of the English domination over Hindostan. Those who personally fight in the holy war and those who help with money will both be blessed, and will achieve salvation in this world and the next. But if anyone opposes his country, he will be hurting only his own self and committing suicide as a Hindostani."

Bakht Khan Marches on Delhi

Bakht Khan, the supreme commander of all the Rohilkhand revolutionary forces, led them to Delhi with the arms, heavy guns, ammunition and the money seized from the Company's possession in Rohilkhand.

Bakht Khan and Khan Bahadur Khan were two of the ablest leaders of the revolution.

Azamgarh

On 3rd June, Rs. 7 lacs were in transit, from the Company's treasuries at Azamgarh and Gorakhpur to Banaras. The Indian Infantry stationed at Azamgarh revolted that very night. The sepoys, however, not only spared the lives of all but two of the Englishmen residing there, but also arranged for carriages to take them and their families to Banaras. The revolutionaries, with the full co-operation of the armed police, also seized the above-mentioned money and the Company's store of arms and ammunition. They took possession of the jail and the Company's offices and hoisted the green flag over the town that very night.

Banaras

About the time of the revolution's outbreak, no white troops of the Company were stationed anywhere between Agra and Calcutta, except a single regiment at Dinapore. On receiving reports of the events at Meerut and Delhi, Governor-General Lord Canning began to collect in Bengal white troops from Bombay, Madras and Rangoon. The war with Iran had ended just then, and a large English force relieved from that theatre was on its way to China for the invasion of that country. But the Indian revolution compelled the English to abandon the invasion of China, and the English troops from Iran were diverted to India. A large contingent of these troops was forthwith led by the famous General Neill to Banaras, where the Indian Infantry, a battalion of Ludhiana Sikhs, a regiment of Cavalry and an Artillery corps (manned by white soldiers exclusively) were already stationed.

The military barracks at Banaras had been fired on 31st May, but the arrival of Gen. Neill with his force heartened the English there very much. The news about Azamgarh reached them on 4th June. That very afternoon the English officers decided to disarm their Indian soldiers, who were summoned to a parade. When the soldiers had formed up on the parade ground, they were ordered to lay down their arms.

The sepoys instead of laying down their arms, forthwith attacked their English officers and the Company's magazine. The Sikh battalion advanced to oppose the sepoys. The artillery came up just as the fighting had started and went into action. But the English artillery officers who were directing the fire were unable, in the melee, to distinguish the Sikhs from the Mussalman and Hindu sepoys, and all the three were shelled indiscriminately. The Sikhs thought it would be safer to desert and did so.

The people of Banaras were, one and all, for the revolutionaries. But the Sikhs, the wealthy citizens of Banaras, and the titular "Raja" of Banaras (a descendant of Raja Chet Singh) co-operated with the English to the fullest possible extent, and helped them retain the city of Banaras.

Most of the Banaras region was, however, taken by the revolutionaries who removed a number of Zamindars recently appointed by the English and re-instated the old hereditary Zamindars. In numerous places English courts, jails and offices ceased to exist. Telegraph wires were cut and railways were disrupted by the tearing up of rails.

Jaunpur

In Jaunpur the revolution started on 5th June. Some Englishmen were killed but a good many who surrendered were allowed to leave in boats for Banaras. The revolutionaries took possession of the Company's treasury. The green flag was hoisted over the town, and the sepoys, like the sepoys of Azamgarh, proceeded towards Fyzabad.

The Importance of Allahabad

For the English as also for the revolutionaries, Allahabad was of far greater importance than Banaras. All the trains from Calcutta to north-west India had to go through Allahabad. The Fort there was one of the strongest in the country and huge quantities of-arms and ammunition were stored therein.

It has been stated that the *Pandas* (Hindu priests) of Prayag (the Hindu name for Allahabad) had been busy for some time in doing propaganda work for the "war of independence". The Mussalmans were even more enthusiastic about it. According to Charles Ball, all the Indian officials of the Company, from the highest to the lowest, had joined the revolutionary organisation.

Allahabad (Town) Occupied by the Revolutionaries

When the news of the Meerut uprising reached Allahabad, not a single English soldier was stationed there. The Fort was garrisoned by the VI Indian Infantry, some 200 Sikh soldiers, and a handful of English officers. A regiment of Indian cavalry later arrived from Oudh as a re-inforcement. The sepoys of the VI had led their English officers up the garden path successfully and, when the news of the liberation of Delhi came, they asked to be sent to Delhi "to cut down the mutineers to pieces". The night of 6th June had been fixed for the outbreak at Allahabad. The sepoys saw to it that their relations with their English officers became even more cordial during the day. The sepoys' barracks were situated outside the Fort. When night fell and the English officers were at dinner, a bugle call was sounded by the sepoys as the signal for starting the revolution.

Some Englishmen were killed and those who could escaped and took refuge in the Fort. The Indian cavalry from Oudh was then called to arms to help the English. But the cavalry too joined the sepoys. Fighting ensued in which English officers of both the VI Infantry and the Oudh Cavalry were killed. The revolutionaries could not, however, take the Fort, mainly because the Sikh contingent quartered in it sided with the English and fought for them. Had the Sikhs remained even neutral, the Union Jack over the Fort would have been hauled down within half an hour of the outbreak.

The town, however, had a different story to tell: Prisoners were released from jails, the Company's treasury with Rs. 30 lacs was seized, telegraph wires were cut and railway lines were disrupted. On the evening of 7th June, the green flag was taken out in procession through the town and the Cantonment, and was hoisted over the Central Police Station, after which the townspeople and the sepoys saluted it. In hundreds of adjoining villages, Hindus and Mussalmans, *Ryots* and Zamindars proclaimed the end of the English Raj and hoisted the green flag.

> "... Not only in the districts beyond the Ganges but in those lying between the two rivers, the rural population had risen ... and soon there was scarcely a man of either faith who was not arrayed against us." (Kaye's *Indian Mutiny*, Vol. II, p. 195)

Within a few days, law and order was restored. The townspeople and some neighbouring Zamindars unanimously appointed Moulvi Liaqat Ali as the Emperor's Subedar of the Allahabad region. He was a man of exceptional ability and probity, and was universally respected. He established the headquarters of his administration at Khusro Bagh and maintained peace and the rule of law in the town and throughout the territory under his administration. He submitted periodical reports to the Emperor. He even tried to occupy the Fort, and appealed to the Sikh soldiers inside it to come out and join the revolutionaries but the appeal fell on deaf ears.

At this stage the English started their campaign of reprisals, which we propose to describe in the next chapter.

REPRISALS

General Neill's Plan

Lord Canning had despatched a large force to Banaras under the command of General Neill. It was composed mostly of white soldiers, Sikhs and Madrasis. When Gen. Neill arrived, the city of Banaras was still in the hands of the English. His arrival was followed by wholesale arrests throughout the town. He sent out several detachments composed of white soldiers and Sikhs to re-conquer the countryside. The "exploits" of these detachments have been described by more than one English writer of history.

Hangings in Diverse Ways

Gen. Neill's soldiers cut down, shot dead or hanged indiscriminately every man that they came across, whilst going from one village to another. Gallows were set up at a number of places and were kept busy round the clock. Even so, they could not cope with the hangings and branches of trees were used as improvised gallows. The victim was brought on an elephant under an overhanging branch. The noose tied to the branch was put round his neck and the elephant was moved away, leaving him dangling in mid-air (*Narrative of the Indian Revolt*, p. 69).

> "Volunteer hanging-parties went out into the districts, and amateur executioners were not wanting ... the victims of this wild justice being strung up, as though for pastime, in the form of the figure of 8 (eight)" (Kaye and Malleson's *History of the Indian Mutiny*, Vol. II, p. 177)

Incendiarism

When in the opinion of the English officers commanding the detachments, the above methods did not fully meet the situation they resorted to setting on fire whole villages, one after the other. We quote below from the private letters written by some of these officers to their friends. One officer wrote:

> "We set fire to a large village which was full of them (men, women, children and cattle). We surrounded them, and when they came rushing out of the flames, we shot them." (Charles Ball's *Indian Mutiny*, Vol. I, p. 244)

Another officer writing to his friend said that the latter would be glad to know that the writer had, *in a single day,* razed to the ground *twenty villages.* The total number of villages destroyed in the countryside can thus be estimated.

It is just *possible* that the English officers commanding the detachments had acted on their own without any instructions from Gen. Neill. But the following incident at Banaras, where Gen. Neill himself was personally in command, tends to reduce that possibility to an improbability:

> "On one occasion, some young boys, who, perhaps in mere sport had flaunted rebel colours and gone about beating tomtoms, were tried and sentenced to death." (*History of the Sepoy War in India, 1857* by J.W. Kaye, Vol. II, p. 236)

From Banaras, General Neill marched to Allahabad with his "conquering" army. On the way, he reduced to ashes thousands of villages with all their inhabitants and the latter's belongings.

At Allahabad

General Neill reached Allahabad on 11th June. It has been stated that when he got within sight of the Allahabad Fort, he was pleasantly surprised to see the Union Jack still flying over it. Apparently, he had expected that the Sikh soldiers in the Fort would join the revolutionaries and would hand over to the latter the Fort with its huge stock of arms and ammunition.

Had that happened, it would have become extremely difficult, if not impossible, for General Neill to retake Allahabad.

But even though the Sikhs had remained loyal to their foreign masters, General Neill would not trust them enough to let them be in the Fort, which he intended to garrison with white troops exclusively. He, therefore, sent all the Sikh soldiers out of the Fort, with orders to plunder the town and to pillage and set fire to the neighbouring villages. The Sikhs gladly carried out the orders.

As mentioned above Allahabad city was then under the administration of Moulvi Liaqat Ali. The latter's headquarters at Khusro Bagh were attacked by Gen. Neill's force on 17th June and a fierce battle raged the whole day. The revolutionaries fought desperately against fearful odds. At the end of the day, however, Liaqat Ali saw clearly that resistance could not last much longer. He had Rs. 30 lacs in cash in his treasury, which he wanted to save from the English. So during the night he slipped away with the money and his men and proceeded towards Kanpur.

On 18th June, Gen. Neill helped chiefly by the Sikh soldiers entered the town of Allahabad. What followed was a veritable reign of terror for the townspeople. Says Sir George Campbell:

> "... And I know that at Allahabad there were far too many wholesale executions ... And afterwards Neill did things almost more than the massacre, putting to death with deliberate torture in a way that has never been proved against the natives." (Sir George Campbell, Provisional Civil Commissioner in the Mutiny, as quoted in *The Other Side of the Medal* by Edward Thompson, p. 81)

In the Chowk Bazar of Allahabad can be seen today (1930) three of the seven *neem* trees whose branches were used, it has been stated, as gallows for hanging some 800 innocent men within three days. Some people tried to escape death by getting away in boats which, however, had to pass the English troops stationed on the river bank. The boats were fired upon and sunk.

One English officer has described his doings on a single day in the following words:

> "One trip I enjoyed amazingly; we got on board a steamer with a gun, while the Sikhs and the fusiliers marched up to the city. We steamed up throwing shots right and left till

we got up to the bad places, when we went on the shore and peppered away with our guns, my old double-barrel bringing down several niggers. So thirsty for vengeance I was. We fired the places right and left and the flames shot up to the heavens as they spread, fanned by the breeze, showing that the day of vengeance had fallen on the treacherous villains. Every day we had expeditions to burn and destroy disaffected villages and we have taken our revenge ... We have the power of life in our hands and, I assure you, we spare not ... The condemned culprits placed under a tree, with a rope round his neck, on the top of a carriage and when it is pulled off, he swings." (Charles Ball's *Indian Mutiny*, Vol. I, p. 257)

Commander-in-Chief Sir Collin Campbell is stated to have told Sir William Russell, the correspondent of the London *Times,* that in those days a certain English merchant was appointed the Special Commissioner in Allahabad to ferret out the rebels. The merchant owed money to several Indians in the city, and about the first thing which he did after his appointment was to hang every one of his creditors (Sir W. H. Russell's private letter to John Delane, Editor of the London *Times,* written from Lucknow).

Sir John Kaye, in his *History of the Sepoy War* (Vol. II), has written:

"Soldiers and civilians alike were holding bloody assizes, or slaying Natives without any assize at all, regardless of sex or age. Afterwards the thirst for blood grew stronger still. It is on the records of our British Parliament, in papers sent home by the Governor-General of India-in-Council that 'aged women and children are sacrificed, as well as those guilty of rebellion'. They were not deliberately hanged, but burnt to death in their villages and then accidentally shot. Englishmen did not hesitate to boast or to record their boast in writing, that they had spared no one and that peppering away at niggers was a very pleasant pastime. And it has been stated, in a book patronised by official authorities, that 'for three months eight carts went their rounds daily from sunrise to sunset to take down the corpses which hung at the cross-roads and market places and that *six thousand beings had* been thus summarily disposed of and launched into eternity... An Englishman is almost suffocated with indignation when he reads that Mr. Chambers or Miss Jennings was hacked to death by a dusky ruffian, but in Native histories or history being written in Native legends and traditions, it may be recorded against our people that mothers and wives and children, with less familiar names, fell miserable victims to the first swoop of English vengeance."

Holmes, the historian, thus summarises the holocaust:

"Old men who had done us no harm; helpless women, with suckling infants at their breasts, felt the weight of our vengeance no less than the vilest malefactors." *(Sepoy War, pp. 229–30)*

Agreeing with another English historian, we too think "It is better not to write anything more about General Neill's revenge," except to say that, by all accounts, many more Indians were done to death in the Allahabad region alone than the total number of the revolutionaries' victims in the whole of India during the fateful 1857–58 period. We might also mention that on numerous occasions the revolutionaries had spared the lives of the English men, women and children. In numberless villages the villagers had given asylum in their homes to the English fugitives, whose countrymen exacted much more than full retribution from the people of Allahabad, before and after occupying the town.

Repercussions in Towns and Rural Areas

People in both towns and rural areas completely boycotted the English. According to Charles Ball, the English could not get *Doli*-bearers or even ordinary labourers at any price. No one, particularly in the villages, dared to sell provisions to the English or to work for them. If anyone ventured to do so, his nose and ears were cut off, if he was not killed outright. Added to all this was the intense heat of the month of June. It led to an outbreak of cholera in the English camp.

We now proceed to narrate the developments in Kanpur, following the liberation of Delhi.

Kanpur

Kanpur was the birth-place of the idea and the plans of the revolution. The principal leaders of the revolution in Bithoor near Kanpur were Nana Sahib, his two brothers, Bala Sahib and Baba Sahib and, last but by no means the least important, the shrewd and exceptionally capable Azimulla Khan (see Chapter XVIII). Also present at the Bithoor *Durbar* was the famous Tatya Tope, the Maratha military leader. Sir Hugh Wheeler was the English General commanding the Company's army at Kanpur.

The news of Delhi's liberation reached Nana Sahib on the 15th May, three days before it reached General Wheeler, who received the report on the 18th. An English writer has commented that one of the most astonishing features of the "revolt" was the speed with which authentic news from distant places was conveyed to its leaders by special messengers who moved amazingly fast (*Narrative of the Indian Revolt*).

The Hindus and the Mussalmans of Kanpur celebrated the regaining of Delhi's independence with eclat. Festive parties were held everywhere. The imminence of India's freedom from foreign rule was openly talked about in bazars and other public places. The sepoys in the cantonment were holding secret meetings to formulate their final plans for "the day". Notwithstanding all this enthusiasm, Nana Sahib decided to hold his hand till the appointed date, viz., 31st of May.

On the other side, the English had not been idle. Some reinforcements from Lucknow had arrived at Kanpur to help General Wheeler's force of 3,000 sepoys and about a hundred white soldiers. A "fort" was hastily improvised on the south of the Ganges, primarily as a place of refuge for the English should the need for it ever arise.

Strangely enough, General Wheeler had so complete faith in Nana Sahib's loyalty to the English as to send him an appeal for armed help. Nothing loth, Nana Sahib left Bithoor and on 22nd May arrived in Kanpur with a few hundred of his armed retainers and two pieces of cannon. On his arrival, General Wheeler entrusted to him for safe custody the Company's treasury and magazine. Nana Sahib immediately put a guard of 200 of his own soldiers over both.

Two of the principal revolutionary leaders of the Company's sepoys were Subedar Teeka Singh and Subedar Shamsuddin, whilst Nana Sahib's two chief lieutenants in Kanpur were Jwala Prasad and Mohammad Ali. All four of them held secret conferences at night on a boat in midstream with Nana Sahib and Azimulla Khan. The news about the revolutionary activities at Delhi had reached the English at Kanpur, and when they became aware that something like it was afoot in Kanpur too, they appeared to have lost their nerve. According to an English writer the flimsiest rumour about the outbreak having occurred somewhere in Kanpur would send them scurrying to the improvised fort with their women and children. 24th May was Queen Victoria's birthday; but in 1857, the usual gun-salute was not fired at Kanpur because the English feared that the sepoys might misconstrue the firing as a signal for starting the revolt.

The Actual Outbreak

The pre-arranged signal for starting the revolution was the firing of three shots in quick succession. It was given at midnight on 4th June, and the revolution broke out immediately. Subedar Teeka Singh rode out of the lines followed by a few hundred horsemen and a few thousand foot soldiers. Some of them burnt the English buildings according to plan. Others went round from place to place pulling down the Union Jack and replacing it by the green flag. Nana's soldiers joined the sepoys, and the Company's treasury and magazine came into the possession of the revolutionaries. All this happened during the same night.

In the morning on 5th June, the sepoys of the Company's army and the Kanpur citizens unanimously elected Nana Sahib as their "Raja" under the suzerainty of the Delhi Emperor. Later in the day, the Emperor's green flag mounted on an elephant was taken round the city and the cantonment in a huge and magnificent procession.

Nana Sahib discarded the role of a loyal friend of the English and openly assumed the leadership of the Kanpur revolutionaries.

Nana Sahib's Ultimatum to General Wheeler

Next morning (6th June), Nana sent a warning to General Wheeler that if the latter did not vacate and hand over the fort to the revolutionaries during the day, it would be attacked that very evening. The fort was not surrendered and at sunset the attack was duly launched. By then, almost all the English living in Kanpur had taken refuge in the fort with their women and children. Those who, for one reason or another, could not get in, or were left in the city, were done to death. The fort was then besieged.

The Siege

Nana Sahib had plenty of guns and shelled the fort heavily. The shells falling inside the fort killed the English in such numbers that it became difficult to bury all the dead. A single well in the fort was the only source of water for the besieged. Nana's guns directed their firing on the well and the English were without any water. They suffered agonies due to thirst in the intense June heat of Kanpur. Those who were not killed by the shells, fell victims to fever, dysentery and cholera. All the same, the guns on the walls of the fort continued to work steadily, thanks to the remarkable courage of the English gunners. The extreme difficulty of sending a message for relief out of the beleaguered fort was overcome with the help of a loyal Indian servant of the Company who volunteered to take General Wheeler's note to Lucknow. The note was tied under the wings of a bird, which the volunteer carried. It was written, partly in English, partly in Latin and partly in French. The words read:–

> "Help! Help!! Help!!! Send us help or we are dying. If we get help, we will come and save Lucknow."

Nana Sahib's spies in the fort were daily bringing to him reports of the conditions therein.

Help for Nana Sahib

During the siege, help for Nana's cause, in money and men, kept pouring in from the zamindars all around Kanpur. This encouraged him and his colleagues to no end. His own force increased to 4,000 men.

Service by Women of Kanpur

The women of Kanpur, both Hindu and Muslim, discarded their seclusion to render service to the besiegers. They took to the latter ammunition, food and other necessities and boldly went right up to the walls of the fort. Amongst them, Azeezan, a public dancer and singer, earned well-deserved renown. A historian has stated that Azeezan, fully armed, rode about for hours, day after day, through the town and the cantonment, with "lightning speed", helping and ministering to the needs of the wounded, taking them food and milk. Quite often she rode right up to the walls of the fort, utterly regardless of guns firing from both sides and cheered up the revolutionaries.

At the same time, the civil administration and the problems of keeping up the supplies to the men fighting at the front was not overlooked. Under Nana Sahib's guidance, the prominent citizens appointed Hulas Singh as the Chief Judge. The duty of arranging for supplies to reach the fighting line was entrusted to Mulla. For civil cases, a court, with Jwala Prasad, Azimullah Khan and Bala Sahib as judges, was established. The citizens cheerfully obeyed all orders promulgated by Nana Sahib. According to the historian, Thompson, those who were found guilty were severely punished, and law, order and peace reigned in the city (*The Story of Cawnpore* by M. Thompson).

Surrender of the Fort

After two fierce battles on 18th and 23rd June, General Wheeler on the 25th hoisted the white flag over the fort. Nana Sahib ceased firing immediately and sent a letter to General Wheeler, which translated into English reads:

"To the subjects of Queen Victoria – All those who have had nothing to do with the implementation of Dalhousie's policy, and are ready to lay down arms, will be safely conducted to Allahabad."

Next day, on the 26th, representatives from both sides met for negotiations. A remarkable feature of the negotiations was that they were conducted in the Hindustani language, because Nana Sahib's representative, Azimulla Khan insisted on it, even though he knew English quite well. The English representatives had, therefore, to talk in Hindustani.

Ultimately, all the English survivors of the siege surrendered to Nana Sahib. The fort with its guns, arms, ammunition and treasury was also delivered to Nana Sahib. On behalf of Nana Sahib an undertaking was given that all the English would be safely conveyed in boats to Allahabad. That very night, 40 boats were collected, stored with provisions for the journey and moored at Sati-Chowra Ghat, ready to start for Allahabad as soon as the English got into them. In the morning on 27th June, the English were carried from the fort in palanquins and on elephants to the Sati-Chowra Ghat, about a mile-and-a-half away.

As soon as the last of the English had departed from the fort, the Union Jack flying over it was hauled down and Emperor Bahadur Shah's green flag was hoisted in its place.

The Massacre at Sati-Chowra Ghat

During the previous eight or ten days, thousands of refugees from Allahabad and from the rural areas adjoining it, whose homes, relatives, women and children had been burnt to ashes by Gen. Neill's soldiers, had poured into Kanpur. The accounts of the horrible atrocities perpetrated on them had inflamed the townspeople and enraged the sepoys at Kanpur.

The boats carrying the English refugees were due to start for Allahabad at 10 a.m. on 27th June. But from early morning, thousands of angry sepoys and townspeople had begun arriving at the Sati-Chowra Ghat. Nana Sahib was then in his palace.

It has been stated that as soon as the English refugees arrived at the Ghat, Col. Ewart was assaulted by an angry sepoy. Then, as narrated in Kaye and Malleson's *Indian Mutiny* (Vol. II, p. 263), the men amongst the English refugees were made to stand in a line. One of them, probably a clergyman, requested and was given permission and time to read aloud to his brethren some prayers from the Bible. As soon as the reading was over, the sepoys started cutting off the heads of every Englishman in the line one by one. Four of the refugees succeeded in slipping away in boats during the confusion. They and the 125 women and children, whose lives had been spared and who were sent in custody to Sowda Kothi, under Nana Sahib's orders, were the only survivors of about a thousand English who had taken refuge in the fort before it was besieged. It is seated that the sepoys who had collected in large numbers at the Sati-Chowra Ghat, and who were responsible for the massacres were not on duty there.

The hanging at Banaras of young boys who were flaunting the "rebel" colours in a sportive mood can in no way be justified. Similarly, the cold-blooded murder of hundreds of unarmed men, who had surrendered only after Nana Sahib had solemnly promised them safe conduct, is unjustifiable. An atrocity is an atrocity and must be condemned as such, whoever might be the culprit.

Nana Sahib's Responsibility

Nana Sahib was not very far away from Sati-Chowra Ghat at the time of the massacre and as narrated in Kaye and Malleson's *Indian Mutiny* (Vol. II, p. 258) he did give the sepoys a free hand to do what they liked with the Englishmen, so long as they (the sepoys) did no harm to any English woman or English child.

Nana Sahib's Treatment of English Women & Children

After the stain which had thus attached itself to Nana's reputation, it is not to be wondered at that numerous reports about the inhuman treatment meted out by him to English women and children became current in India and in England. But we would, in this connection, invite attention to the following facts:

(i) The Commission which was later appointed by the English to investigate the accusation against Nana Sahib held that the accusations were "false" (Muir's Report and Wilson's Report. Also Kaye and Malleson's *Indian Mutiny*, Vol. II, p. 267)

(ii) Justin McCarthy has stated in his *History of Our Own Times* (Vol. Ill):

> "The elementary passions of manhood were inflamed by the stories, happily not true, of the wholesale dishonour and barbarous mutilation of women... As a matter of fact, no indignities, other than that of compulsory corngrinding, were put upon the English ladies.... There were no outrages, in the common acceptation of the term, upon women. No Englishwomen were stripped or dishonoured, or purposely mutilated."

(iii) Sir George Trevelyan (*Cawnpore*, p. 299) has stated that during the melee at Sati-Chowra Ghat's some sepoys abducted four English women. As soon as Nana Sahib heard of it, he rescued the women, and severely punished the sepoys.

As a matter of fact, Nana Sahib's treatment of the English women and children was humane and even generous. Meat formed part of their diet and the children were also given milk. The children were allowed to go out for fresh air three times a day.

Finally, we would quote General Neill himself:

> "At first they (Englishwomen) were badly fed but afterwards they got better food and clean clothing and servants to wait upon them." (General Neill's Report)

Nana Sahib's Installation as Peshwa

On 28th June, 1857, Nana Sahib held a huge *Durbar* at Kanpur. It was attended by six battalions of infantry, two regiments of cavalry, numerous zamindars and numberless townspeople.

First of all, a salute of 101 guns was fired for the Emperor Bahadur Shah, then a salute of 21 guns was fired for Nana Sahib as Peshwa.

Nana Sahib thanked the people and the sepoys for all that they had done and the help which they had given for the success of the revolution in Kanpur.

A lac of rupees was distributed in rewards to the assembled sepoys.

Three days later, on 1st July, Nana Sahib formally installed himself at Bithoor on what was termed "the Peshwa's *Gadi*". It appeared that with Nana Sahib's ascension to the *Gadi,* the well-nigh dead Peshwa power was coming to life again.

21

JHANSI AND OUDH

Rani Lakshmibai of Jhansi

As mentioned earlier (Ch. XVII), Jhansi was annexed by Lord Dalhousie in 1854, following the death of its young Raja Gangadharrao in November, 1853. The latter had adopted a son, a child named Damodarrao, whom Lord Dalhousie had declined to recognise as the rightful heir to the *Gadi*. Gangadharrao's widow, Rani Lakshmibai, who was barely 18 then, had after her husband's death, carried on the administration of the State on behalf of her minor son, with amazing efficiency, till Lord Dalhousie annexed the State by a proclamation dated 13th March 1854. Jhansi was then occupied by a contingent of the Company's Indian army. The annexation had given rise to widespread and bitter discontent amongst the people throughout the State—and Rani Lakshmibai protested against it vigorously. Lord Dalhousie completely ignored the discontent and the protest. Not only that; he seized the deceased Gangadharrao's private jewellery valued at rupees four-and-a-half lacs and two-and-a-half lacs in hard cash and deposited the same in the Company's treasury. He also declared in so many words, that although the minor Damodarrao would, on attaining majority, become entitled to get back the private property of his father, he would never become entitled to the *Gadi (Jhansi Papers*, 1858, p. 31).

To add insult to injury, Lord Dalhousie offered to Rani Lakshmibai a monthly pension of Rs. 5,000/- which the latter contemptuously refused to accept. Then followed a campaign of vilification of the young widow.

> "Evil things were said of her... It was alleged that the Rani was a mere child under the influence of others, and that she was given to intemperance. That she was not a mere child was

demonstrated by her conversation; and her intemperance seems to be a myth." (Sir John Kaye, *History of the Sepoy War*, Vol. III, pp. 361–62)

We would also quote the statement of Major Malcolm, who had personal knowledge of Rani Lakshmibai's character and way of life. In an official letter to the Governor-General, dated 16th March, 1855, Major Malcolm wrote that the Rani

"... bears a very high character and is much respected by everyone at Jhansi". (*Jhansi Papers*, p. 28)

Contemporary records also go to prove that Rani Lakshmibai was a young woman of upright character, exceptional courage and acumen, and was extraordinarily capable. As a child she had lived with her parents at Bithoor, at the exiled Peshwa *Durbar* where she was extremely popular as Kumari Lakshmibai. As a girl she had learnt riding, and the use of arms and was a crackshot at the age of seven. She used to go with young Nana and his brothers on their hunting expeditions.

Rani Lakshmibai and the people had never been able to reconcile themselves to the disgrace of the Jhansi *Gadi* implicit in the annexation of the State, even though several years had passed since then. It was therefore only natural that the Rani became one of the most important, and she proved to be the bravest, of the top leaders of the 1857 Revolution.

Jhansi Throws off the English Yoke

As per plans of the revolutionaries, 4th June, 1857, had been fixed for the outbreak at Jhansi. On the appointed date, Havildar Gurbaksh Singh of the Company's 12th Indian Infantry (which had been stationed at Jhansi on its occupation by the English), started it by seizing the Company's magazine and treasury. Then Rani Lakshmibai came out fully armed and placed herself at the head of the revolutionaries. She was hardly 21 then.

On 7th June the Company's fort at Jhansi, then occupied by the English, was attacked on behalf of the Rani py Risaldar Kaley Khan and Tehsildar Mohammed Hussain. The Company's troops in the fort made common cause with the revolutionaries and Jhansi became independent that very day. Rani Lakshmibai once again occupied the Jhansi *Gadi* as the Regent, on behalf of her minor son, Raja Damodarrao. The Union Jack over the fort was hauled down and replaced by the green flag of the Delhi Emperor. The independence of Jhansi was proclaimed throughout the State by beat of drum to the accompaniment of the usual formula: "The world is God's. The country is the Emperor's. The orders are Rani Lakshmibai's."

It has been stated that on 8th June, 67 English men, women and children in the fort were massacred under the orders of Risaldar Kaley Khan. According to Sir John Kaye, Rani Lakshmibai had nothing whatsoever to do with it. None of her own men were present on the spot, nor was her assent asked for, much less given (*History of the Sepoy War*, Vol. II).

Oudh's Preparations for Revolution

The fiercest and hardest-fought battles of 1857–58 were fought on the soil of Oudh. The reason was that the people of Oudh, from the highest to the lowest, had staked everything that they had on the success of the revolution. G.B. Malleson writes:

> "The whole of Oudh was up in arms against us. Not only the Indian sepoys of the Company's regular army, but 60,000 men of the deposed Nawab of Oudh, the zamindars and their tenants were solidly ranged against us. In addition, 250 fortresses, some of them with heavy guns mounted on their walls had also gone to the revolutionaries. All these people had weighed the Company's rule against that of their own Nawab's and had, by and large, decided that the latter had been much better than the Company's administration. Even the pensioners who had retired from our army had openly declared against us and every one of them took an active part in the revolution." (*The Red Pamphlet*)

The smouldering fires of disaffection had been fanned by the intensive revolutionary propaganda carried on over a long period by thousands of *Moulvis* and *Pandits*, who had gone round from barracks to barracks, and from village to village, filling the sepoys and the people with a religious zeal for the revolution. The result was that nowhere else in the country were the preparations made with such meticulous care and efficiency as in Oudh.

Disarming of VII Oudh Irregular Infantry

In the beginning of May, 1857, the news of Mangal Pandey's hanging reached and inflamed the sepoys in the Lucknow Cantonment. Those who could not restrain themselves burned down some English houses.

On 3rd May, according to Charles Ball, four men of the VII Oudh Irregular Infantry

> "... forced their way into the quarters of the adjutant of the regiment (Lieutenant Mecham) and ordered him to prepare for death. They informed him that, personally, they had no quarrel with him but that 'he was a *Feringhee* and must die' ... The mutineers having paused, that he might speak to them, he said 'Men! ... I am unarmed, and you can kill me; but that will do you no good. You will not ultimately prevail in this matter; another adjutant will be appointed in my place ... Why, then, should you destroy me?' The expostulation had a fortunate and unexpected effect upon the intruders, who turned and left the place without further attempting to molest the astonished officer." (*History of the Indian Mutiny*, Vol. I, p. 52)

The same evening news of the incident reached Sir Henry Lawrence, the Chief Commissioner of Oudh, who immediately:

> "... ordered out Her Majesty's 32nd Foot, the 13th, 48th, and 71st Native Infantry, the 7th Cavalry, and a battery of eight guns manned by Europeans, and proceeded to the lines of the mutineers, about seven miles from the city. Darkness had set in before he arrived and his movement had been so sudden, that the men of the 7 regiment were completely taken by surprise. Within five minutes after his troops had reached the parade ground the bugler was ordered to sound the assembly; and the men on making their appearance were

commanded to form in front of their lines ... The Infantry and Cavalry then formed on either side of them—the guns being ranged in front ... and ... the 7th, completely baffled awaited their doom, whatever it might be. They were simply ordered to lay down their arms, and they obeyed without a moment's hesitation." (ibid.)

Further Steps taken by Sir Henry Lawrence

After disarming the 7th regiment, Sir Henry had recourse to diplomacy and adopted conciliatory methods. He held a military *Durbar* on 12th May at which he delivered an impressive speech in Hindustani. In it he drew pointed attention of the Hindu and Mussalman sepoys to the importance of their steadfast loyalty to the Company's Government, which had benefited both. For the benefit of the Muslim sepoys, he related how Maharaja Ranjit Singh had dishonoured Islam. Similarly, he recalled to the Hindu sepoy's mind the various ways in which the Mughal Emperor, Aurangzeb, had laid the axe at the root of the Hindu religion. He emphasised that the English alone could save them from each other. He then distributed shawls, swords and *pugrees* (turbans) as presents to reward the loyalty of the sepoys. For all the effect that the speech and the presents had on the Hindu and Mussalman sepoys, he might as well have saved himself the trouble. The sepoys were not impressed. On the contrary, both saw clearly that the sole object of recalling the past animosities between the two communities was to keep them at daggers drawn with each other and so to keep both under English domination.

Next day, on 13th May, news of the outbreak at Meerut reached Lucknow, followed on the 14th by news of Delhi's liberation.

Sir Henry took precautionary measures immediately. He fortified Machhi Bhavan and the Residency, and all the Englishwomen and children were taken and lodged there. He ordered that all Englishmen in Lucknow should be compulsorily drilled and trained in the use of arms. He even sent a special emissary to General Jung Bahadur, the Prime Minister of Nepal, to request help for the English in their dire calamity.

The Revolution Breaks out at Lucknow

The signal agreed upon for the outbreak was reported to be the firing of some shots in the cantonment on 30th May between 8 and 9 p.m. Accordingly:

> "... before the chimes that told the hour of nine had ceased to vibrate on the ear, a discharge of musketry was heard in the lines of the 71st regiment of native infantry." (ibid., p. 181)

The next morning, on 31st May, Sir Henry Lawrence advanced against the revolutionaries with some white soldiers and the 7th Light Indian Cavalry. The latter were sent in advance; but upon meeting the revolutionaries, some *sowars* went over to them. Later, the 48th Infantry, the 71st Infantry and 7th Cavalry discarded the Union Jack and replaced it by the green flag.

> "Leaving, therefore, 200 Europeans and four guns in the cantonment, he (Sir Henry) moved with the remainder of his force to the city, and dispatched the following report to the Governor-General, dated Lucknow, May 31st, 2 p.m.

> "Most of the houses in the cantonment have been burnt at the outbreak. The mutineers, consisting of half the 48th native infantry, about half of the 71st, some few of the 13th, and two troops of the 7th cavalry, have fled towards Seetapore" (ibid., p. 183)

Sitapur

Sitapur is to the north-west of Lucknow and some 50 miles from it. The three infantry regiments stationed there discarded the Union Jack on 3rd June and raised aloft the green flag. They seized the Company's treasury and killed all the English that they could find. Twenty-four are stated to have been killed, whilst some sought and were given refuge in the houses of the zamindars in the neighbourhood of Sitapur.

Farrukhabad

Tafazzul Hussain Khan, the Nawab of Farrukhabad, had been deposed by the Company. The revolutionary sepoys went from Sitapur to Farrukhabad. The English there had taken refuge in the fort. After some hard-fought battles, the sepoys occupied the fort, killed all the English there and reinstated the deposed Nawab on the *Gadi*. Within a few weeks not a single Englishman was left in the Farrukhabad State.

Fyzabad

Fyzabad town and Division, constituted the most important as well as the most disaffected region of Eastern Oudh. The chief cause of the disaffection has been stated by Sir Henry Lawrence in the letter which he wrote to Lord Canning in April, 1857:

> "The Talukdars have also, I fear, been harshly dealt with. At least in the Faizabad Division, they have lost half their villages. Some Talukdars have lost all." (Quoted in *History the Indian Mutiny* by Kaye and Malleson, Vol. III, p. 266, 1898 Edn.)

Moulvi Ahmed Shah was one of the dispossessed Taluqdars. From the time of the annexation of the Kingdom of Oudh, he had been devoting all his time, attention and energy in preparing the people for "the War of Independence". He toured constantly and extensively in Fyzabad, Lucknow and Agra, and addressed public meetings. The meetings were everywhere attended by thousands of people, who were so impressed by the impassioned eloquence with which he narrated the history of their hundred years' subjection to foreign rule that, before dispersing, they invariably took the pledge to stake everything they had, even their lives, on the success of the coming "war for freedom". Not only by public speeches but also by publishing pamphlets and periodicals be carried on intensive propaganda and agitation. The English ordered his arrest but the Oudh police would not carry out the order and so the English had to detail a military posse to effect the arrest. Moulvi Ahmed Shah was arrested, tried for overt acts of rebellion and sentenced to death. His arrest and conviction added fuel to the smouldering fires of rebellion throughout the region.

The Company's troops stationed in Fyzabad at that time consisted of two infantry regiments, some cavalry and some guns. Immediately after Moulvi Ahmed Shah had been lodged in jail pending his execution, the sepoys, joined by the people, raised aloft the green flag of independence. Assembled on a parade, they plainly told their English officers that, in future, they would obey only such orders as were given to them by their Indian officers. Subedar Dalip Singh forthwith took in custody all the English officers. The walls of the jail were demolished and Moulvi Ahmed Shah's fetters were cut away. The sepoys and the people then unanimously elected Moulvi Ahmed Shah as their leader, and as such, he immediately wrote to all the English in Fyzabad, calling upon them to quit the town. He then arranged for boats to take them away, provisioned the boats and even gave the departing English some money for incidental expenses on the journey. Law and order were established in the town, and on the morning of 9th June, the end of the Company's rule and the re-establishment of King Wajid Ali Shah's rule were proclaimed throughout the town and the entire Fyzabad region. In obedience to Moulvi Ahmed Shah's strictly enforced orders, not a single English life was taken in Fyzabad throughout the upheaval.

Sultanpur and Saloni

Sultanpur hoisted the green flag on 9th June, and Saloni did the same the next day. Sardar Rustam Shah, Taluqdar of Saloni, had publicly declared his determination and taken a pledge not to rest till English rule had been uprooted. His treatment of the Englishmen, women and children was, however, unexceptionable and even generous.

Shahganj

Raja Man Singh of Shahganj had been jailed by the Company's administration in connection with some dispute about revenue. After the outbreak he assumed the leadership of the revolutionaries. With the concurrence of the other local revolutionary leaders, he gave asylum in his fort to 29 Englishwomen and children and kept them safe and sound all the time.

Raja Hanumant Singh of Kala-Kankar

We cannot do better than quote the historians Kaye and Malleson about Raja Hanumant Singh:

> "This noble Rajput had been dispossessed, by the action of the revenue system introduced by the British, of part of his property. Keenly as he felt the tyranny and the disgrace, his noble nature yet declined to regard the fugitive chiefs of the nation, which had nearly ruined him, in any other light than as people in distress. He helped them in that distress; he saw them in safety to their own fortress. But when, on bidding him farewell, Captain Barrow expressed a hope that he would aid in suppressing the revolt, he stood erect as he replied:"
>
> "Sahib, your countrymen came into this country and drove out our King. You sent your officers round the districts to examine the titles to the estates. At one blow you took from me lands which from time immemorial had been in my family. I submitted. Suddenly misfortune fell on you. The people of the land rose against you. You came to me whom you had despoiled. I have saved you. But now,—*now I march at the head of my retainers to Lakhnao to try and drive you out from the country.*" (italics ours. *History of the Indian Mutiny* by Kaye and Malleson, Vol. III, p. 273 (Footnote), 1898 Edn.)

Chivalry of Oudh Aristocracy

Contemporary history reveals a number of Hanumant Singhs both Hindu and Mussalman, whose patriotism was matched by their chivalry. They openly led the revolutionaries but, at the same time, did not hesitate to give asylum in their palaces to fugitive English officers, women and children. Instances are mentioned in the letters and reports of the English survivors.

End of the Company's Rule in Oudh

Barring a small part of the city of Lucknow, the whole of Oudh had freed itself from the Company's clutches between 30th May and 11th June, 1857. Sir George W. Forrest refers to it as follows:

> "Thus in the course of ten days, the English administration in Oudh vanished like a dream and left not a wreck behind. The troops mutinied, the people threw off their allegiance. *But there was no revenge, no cruelty.* The brave and turbulent population, with a few exceptions, *treated the fugitives of the ruling race with marked kindness, and the high courtesy and chivalry of the people of Oudh was conspicuous in their dealings with their fallen masters*, who, in the days of their power, had from the best (?) of motives, inflicted on many of them a grave wrong." (*State Papers*, Vol. II, p. 37. Italics ours).

22

PUNJAB—ITS IMPORTANCE AND REACTION

Sir John Lawrence's View

The vital importance of the Punjab's steadfast loyalty to the English at the greatest crisis in their rule over India is best described in the following words of Sir John Lawrence, the then Chief Commissioner of the Punjab:

> "Had the Punjab gone, we might have been ruined. Long before reinforcements could have reached the upper provinces, the bones of all Englishmen would have been bleaching in the sun. England could never have recovered from the calamity..." *(Life of Lord Lawrence, Vol. II, p. 335)*

It was from the Punjab, in the north-west of Delhi, that the English attack on Delhi was ultimately launched, and we propose to narrate the events in the Punjab preceding the attack.

Lord Canning's Preparations

It has already been mentioned that on getting the ominous news of what had happened at Meerut and Delhi, Lord Canning had sent for troops from Madras, Calcutta, Rangoon, etc. These he had dispatched to Banaras and Allahabad under General Neill's command.

At the same time he had ordered the Commander-in-Chief in India, General Anson, to march on Delhi. Simultaneously, he had issued and published widely throughout India a proclamation aimed at the pacification of the sepoys. It stated that the Company's Government did not ever have the slightest intention to interfere with anyone's religion, nor did it then intend to do so. It also contained an offer to the sepoys of the option of manufacturing their own cartridges. It declared that men who had "eaten" the Company's "salt" would undoubtedly be committing a sin if they took part in the "revolt".

If Punjab had Joined the Revolutionaries

It is quite a big IF, and we have quoted above the views of Sir John Lawrence about the consequences that would have followed inevitably, had the Punjab gone over to the revolutionaries. General Anson could get troops only from the Punjab, and from nowhere else, for the counterattack on the revolutionaries. Had the Punjab, too, followed in the footsteps of Oudh and Rohilkhand, it would have become utterly impossible for the English to reconquer India. Sir John Lawrence, therefore, took immediately the most effective steps that were possible to retain intact the loyalty of the Punjab, particularly of the Sikhs, for the English Government.

Incitement of Sikhs Against Mussalmans

Whilst Sir Henry Lawrence, the Chief Commissioner of Oudh, was, as narrated before, busy inflaming the Mussalman sepoys of Oudh against the Sikhs, his brother Sir John Lawrence, was doing his level best to incite the Sikhs in the Punjab against the Mussalmans. He kept on telling the Sikhs again and again that the Mughal Emperors of India had all along been intensely hostile to the Sikh religion; so much so, that the Emperor Aurangzeb had had beheaded at Delhi the Sikh Guru, Tegh Bahadur. He pointed out to them that, with English help, they could now avenge all those atrocities by destroying Bahadur Shah, the Mughal Emperor, and the "mutineers" who were lighting under him to re-establish the Mussalman rule over the Sikhs too. He appealed to them to march on Delhi and raze it to the ground. The propaganda did not stop there. Copies of a forged proclamation stated to have been issued by Bahadur Shah were found pasted on the walls in every important town of the Punjab. In the proclamation it was stated that Bahadur Shah had ordered that the first step to be taken was the massacre of all the Sikhs everywhere. The historian Metcalfe has stated that at about the same time, Bahadur Shah was in fact constantly going round in Delhi on an elephant, and personally proclaiming that the war was against the *Feringhees* only, and ordering that no Indian was to be touched at all.

Another step taken by Sir John Lawrence was a very shrewd one as it ensured the loyalty of the moneyed classes of the Punjab to the English Government. On behalf of the Company he offered six per cent interest on loans advanced to the Company. The high rate of interest attracted huge investments. From the moneyed classes all over the Punjab. The self-interest of thousands of rich people and therefore, of influential classes, thus became inseparably bound with the existence of the English rule over the country. At the same time it placed at the disposal of the Company plenty of money, more than enough for any emergency that might at any time arise anywhere in the Company's domain. It may be mentioned that in those days people with spare cash could not, and did not, get a return of more than three per cent and that the coins were of pure gold or silver.

Sir John Lawrence's efforts for consolidating the English hold over the Punjab and retaining its loyalty met with complete success as proved by subsequent events.

Revolutionaries' Efforts to Win over Sikhs

The Emperor, Bahadur Shah, and other revolutionary leaders also made every possible effort to win over the Sikh people and the Sikh Rajas. Bahadur Shah sent a special envoy of his, Tajuddin, to the Rajas of Patiala, Nabha, Jind and other Sikh Chiefs and Sardars. Tajuddin waited on all of them. We give below an English rendering of some extracts from Tajuddin's report to the Emperor:

> "The Sikh Sardars of Punjab are lazy and cowardly. There is little hope of their ever joining the Revolution. They are mere puppets in English hands ... I opened my heart to them, and asked them the reason why they were siding with the English against the life-and-death struggle of their own country for its independence ...They replied:
>
> 'Look Sir, all the Sikhs are awaiting the opportune time; the moment the Emperor's order is received, all the *Kafirs* (the English) will be wiped off the Punjab in a single day.' ... In my own opinion, they cannot be trusted at all."

The Emperor then sent personal letters to the Sikh Rajas, Chiefs and Sardars. But all of them treated the letters with contempt and some even had the couriers murdered!

Sir Robert Montgomery

In addition to the Sikh and English regiments, Hindu and Mussalman regiments were also then stationed in the Punjab. The biggest and most important cantonment was at Miyan Meer, near Lahore, and Robert Montgomery was its Commanding Officer. The Indian sepoys at the cantonment numbered one-to-four as against the English soldiers.

The Hindustani sepoys throughout the Punjab had planned that the revolution in the Punjab was to start at Miyan Meer with the sepoys' attack on the fort at Lahore, and its occupation by them. This was the first step to be taken and thereafter the sepoys of the regiments at Peshawar, Ambala, Phillaur and Jullundur were to revolt simultaneously.

The events at Meerut alerted Montgomery; one of his secret agents also informed him that the sepoys at Miyan Meer were on the *qui vive* and might revolt any moment. He immediately ordered out on parade about a thousand Hindustani sepoys. English cavalry and batteries manned by Englishmen were posted all round the parading sepoys, who were ordered to lay down their arms. The sepoys had no choice. They laid down their arms and quietly marched back to their barracks.

At about the same time, a regiment of English soldiers was sent to the fort at Lahore to "relieve" the Hindustani soldiers posted there. The latter were disarmed after being "relieved" and sent to the barracks situated outside the fort. Thereafter the English regiment and some English-manned batteries constituted the sole occupants of the fort.

There can hardly be any doubt that Sir Robert Montgomery's foresight and prompt action at the right time contributed very largely to the saving of the Punjab for the English.

Peshawar

Four Indian regiments, namely, the 21st, the 27th, the 51st Infantry, and the 5th Cavalry were stationed in four cantonments near

Peshawar. Reports were circulating to the effect that all the four had made up their minds to revolt.

As soon as they got news of the happenings at Miyan Meer, the English officers of the regiments collected at Peshawar all the English regiments stationed in the areas adjoining the Jhelum. On the morning of May 22, the English regiments were sent to all the four cantonments where the Indian regiments were stationed. Then the latter were rounded up and disarmed. The disarmed sepoys were then confined to the lines. That evening some of them tried to go into the city. As stated in the *Narrative of the Indian Revolt* (p. 35), they were stopped and some thirteen or fourteen of them were immediately hanged as a lesson for the others. Guns were then placed outside the barracks, so that no one could dare go out. Thereafter, a number of them were either hanged or blown off from the cannon's mouth.

Hoti Mardan—Col. Spottiswood's Suicide

The 55th Infantry was stationed at Hoti Mardan, near Peshawar. It was commanded by Col. Spottiswood, who was confident that his regiment would never revolt. Other English officers in the Punjab insisted that the 57th too should be disarmed. Col. Spottiswood strenuously opposed the disarming. The Punjab Government decided to disarm the regiment, whereupon, it is stated, Col. Spottiswood committed suicide.

For disarming the 55th, English soldiers and batteries were sent to Hoti Mardan. The sepoys attempted to escape, but outnumbered as they were by the English troops, the attempt failed. One hundred and fifty were killed on the spot to teach a lesson to the others, and the rest were imprisoned.

> "Of the prisoners of the 55th, a more awful example was made. They were tried, condemned, and every third man was selected to be blown off from guns." (ibid., p. 36)

According to the historians, Kaye and Malleson:

> "Col. Nicholson and Sir John Lawrence both admitted in their letters the guiltlessness of most of the sepoys of the 55th. But even so, the fugitive sepoys were being constantly ferreted

out from their far-off hiding places throughout the months of June and July and blown off the cannon's mouth. Some were done to death in ways even more horrifying." *(History of the Indian Mutiny,* Book VI, Chap. 4)

An English officer who was present when the men were being blown off wrote at the time:

"That parade was a strange scene. There were about nine thousand men on parade ... The troops were drawn up on three sides of a square, the fourth side being occupied by ten guns ... The first ten of the prisoners were then lashed to the guns, the artillery officer waved his sword, you heard the roar of guns, and above the smoke you saw legs, arms and heads, flying in all directions. There were four of these salvoes, and at each a sort of buzz went through the whole mass of the troops, a sort of murmur of horror. Since that time we have had execution parades once or twice a week, and such is the force of habit we now think little of them." *(Narrative of the Indian Revolt,* p. 36)

Watery Grave

The 10th Cavalry was disarmed, too, on mere suspicion. The horses were the personal property of the men, but were confiscated. So was the money found on them. The horses were later auctioned and are stated to have fetched Rs. 50,000, which were deposited in the Company's treasury. After the men had been disarmed, they were made to get on the boats moored in the Sindhu river. The boats then rowed away and it is not known where the boats went, or what happened to the men. An English officer, who was present when the boats started, wrote "... I expect every mother's son will have a chance of being drowned in the rapids" *(The Narrative,* p. 38).

John Kaye's Testimony

About the inhumanities inflicted on such people in and around Peshawar, as were either revolutionaries as a matter of fact, or were merely suspected of being so, we quote the historian John Kaye:

"Though I have plenty of letters with me describing the terrible and cruel tortures committed by our officers, I do not write a word about it, so that this subject should be no longer before the world." *(Sepoy War,* Book VI, Chap. 4)

Ferozepur, Jullundur, Phillaur and Ludhiana

At Ferozepur the Company had a very big magazine. On May 13, the English officers summoned a parade of the sepoys to ascertain their sentiments from their behaviour and were satisfied. But it appears that the sepoys had deliberately hoodwinked the English officers by their unexceptionable behaviour during the parade, for they revolted within a few hours. The English officer blew up the magazine. The people of Ferozepur sided with the revolutionaries. The houses of the English were burnt down and every Englishman who could be found was killed. The sepoys then started on their march to Delhi. An English regiment pursued them for some time, but finding it fruitless returned to Ferozepur.

The sepoys of the Indian regiments stationed at Jullundur, Phillaur and Ludhiana had been industriously, but quietly, making preparations for the revolution.

At midnight on June 9, the sepoys at Jullundur rose up in arms all of a sudden. The English troops there were taken by surprise. Before they could recover and take any action, the sepoys, instead of wasting time in killing Englishmen, left for Delhi. They sent a horseman, in advance, to Phillaur to apprise and alert the sepoys there.

The Indian regiments at Phillaur revolted forthwith, and on the arrival of the Jullundur sepoys, hugged them and, with them, started for Ludhiana en route to Delhi.

The Sutlej flowed across the way to Ludhiana and there was a bridge of boats for crossing over to the other side. The English officers at Ludhiana had demolished the bridge as soon as they got the report of the happenings at Jullundur and Phillaur. English and Sikh regiments, and some regiments furnished by the Raja of Nabha were massed on the other side of the river to check the advance of the approaching revolutionary sepoys. The latter had got wind of the formidable obstacles barring their way and made a detour to cross the river by wading through it some four miles upstream. Only a few of them had got across when the English and the Sikhs started shelling them. It was 10 p.m. and it was pitch dark. The revolutionaries could not even see from which side they were being shelled. Their own guns had not, till then, got across. In spite of these handicaps, they gallantly fought on for hours till sunrise. Then a stray bullet hit the English Commander Williams and killed him. The English and the Sikhs were pressed back and had to retire. The victorious revolutionaries then continued on their way to Ludhiana. They entered the town at mid-day and helped by the townspeople they got busy immediately. English houses were burnt down, the Company's treasury was seized and the jail was demolished. The combined force of the Hindustani sepoys of Jullundur, Phillaur and Ludhiana then started on its march to Delhi to fight in their country's war of independence. They and the sepoys from Ferozepur constituted the only contribution and help received by the revolutionaries from the Punjab region. It was given mainly, if not solely, by the Hindustani sepoys stationed in the Punjab and the Hindustani people domiciled there.

"Hindustanis" Externed from Punjab

Whilst the English faith and trust in the loyalty of the Punjabis generally and of the Sikhs particularly were amply justified, the Indians from the eastern provinces, who were domiciled in the Punjab—whom the indigenous Punjabis called "Hindustanis"—were regarded with great suspicion by the English. So, during the early days of the revolution, tens of thousands of unoffending and respectable "Hindustani" citizens of the Punjab were forcibly expelled from their homes and were driven across the Sutlej to make it safe for the English to send English and Sikh troops to re-take Delhi, without the risk of any trouble or insurrection breaking out in the Punjab, whilst the English and Sikh troops were away.

General Anson's Difficulties

As mentioned earlier, General Anson the Commander-in-Chief was ordered by Lord Canning to march on Delhi and re-take it.

On receipt of that order General Anson left Simla and came down to Ambala to make the necessary preparations. It took him some time on account of the difficulties which stemmed from the hostile attitude of the people in Ambala and in the country around it, who were most unwilling to give any help at all to the English. General Anson could not get carts for transport or even coolies. Nor could he buy provisions or fodder. As stated by the historian John Kaye:

> "Natives of all classes stood aloof, waiting and watching the issue of events; from the capitalist to the coolie all shrank alike from rendering assistance to those whose power might be swept away in a day." (Kaye & Malleson's *History of the Indian Mutiny*, Vol. II, pp. 120–1)

Sikh Rajas' Betrayal of India

The territories of three important Sikh States, Patiala, Nabha and Jhind, intersected the way from Ambala to Delhi at various points. Even if these States had remained neutral, the English cause would have, very probably, suffered almost as much as it would have, had they joined the revolutionaries. But thanks mainly to the diplomacy of Sir John Lawrence, the Chief Commissioner of the Punjab, the Rajas of the three States were completely won over and came to the help of the English with plentiful supplies of men, money and material. The Raja of Patiala sent his infantry and artillery detachments to keep Thaneshwar safe in English hands, and the Raja of Jhind undertook the responsibility of defending another important English station, Panipat, should it become necessary.

Not only was General Anson's way to Delhi thus cleared of every obstacle, but it was also rendered impossible for the revolutionaries to get any further help or support from the Punjab.

23

ON THE MARCH TO DELHI

General Anson's Death

On May 25, General Anson left Ambala for Delhi at the head of a big army of English and Sikh soldiers. Amongst the latter was the very large body of troops furnished by the three Sikh States. But General Anson got an attack of cholera at Karnal and died on the 27th. General Sir Henry Bernard succeeded him as the Commander-in-Chief of the Company's forces in India.

General Bernard's English and Sikh Soldiers on March

The unspeakable atrocities committed by the English and Sikh soldiers of the invading army along its way to Delhi were no less terrible than those of General Neill's men which have already been narrated. Even the unoffending ordinary wayfarers to Delhi were not spared as they were suspected of going to Delhi to join the revolutionaries. Untold numbers of them were caught hold of and murdered. An English officer of the force wrote:

> "To overawe the people living alongside our way to Delhi from Ambala with the might of the English nation and so re-establish its prestige, thousands of villagers were fearfully tortured before being hanged. They were run through by bayonets and beef was forced down the throats of the Hindu villagers by spear-heads or bayonets." (*History of the Siege of Delhi* by an officer who served there)

Whilst being tortured, the villagers were treated to the sight of gallows being put up to hang them and they were strung up half-dead.

Farce of the Martial Courts

Most of the villagers thus done to death had never lifted a finger against the English Company's Government. But in order to ensure that none of them escaped death, martial courts were set up from time to time.

> "The officers appointed as judges of the martial courts had to take an oath before they assumed office that they will not allow a single person to evade the gallows." (Holme's *History of the Sepoy War*, p. 124)

The procedure of the martial court was that the villagers were drawn up in long lines and the sentence was immediately pronounced and carried out without even the pretence of a trial.

On Outskirts of Delhi

The English troops at Meerut who had been paralysed into immobility by the sudden eruption of May 10 came to life again, and left Meerut to join forces with General Bernard's army. But before a junction between the two could be effected, the revolutionaries sallied forth from Delhi and, on May 30, engaged the Meerut troops at the river Hindon. The left flank of the revolutionaries weakened in the battle that followed and had to retire, leaving behind five guns and their ammunition. A lone sepoy had, however, hidden himself amidst the guns, and when the English soldiers came up to get hold of the guns, the sepoy exploded the magazine, blowing to pieces, the guns, the approaching English soldiers and, of course, himself. The historian, John Kaye, comments on the heroism of the unknown soldier as follows:

> "It taught us that, among the mutineers, there were brave and desperate men who were ready to court death for the sake of the national cause." (*History of the Sepoy War*, Vol. II, p. 138)

The next day, on May 31, the revolutionary troops, who had retired the previous day, returned to resume the offensive against the Meerut troops. The guns on both sides engaged in an artillery duel, in which the English are stated to have lost many lives and were reduced to disorder. The revolutionary troops then returned to Delhi.

Gorkha Reinforcements for General Bernard

On June 1, Gorkha troops commanded by Major Reid joined the English force that had come from Meerut. A week later, on June 7, General Bernard joined both. Large quantities of material needed for the siege of Delhi were supplied by the Raja of Nabha. The vast and well-equipped army of the three combined forces then advanced on Delhi and reached Alipur on the outskirts of Delhi.

Almost immediately, the revolutionary army sallied forth and attacked General Bernard at Bundelay ki Serai. We shall describe this battle later, as we propose to digress here to relate the events in Delhi after Bahadur Shah had again been proclaimed Emperor of India on May 16, 1857.

24

DELHI—ITS EMPEROR AND PEOPLE

Bahadur Shah

*I*mmediately after Delhi had achieved independence, the re-instated Emperor issued a proclamation in Urdu. The English rendering of a part of it is given below:

> "Sons of Hindustan! If we make up our minds to do it, we can finish the enemy in no time. We will destroy the enemy and save our dearer-than-life country and religion from the danger which threatens both." (Lecky's *Fictions Exposed and Urdoo Works*)

A second proclamation followed after some time. Its copies were very widely distributed throughout India, including the cantonments and bazars in the distant South. It was addressed to all the Hindus and Mussalmans of India and was to the following effect:

> "To all Hindus and Mussalmans. We have joined the people only because we were convinced that it was our sacred duty to do so. Anyone who shows the white feather on this critical occasion, or who is simple enough to trust the slippery *Feringhees'* promises, will soon be put to shame. Loyalty to England, shown by anyone, will be rewarded in the same way as the loyalty of the Nawabs of Oudh was. It is therefore absolutely essential that the Hindus and Mussalmans should unite, work and fight not only to win the war but also to maintain peace and order on the home front, under the guidance and according to the instructions of a universally respected leader. The contentment of the poor must also be secured … Everyone should see to it that copies of this proclamation are exhibited in as many public places as possible."

A third proclamation was published in Bareilly in the name of Bahadur Shah and contained the following appeal:

"Hindus and Mussalmans of Hindustan! Be up and doing, brothers! Of all the gifts with which God has blessed man, freedom is the most precious. Will the cursed tyrant, who has cheated us out of it, be able to keep us deprived of it forever? Can such deeds against the Will of God continue for all time? No! Never! The *Feringhees* committed so many sins against God and men, that the cup of their inequities has become full almost to its brim. They are now consumed with the unholy ambition to destroy the sacred religious faiths of us all. Will you still keep quiet? God does not wish that you should, because He has kindled in the hearts of Hindus and Mussalmans the fire of the determination to drive the English out of the country. By God's grace and with the help of your valour, the English will, before long, sustain such a disastrous defeat that not a trace of the English will be left in our country. All those who draw their swords in this sacred war for the defence of their religion will share equally the glory as brothers. We appeal once again to all our brothers in Hind to rush to the field of battle for doing the duty assigned to them by God."

Bahadur Shah himself frequently went round the city on an elephant and personally congratulated, complimented and encouraged the sepoys and the people on their whole-hearted devotion to the cause and boosted up their morale by exhortations for the continuation of the noble work till the country was made free.

He took another step. Slaughter of cows in India had been forbidden by all the Mughal Emperors from Babar onwards. Even Aurangzeb, who has been stated by some writers to have been a fanatic Mussalman hostile to the Hindus, had not permitted it. But the English administration had ignored the ban and, as mentioned earlier, cows were freely slaughtered everywhere, even in the sacred town of Mathura, to provide the English soldiers with beef. On his re-investment by the revolutionaries with the authority of the 'Emperor of India', Bahadur Shah re-imposed the ban, and forbade cow-slaughter on pain of the offender's hands being out off, or of the offender being shot.

Delhi and its People

Delhi had been the rallying point of the revolutionary sepoys who had gravitated to it from all sides. Manifestoes of loyalty to the Emperor poured into Delhi every day from all parts of the country. The people of Delhi, with unbounded enthusiasm, immediately set up a number of workshops for manufacturing firearms and ammunition. Cannons were cast in large numbers and thousands of maunds of gunpowder was produced every day. In one arsenal alone in the Chooriwalan Street, the daily output of gunpowder was 700 maunds as stated by Zaheer, a personal attendant of Bahadur Shah, in his book *Dastan-i-Ghadar.*

We would now resume the narration of the first battles for Delhi which were fought around and under its walls.

25

FIRST BATTLES FOR DELHI

At Bundelay ki Serai

On June 8, the revolutionary troops inside Delhi sallied forth to attack the Company's force under General Bernard, which was advancing on Delhi from Alipur. They were led out by one of Bahadur Shah's sons named Mirza Mughal. They were pitted against an English army reinforced by the Gorkhas and Sikhs, and led by veteran military commanders, perhaps the ablest in the Company's employ. The revolutionaries fought furiously the whole day, but by evening, they had to retire behind the walls of Delhi, leaving a number of their guns in the hands of the enemy who closely pursued them right up to the walls.

Occupation of the "Pahadi" Adjoining Delhi

The *Pahadi* is an elevated piece of ground on the western edge of Delhi, and was eminently suitable as the place from which an assault on Delhi could be launched. After the battle at Bundelay ki Serai, the Company's army occupied the *Pahadi,* and its commanders held a number of conferences to decide the time when the assault on Delhi was to be launched. They were still undecided when the revolutionaries again sallied forth and attacked them. In the revolutionary attack of June 12, an Indian detachment of the Company's army went over to the revolutionaries, who inflicted substantial losses on the enemy and returned to the walled city.

General Bernard Awaits Additional Reinforcements

It had become the practice of the revolutionaries to sally forth every morning and attack the invaders. They would fight the whole day, inflict heavy losses and retire behind the walls at sunset. The first thing which every fresh detachment of the revolutionary sepoys did on its arrival in the walled city was to sally forth the very next morning and attack the force threatening Delhi.

The actions fought on June 17 and 20, were marked by the splendid courage and determination displayed by the revolutionaries, for which Lord Roberts and other English Commanders have, in their reports, expressed their unstinted admiration.

Ultimately, Commander-in-Chief Bernard came to the conclusion that it would be impossible for him to reduce Delhi, till fresh reinforcements from the Punjab arrived to join him. The siege of Delhi, thereafter, continued without any assault by the besiegers.

The Centenary of Plassey

June 23, 1857 was the centenary day of the Battle of Plassey. Special preparations had been made in Delhi for the sortie on that day. As the day dawned, the cannons mounted on the city walls started shelling the besiegers. Then the revolutionaries sallied forth and fiercely attacked the combined English forces. We quote from Major Reid's *Siege of Delhi:*

> "At about 12 noon the mutineers attacked our force from all sides. No one could fight better than they did. They charged our entire force again and again, and, at one time it appeared to me that we had lost the day."

But at this critical juncture, fortune smiled on the English. A fresh contingent of Sikh soldiers from the Punjab joined them, and the odds against the revolutionaries became heavier. The latter, however, continued to fight, and, at sunset, the battle ended in a draw, each side having earned the genuine respect of its opponents for conspicuous bravery.

The credit for saving the besiegers from utter rout that day must go to the Sikhs from the Punjab. Had they not arrived on the scene in the nick of time and helped General Bernard's force out of its desperate position, the latter would have been annihilated under the walls of Delhi. Thereafter, it might have become impossible for the English to re-establish their hold on India.

A Dictator for Delhi

On July 2, Rohilkhand's revolutionary army was led into Delhi by Mohammad Bakht Khan and was accorded an enthusiastic welcome on behalf of the Emperor and the people of Delhi. The Emperor had been noticing for some time the weaknesses of the local administrators and their inability to cope with new situations which were constantly arising as revolutionary sepoys from different parts of the country kept arriving in Delhi. The Commander-in-Chief, Mirza Mughal, himself had seemed incapable of enforcing order and discipline. His administration of civil affairs, too, had been far from efficient and numerous complaints on that score against Mirza Mughal had reached the Emperor's ears. So when Bakht Khan waited on the Emperor, the latter offered to him the Supreme Command of the entire revolutionary army and the highest post in the civil administration of Delhi. Bakht Khan was a very capable and brave military leader, a strong administrator, and a strict disciplinarian. He expressed his readiness to shoulder the heavy responsibilities of the posts offered to him, provided he was given an absolutely free hand and unfettered full powers. He made it quite plain to Bahadur Shah that even if any of the Emperor's sons, including Mirza Mughal, ventured to interfere or was high-handed with any of the people, then he (Bakht Khan) would promptly and without any reference to the Emperor punish the meddlesome offender. Bahadur Shah agreed, dismissed his son Mirza Mughal, and appointed Bakht Khan the sole civil and military dictator of Delhi.

Bakht Khan had arrived in Delhi at the head of an army of 14,000 infantry, between two and three regiments of cavalry, and a sizeable artillery. He had also brought for Bahadur Shah a cash present of Rs. 4 lacs. In addition he had paid his soldiers six months' salary in advance (*Dastan-i-Ghadar* by Zaheer). He immediately started the rule of law and justice in the civil administration of Delhi and issued an order that every able-bodied man in Delhi was to bear arms and that arms should be supplied free to those who did not have them. He issued orders calculated to enforce strict discipline in the army under his command and to ensure proper behaviour of the soldiers towards the people. He had it widely proclaimed that if any soldier misbehaved towards the people or attempted to get anything without paying a fair price for it, then one or both of the hands of the offender would be cut off. All this was done within a few hours of his appointment, and that very night, Bakht Khan held a council-of-war in the palace, with the Emperor Bahadur Shah, Begun Zeenat Mahal and other top-rank revolutionary leaders. Next morning a parade of about 20,000 revolutionary soldiers was held (*Native Narratives* by Metcalfe, p. 60).

Bakht Khan in Action at the Fighting Front

On July 4, the day after the parade, Bakht Khan ordered a sortie on the besiegers which played havoc with the latter. Thereafter his soldiers harried the Company's army by sallying forth and attacking it almost every day.

In the English Camp

Fresh reinforcements, led by veteran English Commanders had been continuously arriving from the Punjab to join the army near the walls of Delhi. But even so, Commander-in-Chief Bernard did not venture to launch even a single assault on Delhi during the entire month that followed his arrival. Contemporary and subsequent statements by numerous English officers go to show that the English had confidently expected Delhi to capitulate within a few hours of the arrival of the Company's army under its walls. That expectation was being inexorably replaced by disappointment and even despair when General (Sir Henry) Bernard died of cholera on July 5 and was succeeded by General Reid.

Sortie on July 9 and its Sequel

This sortie was exceptionally disastrous for the besiegers. Their cavalry had to turn tail and run from the field before the fierce onslaught, their guns were silenced, and quite a number of their English officers were killed in action. It has been stated that the ignominious defeat infuriated some English soldiers against all "natives". It is stated in Kaye and Malleson's *History of the Indian Mutiny* (Vol. II, p. 438) that

> "Some of our soldiery ... butchered a number of unoffending camp-followers, servants and others who were huddling themselves together in vague alarm, near the Christian churchyard. No loyalty, no fidelity, no patient good service on the part of these poor people could extinguish for a moment the fierce hatred which possessed our white soldiers against all those who wore the dusky livery of the East."

Despair in the English Camp

The sortie on July 9 was followed by another on the 14th, which was even more disastrous for the besiegers. The Company's Commander-in-Chief, General Reid, fell ill, resigned and left for the hills on July 15. He was succeeded by General Wilson.

The green flag had been proudly fluttering for full two months on the ramparts and minarets of Delhi. Some Englishmen had begun to declare that the besiegers of Delhi had themselves been besieged. We might mention here that Delhi had not been besieged in the strict sense of the term, as the Company's army was encamped only under its western wall. The way to and from Delhi on the other three sides was quite open and unhampered for the partisans of the revolution to come in or go out.

The situation had become so full of despair for the English, that quite a number of responsible Englishmen in authority had begun to consider seriously the advisability of lifting the "siege" and of concentrating their efforts elsewhere.

We propose to leave for the present the scene at Delhi to narrate the events that were happening in other parts of India in connection with the revolution.

26

MARCH OF THE REVOLUTION AND ITS REPERCUSSIONS

At Gwalior

Maharaja Jayajirao Sindhia was then on the *Gadi* of the Gwalior State. His entire well-trained and well-equipped army declared for the revolution and on June 14, hoisted the revolution's green flag against the English Company. The English houses in Gwalior were fired. English officers and other Englishmen in Gwalior were put to death; but no Englishwoman or child was touched. Some Englishmen ran away towards Agra, and the English domination over the State came to an end. Even then Maharaja Sindhia was inclined to keep up his friendly relations with the Company's Government of India. Had he led his army to Delhi, the Company's army near Delhi would have been crushed to pulp between the mill stones of the revolutionary army inside Delhi, and the Sindhia's army from Gwalior. The revolutionaries would then have become irresistible throughout the country. As it was, the Gwalior army remained ineffective as it had no leader.

In Indore State

On July 1, the State's army under Saadat Khan, in sympathy with the revolution, attacked the English Residency at Indore; but spared the lives of all the English people there. The latter hurriedly left Indore. The attitude of Maharaja Holkar has, however, been an enigma which historians have not yet been able to solve and to decide where his sympathies lay.

It is remarkable that whilst several Indian rulers kept sitting on the fence, their own army as also the Company's Subsidiary Armies stationed in their States sided with the revolutionaries. The rulers of Kutch and some Rajputana States may be cited as instances of this phenomenon.

At Jaipur and Jodhpur

According to the historian Malleson, the Rajas of Jaipur and Jodhpur ordered their armies to go to the help of the English but the soldiers and their officers flatly refused to do so (*Indian Mutiny*, Vol. III, p. 172).

Liberation of Agra

The incident at Jaipur and Jodhpur was repeated in Bharatpur and some other States.

On July 5, the revolutionaries attacked Agra where a contingent of English soldiers had been stationed. The Raja of Bharatpur sent his army to help the English at Agra. But at the crucial moment, the Indian soldiers of the Bharatpur army refused point-blank to fight for the "whites" and against their own countrymen. General Polwhele's English soldiers then fought the revolutionaries unaided by the Bharatpur army and had to retreat after a day-long battle. On July 6, the green flag was taken out at Agra in a huge procession by the entire police and the people of Agra, Hindus and Mussalmans, and then the city Kotwal hoisted it over the city and proclaimed that as from that day English Raj over Agra was replaced by the Delhi Emperor's rule, which was thus re-established.

Lord Canning's Headquarters at Allahabad

The English had been able to retain possession of the Fort at Allahabad and, as narrated earlier, had succeeded in re-taking and occupying the city too. Allahabad was situated in a very important and central position, from which measures and activities for the suppression of the revolution in the north could best be initiated and guided. The Company's Governor-General, Lord Canning, therefore, shifted his Headquarters from Calcutta to Allahabad. Thereafter, Allahabad became the *de facto* capital of the Company's Government of India, and continued to be so till the end of the revolution. It was at

Allahabad that Queen Victoria's "Proclamation to the Princes and the People of India" was read out by Lord Canning at a public ceremony on November 1, 1858.

Company's Troops March from Allahabad to Cawnpore

On receipt of the news of the calamity which had befallen the English at Cawnpore, General Neill had sent from Allahabad a contingent to their succour under Major Renaud. About the end of June, 1857, General Havelock arrived at Allahabad, and by then the news of the English defeat at Cawnpore and of the massacre at Sati-Chowra Ghat had also come in. General Havelock immediately proceeded towards Cawnpore with a force of Sikh and English soldiers and some artillery. He caught up with the contingent under Major Renaud and joined it on the march to Cawnpore. We quote below from Sir Charles Dilke's *Greater Britain* about the doings of this force on its way:

> "... A letter which reached home in 1857, in which an officer in high command during the march upon Cawnpore, reported 'good bag today, polished off rebel's, it being borne in mind that the 'rebels' thus hanged or blown from guns were not taken in arms, but villagers apprehended on suspicion. During this march atrocities were committed in the burning of villages and massacre of innocent inhabitants at which Muhammad Tughlak himself would have stood ashamed ... "

At Fatehpur

Nana Sahib sent out from Cawnpore a force under the joint command of Jwala Prasad and Teeka Singh to check the advance of the Company's force marching on Cawnpore from Allahabad. On July 12, a battle between the two forces was fought near Fatehpur, in which Nana Sahib's force was defeated and repulsed. The Company's force then entered Fatehpur. The town had earlier proclaimed its liberation from the Company's rule. Some English officers had been killed by the revolutionaries, who had however spared the life of the English magistrate, Mr. Sherrar, and had allowed him to go away. Mr.

Sherrar was now with General Havelock, and both of them wreaked the most fearful vengeance on the people of Fatehpur. It is stated that under orders from their English Commander, the soldiers freely looted the people, and then set fire to the town burning it down to ashes along with its inhabitants.

It was within two or three days of the burning down of Fatehpur, that the inmates of the Bibi Garh Kothi at Cawnpore, were killed, but we propose to deal with the harrowing event after we have finished the narrative of the fight for Cawnpore.

At Cawnpore

General Havelock and his large force arrived on the outskirts of Cawnpore about the middle of July. Nana Sahib personally led his troops out of Cawnpore to fight the invaders. The battle started with an artillery duel between the two armies and ended in the defeat and retreat of Nana Sahib's force. Nana Sahib rallied his men and, according to an English writer of history, the battle was resumed with renewed vigour. Ultimately Nana Sahib had to retire and he went to Bithoor with the remnants of his force. Havelock's victorious troops entered the city of Cawnpore on July 17.

First of all, Havelock's Sikh and English soldiers were directed to loot the city. Then gallows were put up and kept. Charles Ball writes:

> "General Havelock began to wreak a terrible vengeance for the death of Sir Hugh Wheeler. Batch upon batch of natives mounted the scaffold. The calmness of mind and nobility of demeanour which some of the revolutionaries showed at the time of death was such as would do credit to those who martyred themselves for devotion to a principle." (Indian Mutiny, Vol. I, p. 388)

About one individual, Charles Ball testifies:

> "Without the least hesitation, he mounted the scaffold even as a Yogi enters Samadhi" (ibid.).

It has been stated that there was a large blood-stain on the ground at Bibi Garh and it was thought to be the blood of the "massacred" Englishwomen and children. When Havelock entered the town, some Brahmins, who were suspected of having taken part in the revolution, were brought to the spot, and made to lick off the dried blood and wash the place clean before they were hanged. The reason for this queer punishment has been stated by an English officer as follows:

> "I know that the act of touching *Feringhee* blood and washing it with a sweepers broom degrades a high caste Hindu from his religion. Not only this but I make them do it because I know it. We could not wreak a true revenge unless we trample all their religious instincts under foot, before we hang them, so that they may not have the satisfaction of dying as Hindus." (ibid.)

Shortly afterwards, General Neill arrived in Cawnpore with some troops and relieved General Havelock, who on July 25 left for Lucknow with 2,000 English soldiers and several guns. Nana Sahib left Bithoor with his treasury and some soldiers, crossed the Ganges and went towards Fatehgarh.

27
SLAUGHTER OF INNOCENTS

"The Well" at Cawnpore

The burning down of Fatehpur with all its inhabitants has been related in the preceding chapter. The news soon reached Nana Sahib and other revolutionary leaders at Cawnpore and filled them with horror, anger and indignation.

At about the same time, some spies employed by the English were caught and produced before Nana Sahib. It is said that their statements indicated that some of the Englishwomen held in Bibi Garh Kothi had been carrying on secret correspondence with the English officers at Allahabad against Nana Sahib and the revolutionaries.

> "One of the Christian prisoners in the prison of Nana Sahib told the same thing and an Ayah also corroborated it."
> (*Narrative of the Indian Mutiny*, p. 113)

That very evening, all the 125 Englishwomen and children held in Bibi Garh Kothi are stated to have been brutally massacred. Their dead bodies, it is stated, were thrown into a well. In the books in which these allegations have been made, horrific details have been added. For instance, it has been stated that a number of butchers had been called in from the town to butcher the victims and that the latter's limbs were chopped off, one by one, before they were put to death. About these allegations, one of the most authentic English historians, Sir John Kaye, has said:

> "The refinements of cruelty—the unutterable shame, with which, in some chronicles of the day, this hideous massacre was attended, were but fictions of an excited imagination, too readily believed without enquiry, and circulated without thought. None were mutilated, none were dishonoured... This is stated, in the most unqualified manner, by the official functionaries, who made the most diligent enquiries into all the circumstances of the massacres in June and in July"
> (Kaye and Malleson's *History of the Indian Mutiny*, p. 281).

Another eminent English writer, Sir John Russell, the then correspondent in India of the London *Times* said:

> "... The incessant efforts of a gang of forgers and utterly base scoundrels have surrounded it with horrors that have been vainly invented in the hope of adding to the indignation and burning desire for vengeance which hatred failed to arouse." (Russell's *Diary*, p. 164)

The existence of "The Well" at Cawnpore for years after 1857 does not, of course, prove that the massacre at Bibi Garh Kothi did actually take place. The locale of the notorious Black Hole Tragedy at Calcutta (1756) was believed till the day of India's independence, although Lord Clive himself had, in 1765, written to the Court of Directors in England that the so-called "tragedy" had *not the least foundation in truth*.

It may also be recalled that barely three weeks earlier, on June 26/27, the lives of the supposed victims of the Bibi Garh Kothi massacre had been spared under Nana Sahib's specific orders, and they had only been taken into custody (See Chap. XV).

In fairness, we add the following comments on the incident by Sir George Forrest, as the same may be revealing:

> "The evidence proves that the sepoy guard placed over the prisoners refused to murder them. The foul crime was perpetrated by five ruffians of the Nana's guard... It is as ungenerous as it is untrue to charge upon a nation that cruel deed." (*History of the Indian Mutiny,* Introduction, p. iv)

We also quote from the conclusions arrived at by Sir George Campbell, Provisional Civil Commissioner in the 'Mutiny'. He is quoted by E. Thompson in his book, *The Other Side of the Medal* (pp. 78–79), as having said:

> "It is difficult to say anything in extenuation of the Cawnpore massacre and the terrible scene at the well, and yet we must remember two things: first, that it was done, not in cold blood, but in the moment of rage and despair when Havelock had beaten the rebels and was coming in; and second, that we

had done much to provoke such things by the severities of which our people were guilty as they advanced. At a later time a careful investigation was made into the circumstances of the massacre, and we failed to discover that there was any premeditation or direction in the matter."

Anyway, we have no hesitation in saying that if the massacre of unarmed women and children did take place at Bibi Garh Kothi—and it is difficult to be sure that it did not—then it definitely constituted the darkest stain on the good name of the Indian revolutionaries of 1857.

Slaughter near Amritsar

Within three weeks of the incidents at Cawnpore, some 500 innocent, disarmed and fugitive sepoys of the 26th Indian Infantry were done to death within 25 miles of Amritsar, under the personal direction of Frederick Cooper, the Deputy Commissioner of Amritsar, acting under the authority of Sir Robert Montgomery, the commandant at Lahore. Sometime after, Frederick Cooper wrote a book, *The Crisis in the Punjab,* from which it is evident that the massacre was an instance of the measures taken for "overawing" and "striking terror into" the people of the Punjab (pp. 151–52).

The 26th was one of the sepoy regiments stationed at the Miyan Meer cantonment of Lahore. It had been disarmed in May, 1857 (vide Chapter XXII). The disarmed sepoys were refused permission to leave the cantonment, and a guard of Sikh and English soldiers was posted over them. On July 30, however, almost all the sepoys of the 26th and their Indian officers left the cantonment at night. They had no arms and had taken no part whatsoever in any activities connected with the revolution. Next morning they crossed the Ravi and proceeded along its opposite bank. Sir Robert Montgomery ordered Frederick Cooper to have the sepoys held up and dealt with.

The fatigued and hungry sepoys were then resting on the bank of the Ravi some six miles from Ajnala, a Tehsil of Amritsar district, and some 16 miles from Amritsar city. The events that followed have been narrated by Frederick Cooper in his book, *The Crisis in the Punjab,* and in summarising them we shall closely follow his narrative.

At the Ravi Bank

At about mid-day on July 31, Frederick Cooper received information that the fugitive sepoys were going along the bank of the Ravi, within a few miles of Ajnala. The *Tehsildar* (sub-district officer) of Ajnala was immediately sent with a posse of armed Sikh soldiers to hold up the sepoys. A few hours later, Cooper himself arrived at the spot with 80 or 90 Sikh horsemen and started shooting the trudging and fatigued sepoys. The latter numbered about 500 and tried to turn back. Some 150 of them were wounded and fell into the Ravi. Most of them were drowned, as, according to Cooper, they were too exhausted to withstand the strong current which was reddened with their blood. The rest had also tried to swim away, but got out of the river and partly by running and partly by swimming took refuge on an islet in the river about a mile away. They were followed by two boats, which had been kept in readiness each with some 30 armed Sikh soldiers in it. As the boats approached the islet, sixty muskets were pointed towards it. The harassed fugitives saw the boats coming, and, with folded hands, declared their innocence and begged for mercy. About 50 of them, in utter despair, jumped into the river again and were seen no more. Well over 200 had perished by then. The survivors were taken into custody and brought to the bank. The rosaries (sacred religious symbols) round their necks were snipped away and they were securely tied to one another in small groups before being marched off to Ajnala Tehsil under custody of the Sikh horsemen. The cavalcade reached its destination at midnight in pouring rain.

The number of the sepoys that had left the Miyan Meer cantonment barely 24 hours earlier was about 500. By the time they were brought in at the Tehsil their number had dwindled to 282, the rest having perished, barring the few who had somehow got away, but who were rounded up within the next four days, and were hanged or blown off the cannon at Lahore and Amritsar.

At the Ajnala Tehsil Cooper had made his arrangements. He had collected at the Police Station enough ropes for gallows, and 50 armed Sikh soldiers to do the job. But the programme could not be carried out that night as it was raining when the sepoys were brought in, and so it had to be put off till the morning. All the 282 of them, however, could not be lodged in the small Police Station and so only 216 were locked up there. The remaining 66 were crowded into a narrow domed garret in the nearby Tehsil building and all the doors were securely shut on them, so that not even air could get in or out.

Next morning, August 1, was the day of the Muslim festival of Bakrid. Cooper took his seat facing the gate of the Police lock-up. By his side were posted ten Sikh soldiers in a line, with their muskets at the ready for firing. The other 40 Sikh soldiers stood by, fully armed. The unfortunate sepoys were brought out bound together in groups of ten, and as soon as they appeared, they were shot dead. Most of the sepoys were Hindus and some of them, it is stated, called upon Mother Ganges and with their last breath chided the Sikhs for their treachery to their country. When the sepoys lodged in the Police Station were finished, those shut up in the garret were ordered to be brought out. When the number of the sepoys shot dead reached 237, Cooper was informed that the remaining 45 in the garret refused to come out. Cooper states that arrangements were forthwith made for the proper chastisement of the recalcitrant 45 sepoys, and then the garret was entered. Lying about on its floor 45 bodies were discovered, some of them gasping out their last breath, the rest having died of suffocation!

> "Unconsciously, the tragedy of Holwell's Black Hole had been re-enacted." (*The Crisis in the Punjab*)

According to Cooper, the suffocating sepoys in the garret might have shouted themselves hoarse for air and water, but they were not heard on account of the din outside. The 45 dead bodies were dragged out and thrown on the heap of the bodies of the sepoys who had been shot.

The Well at Ajnala

Within a hundred yards of the Police Station was a well. Into it were thrown the 282 bodies. It was then filled up with earth not only to its top but to the height of a diminutive hillock. Frederick Cooper's meaningful boast is:

> "There is a well at Cawnpore, but there is also one at Ajnala." (ibid.)

The above narrative of the horrific happenings at Ajnala might have been unbelievable, but for the fact that it finds a place in the book *(The Crisis in the Punjab)* written by the "hero" of the inhuman drama played at Ajnala, Frederick Cooper himself. Letters written to Frederick Cooper the very next day by Sir John Lawrence, the Chief Commissioner, and Sir Robert Montgomery the Commandant at Lahore also find a place in the book. These express unstinted admiration and appreciation of Cooper's services. Nor were the Hindu Tehsildar of Ajnala and his Sikh accomplices forgotten. Both received munificent rewards in cash. The "well" turned into a small hillock and the garret existed at Ajnala till a few years ago and were called by the local people *Kaliyan-da-Khooh* and *Kaliyan-da-Burj,* respectively.

Baba Jagat Singh of Ajnala who was 20 and an eye-witness to all that happened at Ajnala on August 1, 1857, gave us a statement in writing (September 1928) which does not differ materially from Cooper's account. He (Baba Jagat Singh) states that the name of the Hindu Tehsildar was Pran Nath and that loud groans, coming out of the bodies as they were thrown into the well, were occasionally heard.

28

FALL OF DELHI

The English Army Near Walls of Delhi

We now resume the narration of events at Delhi. As mentioned in Chapter XV, the situation there about the middle of July, 1857, was that the morale of the Company's army had deteriorated considerably on account of the disastrous raids to which it had been subjected by the besieged on July 9 and 14, and it had encamped at a safe distance from the walls of Delhi.

But the sorties by the besieged continued. They would suddenly come out and attack the besiegers either from the right or from the left. Then after inflicting substantial losses, they would slowly retire, luring on the Company's troops after them. When they reached the walls, the revolutionary raiders would disappear behind the walls, leaving their pursuers almost right under the walls. The guns on the walls then played havoc with the Company's troops and men fell like autumn leaves. These tactics were repeated so often and inflicted such heavy losses on the Company's army, that General Wilson ordered that the raiders were not to be pursued under any circumstances.

Inside the Walls

The revolutionary army lacked neither men nor munitions. The men had proved their mettle and were in high spirits. What the army did suffer from, however, was the want of a master-mind, in whom the men and their officers had the most implicit confidence, and who was capable of welding together into a solid body the sepoys who hailed from different parts of the country. The latter naturally had differing views and prejudices, as between one unit and another. The differences were not always latent and, more often than not, resulted in disorganisation and even indiscipline.

Bakht Khan was an extremely competent military leader. But he was not of "noble" birth, and could claim no exalted connections. Most of the other commanders of the revolutionary units were either princelings or were scions of one ruling prince's family or another. The prejudice in favour of men of "noble" birth, and against men of common stock, persisted in India, too, as it did in other countries then. Birth or family, not competency, ability or high character of an individual was what led people generally to respect him and to have confidence in his leadership. It was particularly so in war. The tension between the unit commanders of higher and lower birth and that between those hailing from different parts of the country grew alarmingly in Delhi. Thus it was that although vastly superior in numbers and equipment as compared with the Company's army, and the latter's equal in fighting qualities, the revolutionaries did not come out in a body to fight a pitched battle with the besiegers. Had they done so, their superior numbers and equipment would have enabled them to rout the Company's army, and their prestige and power throughout India would have gone up immeasurably.

Bahadur Shah had realised the extreme gravity of the situation created by the want of an overall Supreme Military Commander who could command the respect, the confidence and the implicit obedience of the entire revolutionary army. His son Mirza Mughal might have commanded unchallenged prestige and influence, but he had proved to be an incompetent military leader. Bakht Khan, who was capable of planning and executing a successful campaign for defeating the Company's army, was not getting the necessary co-operation from some important elements in the revolutionary leadership, because of the latter's jealousy and umbrage at being ordered about by a commoner. Bahadur Shah tried to reconcile the conflicting elements but did not succeed. He himself was too old to be an active military leader. In despair, he wrote letters to rulers of Jaipur, Jodhpur, Bikaner, Alwar and other States. The important part of the letter, translated into English, reads as follows:

> "It is my heartfelt wish that the *Feringhees* be driven out of Hindustan by every possible means and at any cost. It is my keenest desire that the whole of Hindustan be freed. But the

revolutionary war started with that object cannot succeed so long as someone capable of shouldering the burden of the leadership of the entire movement does not come forward to take it up, and integrate the scattered revolutionaries into one solid body. That man will then be a real national leader and as such will stand out prominently in the field of the struggle for independence."

"I have not the slightest wish to rule over Hindustan, and do not want the English to be driven out for any personal gain. If all of you Indian rulers be ready to draw your swords for the expulsion of the common enemy, then I am most willing to divest myself of all my rights, powers and authority as Emperor of India, and to hand over the same to any group of Indian rulers that may be elected for the purpose."

The poignant and pathetic appeal met with no response. As a consequence, the revolution collapsed mainly, if not solely, because it had no master-mind to lead and control it.

Reinforcement of Company's Army at Delhi

General Nicholson's arrival at Delhi with fresh troops from the Punjab revived the drooping spirits of the Company's army besieging Delhi. The reinforced army now consisted of 3,500 English, 5,000 Sikh with Gorkha and 2,500 Kashmiri soldiers. In addition, the Jhind State army led by the Raja personally had also arrived to join the Company's army. But even so the latter did not venture to get too near the walls of Delhi and stayed put at a safe distance, till about the last week of August, in spite of the harassment of the revolutionary raids which continued unabated as before.

Crack of Delhi's Doom

The two most important components of the revolutionary army, both as regards numbers and fighting qualities, were the unit of sepoys from Neemuch, and the unit of sepoys from Rohilkhand. The latter had been led to Delhi by Bakht Khan, who was now the Commander-in-Chief of the revolutionary army in Delhi. Unfortunately for the revolutionaries, the Commanders of the Neemuch unit were jealous of Bakht Khan's appointment. We have alluded to the disunity and latent hostility prevailing between the units composing the revolutionary army. Bakht Khan's appointment exacerbated the existing ill-feelings between the Neemuch and the Rohilkhand units to the extent of rank indiscipline.

Bakht Khan planned an all-out attack on the besieging army's main camp at Najafgarh, where General Nicholson had arrived with the reinforcements. The attack was scheduled to be delivered on August 25 by the Neemuch and the Rohilkhand units led by Bakht Khan in person. He had instructed the Neemuch unit quietly to occupy a certain strategic position a little before he himself led the Rohilkhand units to attack Najafgarh from a different direction, after which the Neemuch unit was also to attack Najafgarh on the side nearest to it and a junction between the two units could be effected in a pincer movement. The Neemuch unit, however, decided to ignore Bakht Khan's orders, and, acting on their own, occupied a different position very much earlier than the appointed time.

Bakht Khan had timed his attack according to the instructions given by him to the Neemuch unit. So before he could lead out his attack, General Nicholson heard about the Neemuch unit's arrival at the position selected by it, and, without a moment's delay, attacked the Neemuch unit with all the force under his command. The Neemuch unit was totally caught unawares but the men fought most gallantly against heavy odds, till every one of them lay dead on the field. Foiled by a unit under his own command, Bakht Khan returned to the walled city of Delhi.

This was the last effort made by the revolutionaries to drive away the besieging army and its failure doomed Delhi. After May 16, August 25, was the first day on which dark clouds of gloom and despondency cast the shadows of coming events all over Delhi.

In the opposite camp, General Nicholson's exploit provided the much-needed tonic for the drooping spirits of the Company's troops, which soared up jubilantly. Plans for taking Delhi by storm were now taken in hand enthusiastically.

A Contrast

We pause here to emphasise the difference between the mentality of Indians fighting for the revolution and of those fighting for the English, which became apparent on the fateful day of August 25. Indians on both sides faced death unflinchingly. The Neemuch unit fought to the last man, and the Indian soldiers fighting under Nicholson and other English Commanders throughout the revolution blindly obeyed their officers' orders even when it meant certain death. The English historian Forrest has paid a well-deserved tribute to the latter's "extraordinary valour". The revolutionary soldiers and officers too never flinched from certain death, but they sadly lacked discipline without which no military unit howsoever gallant and patriotic can ever achieve success in war or escape disaster.

Company's Secret Service

The Company's secret service department had also been expanded and strengthened considerably under the capable administration of Capt. Hudson. Spies and traitors had been raised inside Delhi chief amongst whom was Mirza Elahi Baksh, whose family was connected with that of Bahadur Shah by marriage. Elahi Baksh had thus easy and unhindered access to Bahadur Shah and kept constantly close to the latter. In this way, Elahi Baksh was able to acquire first-hand knowledge of all that took place at the Emperor's palace, and at the conferences held by Bahadur Shah, as well as of everything which the latter said or did. This knowledge Elahi Baksh faithfully conveyed to his employer, Hudson.

Delhi Stormed

From September 7 to 13, the Company's army made repeated assaults with great vigour on the walled city. It lost many lives but could not effect an entry. The continuous shelling of the walls had, however, cracked them here and there and they had been breached too at one or two places.

Then an all-out assault was planned for September 14. General Wilson divided his entire besieging force into five storming parties. The first of these was commanded by General Nicholson and the second, third, fourth and fifth by Col. Campbell, Brigadier Jones, Major Reid and Brigadier Longfield, respectively.

The assignment of the first three parties was to effect an entry through the Kashmir Gate of Delhi. Gen Nicholson led them. Simultaneously, the fourth party under Major Reid was to advance to the Kabuli Gate of Delhi from the Sabzi Mandi side.

Consequently, soon after dawn on September'14, General Nicholson led his men towards a breach in the city-wall near the Kashmir Gate. The guns on the wall furiously shelled the advancing troops, and numberless English and Sikh soldiers fell down dead. But undeterred by the murderous firing, General Nicholson marched towards the breach over the dead bodies, with a compact storming party. A ladder was propped up against the breach and under the hailstorm of bullets and shells the intrepid Nicholson climbed up. He was the first Englishman to get on top of the city wall, from where he blew the trumpet-call of victory. He then jumped down on the cityside of the wall. The second storming-party climbed up the wall at another place and jumped down into the city. The third advanced to the closed and barred Kashmir Gate itself. Some officer tried to blow it up but bullets were raining down on them and a number of English and Indian officers lost their lives in repeated attempts. One officer did succeed in putting a bag of powder in position and another, Captain Burgess, risked and lost his life in igniting it. A part of the gate was demolished by the explosion and the rest of the storming parties poured in through the opening.

The fourth storming party under Major Reid proceeded to the Kabuli Gate to deliver an assault at that point. It came face to face with a detachment of the revolutionary army near Sabzi Mandi which gave battle to it. In the first clash of arms, Reid fell down wounded and his troops were pressed back. Then Hope Grant rode out to the front with some horsemen, most of whom were Indians. Blood was freely shed as men on both sides performed prodigies of valour. Finally, the Company's troops were forced to retreat.

Company's Army Enters Delhi

The other three parties under Nicholson, Campbell and Jones, having entered through the Kashmir Gate, began raiding the city, but they had to fight opposite every house which they passed. On every house or minaret taken by them, they planted the Union Jack as a mark of their conquest.

Thus fighting all the way, at almost every step, they proceeded towards the Kabuli Gate. From Burn Bastion onwards, they had to pass through a narrow lane, about 200 yards long, and flanked on either side by houses more than one storey high. As the Company's troops entered the lane, they were greeted with murderous firing from the windows, the balconies and the terraces of the houses on both sides. The raiding troops wavered. Then the gallant Nicholson, like a true soldier that he was, fearlessly put himself at the head of his flinching men to lead them on. For one reason or another, he had to go back after a short while, and Major Jacob advanced to take his place, but was shot down dead almost immediately. Nicholson turned back and went to the front for the second time and he too fell down fatally wounded. Ultimately, the Company's troops had to retreat from the lane which was by then full of dead bodies and literally flowing with blood. They went back towards the Kashmir Gate.

At the Jama Masjid

Simultaneously with Nicholson's advance towards Burn Bastion, Col. Campbell was sent towards the Jama Masjid with a contingent. He met with no obstruction or difficulty on the way. Several thousand Mussalmans had, however, collected by then inside the Masjid. They had no firearms, only swords. As the Company's troops approached the Masjid, the Mussalmans came out in a body, drew their swords and threw away the scabbards. The Company's troops fired a volley at them, and some 200 of them fell down on the steps of the Masjid, shot dead. Yet the others rushed with drawn swords on the attackers with such speed that the latter had no time to reload their muskets. Then both sides were locked in a hand-to-hand fight with swords.

Campbell was wounded and his troops were forced to scuttle back towards the Kashmir Gate. Campbell afterwards stated that had help and bags of powder reached him in time, he would have certainly blown up the Delhi Jama Masjid that day.

Thus concluded the crucial battle of September 14. It marked the end of the siege of Delhi, which lasted four months. It was the first day since the beginning of the revolution on which the Company's troops were able to occupy a part of Delhi city. It had been an extremely hard-fought battle in which men on both sides had unremittingly shed their blood for every inch of ground. There of the four principal English commanders of the Company's army who were casualties—the bravest of them, General Nicholson, died of his wounds a few days later. The other losses sustained by the Company's army were 66 officers and over 1100 men killed. The revolutionaries lost, it has been stated, about 1500 killed.

Bahadur Shah taken Prisoner—Princes Murdered

The entry of the Company's army into Delhi and the occupation by it of certain parts of the city demoralised the revolutionary army, and it began to disintegrate. Some of the sepoy units left Delhi immediately after the battle of September 14. Others stayed on, and continued the fight valiantly. A number of battles were fought during the next ten days in which the revolutionaries stubbornly contested every bit of ground and inflicted a loss of 4,000 killed. Their own losses were, it is stated, somewhat heavier. But bit by bit, nearly three-fourths of the city fell into the hands of the Company's army.

On September 19, Bakht Khan went to see Bahadur Shah at night, and tried to instill some courage and confidence into him by saying:

> "The loss of Delhi has not deteriorated our position very much. The whole country is still ablaze. Do not accept defeat at the hands of the English, but leave Delhi with me. There are several places which, from a military point of view, command a far more important position than Delhi. We must establish

ourselves at one of these, and continue to fight from there. I am quite confident that if we do that, victory will be ours ultimately." (Translated from the Hindustani)

Bahadur Shah appeared to be impressed by Bakht Khan's plan and asked the latter to come again the next morning for his (Bahadur Shah's) final decision.

The English got wind of what was afoot through their chief spy Elahi Baksh, and pressed the latter anyhow to prevent Bahadur Shah's departure from Delhi. They promised Elahi Baksh a munificent reward if he succeeded in doing so. Elahi Baksh succumbed and succeeded and the English kept their promise, so that at least up to 1930 the descendants of Elahi Baksh were in receipt of a monthly pension of Rs. 1200/- from the British Government. We will now narrate what Elahi Baksh did. He immediately told Bahadur Shah:

> "There is not the slightest chance of the revolution succeeding. If you go with Bakht Khan, you will get nothing but untold calamities and do yourself irreparable harm. On the other hand, if you stay on at Delhi, then I definitely promise an amicable and satisfactory settlement with the English, by which you and your family will not suffer in any way. I undertake the responsibility of getting the English to agree to such a settlement. Only please be guided by me." (Translated from the Hindustani)

Early the next morning, Bahadur Shah went to Humayun's tomb, with his wife, Begum Zeenat Mahal, and son Prince Jawan Bakht. A message was sent to Bakht Khan to come there for the interview which had been arranged the previous night. Bakht Khan's troops and he himself were encamped on the sandy bank of the Jumna, outside the eastern entrance into the tomb's compound. As directed, Bakht Khan came for the interview through the eastern entrance. He repeated his advice and pressed Bahadur Shah to accompany him immediately. Elahi Baksh had taken care to be present at the interview, and, it has been stated, when Bahadur Shah appeared willing to go with Bakht Khan, he (Elahi Baksh) played another card. He roundly accused Bakht Khan of trying to get hold of Bahadur Shah's person by a ruse, because Bakht Khan was a Pathan and the

Pathans had a longstanding grudge against the Mughal regime, which so Elahi Baksh stated, Bakht Khan intended to satisfy by wreaking vengeance on Bahadur Shah. The accusation led to hot words, and the indignant Bakht Khan flashed out his sword to strike Elahi Baksh. Bahadur Shah intervened and caught hold of Bakht Khan's uplifted arm, and so doomed himself. Had Elahi Baksh met, at the hands of Bakht Khan, the traitor's fate which he so richly deserved, Bahadur Shah's future and the future of India might have been different. But, apparently, Bahadur Shah did not disbelieve Elahi Baksh, and decided to follow his advice. He said to Bakht Khan;

> "I have full faith in you my gallant man and whole-heartedly appreciate the soundness of your counsel, but my physical strength has given way, and I must resign myself to whatever destiny has in store for me. Leave me to my fate, go anywhere and do what you like. I shall be quite content if anyone else, besides myself or any member of my family, saves the honour of Hindustan. Do not worry about us, but go and do your duty. I wish you Godspeed." (Translated from the Hindustani)

The above decision of Bahadur Shah in whose name and under whose flag the revolutionaries were still fighting broke the heart of Bakht Khan, the brains and the fountain-head of the energetic prosecution of the revolutionary war. His spirits sank, and with bowed head, he silently departed. He went out through the eastern gate of Humayun's tomb, took his troops across the Jumna and disappeared, no one to this day knows where.

As soon as Bakht Khan had departed, the arch-traitor Elahi Baksh came out through the western door of the tomb and suggested to his masters, the English, that Bahadur Shah be immediately taken into custody. Within minutes 'Captain Hudson reached the western door of Humayun's tomb with 50 horsemen to effect the arrest. When Bahadur Shah became aware of Captain Hudson's arrival and his intention, he cast a withering glance at Elahi Baksh and said, "You prevented me from going away with the faithful brave Bakht Khan ..." Elahi Baksh simply looked down and stood quietly by, whilst Bahadur Shah, Begum Zeenat Mahal and Prince Jawan Bakht were being taken into custody by Hudson. All the three were forthwith whisked to the Red Fort and confined there. General Wilson and Captain Hudson were of opinion that Bahadur Shah be executed immediately. But the English had not been able, till then, to subdue most of that part of India which had joined the revolution. For that reason, other English officers were against it and so Bahadur Shah was allowed to live for the time being as a prisoner of the English Company.

Murder of Princess

After Bahadur Shah, his wife and son had been taken away, two of Bahadur Shah's sons, Mirza Mughal and Mirza Akhtar Sultan, as also a grandson, Mirza Abubakar, were left behind in Humayun's tomb. Elahi Baksh informed Hudson accordingly. Hudson returned to the tomb and took all the three princes into custody. Elahi Baksh who had returned with Hudson persuaded the princes to go peacefully by giving them an assurance of free pardon by General Wilson. Hudson put them in chariots and took them towards the city, accompanied by his horsemen, Elahi Baksh and two of the latter's accomplices. When the cavalcade reached within a mile of Delhi, Hudson stopped the chariots, ordered the princes to get down and to take off their clothes. Then Hudson suddenly grabbed a musket from one of his soldiers and shot them dead!

A Barbarous Act

According to Khwaja Hasan Nizami, the dead princes were decapitated and the three heads were presented by Hudson to Bahadur Shah with the words:

> "Here is the Company's *Nazar* (a tribute made in token of homage) to you which had not been presented for years." (Translated from the Hindustani)

Khwaja Hasan Nizami further states that the aged Bahadur Shah saw the heads of his young sons and grandson with the most extraordinary self-control and calmly said:

"Praise be to God. Timur's descendants, returning from an expedition, presented themselves before their father with their faces invariably crimson, either with the flush of victory or with their life-blood." (Translated from the Hindustani)

The three heads were hang up in front of the city gate which has since then been popularly known as the Khooni Darwaza (The Gate of Murder) and were exhibited for three days. The bodies were hung up in front of the city *Kotwali* (Head Police Station) and exhibited for three days after which they were thrown into the Jumna.

End of Delhi as a Free City

Delhi's freedom from the English came to an end with the arrest and incarceration of Bahadur Shah, and its complete occupation by the Company, after 134 days of continuous and bitter fighting, became an accomplished fact.

29

DELHI AFTER ITS FALL

Atrocities

Lord Elphinstone wrote at the time to Sir John Lawrence:

> "After the siege was over, the outrages committed by our army are simply heart-rending. A wholesale vengeance is being taken without distinction of friend and foe. As regards the looting, we have indeed surpassed Nadirshah!" (*Life of Lord Lawrence*, Vol. II, p. 262)

An Indian historian, Shamsul-ulema Munshi Zakaullah Khan, has recorded in his *Tareekh-i-Hind* (p. 646) that:

> "There was a hospital inside the Red Fort, in which a a number of ill and wounded sepoys were lying. When the Company's army entered the Fort, it put an end to their suffering by shooting all of them. Also wounded or ailing persons found anywhere else were similarly put to death." (Translated from the Hindustani)

General Massacre

Montgomery Martin published at the time a letter in *The Bombay Telegraph* in which he wrote:

> "All the city people found within the walls when our troops entered were bayoneted on the spot; and the number was considerable, as you may suppose, when 1 tell you that in some houses forty or fifty persons were hiding. These were not mutineers, but residents of the city, who trusted to our well-known mild rule for pardon, I am *glad* to say, they were *disappointed*" (italics ours)

In *The Chaplain's Narration of the Siege of Delhi* quoted by Kaye, another English writer, states:

"A general massacre of the inhabitants of Delhi, a large number of whom were known to wish us success, was *openly proclaimed*." (italics ours)

Khwaja Hasan Nizami quotes in his book, *Delhi-ki-Jankani* (pp. 66–67) the following passage (translated into Hindustani) from Lord Roberts' book, *Forty-one Years in India:*

"In the morning we went into Chandni Chowk through the Lahori Gate. It appeared to be a veritable city of the dead. No sound except the hoof-beats of our horses broke the all-pervading silence. We did not see a single living human being. Inert human bodies carpeted the ground and some of the victims could be heard gasping out their last breath even then."

"As we went along we conversed in low tones, subconsciously fearing to startle the dead."

"On one side dogs were feeding on the dead; on another, vultures were pecking at and feasting on the corpses. At the sound of our approach, the vultures would fly up to perch nearby."

"In short, the bodies were in an indescribable condition. We could not look at them without trepidation, and our horses shied at them and neighed with fright. The bodies decomposing and the stinking poisonous gases emanating from them tilled the air all around." (Translated from the Hindustani of Khwaja Hasan Nizami)

Khwaja Hasan Nizami has also stated that in the general massacre, no distinction of sex or age was made.

Torture of Victims before Murder

Lieut. Majendie narrates in his book, *Up Among the Pandies* (p. 187), an incident to which he was an eye-witness. He states that some Sikh and English soldiers repeatedly stabbed their bayonets in a wounded man's face, and then roasted him alive on a low fire, "the horrible smell of his burning flesh as it cracked and blackened in the flames, rising up and poisoning the air." With regard to this particular horror, Sir William Russell, the *Times* correspondent in India at that lime, avers in his book. *My Diary in India in the Year 1858–59:*

> "I saw the bones of this man lying about in the open for several days."

Mowbray Thompson told Sir Henry Cotton that some Mussalmans were stripped bare, tied to stakes and branded from head to foot with red-hot pieces of copper (*Indian and Home Memories* by Sir Henry Cotton, p. 143).

An English clergyman's widow has stated that many arrested persons were first forced, at the point of the bayonet, to sweep the church-floor and were then hanged (*A Lady's Escape from Gwalior,* p. 243).

Russell mentions instances of:

> "...... sewing Mohammedans in pig-skins, smearing them with pork-fat before execution and burning their bodies, and forcing Hindus to defile themselves ..." (Russell's *Diary,* Vol. II, p. 43)

Pollution of Temples and Mosques

Relating the various ways in which the religious sentiments of the citizens of Delhi were grievously wounded, Khwaja Hasan Nizami writes in his book *Delhi-ki-Jankani* (p. 84):

> "The soldiers of the Company's army forced their way into Hindu temples and Muslim mosques and defiled them. In the Jama Masjid a barrack was established for Sikh soldiers. It had lavatories and urinals attached to it. Under its minarets pigs were slaughtered and pork and piglets were cooked on open fires. Dogs owned by the English roamed inside the Jama Masjid. Another mosque, Zeenat-u1-Masjid, was used as a mess for English officers and men. Donkeys were tethered in the famous mosque of Nawab Hamid Ali Khan. The magnificent Akbarabadi Masjid under the walls of the Fort was razed to the ground. Many other mosques met a similar end." (Translated from the Hindustani)

Loot and Prize Agency

After the city had been completely occupied, all the soldiers of the Company's army were rewarded by tacit permission freely to loot the city for three days. Holmes writes in his book *A History of the Indian Mutiny* (p. 386):

> "... the soldiers, going from house to house and from street to street, ferreted out every article of value, and smashed to pieces whatever they could not carry away".

Thereafter, a prize agency was set up. It was assigned the work of seizing and collecting the movables from all the houses in Delhi and to auction them or store them in godowns. The prize agency was instructed and authorised to distribute to the Company's soldiers the proceeds of the auction sales. Needless to say, the department did its work so thoroughly that it seized and removed from all the houses all books, utensils, charpoys, hand-grinding stones, buried valuables and money found therein. Not even the doors of houses were left standing nor was anything made of iron or brass spared. We quote Khwaja Hasan Nizami (ibid., p. 67) again:

> "Col. Burn was appointed the Military Governor of Delhi. He detailed a detachment of his troops to carry on the work of the prize agency. His instructions were that all men, women and children found living in any inhabited locality were to be taken into custody, their household goods were to' be seized and both produced before him. Consequently, men with bundles of their belongings on their heads, followed by their weeping women and children, some of the women with children in their arms, were made to walk all the way. On the way, some of the women who were not accustomed to walking stumbled and fell down or their children slipped down from their arms, whereupon the soldiers heartlessly pushed and prodded them forward."

> "When they were produced before Col. Burn, their goods were diligently searched and anything of any value was promptly confiscated. Only such articles as were useless were restored to the owners. The people were then ordered

to be taken away under guard to the Lahori Gate and from there driven out of the city.

"Thousands of helpless, bare-headed, bare-backed, barefooted, hungry and thirsty men, women and children were thus condemned to wander about without hope for the future, in the country outside the walls of Delhi. Hundreds of crying hungry and thirsty children died in their mothers' arms. Hundreds of mothers, unable to bear the sight of of their children's agony, sought relief from their misery by drowning themselves in wells."

"Inside the city itself, thousands of women hearing about the approach of the Company's soldiers committed suicide, for fear of dishonour and unbearable miseries. The number of women who died by drowning was so great that the wells were soon overflowing with dead bodies. A military officer has stated: 'We took out of wells hundreds of women who were not drowned because there was not enough water left in them, and were either lying or sitting on the dead bodies. When we proceeded to take them out, they piteously cried aloud to be left alone 'for God's sake'. They begged to be shot rather than be touched, because they were respectable and belonged to good families'."

"From a certain well in Farrashkhana street, two women were taken out. One of them was young but blind. The other was old. The latter stated that she had only one son who had been killed by the soldiers in trying to save his blind sister's chastity. When he died, the blind girl, who knew where the well of the house was, rushed to it and jumped in. She (the mother) followed the girl and jumped in too. Both were floundering in water when someone took them out."

"Some householders, in face of the imminent assault on the honour of their womenfolk, instantly killed their young daughters, daughters-in-law, and other young women and then committed suicide."

Delhi Depopulated

The veritable reign of terror described above turned Delhi into a barren silent city. With the exception of the very few families, from whom the Company was receiving help and co-operation, all the other inhabitants of Delhi, who had not been killed or banged were driven out of the city.

> "The people of Delhi had expiated, many times over, the crimes of the mutineers. Tens of thousands of men, women and children were wandering, for no crime, homeless over the country. What they had left behind was gone for ever ..."
> (Holmes' *A History of the Indian Mutiny*, p. 386)

Rehabilitation of Delhi Begun

The empty shell of Delhi was of little use to the Company and the latter began to rehabilitate the city, but very slowly and with great caution. A beginning was made with the grant of permission to some Hindu families to settle in certain streets. Then in March, 1858, Mussalmans also could come back if they were granted permits for living in the city. Their own houses, however, remained confiscated to the Company till 1859, and no Mussalman could move about in the city without a pass granted by an officer of the Company.

End of Mughal Royal Family

We have earlier mentioned the cold-blooded murder of two of Bahadur Shah's sons and a grandson. Before we write "finis" to the tale of Delhi, it is necessary for us to relate what happened to the other members of Bahadur Shah's family, who were living with him in the Red Fort when the revolution broke out.

Quite a number of them were unceremoniously hanged, regardless of the fact whether or not any of them did or could have taken any part in the revolution. Amongst them was the extremely old men, Prince Mirza Qaisar, a son of Emperor Shah Alam who, on account of his age, was physically incapable of taking any part in the revolution. Another victim was Prince Mirza Mohammad Shah, a grandson of Emperor Akbar Shah, the immediate predecessor of Bahadur Shah. Mirza Mohammad Shah had been suffering from gout all his life and could not even stand up erect. Yet he was dragged to the scaffold and hanged. Other princes were jailed and were made to grind corn. Those who could not grind the full fixed quantity were flogged. The floggings became so frequent that they fell ill and suffered agonies till death released them from the bondage of life. Mirza Koyash, the son of Bahadur Shah, whom the Governor-General had, in the previous year, declared to be Bahadur Shah's heir apparent, disappeared mysteriously. He was last seen near Delhi, riding a horse. He was bare-headed and had a dusty face. Hudson had been looking for him everywhere. What happened to him has never been discovered to this day. The princes who succeeded in evading death or imprisonment by escaping from Delhi wandered about destitute from door to door. Such was the fate of the direct male descendants of Babar and Akbar the Great.

The princesses too wandered outside Delhi, utterly destitute. Two of them stayed on in Delhi. One of them, Rabia Begum, a daughter of Bahadur Shah, was reduced to a plight which was next to starvation, and, in desperation married Hussaini, a Muslim cook in Delhi. Fatima Sultan, another daughter of Bahadur Shah, had to work for her living in a Christian missionary school for women in Delhi.

End of Bahadur Shah

Whilst Bahadur Shah was in captivity in the Red Fort,

> "... a rumour gained currency that an attempt was to be made by Nana Sahib to rescue the King ... The effect of this report was simply a strengthening of the guards to whom the safe keeping of the prisoner was entrusted, and the issue of an order from the military commandant to dispatch His Majesty at once in the event of an attempt to rescue him from his captivity ..." (Charles Ball's *Indian Mutiny*, Vol. II, pp. 183-4)

Emperor Bahadur Shah, deported in captivity to Rangoon, died there in 1863 as a prisoner of the British Government. With his death disappeared the last vestige of the Mughal dynasty.

30

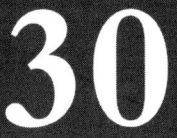

LUCKNOW–OUDH–ROHILKHAND

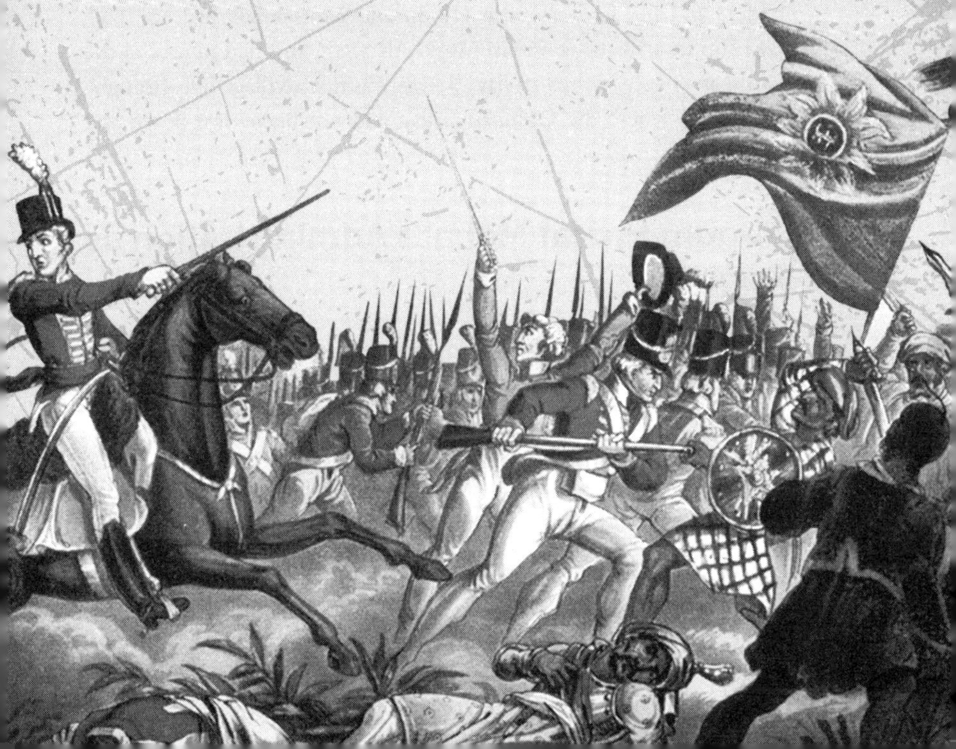

Wajid Ali Shah

We now resume the narration of the events at Lucknow, the capital of Oudh. As stated in Chapter XVIII, the whole of Oudh, barring a tiny part of the city of Lucknow, had freed itself from the English clutches by June 11, 1857.

It will be recalled that, sometime earlier in 1856, Wajid Ali Shah, the Nawab of Oudh, was taken into custody under the orders of Lord Dalhousie and deported to Calcutta as a captive and Oudh was annexed (Chapter XVIII).

Lord Dalhousie had justified the deposition and deportation of Wajid Ali Shah, and the annexation of Oudh, on the ground that the people of Oudh had been groaning under Wajid Ali Shah's despotic misrule. But a clear indication of the Oudh people's feelings towards the administration of Wajid Ali Shah, and towards that of the Company, is furnished by the events of 1857 in Oudh.

The Rajas, the *Jagirdars,* the landholders and the farmers, the traders and the soldiers, both Hindu and Mussalman, had, in 1857, risen up in arms to re-instate Wajid Ali Shah, and had uprooted the Company's rule within 10 days. There was not a village left throughout Oudh where the Company's flag had not been torn down and thrown away.

Begum Hazrat Mahal's Administration as Regent

Sepoys of the *Zamindars* and volunteers from every part of Oudh flocked in their thousands to Begum Hazrat Mahal's standard at Lucknow. The women of Oudh did not lag behind either. Inspired by the leadership of Begum Hazrat Mahal, they put on men's military uniform, armed themselves and formed their own battle-units for Oudh's war of independence, in which they fought bravely.

As already mentioned, a part of Lucknow city was still in English hands. Sir Henry Lawrence then had under him two regiments of Sikh and one regiment of English soldiers, besides some artillery. The news of the English defeat at Kanpur reached Lucknow on June 28 and very much disheartened Sir Henry. Next day, on the 29th, the revolutionaries attacked Chinhat near the iron bridge where the Company's troops had collected. A furious battle was fought in which the Company's troops were defeated and Sir Henry had to retreat, abandoning some heavy guns on the battlefield. He had to take refuge in the Residency. About a thousand Englishmen and some 800 Indians were thus cooped up in the Residency. They, however, had enough of munitions and provisions. The revolutionaries then besieged not only the Residency, but also Machhi Bhawan where the Company's magazine was housed. The English set fire to the magazine, but Machhi Bhawan itself fell into the hands of the revolutionaries.

The English domain and rule over Oudh was now limited to the Residency. The rule of Wajid Ali Shah's minor son Birjees Qadar was proclaimed and established over the rest of Lucknow City, as it had already been over the rest of Oudh. Birjees Qadar being a minor, his mother, Begum Hazrat Mahal, acted as Regent and carried on the Government in his name. The *Zamindars* and the people of Oudh acknowledged her as their suzerain with acclamation.

The Begum-Regent, first of all, on behalf of Birjees Qadar, Nawab of Oudh, sent the good news of Oudh's liberation from English rule to Delhi. She also sent appropriate presents in token of homage to Bahadur Shah, under whose flag the revolution had started and was going on. Then she appointed Raja Bal Krishan Singh as her Prime Minister. Even at that critical period and in spite of it, she overhauled and organised afresh all the State departments, and established peace and good government throughout Oudh. We quote below Russell's tribute to her capability:

> "The Begum exhibits great energy and ability ... The Begum declares undying war against us. It appears from the energetic characters of these Ranees and Begums that they acquire in their *Zenanas* and Harems a considerable amount of actual mental power ..." (Russell's *Diary*, p. 275)

Revolutionary Assaults on the Residency

The assaults began on July 20, with an artillery duel and were continued for several days. The English flag over the Residency was shot down more than once but every time it was replaced almost immediately. The Sikh soldiers inside the Residency did not spare themselves in helping the English, and the repeated efforts of the revolutionaries to win them over had no effect. The walls of the Residency were breached at several places and attempts were made again and again by the revolutionaries to take the Residency by storm but without success. In one of these attempts, Sir Henry Lawrence, who had been appointed the Company's Chief Commissioner of Oudh, was shot dead. His place was immediately taken by Major Becks. He too was killed shortly after, and was succeeded by Brigadier Inglis. Hopes of relief steadily decreased inside the Residency. The besieged Englishmen sent out secret messengers to Kanpur asking for help. Some of the messengers were intercepted by the revolutionaries. At last, on July 25, Brigadier Inglis received the heartening news that General Havelock had left Kanpur with a force and would be arriving at Lucknow within a few days. But days passed, one after another, and Havelock did not arrive. In the meantime the Residency wall on one side had been demolished by the besiegers. They then delivered an all-out and fierce assault, fighting hand-to-hand with bayonets and swords at the breach, but achieved nothing. The assault was repeated on August 18, with the same result. There were no signs yet of Havelock. Brigadier Inglis later received a letter from Havelock, saying that he (Havelock) could not reach Lucknow for at least another 25 days. The spirits of the besieged sank. To add to their difficulties, the provisions in the Residency had by then been depleted to such an extent that everyone had to be put on half-rations.

Havelock's Way to Lucknow Blocked

Lucknow is less than 45 miles from Kanpur, yet it took Havelock more than 60 days to get there. He was held up and had to retreat no less than three times in face of stiff revolutionary opposition. Till

August 11, that is, for about three weeks, he was continuously moving forward a little and then retreating. His net advance from Kanpur came to no more than three miles, which brought him to Magarwara from where he finally went back to Kanpur the next day. In the engagements with the revolutionaries he had lost hundreds of men. His force of about 1500, with which he had started from Kanpur for the relief of the Lucknow Residency, was reduced to 850 when he finally returned to Kanpur.

The reason why Havelock was unable to set foot on Oudh's soil is to be found in the paragraph headed "Oudh's Preparations for Revolution" in the earlier Chapter XXI. As stated by the historian G. B. Malleson in his *Red Pamphlet,* the whole of Oudh was up in arms against the English. So far as sacrifice and unyielding revolutionary spirit were concerned, Oudh put up an even infinitely better show than Delhi. For six months after the fall of Delhi, the flag of independence continued to fly over Lucknow and the whole of Oudh. Lieut-Gen. McLeod Innes, V. C., has quite rightly observed:

> "At least the struggle of the Ouddhians must be characterised as a War of Independence" (*The Sepoy Revolt*).

On crossing the Ganges at Kanpur, Havelock had discovered that he would have to fight all the way to Lucknow. In the battles with the revolutionaries he was repulsed time and again and could not make a break-through. The credit for thus stopping him must also go to the villagers of Unnao and Bashirat Ganj who successfully barred his way, almost literally, with their bodies.

Havelock's Return to Kanpur and its Effect

Whilst Havelock was away from Kanpur, struggling for a passage to Lucknow, Nana Sahib again got active. He had received substantial military help from Saugar, Gwalior, etc. So he crossed the Ganges at another point and re-occupied Bithoor. General Neill who was then at Kanpur did not have with him a force strong enough to fight Nana Sahib with any chance of success. He, therefore, immediately informed Havelock of the new military situation at Kanpur. Havelock had thus to abandon his plan of going to Lucknow. He, therefore, crossed back to the Kanpur side of the Ganges on August 12.

The effect of Havelock's return on the revolutionaries and their supporters is thus described by Lt.-Gen. Innes:

> "But this retirement from Oudh produced a result which he (Havelock) had doubtless never contemplated. The Talukdars openly construed it as the British evacuation of the province and now formally recognised the rebel *Darbar* at Lucknow as the *de facto* Government; and though they refrained from supporting it by their own presence, they obeyed its orders, which they had hitherto disregarded, and sent to the scene of warfare the contingents which they had been called upon to provide." (ibid., p. 174)

Havelock's Dilemma

Back at Kanpur, Havelock found himself in a difficult position. Nana Sahib had not only re-occupied Bithoor; he had also collected a very large force at Kalpi on the banks of the Jumna for the invasion of Kanpur. If Havelock resumed his march to Lucknow, Nana Sahib would sack Kanpur. Havelock tried to get over the difficulty by forthwith launching an attack on Nana Sahib's force. In the hard-fought battle that followed, neither side could get the better of the other, and both had to retire to their original positions, leaving Havelock still on the horns of a dilemma. He could neither leave Kanpur, as that would invite an immediate attack by Nana, nor could he leave the Lucknow Residency to its fate, because it would lead to very grave consequences, little short of a calamity for the English. He, therefore, sent an urgent message to Calcutta, saying:

> "We are in a terrible fix. If new reinforcements do not arrive, the British army cannot escape the terrible fate of abandoning Lucknow and retreating to Allahabad."

Calcutta's response was prompt and saved the situation for the English. Sir James Outram left Calcutta with reinforcements and arrived at Kanpur on September 15.

Havelock's Second March to Lucknow and its End

On September 20, Havelock advanced towards Lucknow for the second time. He was accompanied by veteran English Generals like Neill, Outram, Cooper, and others and had under him a force consisting of 2,000 English soldiers and one regiment of Sikhs. He also had better heavy guns than those which he had during his first march of July 25. But these were only some of the reasons why he succeeded this time in reaching Alambagh, on the outskirts of Lucknow, within three days. The other and the more important reason was that the *Taluqdars,* under the impression that the Company's army had abandoned Oudh for good, had diverted to Lucknow their contingents which guarded the roads. When Havelock returned, only the inadequately armed villagers of Unnao and Bashirat Ganj were there to try and check him. The villagers fought most gallantly and, with the courage of despair, offered the most resolute resistance that they could. They could not, however, stop Havelock who continued to advance, albeit over their dead bodies. He had literally to cut his way through to Alambagh where a contingent of the revolutionary army barred his further progress. A fierce battle was fought continuously for the next 36 hours and more. Just about then, the news of the fall of Delhi came in, and the spirits of Havelock's army soared up.

On the morning of September 25, Havelock's force retired a little from Alambagh, and made a detour to reach the Residency from another direction. The revolutionaries turned round and shelled Havelock's force, which braved the fire and continued to advance under it, till it reached the Charbagh bridge, across which was the city of Lucknow. Another revolutionary contingent was in position commanding the bridge. An artillery duel followed and the number of casualties on both sides went up and up. One of Havelock's sons was in the thick of the battle which raged over the bridge. Ultimately Havelock's troops forced their passage to the other side, over the dead bodies of their comrades and enemies which covered the bridge. But the battle was not over as, across the bridge, Havelock's force had to fight the revolutionaries at every step. When it reached Khas

Bazar, a stray revolutionary bullet hit General Neill, killing him on the spot. This was a terrible blow to the Company's army, but it did not stop it from going on till it reached the Residency and, pressing the revolutionaries back as it advanced, entered it.

Inside the Residency

The joy of the English in the Residency knew no bounds at Havelock's arrival in their midst. During the last 87 days of the siege 700 inmates of the Residency had died. The survivors numbered 500 Englishmen and 400 Indians. Havelock's force had lost 722 men killed in the engagements during its march from Kanpur to Lucknow. Notwithstanding the heavy loss of lives, the success in reaching the Residency for the rescue of its despairing English inmates was a matter of no small satisfaction to Havelock and his colleagues. But the satisfaction was short-lived because the revolutionaries again besieged the Residency and Havelock found himself and his force virtual prisoners inside it. His exploit had not relieved the beleaguered Residency. On the other hand, it had very much increased the number of half-starved people already cooped up within its walls. This was the situation in the last week of September 1857.

Preparations to Retrieve Situation

On August 13, 1857, Sir Collin Campbell, new Commander-in-Chief of the Company's armies in India, had arrived at Calcutta, and had got busy forthwith. He summoned to Calcutta some regiments of English soldiers from Madras, Bombay and China, and had additional heavy guns cast in the Company's kasimbazar foundry. It took him over two months to complete his preparations, after which he himself left Calcutta for Kanpur on October 27, 1857, with the force and equipment collected by him.

At the same time, some men-of-war commanded by Col. Powell and Capt. Peel were sent by the river Ganges to Kanpur *via* Allahabad. They had, however, to fight the revolutionaries at several places along their route, at one of which Col. Powell was killed in action.

Sir Collin Campbell reached Kanpur on November 3. The fleet from Calcutta, too, arrived at about the same time.

By then, Delhi had been re-taken, and the Company's army engaged there was sree. General Greathead also led his army to Kanpur.

Gen. Greathead's Devastations along his Way to Kanpur

An English writer has stated that although the entire region east of Delhi had been in the hands of the revolutionaries since the beginning of the revolution till November, 1857, the people of that area had not thereby suffered the least bit. He writes:

> "The people not only cultivated but in many districts as extensively as ever. In fact beyond supplying their necessity, the rebels did not venture to assume the character of tyrants of the country." *(Narrative of the Indian Revolt)*

But General Greathead, in his march from Delhi to Kanpur, outdid even General Neill in burning villages and killing the innocent villagers of the country along his route.

Arrival of Company's Army at Alambagh

With the arrival of General Greathead's army at Kanpur, the considerable force already collected there by Sir Collin for the relief of the Lucknow Residency and the re-conquest of Lucknow and Oudh grew into a very large and well-equipped army. The bulk of this army was placed under the command of General Grant and sent to Lucknow.

As Nana Sahib was still very active between Kalpi and Kanpur, and the latter was not yet quite immune from danger, Sir Collin stationed a strong contingent of Sikh soldiers and some artillery under Wyndham's command in Kanpur and himself followed General Grant. He crossed the Ganges, and on November 9, 1857, arrived at Alambagh, where General Grant was already encamped. Thereafter, Sir Collin personally was in command of the entire army of the Company at Alambagh.

It was extremely difficult to get in touch, even by letter with the English inside the Residency. So Sir Collin disguised an Englishman, Cavannagh, dressed him in Indian clothes and had him smuggled into the Residency along with an Indian secret agent of his. Cavannagh returned safely and gave Sir Collins a description of the conditions inside the Residency.

Sir Collin's Army in Action

Early on November 14, Sir Collin's army advanced towards the Residency pressing back the revolutionaries encircling it. At the same time, Generals Havelock and Outram attacked the besiegers from inside the Residency. The revolutionaries had thus to fight on two fronts simultaneously. Sir Collin's army reached Dilkush Bagh the same evening (November 14) and on the 16th attacked Sikandar Bagh.

Battle at Sikandar Bagh

Sikandar Bagh was a walled-in group of buildings occupied by the revolutionaries. When it was attacked the revolutionaries put up a strong and courageous defence. In the furious battle that followed in which every foot of ground was stubbornly contested, the defenders, as well as the Sikhs in the attacking army, were conspicuous for their bravery. A Sikh soldier was the first to climb up the wall under the hail of the defenders' bullets. He was shot in the chest and fell down. Later, General Cooper and General Lumsden were also killed in action. Ultimately, the Sikh and English soldiers succeeded in cutting their way through, and entered Sikandar Bagh, stepping over the dead bodies of their comrades. At the same time, another detachment stormed Sikandar Bagh from a different direction and entered it. Sir Collin's army had won the day. We quote below the English historian Malleson about the unflinching and wonderful courage with which Sikandar Bagh was defended:

> "The battle for the possession of Sikandar Bagh was desperate and bloody as men on both sides fought and faced

death unflinchingly. The revolutionaries would not give in even when our force had cut its way in. Every room, every staircase and every corner of the *minars* had to be fiercely fought for. No quarter was given or asked for on either side. The attackers succeeded in the end and occupied Sikandar Bagh, which was by then a pool of blood, with the bodies of over 2,000 defenders lying about in heaps. Every one of the defenders had died fighting. It has been alleged that only four had deserted their posts but it is extremely doubtful that they did so." (G.B. Malleson's *Indian Mutiny*, Vol. IV, p. 132)

Relief of the Residency and After

After Sikandar Bagh, the battle for the relief of the Residency had to be fought for another week at other places. The last engagement, fought even more bitterly than the others, was at Moti Mahal and lasted till November 23, on which date Sir Collin's army, after nine days of bitter and continuous fighting, relieved the besieged army of the Company and joined it. The English, incarcerated in the Residency for so long, were at last freed. They had, however, a stroke of bad luck, as General Havelock died the very next day.

The siege of the Residency was over, but the entire city of Lucknow was still in the hands of the revolutionaries and the next task facing Sir Collin was its conquest. He left the Residency and established his base at Alambagh for the conduct of operations against the city. He began concentrating men, munitions and guns for the attack. In the midst of these preparations, news reached him that Tatya Tope, the famous Maratha General of Nana Sahib, had defeated the English force at Kanpur and taken the town. Sir Collin, therefore, left with his force with the intention of re-taking Kanpur, leaving General Outram in charge at Lucknow.

Tatya Tope

We have to go back a little and narrate briefly the events leading up to the above-mentioned conquest of Kanpur by Tatya Tope.

It will be recalled that General Havelock had, about the middle of July, 1857, marched on Kanpur from Allahabad, defeated Nana Sahib and taken Kanpur. Nana Sahib had then retreated to Bithoor and, on July 17, had to retreat further from there to Fatehpur with his family and treasury. His brother Bala Sahib, his nephew Rao Sahib and his General Tatya Tope accompanied him. Bithoor was then occupied by the English. From Fatehpur Nana Sahib sent Tatya Tope to Shivrajpur where the XLII Regiment of the Company's army was then stationed. Tatya Tope won over the sepoys of the XLII and returned with them to Bithoor, which he succeeded in re-taking with their help. He then attacked the rear of the army which Havelock was about to take to Lucknow for the relief of the Residency there. Havelock had to give up this plan. Instead, he engaged Tatya Tope and defeated him on August 16. Tatya Tope took the remnants of his force to Fatehpur, and, leaving them there, went to Gwalior. Sindhia's large Subsidiary Army, consisting of infantry, cavalry and artillery, was then stationed at the Morar Cantonment near Gwalior. Tatya Tope won over the entire Subsidiary Army to the revolutionary cause, and led it to Kalpi. The fort at Kalpi occupied a position of considerable strategic importance. It was on the other side of the Jumna, some 46 miles from Kanpur. Tatya Tope occupied the fort on November 9, and Nana Sahib made it the base of his operations against Kanpur. He appointed his brother Bala Sahib, the Commandant of the fort. Tatya Tope then marched on Kanpur which was being defended by Gen. Wyndham. On November 19, Tatya Tope encircled Wyndham's force so effectively that it became impossible for any provisions to reach them. Wyndham then sallied forth from Kanpur and on November 26 engaged Tatya Tope's force in battle on the Pandu river. It is stated that Tatya Tope suffered substantial losses in the first round; but it was not due to any lack of ability on Tatya Tope's part. We quote the historian Malleson on the subject:

> "The Commander of the rebel army was no fool. Instead of being unnerved by the losses inflicted by Wyndham, he exploited the opportunity of discovering the weak points in the English General's onslaught ... in fact, he studied them like one studying book. Tatya Tope had all the qualities with which a real army leader is naturally gifted, and took full

advantage of his adversary's weakness." (Malleson's *Indian Mutiny*, Vol. IV, p. 167)

The very next day Tatya Tope's troops pushed back Wyndham's force and, advancing from three directions, occupied half of Kanpur. The battle continued for three days and ultimately the whole of Kanpur was taken by Tatya Tope. Wyndham's force was completely routed and lost many officers in action. A personal letter of an English officer provides some reliable details of the battle on the third and last day:

> "You will read the account of this day's fighting with astonishment; for it tells how English troops, with their trophies and their mottoes and their far-famed bravery, were repulsed, and lost their camp, their baggage, and their position to the scouted and despised natives of India. The hated *Feringhees*, as the enemy has now a right to call them, have retreated to their intrenchments, amid overturned tents, pillaged baggage, men's kits, fleeing camels, elephants, horses and servants. All this is most melancholy and disgraceful." (Charles Ball's *Indian Mutiny*, Vol. II, p. 190.)

It was the news of this disaster which had compelled Sir Collin to leave Lucknow and start for Kanpur. As soon as Tatya Tope heard about it, he demolished the bridge over the Ganges and placed guns commanding its bank. Sir Collin thereupon made a detour and crossing the Ganges at another point reached near Kanpur on November 30. By that time Nana Sahib too had arrived at Kanpur to help Tatya Tope.

Kanpur Re-taken by the English

Tatya Tope was, according to Malleson, "a man of very great natural ability as a leader ..." (ibid., Vol. I, p.186). He did not wait for Sir Collin's army to advance much after crossing the Ganges, but engaged it in a long drawn-out battle which lasted a whole week. The Gwalior army which was supporting Tatya Tope on his right gave way before the combined attack of the English and Sikh soldiers. Ultimately, Sir

Collin won and re-occupied Kanpur. Tatya Tope retreated southwards with his artillery and the remnants of his army. He was pursued by Sir Collin's army, which caught up with him at Shivrajpur, where another battle was fought in which Tatya Tope was irretrievably defeated and lost some of his guns. He saved what was left of his force by escaping towards Kalpi. The Company's army returned to Kanpur. On his way back to Kanpur, Sir Collin razed to the ground Nana's palatial buildings at Bithoor.

Repressive Atrocities

After the fall of Delhi, the revolutionaries had gravitated to the Oudh and Rohilkhand province and had begun collecting there in large numbers. The region was fast growing into their most important stronghold. But before operations against them were undertaken, it was considered necessary first to subjugate the area to the west of Oudh and Rohilkhand and to the east of Delhi. Consequently, several detachments of the Company's army were dispatched in different directions from Delhi, Kanpur etc., for bringing the area under full and undisputed control of the Company. To accomplish it, methods similar to those previously used by English Generals like Neill, Havelock and Greathead were adopted to subdue and overawe the villagers and the people throughout the region. Mentionable amongst the places where resistance was offered are Etawah and Farrukhabad.

Etawah

On December 28, General Walpole started with his detachment northwards from Kanpur. There were minor engagements with the revolutionaries who barred his progress at several places; but he was held up near Etawah by only 25 revolutionaries in a small house by the roadside. The house was bristling with muskets on its roof, and protruding from portholes in the walls. Walpole had with him a regular military detachment and some artillery; but even so, the handful of revolutionaries would not let him pass without a fight. Walpole made overtures, and, when these were rejected, threatened them with a cannonade. But that threat too had no effect. The incident is thus described by Malleson in his *Indian Mutiny*:

> "These men were but few in number and were armed only with common muskets. But fired by an indomitable spirit, they were determined to martyrise themselves for their cause ... hand-grenades were hurled into the house; then an attempt was made to smoke them out by burning piles of hay under the walls of the house. Both proved fruitless. These rebels subjected the attackers to a continuous murderous fire from their muskets and checked their advance for three hours. It was then decided to blow up the house ... when the house went up, its defenders attained the glory they had desired. All of them were killed and buried in the ruins of the house."

Farrukhabad

The Nawab of Farrukhabad had declared himself to be independent of the Company's rule. It was decided that three detachments, commanded by Walpole, Seaton and Sir Collin, should simultaneously advance on Fatehgarh, the capital town of Farrukhabad, from three directions, and encircle it. It was done, and the battle lasted several days. Ultimately Fatehgarh fell to the invaders on January 14, 1858, and the Nawab was taken prisoner. The historian Forbes Mitchell states in his *Reminiscences* that the body of the Mussalman Nawab was smeared with pork-fat before he was hanged. A prominent commander of Nar.a Sahib, Nadir Khan, was also taken prisoner at Fatehgarh and hanged. Charles Ball writes about Nadir Khan in his *Indian Munity* (Vol. II, p. 232):

> "... he died calling upon the people of India to draw their swords and assert their independence by the extermination of the English".

Eventually, Sir Collin Campbell succeeded in subjugating practically the entire region along the Jumna from Delhi to Allahabad, and thereafter speeded up his preparations for marching on Lucknow as a preliminary step towards the ultimate goal of the conquest of Oudh and Rohilkhand province.

Campbell's Preparations

Lucknow was then the biggest revolutionary centre. For conquest, Campbell bad collected at Kanpur a force of 17,000 infantry, 5000 cavalry and an artillery of 134 guns, with which to march on Lucknow from its west. From its east, two other detachments of the Company's army, one commanded by General Franks and the other by General Rowcroft, also advanced on Lucknow. On their way they were joined according to plan, by a contingent of 9,000 Gorkha soldiers commanded by the Nepalese General, Jung Bahadur.

Help from Nepal

We revert to the early days of the revolution to relate the events leading up to the joining of Jung Bahadur's force in the march on Lucknow.

It will be recalled that after the revolution had broken out, the English had approached the Nepal *Durbar* for help in quelling it. At that time the monetary help of Rs. 2.5 crores given to the English in the Nepal War by the then Nawab of Oudh, was apparently still rankling in the hearts of the Nepalese, for they seized upon this opportunity of wreaking their vengeance on Oudh. In response to the English appeal for help, a force of 3,000 Gorkha soldiers had, in August, 1857, invaded Azamgarh and Jaunpur in eastern Oudh. The revolutionary leaders, Mohammad Hussain, Beni Madhava and Raja Nadir Khan had however, successfully defended that region. Thereafter, some understanding, it is stated, had been arrived at, about future action between General Jung Bahadur and the English. On December 23, 1857, Jung Bahadur with 9,000 Gorkha soldiers advanced on Lucknow from its east and, as stated above, joined the two detachments of the Company's army under Generals Frank and Rowcroft. All the three crossed the river Ghogra on February 25, 1858, and marched onwards with the Nepalese contingent leading the way.

At about the same time Campbell himself left Kanpur for Lucknow at the head of the large force which, as mentioned before, he had collected at Kanpur. He marched on Lucknow from its west.

Opposition on the Way

The first opposition offered by the revolutionaries to the Nepalese force was at Amberpore, after it had crossed the Ghogra.

There was a small fortress at Amberpore with a garrison of only 34 sepoys. The latter nevertheless gave battle to the Nepalese and every one of the 34 defenders died fighting at his post. The fortress fell to the Nepalese, who, thereafter continued their march.

The Lucknow *Durbar* sent Ghafoor Khan with a force to check the detachment advancing under General Franks. There were desperate actions fought at Sultanpur and other places between the advancing forces and the revolutionaries, in none of which the latter were able to stop or push back the former. The combined Nepalese and the Company's detachments continued their march on Lucknow, conquering the eastern region of Oudh along their way.

The Unconquered Daurara Fortress

There was, however, one place where the advancing force was repulsed and had to make a detour. It was at Daurara where General Franks failed to take the fortress by assault and had to fall back. The advancing force, unable to get past the Daurara fortress, had to abandon that route and to continue their march by another route. Later, Campbell punished General Franks by demoting him.

Junction with Campbell's Force

Campbell's large force which had advanced from Kanpur on the west of Lucknow was joined there on March 11, 1858, by the Nepalese contingent and by the Company's two detachments advancing on Lucknow from its east.

Inside Lucknow

From November, 1857 to March, 1858, the city of Lucknow had continuously been the main battlefield where the War of Independence was fought out. A vast majority of the people and the landed aristocracy of Oudh were enthusiastically participating in the war. As Lord Canning wrote in one of his letters to General Outram, a good number of the Rajas and Taluqdars participating in the war against the English had suffered no loss whatsoever as a result of the English rule. They had, on the contrary, benefited by it. Yet they had turned into bitter enemies of English rule, and were ready and willing to sacrifice their all for the minor Nawab Birjees Quadar and Begum Hazrat Mahal. The historian Holmes writes in his book *The Sepoy War:*

> "There were numerous Rajas and Chiefs, big and small, who were constantly anxious to free themselves from the English bondage, not because they themselves had thereby suffered any personal loss, but because the very existence of the English rule reminded them unceasingly that they belonged to a subject nation ... Hundreds of thousands of Indians did not have in their hearts any feeling of real loyalty to the English ... To arrive at a correct estimate of the attitude of Indians during the Revolution, we must first realise that it would have been against human nature for them to be loyal, consistently with their patriotism, to a foreign rule like ours ... There was not a single man amongst them who would not have risen up in arms against us, had he been convinced that the English Raj could be uprooted and thrown on the scrap-heap."

Russel has stated that the people of Oudh were:
"engaged in a patriotic war for their country and their sovereign" (*Diary,* p. 275).

Moulvi Ahmed Shah

The ablest of the revolutionary leaders in Lucknow was Moulvi Ahmed Shah, who was in command of the revolutionary army. We have said a good deal about him in an earlier chapter. Holmes writes this about him:

> "A man fitted both by his spirit and his capacity to support a great cause and to command an army. This was Ahmedullah (Ahmed Shah?), the Moulvi of Fyzabad." (*The Sepoy war*)

But unfortunately for the revolutionaries, at Lucknow too indiscipline had raised its ugly head in their army. As in the case of Bakht Khan at Delhi, Ahmed Shah's instructions were not followed to any desirable extent due to the jealousy felt by some influential elements of noble birth against him. Ahmed Shah was not one of them but belonged to the people. It has been stated that hostility towards him had at one time acquired so much strength that Begum Hazrat Mahal, pressed hard by some of her influential supporters, had to put him into prison. But so great was his popularity with the army and the people, that he had to be set free within a short time and re-instated as the Commander of the revolutionary army in Lucknow. He then sallied forth a number of times and leading his troops in person attacked Outram's force at Alambagh. In these attacks he was always in the thickest of the fight on a horse or an elephant. On January 15, his hand was hit by a bullet. On the 17th, another revolutionary Commander, Videhi Hanuman, was wounded and taken prisoner. At about the same time, Raja Balkrishna Singh, Begum Hazrat Mahal's Prime Minister, died too. A month later, Moulvi Ahmed Shah returned to the fighting line even though his hand had only partially healed. Then Begum Hazrat Mahal herself, fully armed and riding a horse, led her troops in person. Personal jealousies and the consequent disorganisation, however, still persisted in the revolutionary camp at Lucknow.

The regular revolutionary army inside the city was 30,000 strong and the armed volunteers supporting it numbered another 50,000. Barricades were erected in every street and bazar. Portholes for musket-barrels were bored through the walls of practically every house. Heavy guns were emplaced at every barrier and all round the Palace. The city was bounded on the north by the river Gomti flowing close to it. On the other three sides it had strong fortifications.

Outside the city and threatening it was the well-trained and well-equipped Company's army about 40,000 strong and commanded by Sir Collin Campbell himself.

The Battle of Lucknow

No attack on Lucknow by the English had ever been launched from its northern side. But this time the city was attacked from the north and the east simultaneously. The battle that followed was furiously fought for over a week, almost continuously, till March 15, 1858. For the third time the streets of Lucknow flowed with blood. The Company's army stormed and carried the barricades, one after the other. Captain Hudson, of Delhi fame, who had shot the Princes in cold blood, was killed in action. Ultimately Lucknow, too, fell like Delhi. On March 14, the Company's army entered the Nawab's Palaces. According to the historian Wilson, most of the credit for this success was due to the Sikhs and the X Regiment.

Moulvi Ahmed Shah, however, continued the fight. After leaving the city with Begum Hazrat Mahal and the minor Nawab Birjees Quadar, he made a detour and returned to attack Lucknow from another direction. He reached the Shahadat Gunj Street in Lucknow and engaged the Company's army in battle there. He had but little more than a handful of men and only two guns. Nevertheless he fought two regiments. English historians have stated that Moulvi Ahmed Shah fought that day with unprecedented bravery and inflicted on his adversaries the heavy loss of many lives. Realising that it was utterly impossible for him to win, he got out of Lucknow once again. The English pursued him for six miles but he eluded them. The engagement at Shahadat Gunj was the last one in the battle of Lucknow, after which the entire city was occupied by the English.

Atrocities

"General massacre" and "loot of all and sundry" are the only phrases which can adequately describe the treatment meted out by the victorious Company's troops to the citizens of Lucknow after its fall. Lt. Majendie, writing about it, states that no distinction of any kind whatsoever was made in the general massacre of the people (*Up Among the Pandies,* pp. 195,196).

Russell has given many instances of unbelievably brutal atrocities. We quote only one below:

> "Some of the sepoys were still alive and they were mercifully killed; but one of their number was dragged out to the sandy plain outside the house; he was pulled by his legs to a convenient place, where he was held down, pricked in

the face and body by the bayonets of some of the soldiery, while others collected fuel for a small pyre; and when everything was ready, the man was roasted alive. These were Englishmen, and more than one officer saw it; no one offered to interfere. The horrors of this infernal cruelty were aggravated by the attempt of the miserable wretch to escape when half burnt to death. By a sudden effort he leaped away and, with the flesh of his body hanging from his bones, ran for a few yards ere he was caught, brought back, put on the fire again and held there by bayonets, till his remains were consumed." (*Diary*, p. 302)

A Contrast

Some six months earlier, the revolutionaries had taken captive at Lucknow some English people—men and women. Throughout the months that followed they were not molested in any way or ill-treated. In the early stages of the entry of the Company's soldiers into Lucknow, when the latter started the indiscriminate massacre of the guilty and the innocent, some revolutionaries pressed Begum Hazrat to have all the English captives handed over to them. The Begum handed over only the men, who were forthwith shot, but she refused to hand over the women. The historian, Charles Ball, writes:

> "To the honour of womanhood, the demand was imperatively refused by the Begum so far as the females were concerned, and they were immediately taken under her care in the Zenana of the palace." (*Indian Mutiny*, Vol. II, p. 94)

Other Begums in the Palace

Massacre and loot were carried into the Palace by the Company's soldiers. Some Begums in the Zenana were slaughtered and others were taken captive. Some historians have related an incident which brings out the captive Begums' undiminished faith in the sanctity of the revolutionary cause and their unshaken confidence in its ultimate success. One day, it is related, some of the English soldiers asked them with a smile "Don't you think that this war has now ended?" The Begums' prompt answer is stated to be "No, we do not. On the contrary we are convinced that in the end it will be you who will be defeated" (*Narrative of the Indian Mutiny*, p. 348, Russell's *Diary*, p. 400).

The Battle near Bari

Moulvi Ahmed Shah was at Bari some 30 miles away from Lucknow. Hope Grant started from Lucknow for Bari with a detachment of 3,000 soldiers and some guns. Moulvi Ahmed Shah came to know of it and planned accordingly. He posted his infantry at a village four miles from Bari in the direction of Lucknow. He sent his horsemen to another place and ordered them to keep under cover until the Company's force attacked his infantry at the village. Then, and not till then, the horsemen were to come out and attack the rear of the Company's force, so that it had to fight, in front and at its rear, at the same time. These orders were, however, disobeyed, and the horsemen attacked the Company's force as soon as they saw it. This indiscipline resulted in the defeat of Moulvi Ahmed Shah's infantry after a short engagement at the village near Bari. The English won the day and Moulvi Ahmed Shah had to retreat.

General Hope killed in Action at Rui-ya Fortress

Rui-ya was 50 miles from Lucknow. Its *Taluqdar* was Narpat Singh. He had a small fortress garrisoned by 250 soldiers. On April 15, 1858, Walpole, who had several thousand soldiers and some guns, attacked the fortress. A party of 150 soldiers led the assault. A hailstorm of bullets fired from its walls decimated them and 46 Englishmen were killed. The rest beat a hasty retreat. Walpole then started shelling the fortress from another side but the shells passed over the fortress, and dropped on the Company's troops stationed there. Walpole was nonplussed and General Hope advanced to help. He was killed and the entire attacking force had to retreat. General Hope was one of the most noted and experienced English Generals and his death was deeply mourned by the English in India and in England. But Narpat Singh, although he had won a victory, realised that the small fortress could not hold out for long against such a large body of troops. Consequently he abandoned the fortress and escaped with a handful of his men.

Shahjehanpur and Bareilly

Nana Sahib and Moulvi Ahmed Shah then went to Shahjehanpur. Commander-in-Chief Sir Collin Campbell marched on Shahjehanpur and surrounded it. His objective was to get hold of Nana Sahib and Moulvi Ahmed Shah, but both these leaders succeeded in getting away through the encircling troops.

Khan Bahadur Khan had kept intact the independence of Rohilkhand's capital, Bareilly. One of the Delhi Princes, Mirza Firoz Shah, Nana Sahib, Moulvi Ahmed Shah, Bala Sahib, Begum Hazrat Mahal, Raja Tej Singh and several other revolutionary leaders were in Bareilly. Sir Collin advanced towards Bareilly with his force. The revolutionary leaders had, however, already decided to abandon Bareilly and disperse with their followers all over Rohilkhand. The English troops surrounded Bareilly on May 5, 1858. Innumerable revolutionaries armed only with swords and shields sallied forth determined to die fighting, and attacked the English troops. Both sides lost many lives. On May 7, 1858, Khan Bahadur Khan accompanied by the other leaders and his soldiers left Bareilly and the English force occupied it.

The Battle at Shahjehanpur

Sir Collin Campbell was at Bareilly when Moulvi Ahmed Shah returned to attack Shahjehanpur. He defeated the English force there and re-occupied the town. Campbell hurried to it and attacked it. After the battle had lasted three days, it appeared impossible for Moulvi Ahmed Shah to get away. The other revolutionary leaders rushed to his help from all directions. Prince Firoz Shah, Begum Hazrat Mahal, Nana Sahib and others reached Shahjehanpur with their forces on May 15, 1858. With their help, Moulvi Ahmed Shah got away. He turned his back on Rohilkhand and entered Oudh again.

Moulvi Ahmed Shah Treacherously Shot

The English could not subdue Moulvi Ahmed Shah, howsoever hard they tried. On re-entering Oudh, he started fresh efforts to increase his strength to fight the English. Along the road taken by him was a small Hindu state called Pavan. Its Raja was Jagannath Singh. Moulvi Ahmed Shah sent him a dispatch bearing the seal of Begum Hazrat Mahal and calling upon him to render help. Raja Jagannath Singh immediately invited Moulvi Ahmed Shah for an interview. The latter went to Pavan on an elephant. He met and talked with Raja Jagannath Singh, whose brother was also present. They were still talking when Raja Jagannath Singh's brother fired at him pointblank. Moulvi Ahmed Shah could not save himself from the treacherous shot. The Raja forthwith decapitated him, wrapped up the head and took it to the nearby English camp. The head was later hung up in front of the Kotwali at Shahjehanpur. Raja Jagannath Singh was rewarded with Rs. 50,000 by the English Government.

Thus ended the life of the brave patriot, Moulvi Ahmed Shah.

Tributes to Moulvi Ahmed Shah's Memory

We have earlier quoted the opinions of some English writers of history about Moulvi Ahmed Shah's skill and character. We would supplement them by two more quotations. Holmes refers to him as:

> "The most formidable enemy of the British in Northern India".
> *(History of the Indian Mutiny*, p. 339)

Another English historian writes:

> "The Moulvi was a very remarkable man ... Of his capacity as a military leader many proofs were given during the revolt ... No other man could boast that he had twice foiled Sir Collin Campbell in the field ... Thus died the Moulvi Ahmed Shah of Fyzabad. If a patriot is a man who plots and fights for the independence, wrongfully destroyed, of his native country,

then most certainly the Moulvi was a true patriot. He had not stained his sword by assassination; he had connived at no murder; he had fought manfully, honourably, and stubbornly in the field against the strangers who had seized his country; and his memory is entitled to the respect of the brave and the truehearted of all nations." (Malleson's *Indian Mutiny*, Vol. IV, p. 381)

These are the words of an Englishman. There can be no doubt whatsoever that amongst the martyrs in the cause of India's freedom, the name of Moulvi Ahmed Shah will always evoke unusual respect and shine with glory forever.

31

BIHAR

Organisation for the Revolution

The Province of Bihar had joined the movement from its inception and had organised itself to take part in the revolution when it broke out. Although the organisation there was not as extensive as it was in the Delhi and Oudh regions, Bihar had a few sizable revolutionary centres of which the most powerful was at Patna, which had branches all over the province. Before 1857, secret meetings were held there from time to time. The police there had also joined the organisation. There was no lack of funds. Hundreds of paid and honorary workers toured the countryside in all directions to propagate the cult of the revolution. The leaders at the centre kept themselves in constant touch with the revolutionary leaders at Delhi, Kanpur and Lucknow by carrying on secret correspondence with them.

Precautionary Measures taken by the English

When the English got scent of the above-mentioned activities, they sent a contingent of Sikh soldiers to Patna for the security of their rule there. It is stated that the people of Patna expressed their dislike of the Sikhs by shunning even the shadow of the latter.

A Police Jemadar of Tirhoot district, Waris Ali, was arrested and hanged on suspicion of his complicity in revolutionary activities. Amongst the letters found in Waris Ali's possession, one gave away the revolutionary leader, Ali Kareem. A posse of troops was sent to apprehend him. Ali Kareem escaped on his elephant and disappeared in the countryside. The Company's posse pursuing him was deliberately misled into going the wrong way by the people of the neighbouring villages, who were in collusion with Ali Kareem. The pursuit became infructuous and the pursuers returned unsuccessful. Taylor, the Commissioner of Patna, was informed that three influential Moulvis in the city were involved in the revolutionary organisation. He resorted to the ruse of inviting them to his house for an interview and had them arrested when they came.

The Revolution Breaks Out

On July 5, 1857, there was an uprising in Patna, but it was easily put down with the help of the Sikhs. The principal revolutionary leader, Pir Ali, was hanged. It is stated that he was tortured before he was hanged. Taylor himself has written that Pir Ali endured the tortures with great fortitude and met his death with the courage of one whose faith in the justice of the cause was almost religious.

After Pir Ali had been executed, the three sepoy regiments stationed at Dinapore declared their independence and marched to Jagdeeshpur.

Raja Kunwar Singh of Jagdeeshpur

Jagdeeshpur was the capital of a small old Rajput State in the Shababad district of Bihar. It dated back to the reign of the Mughal Emperor Shah Jehan, whose *Durbar* had conferred upon its owner the title of Raja. This state too had been victimised by the Dalhousie policy of annexation by usurpation; but its Raja, Kunwar Singh, was still intensely very popular in that region. He was over 80, but even so, he became an outstanding revolutionary leader in the Bihar Province, and proved to be one of the most brilliant fighters in the revolutionary war of 1857.

Siege of the Arrah Fortress

When the sepoys of the three revolting regiments of Dinapore arrived at Jagdeeshpur, old Kunwar Singh immediately took up arms, came out of his palace, and placing himself at their head, led them to Arrah. He seized the Company's treasury there, set free the prisoners in its jail, and razed its offices to the ground. Then he besieged the Arrah fortress which was garrisoned by a few English and some Sikh soldiers. Then occurred an acute shortage of water in the fortress from which the English began to suffer. To relieve their distress the Sikh soldiers dug up a new well and had it ready within 24 hours. Kunwar Singh offered their lives to the besieged if they surrendered the fortress but the offer was not accepted by the garrison. Kunwar Singh also tried to win over the Sikh soldiers but did not succeed. The siege continued.

Surprise Attack

On July 29, a contingent of some 300 English and 100 Sikh soldiers, commanded by Capt. Dunbar, started from Dinapore for the relief of the Arrah fortress. They had to pass through a mango-grove near Arrah. Kunwar Singh had hidden a number of his men in the branches of the mango trees who started shooting as soon as the English and the Sikh soldiers got under them. Well over 360 of them, including Capt. Dunbar, were killed. The survivors numbering about 50 fled back towards Dinapore.

The Bibigunj Battle

Major Eyre was then sent with a large force and some guns to help the English in the Arrah fortress. On August 2, a battle was fought near Bibigunj between his force and that led by Kunwar Singh, during which an English officer, Capt. Hastings, told Major Eyre, that victory seemed to be slipping out of their hands. Major Eyre, however, won the day and Kunwar Singh's force had to retreat. The fortress was relieved after a siege that had lasted eight days, and the English re-occupied the town.

Kunwar Singh Abandons His Capital

Kunwar Singh retreated towards his capital, Jagdeeshpur, and Major Eyre followed him in hot pursuit. The battle for Jagdeeshpur lasted several days and then Kunwar Singh abandoned his capital and left his palace with his family and 1,200 soldiers. On August 14, Major Eyre occupied the palace.

Kunwar Singh Fights Again

After leaving Jagdeeshpur, Kunwar Singh increased his force by enlisting the revolutionaries in the neighbouring region and advanced towards Azamgarh. He established his camp on March 18 at Atraulia, some 25 miles short of Azamgarh.

When the English came to know of it, they immediately dispatched a force consisting of infantry, cavalry and artillery to attack Kunwar Singh's camp. It was commanded by Milman.

On March 22, the two forces joined battle on the Atraulia plain which adjoined a forest. A little after the battle had begun, Kunwar Singh was in full retreat with his force. Milman concluded that Kunwar Singh was defeated and had run away. Delighted with his easy victory, Milman rested his troops and ordered them to have their meal. Whilst they were having it, Kunwar Singh suddenly pounced upon them. He knew every inch of the forest and, notwithstanding his age, was amazingly active. Milman's force was routed. Many were killed and the rest ran away and kept running till they reached the shelter of Kaushila. Milman's Indian servants deserted him and it is stated that they took away the bullock-carts. The abandoned baggage and guns fell into the hands of Kunwar Singh. Milman and his troops escaped towards Azamgarh.

Col. Dames Defeated—Lord Canning Worried

To help Milman's retreating force, another detachment of troops called in from Banaras and Ghazipur and commanded by Col. Dames reached Azamgarh, and joined Milman. On March 28, the combined forces commanded by Col. Dames sallied forth and engaged Kunwar Singh's force at a place a little beyond Azamgarh. Kunwar Singh was victorious once again, and Col. Dames was forced to retreat to the fort at Azamgarh. Kunwar Singh pursued him and occupied the town. Kunwar Singh appears to have put off the siege of the fort, for he advanced towards Banaras with the bulk of the force, leaving only a detachment at Azamgarh for the siege of the fort at a later date.

The historian Malleson states that the news of Kunwar Singh's victories and his march on Banaras upset Lord Canning who was then at Allahabad.

Lord Mark Kerr's Strategy

Kunwar Singh had by then travelled over a hundred miles from his capital Jagdeeshpur and had reached a point due north of Banaras. A large number of revolutionaries retreating from Lucknow joined his force there. Lord Canning immediately sent Lord Mark Kerr with a considerable force and a number of guns to check Kunwar Singh, and the first battle between the two was fought on April 8. It is stated that during the battle, the 81-year-old Kunwar Singh was seen dashing on his white horse with lightning speed, from point to point, wherever the fight become fast and furious. Lord Mark Kerr began to fall back with his guns. He left the battle-field with his force and proceeded towards Azamgarh, pursued by Kunwar Singh. According to the historian Malleson, Kunwar Singh made a tactical mistake in not continuing his march on Banaras and in giving it up to pursue Lord Mark Kerr. Apparently the latter had pretended to retire in order to lure Kunwar Singh on in his pursuit, and so to draw him away from his march on Banaras. The stratagem succeeded. Lord Mark Kerr reached Azamgarh fort and entered it. Kunwar Singh laid siege to it.

Kunwar Singh Changes His Plan

Another detachment of the Company's army under Lugard then advanced from the west to help Lord Mark Kerr who was besieged at Azamgarh.

Kunwar Singh, when he came to know of this, decided to abandon Azamgarh, and to go to Ghazipur. His plan was to cross the Ganges there and to proceed thence to Jagdeeshpur for re-conquering his ancestral State. At the same time he took measures to bar Lugard's way to Azamgarh, which lay across the river Tanoo. Kunwar Singh posted a detachment at the bridge which Lugard's force had to use for the crossing, whilst he himself proceeded towards Ghazipur. The detachment gallantly contested Lugard's passage over the bridge till it learned that its own main body had reached a safe distance. It then retired slowly and went to join the main body. Lugard never realised that the opposition at the bridge followed by the retirement of the force was only a ruse. The historian Malleson has expressed his unstinted admiration for it and for the gallantry with which the small detachment fought against heavy odds at the bridge. Kunwar Singh was pursued by Lugard for 12 miles and got away, only to return after a short detour and deliver another sudden attack on Lugard's force. The latter lost several officers and a number of men killed in action and had to retreat. Kunwar Singh then continued on his way to the Ganges.

Battles at Naghai and Manohar

Another contingent of the Company's army under Brigadier Douglas then advanced to subdue Kunwar Singh. A battle was fought near the village Naghai. Kunwar Singh divided his force into three detachments. One engaged the force under Douglas, whilst the other two made a short detour. The first detachment put up a stiff fight although it was heavily outnumbered. Douglas's force pressed it back four miles and then, getting tired, rested for a while. Whilst resting it was suddenly pounced upon by the other two detachments of Kunwar Singh's force which had returned by another route. Douglas was defeated and had to retreat.

All the three detachments of Kunwar Singh's force then continued on their way to the Ganges. Douglas's force, having recovered from its defeat, followed in pursuit which proved infructuous. Kunwar Singh marched on with amazing speed and reached Sikandarpur. He crossed the river Ghogra there and, reaching Manohar village, halted his force for a short rest.

It would, however, appear that Douglas had not abandoned the pursuit. His force caught up with Kunwar Singh's force at Manohar and attacked it, this time not without some success. Kunwar Singh lost to Douglas some elephants, munitions and provisions. Then Kunwar Singh divided his force into a number of small parties and instructed each of them to go by a different route to a specified place where all of them were to meet. It was not possible for Douglas to pursue every one of the parties, each going in a different direction. Eventually all the parties met at the rendezvous and went forward towards the Ganges.

Kunwar Singh Wounded

When he neared the Ganges, Kunwar Singh put in circulation a rumour to the effect that his plan was to go to a place near Ballia and to transport from there his troops across the Ganges on elephants. The English believed the rumour and stationed their force at that place to prevent Kunwar Singh's force from crossing the river. Actually Kunwar Singh had taken his force to Shivpur Ghat, some seven miles down the river from the place where the English force was stationed. When the English discovered that they had been tricked, they took their force post-haste to Shivpur Ghat. But by then, Kunwar Singh's force had got across by boats, and when the English force arrived at Shivpur Ghat, Kunwar Singh himself was going away in the last boat towards the opposite bank. He was in midstream when the English started firing on the boat. A stray bullet hit Kunwar Singh's right wrist. He realised that there was a risk of the wound getting septic and poisoning his whole body. The 81-year-old man immediately drew his sword with his left hand and at one stroke, cut off his right arm above the elbow. He threw the severed limb into the Ganges and wrapped a piece of cloth round the bleeding stump. His boat reached the opposite bank and, without a moment's rest, he marched his troops towards Jagdeeshpur, which was at some little distance from the Ganges. The English could not get across the river to pursue him further.

Kunwar Singh Enters Jagdeeshpur

Some eight months earlier Kunwar Singh had to leave his capital, which was then occupied by the English and was still occupied by them. On April 22, Kunwar Singh re-took possession of it. During the past eight months, his brother Amar Singh had not been idle. He had collected a small force of volunteers ready to join Kunwar Singh's force.

Captain Le Grand's Defeat and Death

The English were taken aback completely by Kunwar Singh's sudden re-occupation of Jagdeeshpur. The very next day, on April 23, a detachment of the Company's troops, composed mostly of Sikhs and some English soldiers and sailors, left Arrah under Capt. Le Grand to oust Kunwar Singh once again from Jagdeeshpur. The latter had entered Jagdeeshpur less than 24 hours earlier. His right forearm was gone. His men numbered about a thousand. He and his men had spent the previous eight months in almost continuous fighting and in journeying from place to place under difficult conditions. Opposed to him were fresh troops and equipped with guns too. Kunwar Singh had no guns. When Le Grand's force got within a mile-and-a-half of Jagdeeshpur, it was engaged in battle by Kunwar Singh's troops and routed. The historian White states:

> "The English sustained on this occasion a complete defeat of the worst kind." (*History of the Mutiny*).

For a description of the retreat of Le Grand's force, we give below an extract from what an English officer, who took part in the battle, wrote at the time:

> "I have proceeded thus far, but I am really ashamed to write further; however, as I have begun I will end it. We began our retreat in a most orderly manner out of the jungle, driving the enemy back wherever they approached too near, till we reached a tank in the open plain, where soldiers, sailors, Sikhs and followers began swallowing stagnant water, as they could get no better, and were fainting with thirst, when a cry was raised that the cavalry was thundering down on us ... After this the retreat was disgraceful; every man had his own way; no commands were listened to; the men were raving wild; and when we gained the main road, a more dreadful

scene as never before was beheld. The European portion of the force were falling from apoplexy by sections and no aid could be administered, as the medical stores were captured by the enemy, the dhooly-bearers having fled, notwithstanding the utmost exertions of the medical officers to keep them to their post. What aid could be given them, nothing. There were sixteen elephants, but they carried the wounded; so the poor unfortunate beings were left behind … About two miles from the village, on the retreat, Capt Le Grand was shot through the breast and died … When we had got five or six miles on the road, the soldiers and sailors were unable to load and fire their pieces through exhaustion, while the main body of the Sikhs who were accustomed to marching under a burning sun kept ahead with the elephants instead of covering our retreat … there were only about eighty Europeans left from 199." (Charles Ball's *Indian Mutiny*, Vol. II, p. 288)

All the guns and the baggage of the English force fell into the hands of Kunwar Singh.

Death of Kunwar Singh

On April 23, 1858, the victorious Raja Kunwar Singh became the *de facto* ruler of his ancestral state once again. He had won full freedom from the English Company's rule over it and over his people. The green flag of the War of Independence was flying over his capital. But only three days later, he died in his palace at Jagdeeshpur. The cause of his death was the self-inflicted wound on his right arm which had not healed. In the words of the historian Holmes:

> "The old Rajput who had fought so honourably and so bravely against the British power died on April 26th, 1858." *(History of the Sepoy War)*

Kunwar Singh's personal character was without a blemish and his life abstemious. His people respected and loved him to such an extent that out of regard for his abstinence, no one smoked in public.

Raja Amar Singh

On Kunwar Singh's death, his younger brother Amar Singh, succeeded to the Jagdeeshpur *Gadi*. He was in action within a few days, because he was not content to rule over Jagdeeshpur state only. He soon collected an army and marched at its head on Arrah.

On Way to Arrah

The detachments commanded by Gen. Douglas and Gen. Lugard had in the meantime crossed the Ganges and arrived at Arrah. The battle between them and Raja Amar Singh was fought on May 3, and was followed by battles at Bihia, Hatampur, Daleelpur, etc. In all of them Amar Singh closely followed the policy and the tactics of Kunwar Singh, and inflicted defeats on his adversaries time and again.

In despair Gen. Lugard sent in his resignation on June 15, and thereafter, the entire burden of the campaign was shouldered by Gen. Douglas alone. He had under him a force 7,000 strong and bad sworn to crush Amar Singh. But the months of June, July, August and September passed, and Amar Singh was still undefeated. On the contrary, he had succeeded in reaching Arrah and had entered the town. The frustrated Gen. Douglas then announced that anyone bringing him Amar Singh's head would be richly rewarded. But that too was of no use. All this time Amar Singh had kept intact his hold on Jagdeeshpur and the town became the next target of the English attack.

Jagdeeshpur Encircled

On October 17, seven big detachments of the Company's army simultaneously marched on Jagdeeshpur and surrounded it completely. Amar Singh realised that it would be impossible for him to win a fight against such heavy odds. So with a few hundred followers, he left Jagdeeshpur, and cut his way through the encircling enemy troops. Jagdeeshpur was then re-occupied by the English.

Battle at Now-nadi

The Company's troops pursued Amar Singh and caught up with him at Now-nadi village. He had only 400 men with him. But they put up a very stiff fight and at one time pressed back the pursuers. Amar Singh lost 300 men in the fight who had died fighting. The surviving 100, however, would not give in and continued to fight desperately. Then more English troops arrived on the scene. Amar Singh left the battle-field with only two companions. The other 97 covered his retreat and continued to fight till the last man lay dead on the field.

Amar Singh's End

The Company's troops pursued the fleeing Amar Singh. Some horsemen caught up with him. Amar Singh was riding an elephant which was stopped by the horsemen. Amar Singh jumped down from the elephant and escaped to the nearby Kai-moor Hills. He was then pursued till he disappeared in the hills and was never heard of thereafter.

Heroic Women of Jagdeeshpur Palace

The women in the palace could not bear the idea of falling into the hands of the enemy. So, when they saw that it had become inevitable, they preferred death. It is stated that all the 150 of them determined to get themselves blown off a cannon's mouth. They stood at the cannon's mouth and calmly fired them, thus ending their life on earth.

Revolutionary Leaders' Directive

We pause here to describe the situation as it had developed by April, 1858.

After the fall of Lucknow no revolutionary centre of importance was left anywhere in India. The Company's troops had spread out in all directions. Regiments had been recruited in England and sent out to India. On April 1, 1858, the number of English soldiers in India had reached a total of 97,000. The rulers of England had realised that their vast Indian Empire was slipping out of their grasp, and had gone all-out to put down the revolution. Some of the topmost and most experienced military Commanders which the English nation possessed were sent to India. Besides the English soldiers drafted from England, the Company had its own Indian army, as also the armies of a number of Indian States. The Sikhs and the Gorkhas were also supporting the English with all their strength.

On the other side the revolutionaries were getting more and more disorganised. They had lost important revolutionary centres like Delhi, Kanpur and Lucknow. In these circumstances, the revolutionary leaders of Oudh and Rohilkhand published their directions to the scattered revolutionaries who were still fighting. The directions were as follows:

> "Avoid meeting the regular troops of these irreligious people (i.e., the English) in an open fight on a battle-field. They are better equipped and better organised than we are. They have a number of big heavy guns too. Watch their movements closely. Post your men on all the *ghats* of the rivers, Intercept the stores and provisions going for them as also their correspondence. Disrupt their system of carrying mail and demolish their out-posts. Keep going about around their camps. Above all do not give the *Feringhee* any respite." (*Russell's Diary*, p. 276)

Russell's comments on the above directions are to the following effect;

> "This public announcement is indicative of the wisdom of the revolutionary leaders as also of the fact that never before had we to fight such a fearsome war." (ibid. p. 276)

32

RANI LAKSHMIBAI OF JHANSI

Sir Hugh Rose on the War-Path

For eleven months the revolutionaries had been in occupation of the entire region to the south of the Jumna, right up to the Vindhyachal Mountains. Chief credit for it was due to Rani Lakshmibai. A large force was sent to re-conquer this region. It included the troops of Hyderabad, Bhopal and other Indian States, and was commanded by Sir Hugh Rose.

On January 6, 1858, Sir Hugh started from Mhow and marched on Jhansi. On his way he took Raigarh, Banapur, Chanderi, etc., and arrived near Jhansi on March 20. Jhansi was then the most important revolutionary centre in that region. Several Rajas and Sardars, including Raja Mardan Singh of Banapur, had arrived there to help the Rani.

Rani Lakshmibai, on hearing of Sir Hugh's march, resorted to "scorched-earth" tactics. For a long distance from Jhansi, the country along Sir Hugh's line of march had been laid waste and was deserted, in order to ensure that Sir Hugh's force did not get any provisions on the way. Not an ear of corn was left in the fields. Not a blade of grass could be seen anywhere. Not a tree to provide shade was left standing.

But Maharaja Sindhia and the Raja of Tebri-Tikamgarh had made efficient arrangements for the supply of provisions, fodder, etc., to the advancing army, and Sir Hugh had no difficulty about getting them.

Rani Lakshmibai in Command of Operations

The Rani assumed command of the revolutionary army. She personally supervised the erection of barricades and barriers, and the mounting of guns on the ramparts of the fort. Sir Hugh has recorded that hundreds of women of Jhansi had joined Rani Lakshmibai, and could be seen working in the arsenal and the artillery of the revolutionary army.

The duel started on March 24, with the shelling of Sir Hugh's force by a Jhansi gun called 'Ghangarj' (Thunderer). It continued for eight days during which fortune alternately, favoured, with a temporary advantage, first one side and then the other. We give below some extracts from an eye-witness's account of the duel:

> "... Rani Lakshmibai was constantly on the walls directing and looking after everything ... Wherever she found the wall weakened she had it strengthened immediately ... Her presence in the midst of her gunners and soldiers boosted up their morale ... She rewarded conspicuous deeds on the spot; for instance, she promptly presented a gold bracelet to the gunner Ghulam Ghaus Khan who blew up the best gunner of the enemy ... Gunners and soldiers who fell fighting were immediately replaced by others ... Heavy losses in lives were sustained by both sides ... An arsenal inside the fort was hit and blown up, killing 30 men and 8 women ..."

The defenders, however, would not give in, although their position was well-nigh hopeless, and it had become impossible for them to hold out much longer against such heavy odds, in numbers and in equipment, unless they received help. Rani Lakshmibai wrote to Tatya Tope for assistance.

Tatya Tope Foiled

Tatpa Tope had, in the meantime, crossed the Jumna with his force, and had reached Charkhari, whose Raja had declined to join the revolutionaries. Tatya attacked Charkhari, seized 24 guns of the Raja, and exacted from him a contribution of 3 lacs of rupees for the revolutionary war-chest. Then he reached Kalpi where he received Rani Lakshmibai's letter, and advanced towards Jhansi to help the Rani in its defence. It is stated that he had a large force with him, and his arrival put the Company's force in a very difficult position, as Tatya Tope now threatened its rear, whilst it was fighting Rani Lakshmibai on its front. Yet it faced the situation with indomitable courage and on April 1, 1857, attacked Tatya's force on its rear, and routed it. Tatya lost some 1500 killed in action, and all his guns fell into the hands of the English.

Last Attack on Jhansi

With the rout of Tatya's force, the position of the defenders of Jhansi became even more precarious. Rani Lakshmibai, however, did not lose heart, and continued to fight courageously. On April 3, the English force attacked Jhansi from all sides simultaneously. Rani Lakshmibai, riding a horse, was invariably in the thick of the fight, and flashed, like lightning, from one spot to another, encouraging her soldiers and their officers. The English pressure was directed on the northern gate of the city. Ladders were put up against the city wall at eight places, under fire from the Rani's guns. Two English officers, Dick and Micklejohn, climbed up the ladders shouting to the others to follow. Both the brave Englishmen were shot dead. Their places were immediately taken by two other Englishmen, Bonus and Fox. They too were shot down. Then the ladders collapsed. According to the historian Lowe, the firing from the walls was so furious and so murderous that the English troops had to retire.

Treason at Work

Whilst fighting was going on at the northern gate, some traitor, it is stated, helped the English troops to enter the city through its southern gate, and they then advanced towards the Palace, massacring the city people on the way. The Rani saw from the ramparts the indiscriminate slaughter of her people. She collected a thousand soldiers and rushed to the scene of slaughter. Soldiers on either side discarded their muskets and fought with swords. Many lives were lost on both sides. The English troops were being pressed back, when news was brought to the Rani that the officer defending the northern gate, Sardar Khuda Baksh, and the artillery officer posted there, Sardar Ghulam Ghaus Khan, had both been killed fighting. It meant that the northern gate too was now open for the English. The Rani lost her heart completely, and her first impulse was to blow herself up with her powder-magazine. But on second thoughts she decided to abandon Jhansi and to continue the fight from somewhere else, and thus help the revolution. Jhansi fell to the English.

Rani Lakshmibai Leaves for Kalpi

That very night Rani Lakshmibai left Jhansi. She dressed herself in male attire, fastened her adopted child Damodar to her back, and, fully armed, jumped down from the wall of the fort on an elephant. She then mounted her favourite white horse and sped towards Kalpi, with some 10 or 15 horsemen.

A Hundred-mile Ride

Lt. Bokker with some picked troopers followed the Rani in hot pursuit. It developed into a race between the pursuers and the pursued, but the latter could not be overtaken. At daybreak, the Rani reached the village of Bhander, where she stopped to get some milk to feed the child. Then the pursuers having got close behind her, she and her horsemen galloped away. The pursuers, however, caught up with her, and Lt. Bokker got close to the Rani, who immediately drew her sword, struck and wounded him. He fell down. Then the horsemen of both engaged in a running fight with swords. Ultimately the Rani and her followers succeeded in getting away, leaving the wounded Lt. Bokker and his troopers far behind. They kept going as fast as possible throughout the day and without a moment's respite. Night fell, the stars came out but they kept on riding. At about midnight. Rani Lakshmibai, with Damodar still fastened to her back, entered Kalpi. She had ridden non-stop all the 102 miles from Jhansi. Her favourite horse, who had gamely stood up to the gruelling speed all the way, collapsed, as she got down, and died. Next morning the Rani held a conference with Tatya Tope and Rao Sahib, the nephew of Nana Sahib.

Nawab of Banda

On February 17, 1858, General Whitlock started from Jubbulpore with a large force of English and Indian regiments. His purpose was similar to that of Sir Hugh Rose—the reconquest of Saugar and its adjoining region. On the way he was joined by the Raja of Orcbha. After Saugar, Whitlock proceeded towards Banda. The Nawab of Banda had granted asylum in his palace to many Englishmen and had treated them very considerately, although he was a prominent revolutionary leader in his province. At the start of the revolution, he had uprooted every emblem of the English Raj and had hoisted over the city the green flag of Emperor Bahadur Shah.

On hearing of Whitlock's approach, the Nawab got ready to fight him. There were many engagements, but, ultimately, the Nawab was defeated and leaving Banda with some of his troops, he proceeded towards Kalpi. The victorious Whitlock entered the town of Banda on April 19, 1858.

Rao of Karvi

From Banda, Whitlock marched on to Karvi. The Rao of Karvi, Madho Rao, was a boy of ten. During his minority, the administration of the Karvi State was carried on by a *Karbhari* (administrator) appointed by the Company. The Rao had taken no part whatsoever in the revolution. When he heard of Whitlock's approach, he came out of his palace to welcome him. The boy Rao was immediately taken into custody. His palace was demolished, his capital was looted and his State was annexed to the Company. The historian Malleson states:

> "Not a shot had been fired against him (Whitlock), but he resolved nevertheless to treat the young Rao as though he had actually opposed the British forces. The reason for this perversion of honest dealing lay in the fact that in the palace of Karvi was stored the wherewithal to compensate soldiers for many a hard fight and many a broiling sun. In its vaults and strong rooms were, jewels and diamonds of priceless value ... The wealth was coveted." (Kaye and Malleson's *Indian Mutiny*, Vol. V, pp. 140–41)

Then Whitlock moved to Mahoba, and from there he sent out detachments to subdue the revolutionaries in the adjoining areas.

Battle at Kanchgaon

The revolutionaries had assembled at Kalpi in considerable strength. Rani Lakshmibai, Rao Sahib, Tatya Tope, the Nawab of Banda, the Rajas of Shahgarh and Banapur were all there with their troops, besides a number of other revolutionary leaders. It would not have been very difficult for such a large force to get the better of the enemy, provided it was commanded by a single overall leader. But there was no one amongst the revolutionary leaders assembled there, who could command the unquestioning obedience of the rest to whatever orders he might dictate. The Rani was undoubtedly the ablest of them all, but she was a woman, and only 22 years of age. Tatya Tope was a brave and clever army leader, but he was a commoner. It had not till then become easy for the scions of old ruling families to reconcile themselves to their being commanded by a woman or a commoner. The same prejudice had been the chief cause of the fall of Delhi.

The Rani, however, took the initiative and advanced 42 miles from Kalpi to check the oncoming force of Sir Hugh Rose. The two forces joined in battle at Kanchgaon, which was lost by the Rani, because, on account of the differences between the revolutionary leaders, she did not get from them the necessary co-operation and help. The historian Malleson very admiringly states that in spite of her defeat, the Rani brought her force back to Kalpi in amazing order *(Indian Mutiny,* Vol.V, p. 124).

Battle at Kalpi

Sir Hugh Rose then marched on Kalpi. Rani Lakshmibai rallied her defeated troops and sallied forth from Kalpi with her horsemen to fight him. The battle that followed was furious and at one time Sir Hugh's right flank had to fall back. His gunners abandoned the guns and ran away. Then Sir Hugh retrieved the situation by leading his left flank in a turning movement to attack Lakshmibai from that side. Ultimately, he won the day. On May 24, his force entered Kalpi. Some 700 maunds of gunpowder and innumerable arms in the Kalpi arsonel fell into his hands. Rani Lakshmibai left Kalpi with a small body of troops. Rao Sahib and the Nawab of Banda also left with her.

Sir Hugh Rose was no doubt one of the ablest and bravest of the Company's generals. His achievement was brilliant. He had marched a thousand miles through difficult terrain, crossed mountains and rivers and got through dense forests. He had won victories over large forces opposing him, and he had re-conquered for the Company the entire region between the Narmada and the Jumna rivers.

Revolutionaries Take Gwalior

Driven out of Kalpi, the revolutionaries of that region were now bereft of all resources. They had no troops worth the name, no equipment and no stronghold. But Rani Lakshmibai and Tatya Tope had not lost courage. The latter went to Gwalior secretly and won over to the revolution, not only the people of Gwalior but a goodly portion of Maharaja Sindhia's army too, which he led back to Gopalpur. He was joined there by Rani Lakshmibai, the Nawab of Banda and Rao Sahib. In a conference between them the Rani proposed that the first thing to do was to take Gwalior in the name of Rao Sahib as the representative of the Peshwa, Nana Sahib. Gwalior could then be made their new headquarters. Accordingly, on May 28, 1858, the revolutionary leaders arrived at Gwalior and sent a letter to Maharaja Sindhia to the following effect:

> "We have come to you in all friendliness, and would remind you of your past relations with the Peshwa. We look to you for help to enable us to proceed southwards, etc."

Instead of extending a friendly hand to the revolutionary leaders, Maharaja Jayajirao Sindhia decided to fight them and on June 1 sallied forth with that intention. Rani Lakshmibai immediately charged his artillery with 300 horsemen. Most of the Sindhia's army had already given a pledge to Tatya Tope to join the revolutionaries, and the men and their officers honoured their pledge and defected. Maharaja Jayajirao Sindhia and his Minister Dinkarrao had to run away towards Agra. The people of Gwalior welcomed the revolutionaries enthusiastically. The Gwalior army fired a salute in token of their acknowledgement of Rao Sahib as the Peshwa. The Finance Minister of Gwalior, Amar Chand Bhatia, handed over Sindhia's treasury to the revolutionary leaders.

On June 3, 1858, a grand *Durbar* was held in the Phool Bagh of Sindhia's Palace, which was attended by all the military commanders, Sardars and noblemen of Gwalior. The Arab, Rohilla, Rajput and Maratha battalions in uniform formed up in front of the assemblage. The plumed head-dress, traditionally worn by the Peshwas, was placed on Rao Sahib's head in token of the *Durbar* acknowledging him as the Peshwa. The Peshwa's Ministers were appointed. Tatya Tope was appointed the Supreme Commander-in-Chief of the Gwalior Army. Rs. two lacs were distributed to the army as guerdon. The *Durbar* concluded with a gun-salute for the Peshwa.

Thus it was that Rani Lakshmibai provided the revolutionaries with a new stronghold in place of Delhi, Kanpur and Lucknow which they had lost, one after another.

> "But no one, not even Sir Hugh Rose, had imagined the height of daring to which the Rani of Jhansi would carry her audacious plans. The rebels might march to Gwalior but no one believed they would carry it by a *coup de main* ... How the 'impossible' happened has been told. The information of it reached Sir Hugh Rose on the 4th June ... In a moment he realised the full danger of the situation ... He realised, moreover, the great danger which would inevitably be caused by delay. No one could foresee the extent of the evil possible, if Gwalior were not promptly wrested from rebel hands. Grant them delay, and Tatya Tope, with the immense acquisition of political and military strength secured by the possession of Gwalior, and with all its resources in men, money, and material at his disposal, would be able to form a new army on the fragments of that beaten at Kalpi, and to provoke a Maratha rising throughout India. It might be possible for him, using the dexterity of which he was a master, to unfurl the Peshwa's banner in the southern Maratha districts. Those districts were denuded of troops, and striking success in central India would probably decide their inhabitants to

pronounce in favour of the cause for which their fathers had fought and bled." *(History of the Indian Mutiny* by Kaye and Malleson, Vol. V, pp. 149–50)

Rani Lakshmibai's Sound Advice

After the occupation of Gwalior, Rani Lakshmibai tried hard to impress upon the other leaders the absolute necessity of putting in the field immediately a well-organised, well-equipped and strong army. She insisted that everything else must be put aside. But Rao Sahib and the other leaders ignored her sound advice. Invaluable time was wasted in feasts and celebrations, in the midst of which Sir Hugh Rose suddenly appeared outside Gwalior with a strong force. He had brought Maharaja Jayajirao Sindhia with him, and announced that the Company's army had come only to re-instate the Maharaja on the Gwalior *Gadi*.

Failure of Tatya Tope's Resistance—Rani to the Rescue

Tatya Tope sallied forth to fight Sir Hugh's force. But the troops led out by him were shaky because they had been formerly routed in northern India by the Company's army. Consequently, they degenerated into a disorderly rabble soon after the battle had started. Rao Sahib lost his head. Rani Lakshmibai rallied the men, inspired them with courage and united them into a solid formation. She then took personal charge of the defence of the eastern gate of the city and posted herself there.

Battles for Gwalior

On June 17, 1858, the noted English general, Smith, advanced to attack the eastern gate. His troops repeatedly assaulted the gate but were driven back every time by Rani Lakshmibai. Each time she pursued the retreating storming party in a sortie and, after playing havoc with them, returned to her post at the gate. She fought personally, and by her side fought her two girl-friends, Mandra and Kashi. It has been stated that throughout that day, from sunrise to sunset, the Rani was in her saddle continuously and could be seen riding and fighting everywhere. General Smith had to give up his attempt and retired. Rani Lakshmibai had won the day.

On June 18, General Smith again advanced towards the eastern gate, this time with a stronger force., Sir Hugh Rose too appeared in front of the gate. The English force attacked Gwalior that day from more than one direction. It is stated that early in the morning on that day, whilst Rani Lakshmibai was drinking sherbet with her two girl-friends, she was informed of the approach of the English detachments. She forthwith threw away her drinking bowl and, with her girl-friends, advanced to fight the approaching enemy. The Rani was in male attire.

An Englishman, who was an eye-witness of the battle that followed, describes it thus:

> "The beauteous Rani immediately reached the field of battle. She posted her troops in strong formations in front of Sir Hugh's force and subjected the latter to furious attacks again and again, which she led in person. Her troops were decimated by the fire of the guns of the enemy and their number was steadily growing less and less. But the Rani continued to fight and was invariably in the forefront. Again and again she rallied her faltering soldiers and led them to attack. She displayed superhuman courage and bravery at every step. But it all led to no decisive result. Sir Hugh personally led his subsidiary army to break through the last phalanx formed by the Rani. The intrepid Rani, however, bravely stuck to her post."

The Rani Fights On

Whilst the Rani was thus desperately fighting against Sir Hugh's force in front of her, the rest of the English force cut its way through the revolutionaries on her rear and attacked her.

By then, the Gwalior guns had been silenced, and the main body of the Gwalior army had been scattered. The victorious English troops were bearing down upon the isolated Rani, whose followers were now reduced to a pitiful 15 or 20 horsemen and her two girlfriends who had stuck to her and were fighting by her side. The Rani put her horse to a gallop and made a gallant attempt to cut her way through to the revolutionaries fighting on the other side. English horsemen pursued her. Then her friend Mandra was shot and fell down dead from her horse. The Rani turned and cut down with her sword the English horseman who had shot Mandra. She then went forward again. A deep drain confronted her. Had the Rani's horse jumped over it, it might have become impossible for the English horsemen to pursue her further. But all the trained and favourite horses of the Rani had been killed under her, and the one she was riding was a new and untrained one. It would not jump over but went round and round in circles. The pursuing English horsemen closed in and surrounded her on all sides.

Lakshmibai's Martyrdom

Alone and hemmed in, but quite undismayed, the Rani continued to fight single-handed. An English horseman cut open her head from behind. Another, in front of her, wounded her in the chest. Her right eye was blinded. Blood welled out from her head and her chest. She was losing consciousness. With a last superhuman effort, she used the last ounce of her strength in cutting down the horseman confronting her. Then she collapsed and fell—never to rise again.

Rani Lakshmibai died sword in hand, a valiant soldier's death. Her young life bad been without a blemish, so were her heroic struggle and her end. She ranks amongst the rare heroines recorded in human history, who though so young, yet fought so persistently and with such phenomenal courage for the freedom of their country and died fighting for it with extraordinary valour and ability.

Vincent A. Smith describes her as "... the ablest of the rebel leaders" (*The Oxford Student's History of India*, p. 328).

33

INEFFECTUAL OUTBREAKS IN THE SOUTH

South of the Vindhyachal

The 1857 revolution was at its height in northern India up to the Vindhyachal mountain. The country to the south of the mountain did not join the revolution as wholeheartedly. Had it done so, the whole picture would have changed. It would then have become impossible for the Company's Madras and Bombay armies to go north and reconquer Bihar, Banaras, Allahabad, Oudh and Rohilkhand. The result of the revolution would then have been quite different.

The revolutionary propagandists who had gone to that part of the country had not been able to organise it effectively. We have already mentioned (Chapter XVIII) that Rango Bapuji was busy in Satara with the propaganda for the revolution, amongst the rulers and chiefs of the South Indian States, and was also keeping in close touch with Nana Sahib.

There were uprisings at a number of places, but they were so scattered, unorganised and untimely, that the English suppressed them quite easily, before these could materially help the cause of the revolution.

At Kolhapur

On July 13, 1857, the Indian Regiment stationed at Kolhapur revolted. The sepoys killed some of their English officers and seized the Company's treasury. The English suppressed the revolt. Then on December 15, there was a serious outbreak in the city. It was helped by the Maharaja's younger brother, Chimna Sahib. The gates of the city were closed, cannons were mounted on the city wall, and independence was proclaimed by beat of drum. The Company's troops rushed to the city, fought the revolutionaries and won. Thereafter a number of people were blown off the cannon's mouth.

At Belgaum, Dharwar and Satara

In August 1857, the English noticed signs of revolt in the Indian regiment posted at Belgaum. The ring-leaders were immediately blown off the cannon's mouth. Belgaum and Dharwar were thus quietened.

A son of Rango Bapuji was hanged at Satara and two members of the Raja's family were externed. Rango Bapuji got away from Satara. Huge rewards were offered for information leading to his arrest but he was never found.

At Bombay and Nagpur

Some Indian regiments stationed at Bombay had planned to start a revolution and then to march to Poona and seize it. At Poona Nana Sahib was to be proclaimed the Peshwa. The English got wind of these plans and acted immediately. Some were hanged, others were externed and the plans were nipped in the bud.

Some sepoys stationed near Nagpur had decided to revolt on June 13, 1857. A number of prominent and influential citizens of Nagpur had joined in the sepoys' plans. The Indian regiments from Madras, however, arrived before the date and made Nagpur secure for the English.

At Jabalpur

Raja Shankar Singh, the Gond Raja in the Jabalpur region, and his son were sincerely devoted to the revolutionary cause. They won over to the cause the LII Indian Regiment stationed at Jabalpur. The English got wind of what was afoot. On September 18, 1857, Raja Shankar Singh and his son were blown off the cannon's mouth. The LII revolted forthwith. An Englishman was killed. A number of the sepoys left Jabalpur to take part in the revolution at some other place.

Prince Feroze Shah of Delhi

In Dhar State, in Maheedpur, in Goria and other places, Prince Feroze Shah made plans for the outbreak of the revolution. He does not appear to have succeeded much at if, all.

Hyderabad

An English historian has very rightly stated that for three months the fate of Hindustan was in the hands of Nizam Afzal-ud-Daulah and his Vazir, Sir Salar Jung. There can be no doubt that the whole of southern India would have been ablaze had the Nizam of Hyderabad sided with the revolutionaries. During the months of June and July, 1857, there was unstinted public enthusiasm in Hyderabad for the revolution. The Mussalmans were conspicuously zealous in supporting it. Eminent *Moulvis* authoritatively gave *Fatwas* (religious directives) in favour of the revolution. Thousands of handbills and leaflets supporting it were published. Crowded meetings were held in mosques in which speeches against English rule were delivered. Mussalman soldiers were intensely agitated. But the Nizam and his Vazir firmly adhered to the English side and co-operated with the English to the fullest possible extent. They arrested the ring-leaders of the agitation and handed them over to the English. With the help of the Company's troops, all the rebellious Mussalman sepoys were slaughtered. The Nizam and his Vazir thus saved Hyderabad State for the English.

Youthful Raja of Shorapur

Shorapur was the capital of the State of that name near Hyderabad. The State was an ancient Beydur Raj, when the the name of its capital was Shoorpur or "the city of the brave". "Beydur" means "fearless", and the Beydurs were a warlike clan. "They are," writes Taylor, "highly honourable and never break an oath ... Their moral character is high." (Collated from The *Story of My Life* by Meadows Taylor, Chap. XV, 1920 Edn.)

When the 1857 revolution broke out, Raja Enketappa Naik, a young man of barely 23, was the ruler of Shorapur. He collected Arabs and Rohilla mercenaries in addition to calling his own clan (the Beydurs) together, "while he was more than suspected to hold communication with foreign mercenaries at Hyderabad". A force of contingent troops under Capt. Wyndham was sent from Lingsugur to Shorapur, as a precautionary measure, by the English. It arrived at Shorapur on February 7, 1858, and encamped near the town. At night Wyndham was attacked by "the Raja's whole force of Beydurs and foreign mercenaries" and his (Wyndham's) force suffered some losses. Then reinforcements for Wyndham arrived on the morning of the 8th. The battle was renewed. Capt. Newsbury was killed in a charge against the Rohillas and Lt. Stewart was badly wounded. But the Beydurs and the others were pushed back into the town.

> "As the city of Shorapur was very strong ... and the walls and bastions crowded with defenders, they (the English) did not attack it at once, but waited for Col. Malcolm's force, which had moved close to the western frontier of Shorapur."

The Raja heard that "Col. Malcolm's force had with it a large proportion of English troops, who, together with two companies of the 74th Highlanders under Col. Hughes, made a sufficiently imposing army." The Raja saw that he was hopelessly out-numbered and went to Hyderabad to acquire the support of the Arabs there. He did not succeed, and the Hyderabad minister, Salar Jung, promptly had him apprehended and sent in custody to the Resident.

> "The Raja of Shorapur," writes Taylor, "was a prisoner in the main-guard of the Royals at Secunderabad, and I went three times to see him."

The first interview was infructuous, but the Raja pressed Taylor to come again and Taylor promised to do so.

> "I hoped", proceeds Taylor, "that when I next visited the Raja, he would disclose to me all the particulars of his rebellion."

I asked him if he would like to see the Resident ... To my surprise, he drew himself up very proudly and replied haughtily:

> "No Appa" (The Raja always called Taylor "Appa.") He would expect me to ask my life of him, and I won't do that ... I will not ask to live like a coward, nor will I betray my people."

At the next interview, Taylor tried once again to get the the Raja to betray his colleagues and so save his own life. The Raja's refusal was even more emphatic:

> "Shall I... be faithless to those who trusted me? Never Appa. I would rather die than be sent over the black water, or shut up in a fortress ... No; the meanest Beydur could not live if he were imprisoned—shall I, a Raja?"

> "If you have to die," said Taylor "die like a brave man."

> "I shall not tremble when they tie me up to a gun ... only one thing, Appa, do not let them hang me. I have done nothing to be hanged like a robber. Tell the Resident that is all the favour I ask."

> Taylor did so and the Resident was moved to comment.

> "The poor lad has spirit."

> "We will save him if we can, Taylor," promised the Resident, "when the time comes. Just now things must take their course ... I am sure there is good stuff in the lad."

Things did take their course and the Raja was sentenced to death; but

> "The Resident... commuted the sentence to transportation for life, which was the most his power admitted of. This sentence (was) ... however ... still further commuted by the Governor-General to four years' imprisonment in a fortress near Madras ... In addition ... if he (the Raja) showed evidence of reform ... his principality was to be restored to him."

But the Raja's firm resolve was unshaken by this show of clemency, and he carried it out as he was being taken away, under an escort, to the fortress. Next day, a runner brought to Taylor the following few lines hurriedly written by the Resident:

> "The Raja of Shorapur shot himself dead this morning, as he arrived at his first encampment. I will write particulars when I know them."

Such was the end of the heroic young fighter for independence, who, rather than submit to imprisonment, preferred death by his own hand. He was not even 24 then.

The Raja of Nargunda

Bhaskarrao Baba Sahib, the Raja of Nargunda, was a close associate of the Raja of Shorapur. His Rani was a very brave woman and a mortal enemy of the English. It is stated that Baba Sahib hesitated a long time. Pressed by his Rani, he at last declared war against the English on May 25, 1858.

A contingent of the Company's army, led by Monson, marched to Nargunda. When it was in a jungle near Nargunda, Baba Sahib surrounded it at night. In the battle which followed Monson was killed, and his troops ran away. Monson's body was decapitated and next day the severed head was hung from the Nargunda wall.

Sometime afterwards, a step-brother of Baba Sahib went over to the English, who attacked Nargunda again. This time Baba Sahib was defeated, but he succeeded in getting away from Nargunda. He was, however, apprehended a few days later and was hanged. His Rani and his mother committed suicide by jumping into the Malprabha river.

Some Other Infructuous Uprisings

Bheem Rao of Komal Durg who belonged to the Bheem tribe fought the English. So did the Bhil men and women of Khandesh with their bows and arrows. There were some violent disturbances in Burma and in Rangoon which were then part of British India. But all of them occurred too late, and were easily suppressed without having achieved anything.

OUDH'S LAST BID FOR FREEDOM

Revolutionaries Foregather in Oudh

Once again we revert to Oudh, the last and toughest revolutionary stronghold. After Lucknow had been finally taken by the English, Lord Canning had an announcement made throughout Oudh, whereby he promised amnesty and restoration of *Jagirs* to all those who laid down their arms. But it does not appear to have had any particular effect on the revolutionary leaders who had gathered in Oudh.

Khan Bahadur Khan, the revolutionary leader of Rohil-khand, was again in the field with a force 4,000 strong. In Farrukhabad, 5,000 sepoys had collected afresh. Thousands of soldiers were joining up under Nana Sahib, Bala Sahib, Vilayat Shah and Ali Khan Mewati. Begum Hazrat Mahal's force under Sardar Mamoo Khan was at Chowk Ghat on the bank of the Ghogra. Prince Ferozeshah of Delhi too was in Oudh. In addition, a number of big *Zamindars* were busy in hectic preparations for an all-out, collective effort to wrest Oudh from the English by force of arms. Amongst them may be mentioned Raja Narpat Singh of Rui-ya, Raja Rambaksh, Bahu Nath Singh, Chanda Singh, Gulab Singh, Bhupal Singh, Hanumant Singh, and others, who had brought with them their armed followers. The aged Raja Beni Madhav too had started preparations for an attack on Lucknow.

Then as mentioned in Chapter XX, Moulvi Ahmed Shah was treacherously shot dead at the instigation of the English, who had rewarded the murderer. The revolutionaries' indignation boiled over at the foul murder and Oudh was ablaze again. Pilibhit was attacked by Nizam Ali Khan.

Revolutionaries' Battle for Lucknow

The revolutionary forces converged on Lucknow and assembled at Nawabganj, near the city. On June 13, 1858, General Hope Grant suddenly attacked them with a force which consisted, *inter alia,* of a number of Indian regiments. The revolutionaries counter-attacked. General Hope Grant thus described the fighting:

> "Their attacks on us were unsuccessful, although all of them were very strong and we had to fight very hard to repel them. Some handsome and courageous Zamindars brought two guns in the open and attacked our rear. I have witnessed many a battle in India, and have seen many brave men fight with the determination 'to win or die'. But I have never seen a more splendid sight than the way in which these Zamindars fought that day. They first attacked a cavalry regiment of ours. Our horsemen could not stand up to them, and were routed. Our two guns which were with them were imminent danger. I ordered the VII Regiment, which had four guns, to advance. The guns were emplaced at a distance of 500 yards from the enemy whom they started shelling. They fell down in numbers like grass cut under by a scythe. Their leader was a tall, broad-shouldered man with a goitre under his chin. He was not perturbed in the least. He planted two green flags near his guns and rallied his men around them. Our guns were, however, firing so furiously that the men reached the guns only to fall down dead. Then two other regiments arrived to help us, and it was only then that we could force the enemy to retreat. Even whilst retreating, they brandished their swords and lances at us fearlessly, challenging our men to come on and fight. At one spot alone, near the two guns of the enemy we found 125 dead bodies. We won after a murderous battle lasting three hours." (*Incidents of the Sepoy War,* p. 292)

Equally furious battles were being fought at that time at a number of places in Oudh. The people of Oudh had to begin fighting again for every foot of their motherland.

Raja Beni Madhav

Shankarpur, Raja Beni Madhav's palace, was invaded. The fortress was attacked from three sides by an English force far stronger than his. Beni Madhav was short of men and ammunition. But he would not surrender. Commander-in-Chief Sir Collin Campbell called upon him to surrender if he did not want useless bloodshed by fighting when it was utterly impossible for him to win. Sir Collin also held out the promise of a pardon and the restoration of his *Zamindari*. Beni Madhav's answer was:

> "It has indeed become impossible for me to defend the fortress and so I am abandoning it. But I will never deliver my person to you. Because my body is not mine. It is my King's."

End of Company's Rule

After the revolution had lasted a year and a half, an event occurred which is considered to be an important landmark in the history of British rule in India. It had been prophesied, at the start of the revolution, that the English Company's rule over India would end. So it did, on November 1, 1858. The rulers of England considered it not only politic but essential too, in their own interests, to end the rule of the East India Company over the country which had lasted a hundred years. But so far as India was concerned, it was only a change of masters. The Company's domination was replaced by that of the British Crown.

Proclamations by Queen Victoria and Begum Hazrat Mahal

Queen Victoria's "Proclamation to the Princes, Chiefs and People of India" was published throughout India on November 1, 1858. It was read out on that date by Lord Canning himself to thousands of people collected under the Fort at Allahabad.

It announced that Queen Victoria "had taken upon herself the Government of the territories in India", and that her "clemency will be extended to all offenders, save and except those who have been or shall be convicted of having directly taken part in the murder of British subjects". An assurance was also given thereby, that there will be no "interference with the religious belief or worship" of any of the Queen's subjects. It also assured the native princes of India "that all treaties and engagements made with them by or under the authority of the Honourable East India Company", were, by the Queen, "accepted and will be scrupulously maintained", etc., etc.,

Immediately after the publication of Queen Victoria's proclamation, Begum Hazrat Mahal issued a proclamation to the people of Oudh. It was in Urdu. The Chief Commissioner of Oudh had it translated into English, and we happened to get a copy of the latter, as quoted by Charles Ball in his *History of the Indian Mutiny,* Vol. II, pp. 543–44.

Begum Hazrat Mahal's proclamation purports to be a critique of the proclamation issued by Queen Victoria, and contains a warning to the people not to be "deceived" by it.

Proclamation by the Begum of Oudh. (Translation by Order)

> "At this time certain weak-minded, foolish peoples have spread a report that the English have forgiven the faults and crimes of the people of Hindostan. This appears very astonishing, for it is the unvarying custom of the English never to forgive a fault, be it great or small; so much so, that if a small offence be committed through ignorance or negligence, they never forgive it. The proclamation of the 1st of November, 1858, which has come before us, is perfectly clear; and as some foolish people, not understanding the real object of the proclamation, have been carried away we, the ever abiding Government, parents of the people of Oudh, with great consideration, put forth the present proclamation, in order that the real object of the chief points may be exposed, and our subjects placed on their guard."

(i) It is written in the proclamation, that the country of Hindustan, which was held in trust by the Company, has been resumed by the Queen, and that for the future the Queen's laws shall be obeyed. This is not to be trusted by our religious subjects; for the laws of the Company, the settlement of the Company, the English servants of the Company, the Governor-General, and the judicial administration of the Company, are all unchanged. What, then, is there new which can benefit the people, or on which they can rely?

(ii) In the proclamation it is written, that all contracts and agreements entered into by the Company will be accepted by the Queen. Let the people carefully observe this artifice. The Company has seized the whole of Hindostan, and, if this arrangement be accepted, what is there new in it? The Company professed to treat the chief of Bhurtpore as a son, and then took his territory; the chief of Lahore was carried off to London, and it has not fallen to his lot to return; the Nawab Shumshoodeen Khan, on one side, they hanged and, on the other side, they salaamed him; the Peshwa, they expelled from Poona and imprisoned for life in Bithoor; their breach of faith with Tipoo Sultan is well known; the rajah of Benares they imprisoned in Agra. Under pretence of administering the country of the chief of Gwalior, they introduced English customs; they have left no names or traces of the chiefs of Bihar, Orissa, and Bengal; they gave the Rao of Furrukhabad a small monthly allowance, and took his territory—Shahjehanpore, Bareilly, Azimgurh, Jounpore, Goruckpore, Etawah, Allahabad, Futtehpore, etc. Our ancient possessions they took from us on pretence of distributing pay; and in the 7th article of the treaty, they wrote, on oath, that they would take no more from us. If, then, the arrangements made by the Company are to be accepted, what is the difference between the former and the present state of things? These are old affairs; but recently, in defiance of treaties and oaths, and notwithstanding that they owed us millions of rupees—without reason, and on pretence of the misconduct and discontent of our people, they took our country and property worth millions of rupees. If our people were discontented with our royal predecessor, Wajid Ali Shah, how is it they are content with us? And no ruler ever experienced such loyalty and devotion to life as we have done. What, then, is wanting that they do not restore our country? Further it is written in the proclamation, that they want no increase of territory, but yet they cannot refrain from annexation. If the Queen has assumed the government, why does her Majesty not restore our country to us when our people wish it? It is well known that no king or queen ever punished a whole army and people for rebellion; all were forgiven; therefore, the wise cannot approve of punishing the whole army and people of

Hindostan; for so long as the word 'punishment' remains, the disturbance will not be suppressed. There is a well-known proverb—'A dying man is desperate.' It is impossible that a thousand should attack a million, and the thousand escape.

(iii) In the proclamation it is written, that the Christian religion is true, but that no other creed will suffer oppression, and that the laws will be observed towards all. What has the administration of justice to do with the truth or falsehood of religion? That religion is true which acknowledges one God, and knows no other. Where there are three Gods in a religion, neither Mussulman nor Hindoo—nay, not even Jews, Sun-worshippers, or Fire-worshippers can believe it true. To eat pigs and drink wine—to bite greased cartridges, and to mix pig's fat with flour and sweetmeats—to destroy Hindoo and Mussulman temples on pretence of making roads—to build churches—to send clergymen into the streets and alleys to preach the Christian religion—to institute English schools, and to pay a monthly stipend for learning the English sciences, while the places of worship of Hindoos and Mussalmans are to this day entirely neglected; with all this, how can the people believe that religion will not be interfered with? The rebellion began with religion, and, for it, millions of men have been killed. Let not our subjects be deceived; thousands were deprived of their religion in the North-West, and thousands chose to be hanged rather than abandon their religion.

(iv) It is written in the proclamation, that they who harboured rebels, or who were leaders of rebels, or who caused men to rebel, shall have their lives, but that punishment shall be awarded after deliberation, and that murderers and abettors of murderers shall have no mercy shown them, while all others shall be forgiven. Any foolish person can see, that under this proclamation, no one, be he guilty or innocent, can escape. Everything is written, and yet nothing is written; but they have clearly written that they will not let off anyone implicated; and in whatever village or estate the army may have halted, the inhabitants of that place cannot escape. We are deeply concerned for the condition of our people on reading this proclamation, which palpably teems with enmity. We now issue a distinct order—and one that may be trusted—that all subjects who may have foolishly presented themselves as heads of villages to the English, shall, before the 1st of January next, present themselves in our camp. Without doubt their faults shall be forgiven them, and they shall be treated according to their merits. To believe in this proclamation it is only necessary to remember that Hindostanee rulers are altogether kind and merciful. Thousands have seen this, millions have heard it. No one has ever seen in a dream that the English forgave an offence.

(v) In this proclamation it is written, that when peace is restored, public works, such as roads and canals, will be made in order to improve the condition of the people. It is worthy of a little reflection, that they have promised no better employment for Hindostanees than making roads and digging canals. If people cannot see clearly what this means, there is no help for them. Let no subject be deceived by the proclamation."

A True Translation

Secretary to The Chief Commissioner of Oudh.

Oudh Continues to Fight

Queen Victoria's Proclamation had but little effect on the people of Oudh who fought on desperately for their freedom. Charles Ball sums up the situation thus:

> "At that time the cities of Lucknow and Fyzabad were the only two positions of importance in the hands of the British. The country between those two points was, it is true, comparatively quiet; but there were still great armies in the field. On the Oudh side of the Gogra, at least three formidable bodies were in motion. Seven great fortresses were in the hands of the rebels: and the total number of troops arrayed against the Government was officially estimated at 60,000 men. Beyond the Gogra, the Begum Hazrat Mahal still paid some 12,000 men; and a band, perhaps equal in number, occupied Toolseypoor. Nanda had with him a strong body of cavalry; and Ferozeshah was attended by at least 1500 more: and all

these bands of rebels were strengthened and encouraged to an inconceivable degree by the sympathy of their countrymen. They could march without commissariat, for the people would always feed them. They could leave their baggage without guard, for the people would not attack it. They were always certain of their position, and of that of the British, for the people brought them hourly information, and no design could possibly be kept from them, while secret sympathisers stood around every mess-table, and waited in almost every tent. No surprise could be effected but by a miracle, while rumour communicated from mouth to mouth outstripped even the cavalry." (*History of the Indian Mutiny,* Vol. II, pp. 571–2)

Thus it was that for six months after Queen Victoria's Proclamation, there were desperate battles fought at Dhun-dhiya Khera, Rae Bareilly, Sitapur, etc., and the province of Oudh could not be entirely subdued by the English.

Earlier, in October, 1858, Commander-in-Chief Sir Collin Campbell had assigned to a number of English and Indian regiments the task of rounding up the revolutionaries and of driving them northwards. By April, 1859, the last of the Oudh revolutionaries had been driven across the Nepal border.

Revolutionaries in Exile

It has been stated that about 60,000 men, women and children entered Nepal with Nana Sahib, Bala Sahib, Begum Hazrat Mahal and the minor Nawab Birjees Quadar. For some time Nana Sahib had been in correspondence with Maharaja Jung Bahadur of Nepal. Nana's first approach was for the help of Nepal *Durbar* against the English. Later he only requested permission for the Indian exiles to live in Nepal. Maharaja Jung Bahadur not only turned down both the requests, but accorded permission to the English troops to enter Nepal and finish off the Indian exiles. Some of the latter discarded their arms and returned to India. Others were swallowed up by the Nepal forests and hills.

Whilst Nana Sahib was in Nepal, he exchanged some letters with General Hope Grant. An extract from Nana's last letter to Hope Grant reads:

"What right have you to take possession of India and to hold me culpable? Who gave you the authority to rule over India? Do you *Feringeees* have the kingly prerogative of doing 'not wrong', and we Indians are thieves in our own country?"

What happened to Nana Sahib thereafter is not known. The Nepal *Durbar* after some time granted asylum to Begum Hazrat Mahal and her son Birjees Qadar.

Malleson's Comments on the Revolution in Oudh

"At last, then, Oudh was at peace. The province had become British by a right far more solid and defensible than the pretext under which it had been seized in 1856. Then, the country of the ruler who had ever been true to his British overlord was, in disregard of treaty, seized in the dead of the night, against the wishes alike of the sovereign and the people. Fifteen months' experience of British rule... far from reconciling the people to their new master, had caused them to regret the sovereigns whom the British had expelled. They hailed, then, the opportunity...which seemed to promise them a relief from...changes which irritated them. They joined in the revolt inaugurated by their brethren the *Sipahis*—the majority of them Oudh men—and fought for independence. How pertinaciously they waged the contest has been told...No other part of India gave an example of a resistance so determined, so prolonged, as did Oudh. Throughout the struggle, the sense of the injustice perpetrated in 1856 steeled the hearts of its people and strengthened their resolution. If on some occasion they too fled, it was in the hope of renewing the struggle with some chance of success another day. When, finally, the sweep made over Oudh by Lord Clyde (Sir Collin Campbell) forced the remnant of the fighting class to take refuge in the jungles of Nepal, the survivors often preferred starvation to surrender. The agricultural population, the talukdars, the land owners, the traders accepted the defeat, when after that long struggle, they felt that it was final." (*History of the Indian Mutiny* by Kaye and Malleson, Vol. V, p. 207)

35

TATYA TOPE'S FINAL EFFORTS

Tatya's Plan

Tatya had left Gwalior on June 20, 1858. He had no army worth the name, and no equipment. His colleagues were reduced to two, Rao Sahib and the Nawab of Banda, and his followers were a mere handful. But he did not give up hope. He planned to go south and, in Peshwa's name, enlist the active support of the rulers and the people of southern India for the revolution. To execute the plan, he proceeded towards the Narmada, which he intended to cross and go south. The English would not let him do it.

The English in Hot Pursuit of Tatya

The first English attempt to check Tatya was made at Jaora Alapur on June 22, 1858. An English force caught up with Tatya but he got away.

Tatya then headed for Bharatpur. A strong English force immediately reached Bharatpur to get him there. Tatya turned and made for Jaipur. The people and the army of Jaipur were in sympathy with the revolution, and Tatya had sent them word to be ready. An English force was forthwith sent from Nasirabad to Jaipur. Tatya then turned southwards. Col. Holmes pursued him. Tatya hoodwinked his pursuers and neared Tonk. The Nawab of Tonk closed the gates of the city and sent out a detachment of his troops with four guns to fight Tatya. But the detachment, as soon as it came face to face with Tatya, went over to him with the guns. Tatya had now acquired fresh troops and equipment, with which he marched towards Indragarh. It was raining heavily. Holmes was rapidly advancing on Tatya's rear, and General Roberts was leading a force from the Rajputana side to attack him. The river Chambal facing Tatya was in high flood.

Tatya got round all the three obstacles and turned northeast towards Bundi. Tatya stopped at Bheelwara village in the Neemuch-Nasirabad province, for a little while. General Roberts got news of it and, on August 7, 1858, attacked Tatya. The fight lasted throughout the day. In the darkness of the night, Tatya made good his escape with his guns. He reached Kotra village in Udaipur State.

Battle at Kotra and After

On August 14, the pursuing English force caught up with Tatya at Kotra. Tatya was defeated in the battle which followed, and had to abandon his guns. As he retreated, the English force pursued him. Tatya again headed for the Chambal. In addition to the English force that was pursuing him, another was marching on him on his right. A third force was on the bank of the Chambal facing him directly. But with amazing skill and speed, he eluded all of them, reached and crossed the Chambal only a short distance from the position of the English force.

The river Chambal was now between Tatya and the pursuing English forces. But Tatya had lost his guns and had no provisions. He proceeded to Jhalrapattan straightaway. The Raja of Jhalrapattan sallied forth with his army and guns to attack Tatya; but when his army faced Tatya, it went over to Tatya. Tatya thus got more men, guns and provisions. He did not have a single gun when he had started for Jhalrapattan; now he had 32. He had won a bloodless victory, and he exacted Rs. 15 lacs from the helpless Raja for his war-chest. He stayed on at Jhalrapattan for five days and paid his troops. Then, in consultation with Rao Sahib and the Nawab of Banda who were with him, he decided to renew the attempt to cross the Narmada. The English spread out a net far and wide to trap Tatya, who was now headed for Indore.

Six of the ablest English Generals, Roberts, Holmes, Parke, Mitchell, Hope and Lockheart, were now making strenuous efforts simultaneously to round up Tatya. More than once the English pursuers came within sight of Tatya and his force, yet Tatya got away every time.

The English force under Mitchell attacked Tatya near Raigarh. After a short battle Tatya abandoned 30 of his guns, and made good his escape. Later, he acquired four guns whilst on his way northwards.

He entered Sindhia's territory and attacked Eeshgarh (Isagarh) and seized light guns from there.

Tatya's ultimate aim and object was to cross the Narmada anyhow, and the English were trying their hardest to prevent him by encircling him again and again. An English writer sums up the situation thus:

> "Then began the series of Tatya's amazing elusions and escapes, which continued for ten months, and which seemed to render our victory fruitless. His successes in evading capture made his name better known in Europe than that of most of our English Generals. The problem facing Tatya was not an easy one...He had to march his irregular army so continuously, and with such speed as to foil not only the troops pursuing him, but also those that suddenly pounced upon him from his right or his left. Whilst madly on the run with his army he, at the same time, attacked dozens of towns that lay along his route, and thus provided himself with equipment and stores. He also seized guns wherever he could find them. And, more than all that, he enlisted volunteer-recruits in his army—recruits who had to march continuously and, at a run, some 60 miles a day. Tatya's achievements, in spite of his meagre resources, prove that he was not a man of ordinary ability... He ranked with Hyder Ali. It has been stated that Tatya planned to reach Madras via Nagpur. Had he succeeded in doing so, he would have proved quite as formidable for us as Hyder Ali had done. The Nurbudda however, proved to be as great an obstacle in his way as the English Channel had been in that of Napoleon. Tatya did everything but he could not cross the Nurbudda...The English troops pursuing him were used to march at only a reasonable speed, and they did so at first. But later, they schooled themselves to march fast. The detachments led by General Parke and Col. Napier marched with a speed which equalled the speed of half the marches made by Tatya. But even so, Tatya always got away. The summer passed, so did the whole of the rainy season. Winter was practically over and summer had come round again. But Tatya was still at large and on the move, sometimes with only 2,000 tired troops—sometimes with 15,000." *(The Friend of India)*

Tatya Crosses the Narmada at Last

Tatya then divided his force into two detachments. One was led by him personally, and the other was put under Rao Sahib. Both advanced, but by different routes. Their way was barred at a number of places by English forces, but both fought their way through to Lalitpur where they joined. They were, however, encircled by five detachments of the English army. On the south by Mitchell's force, on the east by Col. Liddell's force, on the north by Col. Meade's force, on the west by Col. Parke's force, and by General Roberts' force in the direction of the Chambal. Tatya then had recourse to a ruse to fool the English. He stopped going southwards, turned back and began marching rapidly northwards. The English were misled into believing that Tatya had abandoned his plan of going to the south, and so they relaxed. Suddenly, however, Tatya turned back once again, and with amazing speed, he reached and crossed the river Betwa. He fought an opposing English detachment at Kajoori and from there went on to Raigarh. From Raigarh he raced southwards like an arrow shot from a bow. The English were bewildered by these tactics. Gen. Parke rushed from one direction, Mitchell rushed from behind Tatya. None of them could, however, stop Tatya, who reached the Narmada and crossed it near Hoshangabad. He had baffled some of the highly recognised war-tacticians of the world. The historian Malleson has stated that it is impossible to withhold admiration from the pertinacity with which the scheme was carried out (*History of the Indian Mutiny* by Kaye and Malleson, Vol. VI, p. 237).

The comments of the London *Times* correspondent in India are:

> "Our most amazing friend Tatya Tope is so troublesome and so cunning an enemy, that it is impossible to admire him enough. Since the last month of June, he has been playing havoc with us in Central India. He has trampled upon our places, plundered our treasuries, and emptied our magazines. He has collected armies and lost them. He has fought battles and sustained defeats. He has seized guns of the native rulers and lost them. He has seized some more and lost them too. His marches seem to be like lightning

flashes. For weeks he has marched 30 to 40 miles a day. One moment he was on one side of the Nurbudda, the next he was on the other...He has got away even when our troops faced him, sometimes right through them. He has crossed hills, rivers, marshes, or by-passed them by detouring to one side or the other..." (*The Times,* January 17, 1859)

Tatya Heading for Nagpur—English Apprehensions

After crossing the Narmada, Tatya marched towards Nagpur in October, 1858. Rao Sahib (Nana's nephew and representative) and the Nawab of Banda, with their respective troops accompanied him. Their arrival inside the Maratha territory of Nagpur gave rise to very grave apprehensions in the English rulers' minds. What these were has been described by Malleson as follows:

> "The nephew of the man recognised by the Marathas as the lawful heir of the last reigning Peshwa was on Maratha soil with an army!... Had that event occurred but fifteen months previously, British authority in western India would, for the time, have succumbed. As it was... the event caused alarm of no ordinary character to the Governments of Bombay and Madras... Lord Elphinstone (the Governor of Bombay)... could not view without grave concern the arrival of Tantia Topi and Rao Sahib in the country of the Bhonslas, that country the annexation of which but a few years previously had moved the Maratha heart to its core. He could not but remember that a large proportion of the population of the Bombay Presidency was Maratha, and he could not foresee—who, indeed, could foresee?—the effect which might be produced on the easily kindled minds of a susceptible people by the presence of the representative of the man whom many amongst them regarded as their rightful ruler. Nor could Lord Harris (the Governor of Madras)... listen with an indifferent ear to the tidings that the Maratha leader had crossed the Narbada. True it was that the Madras Presidency was separated from the country now chosen by Tantia as his campaigning-ground by the vast territories of the Nizam. True it was that the Nizam...

had displayed to the British a loyalty not to be exceeded. But the times were peculiar. The population of the Nizam's territories was to a very considerable extent Hindu. Instances had occurred before, as in the case of Scindhia, of a people revolting against their sovereign when that sovereign acted in the teeth of the national feeling. It was impossible not to fear lest the army of Tantia should rouse to arms the entire Maratha population, and that the spectacle of a people in arms against the foreigner might act with irresistible force on the people of the Dakhan." (*History of The Indian Mutiny* by Kaye and Malleson, Vol. V, pp. 239–240)

There can be no doubt that, had Tatya arrived in Maharashtra, a year earlier, the course of Indian history would have changed entirely. But during the past year the spirit of the Indian people had been broken. The Maharashtrians of Nagpur were now afraid of even getting near Tatya.

Tatya's army stayed on at Nagpur for some time. In the meantime, English forces had started hemming in Tatya once again. A large force had crossed the Narmada to the north of Nagpur, and was marching fast upon him. Tatya could not get any help or support in Nagpur. He, therefore, decided to leave Nagpur and proceed towards Baroda.

Swimming Across the Narmada

English troops had been stationed at every *Ghat* on both sides of the Narmada. Tatya advanced to the river. His way was barred by a force under Major Sunderland. Tatya engaged it in battle. Then he ordered his men to abandon the guns, rush to the river, jump into it and swim across. The men obeyed and in no time Tatya and his men appeared on the opposite bank. As Malleson states:

"Now that the guns were lost, his (Tatya's) men were able to display that capacity for rapid marching in which the natives of India are unsurpassed, I might almost say unequalled, by any troops in the world. So quickly did they cover the ground that, when at sunset the following day, Sutherland reached the banks of the Narbada, he beheld the rebel force comfortably encamped on the opposite bank." (ibid., p. 244)

Nawab of Banda Surrenders to the English

Tatya reached Rajpura and, collecting some money and horses from its Chief, arrived at Chhota Udepur the next day. Baroda, for which place Tatya was now headed, was only 50 miles away. But an English force led by Parke in hot pursuit neared Chhota Udepur within less than two hours and Tatya, abandoning his plan of going to Baroda, turned northwards. Rao Sahib was now his only companion, the Nawab of Banda having taken advantage of the Royal Proclamation to surrender in November:

> "But these two men were, in this hour of supreme danger, as cool, as bold, as fertile in resource, as at any previous period of their careers." (ibid., p. 247)

Major Rocke Defeated—Prince Feroze Shah Joins Tatya

Tatya then turned towards Udaipur (Mewar), and was immediately pounced upon by the English troops. He turned aside and entered a forest. It looked as if it would be impossible for Tatya to get away this time. He and Rao Sahib headed for Pratapgarh one afternoon at about 4 p.m. Major Rocke appeared in front and barred their way. Tatya forced his way through Major Rocke's troops and went on. On December 25, 1858, Tatya emerged out of the Banswara forest. At about this time, the well-known Prince Feroze Shah of the Delhi Royal family was hurrying to the help of Tatya Tope. It will be recalled that the Prince had fought in the Oudh battles. The story of his crossing the Jumna and the Ganges to join Tatya is full of interest. On January 13, 1859, Feroze Shah joined Tatya and Rao Sahib at Indragarh. One of Sindhia's Sardars, Man Singh, also joined the trio.

Tatya's Hairbreadth Escape at Dewas

The English troops had been converging on Tatya from all points of the compass. Napier from the north, Showers from the north-west,

Somerset from the east, Smith from the southeast, Mitchell and Bensen from the south and Bonner from the south-west and west, were all closing in on him.

Tatya reached Dewas, and, on the morning of January 16, 1859, when, Tatya, Rao Sahib and Prince Feroze Shah were conferring together in a tent, an English officer's hand suddenly fell on Tatya's back, and English soldiers rushed into the tent. It was given out that Tatya had been captured. But as a matter of fact, all three of them slipped out of the clutches of the English soldiers. They were looked for everywhere but could not be found.

Betrayal by Man Singh

Tatya Tope, Rao Sahib and Prince Feroze Shah were next seen at Shikharji near Alwar. The English were still hounding them from place to place. Tatya's hopes had all been dashed to pieces and he was now a completely exhausted man. Man Singh was hiding in a nearby jungle. Tatya left Feroze Shah and Rao Sahib with his army, and went on a visit to Man Singh, with only three men. Man Singh had, by then, gone over to the English, who had promised him a *Jagir*. Feroze Shah grew suspicious and tried to get Tatya back. Man Singh, however, succeeded in persuading Tatya to stay on. Then on April 7, 1859, at midnight, the sleeping Tatya was delivered into the hands of the English by Man Singh.

End of Last Leaders of Revolution

April 18, 1859 was fixed for the public execution of Tatya Tope. It is stated that thousands of villagers collected that morning on the hillocks around the heavily guarded place of execution, and, when Tatya appeared, they deferentially folded their hands in token of homage. Calmly and courageously Tatya climbed up the scaffold. His fetters were cut away, and, with a wry smile, he himself adjusted the noose round his neck. The plank was whisked away from under his feet, and all was over. The dead body was kept dangling the whole day. In the evening, a number of Europeans plucked from the dead Tatya's head a few hairs to keep as a memento of the hero.

Rao Sahib and Feroze Shah continued the hopeless fight for another month. Then both of them disguised themselves and disappeared in forests. Rao Sahib was taken captive three years later, and was hanged at Kanpur on August 20, 1862. Feroze Shah wandered about in Indian jungles till 1864, and then escaped to Arabia, where he was last seen in 1866, dressed as a faqir, in the company of some other Indian revolutionaries in exile.

Thus failed the greatest and most determined Indian struggle for freedom from foreign rule. The British rule over India was more firmly established than ever, at least for the time being.

36

A RETROSPECTIVE VIEW OF THE REVOLUTION

Chief Reasons Why Revolution Failed

*I*n the foregoing pages we have narrated in detail the causes and the course of the revolution. The reasons for the various failures have also been given in their appropriate contexts. Of these, two appear to us to be the most important.

The first was its premature outbreak at Meerut. We have quoted earlier the opinions of English writers like Malleson, Wilson and White to the effect that it would have been utterly impossible for the English to "re-conquer" India, if the revolution had started simultaneously, according to plan, on May 31, 1857.

The second was the unstinted help and the co-operation of every kind, which the Sikhs, the Gurkhas and numberless other Indians rendered to the English against their own countrymen, the revolutionaries. The Sikhs and the Gurkhas made it possible for the English to re-take Delhi and Lucknow, respectively. We have quoted the clear verdict of Sir Jonh Lawrence, Punjab's Chief Commissioner, to the effect that the picture would have changed completely had the Sikh States, Patiala, Nabha and Jhind, refrained from helping the English at the critical moment, and the English could not possibly have subdued Delhi, whose victorious defenders would then have sallied forth to the East and to the South, pushing the English out of India. About the help given by non-military Indians, we quote from Sir W. Russell's *My Diary in India:*

> "Yet it must be admitted that, with all their courage, they (the British) would have been quite exterminated if the natives had been all and altogether hostile to them. The desperate defences made by the garrisons were no doubt heroic: but the natives shared their glory; and they by their aid and presence rendered the defence possible. Our siege of Delhi would have been quite impossible, if the Rajas of Patiala and Jhind had not been our friends and if the Sikhs had not

recruited in our battalions and remained quiet in the Punjab. The Sikhs at Lucknow did good service, and in all cases our garrisons were helped, fed and served by the natives, as our armies were attended and strengthened by them in the field. Look at us all, here in camp, at this moment, our troops are native troops, natives are cutting grass for our horses and grooming them, feeding the elephants, managing the transports, supplying the commissariat which feeds us, cooking our soldiers' food, clearing their camp, pitching and carrying their tents, waiting on our officers, and even lending us their money. The soldier who acts as my amanuensis declares that his regiment could not have lived a week but for the regimental servants, dolibearers, hospital men and other dependents."

Just as it would have been impossible for the English to have defeated the Delhi defenders without the help of the Sikhs, so it would have been equally impossible for them to have defeated the defenders of Lucknow without the help of the Gorkhas.

Some Less Important Reasons

In addition to the above two all-important reasons, three others, only a little less important and far-reaching in their effects, may also be mentioned.

One of them was that throughout the siege of Delhi, the besieged were not defending under a unified command. They lacked an able, strong and influential military leader, who could have welded together the scattered defence-efforts of those inside the town into a formidable opposition of the besiegers. In the absence of one overall courageous military leader, the defenders, although they far outnumbered the besiegers, could not sally forth and rout the latter. Lucknow, too, laboured under similar handicaps. At times, discipline and obedience to orders seemed to be conspicuous by their absence in the rank and file of the defenders.

Another was lack of faith in the success of the revolution and the consequent indecision and hesitation in certain influential Indian quarters. It was due to this that Sindhia, Holkar and the Rajput princes could not, or did not, make common cause with the leaders of the revolution. Had Maharaja Jayaji-rao Sindhia or, any other strong ruler gone to the rescue of Delhi with his army, the Company's army would have been forced to lift the siege, and the revolutionaries would have got the supreme military leader they so sorely needed. Bahadur Shah did make an earnest appeal to the Indian rulers like Sindhia, Holkar and others but it fell on deaf ears.

The third reason was the lack of support for the revolution, in the country south of the Vindhya range. The people there did not feel even a part of the enthusiasm for the War of Independence, which the people in the north of the Vindhyas did. If Bombay, Madras and Maharashtra had revolted too, then the English would not have been able to send their troops from these regions to the north. Gen. Neill, Gen. Havelock and other English commanders could not have reached even Calcutta, and it would have become *impossible for the English* to have re-taken Banaras, Allahabad, Kanpur, etc. Each of the above reasons contributed its share to the failure of the revolution, but the possibility cannot be ruled out that it may not have failed altogether as it did, even if any *one* of these *five had not been* there.

Atrocities

The revolutionaries fought for the freedom of their country and the security of their religious faiths. The English fought the revolutionaries for the perpetuation of their own despotic rule over the country. There were instances of heroism on either side, just as there were of atrocities committed by both. It is quite possible that some English women and children were done to death at Delhi, Kanpur, Jhansi or other places. But their number has been grossly exaggerated, as is borne out by our earlier quotations from the writings of responsible and unprejudiced Englishmen.

Mr. Layard, M.P., who had, during the revolution, left England and come to India to make an on-the-spot investigation into the revolutionaries alleged atrocities, delivered, on his return to England on May 11, 1858, a public speech, which *The Home News* (May 17, 1858, p. 690) reported thus:

> "While he (Mr. Layard) was in India, he endeavoured with utmost conscientiousness to find out whether or not there had been any case of mutilation, and he had been assured by men who had been employed by the Government to make enquiries, and men who, he was sorry to say, would have joyfully pounced on any case of cruelty on the part of the natives, that they had not found one case of mutilation."

The Times (August 25, 1858) published a letter written to it by Mr. Layard, from which we quote the following:

> "From the information I received from the very best and most trustworthy sources, after the most careful enquiries, I am convinced that the series of horrible cruelties alleged to have been committed upon English women and children at Delhi, Cawnpore, Jhansi and elsewhere were almost without exception shameful fabrications."

Then there are numerous authoritative statements of English writers to the effect:

(i) that if English women and children were, in fact, murdered at Kanpur, then it was without the knowledge even, let alone the permission, of Nana Sahib, who cannot justly be held responsible for the crimes.

(ii) that Rani Lakshmi Bai had no hand whatsoever in the murder of any unarmed Englishman in Jhansi, and

(iii) that the Emperor Bahadur Shah, Nana Sahib, Begum Hazrat Mahal and Rani Lakshmi Bai had, all four of them, made from time to time, adequate arrangements for the safety of English women and children.

According to Forrest, the leaders of the revolution had time and again, issued strict orders by proclamation to their followers not to tarnish the fair name and purity of their cause by attacking defenceless women and children.

In Oudh one comes across numerous instances where the revolting *Zamindars* joining and leading the revolution gave asylum in their houses to English women and children and even, to men who sought it. The people joining the Revolution did the same invariably.

On the other hand, what Generals Neill, Havelock, Cooper, Hudson and other senior English officers did was characterised by the Governor-General-in-Council (Lord Canning) himself in his speech on "state of affairs", thus on December 24, 1858:

> "The indiscriminate hanging, not only of persons of all shades of guilt, but of those whose guilt was at the least very doubtful, and the general burning and plundering of villages, whereby the innocent as well as the guilty, without regard to age or sex, were indiscriminately punished ..." (*The Other Side of the Medal* by E. Thompson, p. 73)

Had There Been No Revolution

In the words of Ludlow quoted earlier, "the natives of India" had to be "less than men", not to be furiously indignant and in "favour of the victims of annexation and against the annexer". In view of all that the English had done in the preceding hundred years of their political domination of India, the 1857 revolution was a natural phenomenon and was inevitable if the Indians had the slightest trace of national or human dignity left in them. Had there been no revolution, it would have been demonstrated that Indians were devoid of all courage, self-respect, sense of duty and the will to live like human beings. Further, there can be no doubt that not a single Indian State, Hindu or Muslim, would have escaped extinction but for the 1857 upheaval. Had the Indians not revolted, they would have been slowly but relentlessly pushed down to the level of serfs. It cannot therefore be rightly asserted that the 1857 revolution achieved nothing worthwhile. It did open the eyes of the power-drunk English rulers, and the fierce and bloody warning made them more careful and a bit more considerate towards their Indian subjects than towards their own interests. It may also be claimed that it did give the Indians the first ray of hope and some confidence for their future national life. Both grew steadily stronger during the ninety years that passed till India became independent. Our conclusion that the English had received "a warning" is supported by Forrest ("State Papers" Introduction), who wrote:

> "The Mutiny reminds us that our dominions rest on a thin crust ever likely to be rent by titanic fires of social changes and religious revolutions."

Effects of Indian Revolution on Other Countries

It is interesting to note that one immediate effect of the 1857 revolution in India was to save China from an English invasion. Early in 1857, England having decided to invade China, her army had actually sailed for China and was in the vicinity of India when the revolution broke out. Lord Canning got this army to disembark on the Indian coast and used it to fight the Indian revolutionaries. Thus China was saved, at least for the time being. It was very weak then, much more than it was 40 years later, at the time of the Buxar uprising.

Japan too was, in 1857, split into 273 small separate States which were frequently fighting with one another. Politically, Japan was no more an integrated and united country at that time than the India of 1857, and was neither better off internally or stronger than the latter. It would, however, appear that the historical letter written by the famous English philosopher, Herbert Spencer, after the Indian revolution of 1857, had a profound effect on the political leaders all over Japan. The latter's attention was pointedly drawn by Herbert Spencer to the case of India, warning them of the English and American political machinations directed against the Asiatic countries. In 1868—eleven years after the Indian revolution—Japan took drastic action. All the 273 separate States were swept away and Japan started on its way to become a world power which defeated Czarist Russia in 1905.

It may be that at least some of the credit for saving the independence of both China and Japan is due to the moving spirits and leaders of the Indian revolution of 1857, who delivered a severe blow to the British Imperialistic designs at a critical juncture in the life of Asia, and so sounded a note of warning to other Asiatic countries against Western political brigandage, greed and chicanery.

37

AFTER 1857— ENGLAND'S REACTION

Second Thoughts

The 1857 'war of independence' opened the eyes of England's statesmen, and they saw the political error of the policy they had till then followed. They had worked diligently to colour the map of India with their own colour, red, by the extinction of all Indian States and the absorption of their territories into the British Empire of their dreams. They now realised that such a policy was not wholesome for the permanence of English rule in India, and that it was much more important to conserve and consolidate what they had than to make further additions to their dominion. During 1857–58, English political circles and papers thrashed out the pros and cons of the proposal to change the prevailing policy. Ultimately, new methods considered essential for strengthening English rule in India were evolved and adopted. Also they, to a large extent, shaped the policy which the English have since followed with regard to India. We now proceed to relate the various steps taken.

Queen Victoria's Proclamation

The first step was taken even before the blaze of the revolution had died out completely. Queen Victoria's Proclamation was read out on November 1, 1858 by Lord Canning at Allahabad.

(i) The Queen notified and declared that "with the advice and consent of the Lords, Spiritual and Temporal, and Commons, in Parliament assembled, we have taken upon ourselves the Government of the territories in India heretofore administered in trust for us by the Honourable East India Company".

(ii) The Queen called upon "all our subjects within the said territories to be faithful, and to bear true allegiance to us, our heirs and successors, and to submit themselves to the authority of those whom we may hereafter, from time to time, see fit to appoint to administer the government of our said territories, in our name and on our behalf".

(iii) The Queen constituted and appointed "Viscount Canning to be our first Viceroy and Governor-General in and over our said territories and to administer the government thereof in our name, and generally to act in our name and on our behalf, subject to such orders and regulations as he shall, from time to time, receive from us through one of our principal Secretaries of State".

(iv) The Queen announced to "the native princes of India that all treaties and engagements made with them by or under the authority of the Honourable East India Company are accepted by us, and will be scrupulously maintained, and we look for the like observance on their part".

(v) The Queen declared "it to be our royal will and pleasure that none be in any wise favoured, none molested or disquieted, by reason of their religious faith or observances, but that all shall enjoy the equal and impartial protection of the law alike and we do strictly charge and enjoin all those who may be in authority under us that they abstain from all interference with the religious belief or worship of any of our subjects on pain of our highest displeasure".

(vi) To those "in arms against the Government", the Queen "promised unconditional pardon, amnesty, and oblivion of all offence against ourselves, our crown, and dignity, on their return to their homes and peaceful pursuits. It is our royal pleasure, that these terms of grace and amnesty should be extended to all those who comply with these conditions before the first day of January next".

The Proclamation concluded with the expression of the Queen's "earnest desire to stimulate the peaceful industry of India, to promote works of public utility and improvement, and to administer its government for the benefit of all our subjects resident therein" and with the pious prayer "may the God of all power grant to us, and to those in authority under us, strength to carry out these our wishes for the good of our people". Perhaps Her Majesty did not realise that the words "our people" could and would be interpreted to mean the English people exclusively, as they were, by those Englishmen who were in authority over India. Anyway, the Proclamation did go a long way in pacifying many of the frustrated revolutionaries, who trusted the Proclamation. The last vestiges of the Mughal rule over India had vanished for ever, and the Indians could not but turn to the English for the administration of the government of the country.

We must point out that the constitutional value of the Proclamation was exactly nil. As Sir James Stephen, the well-known jurist and eminent Law Member of the Government of India, said, it was only a "ceremonial document", it "was not a treaty", it "had no legal force whatever", and as such, was not binding on anybody, including those who actually ruled India thereafter. The Queen was a constitutional sovereign and under the English Constitution could not impose her will either on the British Parliament, or on anyone appointed and authorised by the latter to administer the government of India under its sole control, guidance and supervision. Thus it was that during the ninety years (1857–1947) the British Government and/or the Government of India, could and did, with impunity, treat the Queen's Proclamation as a mere "scrap of paper" on numberless occasions, whenever it appeared to be expedient to do so for the perpetuation of English rule over India or in wider English interests.

Termination of East India Company's Rule Over India

As stated in the Proclamation, the Company's rule was terminated on the advice of the British Parliament. The termination was considered advisable as an olive branch to be extended to the intransigent revolutionaries, inasmuch as it deposed the rulers against whose regime the people had risen up in arms.

Before the Clive regime, the activities of the East India Company were limited to trade only. The Company had been constituted solely with that object under a Charter granted by Queen Elizabeth in 1600 A. D. Thereafter, the British Parliament renewed by enactment every 20 years in confirmation of the Company's rights and privileges.

Sometimes additions to the said rights and privileges were also made by the new Charter Act.

The arrival of Clive in India was followed by the beginning of the Company's rule over some regions of the country. It was during Warren Hastings' regime that Minister Fox of England proposed in the British Parliament that the Indian territories ruled by the Company should be taken away from it and put under the direct rule of the British Crown. The proposition was then agreed to by the House of Commons, but the House of Lords rejected it, as the shareholders of the Company wielded a good deal of influence in the Upper House.

Next year, in 1783, Prime Minister William Pitt set up, with the Parliament's approval, a Board of Control presided over by one of the Ministers which, under the authority of the British cabinet, supervised the direction of the Company's administration in and over India. Thereafter, the government of India was carried on in accordance with the policy, laid down from time to time, by the Board of Control and the Directors of the Company jointly.

The Charter Act of 1813 ended the East India Company's monopoly of trade with and in India, which was thrown open to all English individuals or corporate bodies, who wanted a share in the profits accruing from England's trade with India. We have, in earlier chapters, described how this innovation brought about the ruin and extinction of India's trade, industries and handicrafts, resulting ultimately in the extreme poverty of the Indian people. Whether or not these consequences were intended by the framers of the 1813 Act, the fact remains that they did run counter to the sanctimoniously declared object of the Act, namely:

> "To promote the interests and happiness of the inhabitants of the British Dominions".

In a similar vein, the following clause was inserted in the Charter Act of 1833;

> "That no native of the said territories, nor any natural-born subject of His Majesty resident therein, shall by reason only of his religion, place of birth, descent, colour, or any of them, be disabled from holding any place, office, or employment under the said Company".

When the enactment of the Charter Act of 1853 was due, the English administrators of India were examined as witnesses by the Select Committee of Parliament. Their statements clearly indicated that their sole overriding objective was the enrichment of England at the cost of the Indian people even if it meant the impoverishment of the latter. The Company's system of educating them in English, and the propaganda and its efforts for their conversion to Christianity would also indicate that both were intended to denationalise the "natives" in order that the poverty-stricken demoralised people may be content to remain under the English heel for ever.

In England, a strong and widely-supported agitation had started a little earlier than 1857. It aimed at the transfer of the government of the vast British Indian Empire from the Company to the British Crown. The demand was founded on two declared reasons.

One was that so long as the Company continued to run the government in India, an all-out effort for the "development of the resources of India was impossible". The word "development" was, in fact, a euphemism coined for "exploitation", and covered, as was intended, a multitude of sins against the vital interests of the Indian people. England sorely needed raw materials, particularly cotton, for her rapidly expanding textile and other industries. England did not grow cotton and due to her widespread industrialisation, agriculture had been progressively abandoned. So England needed foodgrains, too. India grew both cotton and foodgrains and if her resources were properly exploited could supply England with either, in sufficient quantities, and at prices far lower than those at which, England could import them from elsewhere. The cultivation of cotton and foodgrains could be increased manifold, and both could be obtained cheaply enough by the adoption of suitable ways and means and by providing facilities, including railways, which could not only transport inexpensively and quickly Indian cotton and foodgrains, etc., to the ports of embarkation for England but could also transport to the Indian markets the goods manufactured by England and exported to India by her. All these efforts could not obviously be made by a profit-making trading concern and so the rule of the East India Company had to be ended.

The other declared reason was that the Company had resolutely set its face against the colonization of India by Englishmen, who were keen on the establishment of their colonies on the fertile soil of India too, as had been done in Australia, America, etc.

But the real and most potent reason for the termination of the Company's rule was the greed of its shareholders, who wanted to monopolise the benefits and the huge wealth accruing from their rule over India, their trade with and loot in the country. Their phenomenal wealth had excited the envy of their countrymen who naturally considered it to be the right of the English nation as a whole to be benefited by its Indian "empire".

This agitation in England derived immense support from the revolution of 1857 and, soon after the Queen's Proclamation, the replacement of the East India Company by the British Crown was formally moved in the British Parliament. In opposition to the motion, the East India Company presented to the British Parliament a petition, praying that the Company's rule over India may be continued on the ground of the benefits accruing therefrom to England during the past hundred years. The Company in proof of the success of its political policy in India, said:

> "How very different would probably have been the issue of late events, if the native princes instead of aiding in suppressing the rebellion, had put themselves at its head, or if the general population had joined in the revolt."

The petition concluded with detailed proposals regarding the objectives intended to be kept in view in formulating the policies to be followed in the future administration of the government of India.

But the pressing demand of the English people could not be denied. Also it was necessary to impress the Indian people with a revolutionary change in their rulers. So in 1858, the East India Company's rule over India was terminated and replaced by the direct rule of the British Crown.

The House of Commons appointed a Select Committee on March 16, 1858.

> "to inquire into the progress and prospects and the best means to be adopted for the promotion of European colonization and settlement in India, especially in the hill districts and healthier climates of that country as well as for the extension of our commerce with Central Asia".

The above quotation from the "Terms of Reference of the Select Committee" makes it quite plain that the change was not made with a view to benefiting the people of India but solely in English interests. As stated in the above-mentioned petition of the Company, "The doctrine" then "widely promulgated" in England was that "India should be administered with a special view to the benefit of the English who reside there". Sir Charles (afterwards Lord) Metcalfe held similar views. He wrote:

> "Although it seems to be a matter of indifference to the 'native population whether India be governed through the Company, or directly by the ministers of the Crown, it is not so to another class of subjects. The Europeans settled in India, and not in the Company's service, and to these might be added generally the East Indians of mixed breed, will never be satisfied with the Company's Government ... *For the contentment of this class, which, for ... the security of our Indian Empire, ought greatly to increase in numbers and importance, the introduction of a King's Government is undoubtedly desirable*" (italics ours).

Need anyone doubt, therefore, that the real aim and objective of the change was not so much the betterment of the condition of the people of India as the colonisation of the country by the English, leading, inevitably, to the reduction of the "natives" to the status of mere "hewers of wood and drawers of water" for their white masters, and the latter's mixed breed.

Maintenance of Indian States' *Status Quo*

After the annexations during the Dalhousie regime, the picture of the plan for further acquisitions was drawn in the House of Commons by Sir Erskine Perry on April 18, 1856, in the following words:

> "It will now be the Nizam's turn. Then the fertile Malwa region will be occupied as its black soil cotton and opium of superior qualities can be cultivated. Then Gujarat, which is even more

fertile—Rajputana and the remaining six crores of the Indian people will be 'conquered'."

But the revolution, which broke out the very next year, changed the picture completely, as it made the English realise that the annexations during the Dalhousie regime were more than anything else the main cause of the upheaval. They could see very clearly that their interests could be served best only by continuing the existence of the remaining Indian States. Consequently, after 1857, not a single annexation (with the solitary exception of some Burmese territory) of any Indian State was made to the British Empire. The policy of non-annexation paid rich dividends during the 88 years, 1859–1947 as the Indian States, instead of being a potential menace to the British rule in India, became its warm and steadfast supporters. Some important States maintained what were called "Imperial Service Troops", to be used by the British Government, at its sole discretion, whenever and wherever it considered it necessary. During the Buxar troubles in China, at the turn of the century, the then Maharaja Sindhia personally headed the Gwalior State's contingent sent to China for the help of the English fighting there. When the First World War broke out, all the several hundreds of the Indian States forthwith placed all their resources unreservedly at the disposal of the English and helped England win a war which had nothing to do with India.

It is, of course, beyond the scope of this book to narrate the treatment received by the Indian ruling Princes generally at the hands of the British Government of England or of India, but the documentary evidence produced by the Princes before the Butler Committee (1927–29) is eloquent enough of the fact that the treaties and engagements made with them were, oftener than not, treated by the British authorities as mere "scraps of paper" whenever they could not be interpreted to suit the then prevailing policy of Britain, which styled itself the "Paramount Power of India".

Colonization of India by the English

The discussions about the colonization of at least some parts of India can be traced back to Warren Hastings' regime. On November 7,

1794, Cornwall wrote to Dundas, the then Secretary of State for India, that it was very important in Britain's interests to check, as far as possible, European migration to India. On February 4, 1801, the Directors of the East India Company passed a resolution against such colonization. When in 1813, the Company's monopoly of English trade with India was abolished and the trade was thrown open to all Englishmen, the movement for the colonization of such hilly tracts in India as had been recently acquired was started and sponsored by English politicians like Sir Frederick Shore. They were supported by Sir Charles Metcalfe and Lord William Bentinck on the ground that the English colonizers' interests would become identified with those of the English Government in India and, in case of trouble, the latter would be helped and supported by the colonizers, their Indian collaborators and employees. Thus the life of English rule in India would be safe and prolonged a good deal. This view was some years later emphatically confirmed by Brian Houghton Hodgson, Resident of Nepal, who advocated the establishment of English colonies in the Himalayas and wrote:

> "... the encouragement of colonization therein is one of the highest and most important duties of the Government, ... greatest, surest, soundest and simplest of all political measures for the stabilization of the British power in India". (On the Colonization of the Himalayas by Europeans.)

After 1857, the movement for colonization gained fresh impetus because of the revolution. As mentioned earlier, the Parliament appointed in March 1856, a Select Committee whose terms of reference have been quoted above. The witnesses examined by the Select Committee gave details of the ways and means till then adopted by the Government of India to attract, facilitate and help in every way the colonization of the country by the English. These may be summarised as under:

(i) The Government carried out experiments for growing tea in Assam and Kumaon, and proclaimed publicly that if the experiments proved successful, the plantations would be handed over to Englishmen desirous of settling in Assam or Kumaon.

(ii) Some Englishmen were sent to China, at the Indian Government's expense, to get trained in tea-planting, and to bring China tea seeds as well as Chinese experts in tea-growing to India.

(iii) Laws were enacted which turned the indentured labour employed on the English tea plantations into veritable but legal slaves of the planters. The treatment of the Indian labourers by the English planters and their employees constitutes one of the blackest chapters in the story of the English occupation of India.

(iv) Similar help and facilities were freely given by the British Government to English foundries in Kumaon and to English indigo planters. The latter were helped financially too.

(v) Special rules to facilitate the cheap and quick transit, by road or rail, of the goods produced by Englishmen were framed.

Of course, India had to foot the bill. It might, moreover, be mentioned that the English Government then never made the slightest effort to render help of any kind to any industry or business carried on solely by Indians.

Some of the witnesses deposing before the Select Committee went so far as to advocate strongly the idea of bringing out from Britain capitalists, agriculturists, artisans and even working people and settling them all over India on the model of Algeria.

In support of our view that the ambition to colonise India was one of the chief reasons why the rule of the East India Company was terminated, we would refer to the statement of J. G. Waller, one of the witnesses examined by the Select Committee. He said that he considered it most essential that the government which the Company was carrying on in trust for the King should forthwith be taken over by the British Crown, if the object was to colonize India. It was equally essential, he said, for the permanence of the English rule over India and that the object could be achieved only if the British Crown, and not the Company, ruled the country directly.

The Company's rule was terminated and no stone was left unturned by the English Government in India, and the British Government in England, in their efforts to colonise India, but the result was little better than a dismal failure. The English writer, Meredith Townsend (*Asia and Europe,* p. 57), has given the reason why. According to him, the English soon got so fed up with life in India, wherein they felt themselves to be outsiders and strangers, that they left the country after a short stay, regardless of the resulting loss of business, prestige or prospects of future wealth.

The real reason why India was spared the visitation appears to be the fact that India was not a small, sparsely-populated and uncivilized or half-civilized country like those which the English had till then colonized by practically obliterating the original tribes living there. India was a vast country, thickly populated by millions of ancient and cultured people who could not be reduced to nonentities for ever by a handful of Englishmen. On the contrary, there was more than a possibility of the English themselves being submerged in the millions of a country, many times the size of the islands they came from. So, after a brief stay, they packed up and returned to the security their "dear old England".

Extermination of Indian Patriotism

Two methods were considered specially effective for extinguishing the Indian national sentiments and the urge for independence. One was the propagation of Christianity and the other was the system of educating Indians in the English language, literature, history and traditions. A beginning had been made as regards both, much earlier than 1857; but after the quelling of the Revolution, both the methods were followed with much greater vigour.

The 1813 Charter Act contained a clause authorising the Government to give every kind of help and facility to the English clergymen who tried to live and work in India for the "religious salvation of the Indian people". An Ecclesiastical Department was accordingly established in the Government of India.

After the Revolution, the English politicians flooded their statesmen with suggestions as to what would be the best thing to do. An English contributor to the English magazine, *The Calcutta Review,* wrote in its issue of March, 1858:

"...On every hand, we hear the voices of the times... urging the popular measure of the hour, 'India must be Christianised'—'India must be colonised'—'The Mohammedan religion must be suppressed'—'We must abolish the vernacular and substitute our mother tongue'..."

In 1859 Lord Palmerston, the British Prime Minister, received a deputation of English clergymen headed by the Archbishop of Canterbury, and told them:

"We seem to be all agreed as to the end. It is not only our duty, *but it is our interest*, to promote the diffusion of Christianity as far as possible throughout the length and breadth of India." (italics ours. *The Conversion of India* by George Smith, C.I.E., LL.D., p. 233)

This contrasts sharply with the Proclamation issued by Queen Victoria, only a little more than a year earlier, in which Her Majesty had "strictly charged and enjoined all those who may be in authority to abstain from all interference with the religious belief or worship" of any of her subjects.

More than one English missionary, whilst commenting on the 1857 Revolution, affirmed that the principal enemies of the English were those very Mussalmans, whom the English had puffed up with pride by praising their Muslim faith, as well as those Hindus whose blind religious beliefs had been strengthened by the English, and the only true friends of the English were those Indians who had been converted to Christianity.

William Edwardes, who was in the Company's service during the Revolution, and was later appointed a judge of the High Court at Agra, expressed his opinion in these words:

"We are, and ever must be, regarded as foreign invaders and conquerors... Our best safeguard is the evangelization of the country...Christian settlements scattered about the country would be as towers of strength for many years to come, for they must be loyal as long as the mass of the people remain either idolaters or Mohammedans."

The creation of such "towers of strength" for the British rule was similarly the object of the system of education advocated by Macaulay, and followed for instructing the Indians in the English language and literature. We have dealt with it at some length in an earlier chapter. It was calculated to create a class of English-knowing Indians who would depend on the British raj to earn their livelihood, and whose own interests would thus make the permanence of the British rule absolutely necessary. It was expected that in this way the patriotic sentiments, and the urge for freedom from the English yoke would by degrees disappear from their minds. It was also expected that, although they would be in a microscopic minority, the English-knowing Indians would exercise a tremendous influence over the rest of their countrymen, who were innocent of the language of their rulers. Both the expectations were fulfilled and the Indian people, by and large, were for a long time hypnotised into willing submission to and even enthusiastic acceptance of the British rule.

"Development" of Resources of India

According to the views of most European politicians, the rule of one country over another has no purpose other than the draining of the latter's wealth to the ruling country. This can best be done by exploiting the resources of the subject-country. So six methods were evolved and adopted for the exploitation of India's resources in the interests of England, some of them under the guise of "development".

(i) *Railways.* These were constructed and run with the money collected by the English from India in various ways and a large part of it was spent in England. "It has been computed," declared Swift MacNeill in the House of Commons, on August 14, 1890, "that out of every shilling spent in railway enterprise, 8d makes its way to England." The Railways were intended and used chiefly for cheap and quick transport of wheat, cotton, and other raw materials to the ports of embarkation for being shipped to England, and for similarly transporting the goods made in and exported from England to every nook and corner of India. They also provided fast-moving transport for the army whenever it became essential to move its contingents within the shortest possible time from one end of the vast country to another. This facility was a *sine qua non* for keeping intact the British hold on the country. The benefit to India, if any, was only a by-product of the railways.

(ii) *Cultivation of Cotton.* As mentioned before, Berar, Sindh and the Punjab were annexed primarily because those regions were famed for growing cotton. Lancashire, Manchester and other textile-manufacturing centres had been wanting good and cheap cotton for some time. So after 1851, a new "East India Cotton Company" was floated, and other strenuous efforts were made to meet the English demand for Indian cotton. The livelihood of numberless inhabitants of England at the time depended upon getting cheap cotton and upon the unrestricted flooding of the Indian markets with goods manufactured by England.

(iii) *Special Privileges for English Capitalists.* These had earlier been granted to a certain extent, particularly to the tea and indigo planters in India. After 1858 they were very largely augmented and hundreds of thousands of Indians, men and women, were by law, forced to live and work on English plantations under conditions comparable with those of the Roman slaves of about 1,500 years ago. Sir Ashley Eden, who later became the Lieut.-Governor of Bengal, said in 1860 that all Indians hated the cultivation of indigo but were compelled by law to do it.

(iv) *Responsible Government Posts.* It was obviously imperative for the maintenance of British rule that only Englishmen should fill all responsible executive posts in India even if they had to be paid what has been admitted to be more than double of what they could earn anywhere else. Needless to say, it became a practice which was seldom, if ever, deviated from.

(v) *Indians kept away from real power in administration.* The interests of England as the ruling country clashed violently with those of India as the ruled country. It was natural and inevitable that the development of industries in England and the monopolization of Indian markets by her products should, as it did, lead to widespread unemployment among the Indian working classes. The prosperity of England meant and resulted in the poverty of India. When interests clashed to that extent, it could not possibly be beneficial for England if Indians were vested with any real power in the administration. As far back as 1819, Capt. P. Page had written in his memorandum dated East India House, April 9, 1819:

> "I would reward good conduct (of natives) with honour but never with power ... *Nullum imperium tutum, nisi benevolentia muniturm*. The good will of the natives may be retained without granting them power; the semblance is sufficient; and although I abhor in private life that maxim of Rochefaucult's which recommends a man to live with his friends as if they were one day to be his enemies, I think it may be remembered with effect by the sovereigns of India."

(vi) *Laws and Law-Courts.* It was after the 1857 Revolution that the penal code drafted by Macaulay was enacted as the Indian Penal Code. We might quote once again Edmund Burke's comments on that code:

> "... A machine of wise and elaborate contrivance, and as well fitted for the oppression, impoverishment and degradation of a people, and the debasement in them of human nature itself, as ever proceeded from the perverted ingenuity of man."

The civil laws, too, followed more or less the same pattern. These laws, added to the complexities of the procedures followed by courts in administering laws, could not but lead to the degradation and debasement of the character of the Indian people foreshadowed by Burke. One cannot help recalling wistfully the thousand-year-old *panchayats* to which the poorest could appeal for justice and obtain relief without spending a copper. One is also reminded of the urban courts of the Mughal regime, whose doors bore an inscription to the effect that *Faqiri*, asceticism, was the one thing which a judge should be most proud of, and whose pious judges deemed it a sin to accept an invitation to dinner or even a *pan* (betel-leaf) offered to them by anyone connected with the litigants before them.

Re-organisation of the Army

A Royal Commission was appointed, shortly after 1857, to recommend measures for the re-organisation of the British Government's Army. Some suggestions made were symptomatic of the feelings and fears aroused by the Revolution in the minds of the English. One sought to limit the recruitment to the army to Englishmen and persons of mixed breed exclusively. Another was that a small number of Arabs, Burmese and Negroes should also be enlisted along with Englishmen. Both the suggestions were held to be impracticable. Ultimately, it was decided that preference should be given to the Gurkhas, Pathans, Dogras, Rajputs, Sikhs and Marathas over the other Indian communities. The employment of Indians in the artillery sections of the army was banned, partly because of distrust, and partly because Indians, according to the English writer Coulfield, made the most efficient artillerymen. The Indian soldiers were armed with weapons which were inferior to those with which the white soldiers were armed. Also as a matter of policy, really responsible military posts, higher than that of a Subedar-Major, were not open to Indians.

The re-organisation very substantially increased the number of English troops in India, downgraded further the status of the Indian elements in the army, and added to the already heavy cost of administration which India had to pay. In 1859, the English military personnel employed in India numbered 91, 817, according to Major Wingate. They were paid by India. In addition, India had also to pay 16, 427 English soldiers, who never came out to India, but stayed in England in the interests of the security of that country.

The re-organisation was obviously intended to fasten more firmly the English chains on India.

Divide et Impera

The policy explicit in the Roman motto had been adopted by the English from the very beginning of their rule in India and had been consistently followed ever since. Sir John Malcolm, one of the leading

English statesmen, who worked for the expansion of England's Indian Empire at the start of the nineteenth century, stated before the Parliamentary Committee in 1813:

> "In the present extended state of our Empire, our security for preserving a power of so extraordinary a nature as that we have established, rests upon the general division of the great communities under the Government, and their subdivision into various castes and tribes; while they continue divided in this manner, no insurrection is likely to shake the stability of our power."

A few years later, an English officer wrote in the *Asiatic Journal* (May 1821):

> "*Divide et impera* should be the motto of our Indian administration, whether political, civil, or military."

After 1857, Lt.-Colonel John Coke, the Commandant at Muradabad, wrote:

> "Our endeavour should be to uphold in full force the (for us—fortunate) separation which exists between the different religions and races, not to endeavour to amalgamate them. *Divide et impera* should be the principle of Indian Government."

Lord Elphinstone, the Governor of Bombay, wrote in a minute dated May 14, 1859:

"*Divide et impera* was the old Roman motto and it should be ours."

Any number of such statements can be quoted from the writings and speeches of responsible British statesmen of those days.

Similar to the exploitation of religion for perpetuating the said differences was the exploitation of provincial prejudices and the different ways of life in the different provinces of India. It had the same objective and was resorted to under the guise of "provincial autonomy". One of the witnesses examined by the 1858 Select Committee, Major G. Wingate, stated that there were several risks involved in the establishment of a unitary Central Government for the whole of India. He said that the creation of a tendency to unite the different communities in India's different provinces would be a great risk. If the decisions of one Central Government affected the entire people, they would unite in opposing a decision unpalatable to them, and the agitation could become countrywide against the one and only Government of India. If, however, such a decision was made by a Provincial Government, acting on its own, then it would affect only that province and if unpalatable to the people of the province, the agitation against it would be limited to that province alone, isolated from the rest of India. Accordingly, the decentralisation of the power and authority of the Government of India was effected, and provincial Governments were set up and vested with autonomous powers to a specified extent. The device succeeded in retarding the integration of the Indian people and deteriorated their development as a united nation inspired by national sentiments and aspirations. The evil effects of this imperialist policy persist up to this day (1971), even long after the attainment of independence by India.

India's Tribute to England

India paid no "tribute" to England in the strict sense of the word, but was made to pay the "Home charges' which, for the 17 years, 1834–51, totalled £ 57,600,000, apart from those remittances to England made by individual Englishmen employed or doing business in India. Besides these, the Englishmen in India had invested at that time, out of their savings, from their earnings in India, 36 million pounds sterling in the Government of India Loans and Promissory Notes.

As mentioned above, India was also paying for the contingent of 16,427 English soldiers stationed in England for the security of that country.

The cost of British rule in India, in terms of money which India had to pay for nearly two centuries, can thus be estimated.

EPILOGUE

Our narrative of how India lost her freedom has come to a close. The story of British rule in India after 1858 is beyond the scope of this book. We would, however, describe briefly how the British domination of India affected, as it was bound to do, not only the ruled but also the rulers, and also the latter's relations with other countries, particularly with those which adjoin India.

The rule of one country over another is basically and therefore, essentially, unnatural. That is why all such empires crumbled after a time.

British rule in India, counting from the Battle of Plassey (1757), lasted 190 years. Amongst other things, it demonstrated the correctness of the memorable words of Abraham Lincoln that "There is no nation good enough to govern another," as also of what Lord Macaulay once said:

> "Of all forms of tyranny, I believe the worst is that of a nation over a nation."

British rule over India was marked by the progressive impoverishment of the Indian people and the deterioration of their character and stamina. The country was periodically visited by famines and epidemics like the plague, cholera, influenza, etc. Such visitations have been held by more than one eminent Western historian to be the inevitable consequences of every foreign rule. The military spirit of the people, where it survived, became merely mercenary and was exploited by the foreign rulers not only to maintain their despotic rule over India, but also to undertake military operations against countries like Nepal, Afghanistan, Burma and such others as were considered to be weak.

The perpetrators of injustice on others, however, cannot escape the nemesis which, sooner or later, overtakes them. The character of those who actually maintain or are employed to carry on the rule of one country over another country also deteriorates rapidly and to an alarming extent. The narrow interests of the ruling nation make it imperative that its representatives, ministers and administrators should become, more or less, blind and deaf to the demands of justice and fairness in their dealings with the ruled when the interests of the two clash. For the rulers, the real interests and the welfare of the ruled cease to exist, unless and only in so far as they are conducive to the enrichment of and aggrandisement by the ruling nation. They naturally become selfish, callous and bereft of humanitarian instincts, and even of decent behaviour, so far as at least the ruled people are concerned. Human nature being what it is, their whole character is affected for the worse by the unnatural conditions in which they live and work. It deteriorates so much that when they retire and go back "home", they are generally treated by their own countrymen as intolerable outsiders. That this happened to Englishmen who had lived and worked in India as India's rulers is a well-known fact.

Industrially, too, England's rule over India did not do England any abiding good. Her industries were so long spoonfed by cheap raw materials obtained from India, and by the creation of Indian markets for goods "made in England", that they (the English industries) were bound to suffer, as the cheap raw materials and the Indian markets became unavailable, as result of the absence of any English hold over India. English domination over India facilitated the most unscrupulous exploitation of India, its people and its resources. In other words, it led to the short-lived prosperity of England at the cost of the poverty and misery of the Indian people.

England's anxiety to preserve her rule over India naturally motivated the shaping of her policy with regard to other countries also, even as distant as Egypt. As the famous Egyptian patriot, Zaghlul Pasha, once said, it was essential for the English to control the Suez Canal for maintaining their Indian Empire, and so it was equally essential for them to undermine the sovereignty and independence of Egypt for preserving intact their control of the Suez. Thus Egypt very nearly lost her independence as a consequence of British rule in India.

Similarly, persistent interference in the affairs of Afghanistan, the domineering over Nepal, and the conquest of Burma were resorted to by the English for the consolidation of their "Empire" in India.

Iraq, Iran and Turkey too were not spared, because England considered them potential dangers to her rule over India, England's rule over India also helped her to maintain her military prestige in Europe. India proved to be an almost inexhaustible source for supplying England with mercenaries whom she could use anywhere, in and outside India, without much cost.

To sum up, the rule of one country over another cannot but be, in the very nature of things, detrimental to the best interests of any third country, although the worst sufferer is always the country under the foreigner's heel.

Manifestly, it will benefit the entire world if such unnatural domination ends everywhere in all countries and all continents. India, which got her freedom in 1947, is a friend of all peoples of the world. She wants all countries to be absolutely free in all their affairs, internal as well as external.

BIBLIOGRAPHY

Ball, Charles: *History of Indian Mutiny,* Vols I & II.
Basu, B.D.: *The Ruin of Indian Trade and Industries.*
Bell, Major Evan: *Retrospects and Prospects of Indian Policy.*
Bell, Major Evan: *Empire in India.*
Bolts: *Considerations on Indian Affairs.*
Briggs, General John: *Memoirs of Briggs.*
Brooks, Adam: *The Law of Civilization and Decay.*
Campbell, Sir George: *The Other Side of the Medal.*
Cobden: *How Wars are Got up in India.*
Crisis in the Punjab.
Cunningham: *History of the Sikhs.*
Dufferin, Lord: *Lord Dufferin's Speeches in India.*
Eastwick, Colonel: *Dry Leaves from Young Egypt.*
Edwards, William M.: *Reminiscences of a Bengal Civilian.*
Forrest, George: *History of the Indian Mutiny.*
Friends of India.
Grand Jacob, George Le: *Western India.*
Grant Duff: *History of India.*
Grant, General Hope: *Incidents of the Sepoy War.*
Grouger, Henry: *A Personal Narrative of Two Years' Imprisonment in Burma.*
Hastings, Warren: *Private Journal.*
Holmes: *History of Sepoy War.*
———— *History of Indian Mutiny.*
Hope, John: *The House of Scindia.*
Hussain, Syed Feda: *Nairang-i-Afghanistan.*
Kashmiri Pandit Mohanlal: *Life of Dost Mohammad Khan.*
Kaye: *Lives of Indian Officers.*
———— *Life of Malcolm.*
———— *Selections from the Papers of Lord Metcalfe.*
———— *History of the War in Afghanistan.*
———— *The Calcutta Review.*
———— *History of the Sepoy War,* Vols I, II, III.
———— *Indian Mutiny,* Vols I, II.
Kaye and Malleson: *History of the Indian Mutiny,* Vols I, II, III, IV, V, VI.
Lawrence, John: *Life of Lord Lawrence.*

Lecky, W. E. H.: *The Map of Life.*
────── *History of England in the Eighteenth Century.*
Lindsay, W.S.: *History of Merchant Shipping.*
Ludlow: *British India.*
────── *Thoughts on the Policy of the Crown towards India.*
────── *Life of Sir Charles Napier.*
Malcolm: *Political History of India.*
Malleson, G.B.: *Indian Mutiny.*
Mecarthy, Justin: *History of Our Own Times.*
Mill, James; *History of India.*
Montgomery, Martin: *The Bombay Telegraph.*
Napier, Charles: *Lights and Shades of Military Life.*
Narrative of Indian Revolt.
Nizami, Khwaja Hasan: *Delhi-Ki-Jankari.*
Nolan S.: *History of the British Empire.*
Origin of Pindaries by an officer in the service of East India Co.
Outram, Colonel: *The Conquest of Sindh, A Commentary.*
Prinsep: *History of Political and Military Transactions in India. Punjab Papers.*
Roberts, Lord: *Forty-One Years in India.*
Russell, Howard: *My Diary in India in the Year 1858–59.*
Russell, John: *Russell's Diary.*
Sedgwick, Major W.: *India for Sale: Kashmir Sold.*
Shore, Frederick: *Notes on Indian Affairs.*
Snodgrass: *Narrative of Burmese War.*
Spencer, Herbert: *Social Statistics.*
Stanford, Edward: *Causes of the Indian Revolt.*
Thompson, M.: *The Story of Cawnpore.*
Watt, George: *Commercial Products of India.*
Wellington, Duke of: *Despatches.*
Williams, G.R.C.: *Memoirs of Dehra Dun.*
Wilson, H.H.: *Narrative of the Burmese War.*
Zakaullah Khan: *Tareekhi-i-Hind.*

ANNALS

	Year
Lord Cornwallis appointed Governor General	1805
Sir George Barlow appointed Governor General	1805
Treaty Between Scindia and East India Company	1805
Mutiny of Vellore	1806
Lord Minto as Governor General	1806
Marquis of Hastings as Governor General	1813
Lord Amherst as Governor General	1823
Lord William Bentinck as Governor General	1828
Sir Charles Metcalfe as Governor General	1835
Lord Auckland as Governor General	1836
Lord Ellenborough appointed Governor General	1842
Lord Hardinge appointed as Governor General	1844
Declaration of War on Sikhs	1845
Lord Dalhousie as Governor General	1848
Annexation of Punjab	1849
Lord Canning as Governor General	1856
Sepoy Mutiny	1858
Queen Victoria's Proclamation and end of East India Company's Rule	1858

INDEX

Abbot, Captain, 255–57
Afghanistan, declaration of war, 185
  financial burden of English, 203
Ajnala Tehsil, Tragedy of, 389
Alambagh, battle of, 421, 423–25, 433
Aliwal, Supposed battle of, 242, 243
Allahabad, 66, 110, 111, 279, 295, 308, 327–28, 331–34, 339, 356, 381–82, 386, 420, 422, 426, 429, 446, 468, 478, 480
Amritsar, Massacre of, 32, 229, 388, 389
Anson, General, 356, 357, 363, 364, 366
Appa Sahib
  arrest and deportation, 111
  occupation of Gadi, 102–103
  signing of coercive terms, 103
  signing of Subsidiary Alliance, 102
Azamgarh, 325–27, 430, 445–47
Azimullah Khan, envoy to London, 304–306, 338

Baba Khan, King of Iran, 25–28, 33
Bakht Khan, Mohammed, 323, 325, 397, 401–403, 433
  as Delhi's Dictator, 376–77
  as a military leader, 376, 395
Ball, Charles, 285, 313, 319, 327, 331, 333, 334, 347, 383, 414, 427, 429, 435, 450, 479, 482
Banaras, 54, 67, 168, 308, 325–27, 330, 331, 340, 356, 445, 446, 468, 498
Bandoola, Menji Maha, 126, 129

Bareilly, 322–24, 370, 437, 480, 483
Barlow, Sir George, appointment, 7, 11–13
  tactics, 11–13
Barrackpore, Mutiny of, 17, 309, 314–16
Barrackpur massacre, 127–29
Basu, B. D., 40, 57
Battles, record
  Alambagh, 423, 425, 433
  Aliwal, 442, 443
  Allahabad, 332
  Bari, 436
  Bibigunj, 444
  Burma, 125
  Chilianwala, 260
  Delhi, 374–78
  Etawah, 428–29
  Fatehpur, 382–83
  Ferozeshah, 240, 241
  Gwalior, 464–65
  Jaitak, 72
  Jhansi, 346
  Kalpi, 461–62
  Kanchgaon, 461
  Kirkee, 99
  Kotra, 487–88
  Lucknow, 419, 431, 433–34, 476–77
  Maharajpur, 227
  Mahidpur, 112–13
  Manohar, 447–48
  Miami, 212–14
  Mudki, 240
  Naghai, 447–48
  Now-nadi, 452
  Oudh, 346, 492

Oudh-Rangpur Frontier, 73
Panniar, 227
Shahjehanpur, 437
Sikandar Bagh, 424–25
Sutraon
Belgaum, 469
Bell, Major Evan, 140, 261, 279, 281, 282
Bengal, Law and Order, 16
  enactment of, 42
Berar, 5, 10, 16, 18, 19, 22–24, 102, 106, 109, 250, 277–78, 517
Bernard, General, 366–68, 374–75, 377
Bhaironwal, Treaty of, 246, 251–53, 257
Bharatpur, siege of, 130–31
Bhaskarrao, Baba Sahib, 473
Bhonsle, Raghoji, 102, 104, 110, 279
Bibi Garh Kothi massacre, 387
Bihar, its revolt, 443
Bithoor, 101, 298, 299, 306–308, 310, 335, 336, 342, 345, 383, 384, 419, 420, 426, 428, 480
Bradshaw, Major, 64, 65, 76
Briggs, General John, 250
Broadfoot, Major, intrigues at Ludhiana Court, 234, 236–40
Brooks, Adam, 39
Burke, Edmund, 114–15, 518
Burma, English relations
  English intrigues, 129
  its people, 122
  plans of invasion of Burma, 123–24
  war, 120–22
Burnes, Colonel, 182–85

Cachar, Acquisition of, 139–140
Calcutta, 3, 5, 8, 17, 56, 66, 92, 118, 121, 123, 125, 126, 128, 138, 141–43, 168, 176, 178, 204, 208, 215, 239, 264, 280, 285, 287, 294, 302, 308, 309, 316, 325, 327, 356, 381, 387, 416, 420, 422, 423, 498, 514
Campbell, George, 332, 387
Campbell, John, 155, 156, 158
Canning, Lord, 178, 292, 300, 312, 325, 330, 350, 356, 363, 381–82, 432, 445–46, 476, 478, 500, 501, 504
Cass, General, 270
Charter Act of 1793, 250
Charter Act of 1813, 46, 49, 55, 150, 167, 507
Charter Act of 1833, 150–60, 507
Chilianwala, Battle of, 260
Christianity, Propagation of, 12, 13, 169, 299–304, 514
Cooper, Frederick, 288, 289, 390, 391
Coorg, annexation of, 138–39
Cunningham, 73, 146, 235, 236, 238, 239, 241, 244
Currie, Frederick, 251, 253, 254, 256, 257

Dalhousie, achievements, 177
  doctrines of lapse and paramountcy, 274, 275
D-Day for Sepoy Mutiny, 304, 313
Delhi, 3, 4, 7, 31, 32, 54, 70, 80, 82, 132–33, 142, 172, 176–78, 231, 241, 292, 294–97, 307, 308, 310, 317–23, 325, 327, 335, 336, 346, 348, 356, 357, 362–68, 370–72, 374–78, 380, 381, 394–405, 408–14, 417, 419, 421, 423, 428, 429, 433, 434, 442, 453, 461, 463, 470, 476, 492, 496–99
Dharwar, 469
Disraeli, British Prime Minister, 313
Divide and Rule, Policy of, 136–37
Dubois, Abbe, 12, 141, 142
Dufferin, Lord, 17, 61, 62

INDEX

East India Company, 4, 12, 16, 19,
20, 22, 39, 42, 43, 46, 58, 62, 158,
162, 163, 166, 200, 218, 219, 274,
275, 277, 283, 287, 292, 293, 300,
478, 479, 504, 505, 506–10, 512,
513
Eastwick, Captain, 186, 187, 201,
202, 204–207, 209, 210, 214–17,
219
Education
before British arrival, 162
Charter Act of 1833 and
education, 157
consequences, 178–79
Education despatch, 177–78
Establishment of Universities at
Bombay, Calcutta, Madras,
178
extinction and its causes, 164–66
orientation, 171
suppression of Indian languages,
172
system, 163–64, 173–75
Edwards, William, M, 240–43
Eighteen Fifty-Seven Revolution,
see Sepoy Mutiny
Elahi Baksh, treachery of, 398,
402–404
Ellenborough, Lord, 191–96, 208,
219, 222–32, 234–37, 266, 296
Elphinstone, 28, 33–35, 90–100,
102, 103, 105, 182, 408, 490, 520
Emblem of Revolution of 1857,
309–10
Etawah, battle of, 320–21, 428–29,
480

Farrukhabad, 350, 428, 429, 476
Fatehpur, battle of, 382–83, 386,
426
Fatehsinh, Gaikwad of Baroda, 91,
92, 94
Ferozepur, 234, 235, 238, 244, 257,
362, 363

Ferozeshahr, battle of, 240, 241, 243
Firozepur, 362–63
Forrest, George, 312, 353, 387, 398,
499, 501
Fyzabad, 327, 350–51, 432, 438,
482

Gaikwad of Baroda, 90
Gangadharrao, Raja of Jhansi, 281,
344
Ghaziuddin, Nawab, 66, 82, 83
Gokhale, Bapu, 99
Govindgarh Fort, 260
Grand Jacob, George Le, 306
Grant Duff, 18, 19, 22
Grant, Hope, 399, 436, 476, 477,
483
Greathead, General, 423, 428
Grouger, Henry, 42, 43
Gwalior, 5, 6, 8, 88, 142, 143,
222–28, 380, 410, 419, 426, 427,
462–65, 480, 486, 511

Hardinge, Lord, 232, 234–41,
245–47, 251
Hastings, Marquis, 38, 59, 66, 82,
153, 285
Hathras, acquisition of, 80, 81, 131
Havelock, General, 382–84, 387,
418–22, 424–26, 428, 498, 500
Hazara, 256–58
Holkar, Jaswantrao, 2–3, 7–11, 16,
18–24, 30, 75, 89, 112, 113, 237,
498
Holmes, 334, 411, 413, 432, 438,
486, 487
Hope, John, 142, 143, 223, 224, 227,
399
Hoti Mardan, 360–61
Hussain, Syed Feda, 59, 192
Hyderabad, 29, 35, 59, 144, 194,
200, 204, 206, 207, 209–14,
216–18, 230, 250, 275, 277, 456,
470, 471

Imamgarh, 210, 211
India
    colonization by British, 508,
        511–14
    exploitation of resources, 516
    extermination of patriotism,
        514–16
India Bill, 114
Indian Revolt, *see* Sepoy Mutiny
Indore, 143–44, 380, 487
Industries and Trade in India, 38–40

Jabalpur, 469
Jadeja, Rajputrao, 80
Jagdeeshpur, 443–46, 448–52
Jaitak, battle of, 71, 72
Jaitpur, annexation of, 277
Jaunpur, 326–27
Jenkins, English Resident at
    Nagpur, 5, 8, 102–108, 110
Jetpur, 231, 298
Jhansi, 144, 281–82, 298, 344–53,
    456–66, 498, 499
Jullundur, 257, 259, 362–63

Kabul, occupation of, 187–88
Kaithal, annexation of, 31, 228
Kala-Kankar, 352
Kalanga, 68–72
Kanpur, 101, 298, 332, 335–39, 341,
    342, 417–20, 422, 423, 425–28,
    430, 431, 442, 453, 463, 494, 498,
    499
Karnatic, annexation of, 274, 282,
    283, 284
Kaur, Jhinda Rani, 235, 246, 254,
    261
Kaye, 12, 32, 34, 100, 127, 128, 131,
    145, 183–86, 189, 190, 197, 203,
    204, 208, 215, 279, 280, 288, 299,
    307, 308, 312, 328, 330, 331, 333,
    340, 341, 345, 346, 350, 352,
    360–62, 364, 367, 378, 386, 408,
    460, 464, 484, 489, 491

Keith, Major, 55
Khairpur, 204–206, 209–12, 215, 217
Khan, Akbar, 188, 191–93, 197
Khan, Alinaqi, 307, 308
Khan, Amir, 9, 18, 19, 21–24, 112,
    113
    Victim of English duplicity, 21
Khan, Dost Mohammad, 146,
    182–85, 187, 188, 191, 193, 197,
    198, 255
Khan, Khan Bahadur, 322–25, 437,
    476
Khan, Nadir, 429, 430
Khan, Risaldar Kaley, 345, 346
Khan, Rustam Mir, 204–207, 209–
    12, 214–17
Khan, Saadat, 380
Khasgiwale, Dada, 223–26
Kolhapur, 468
Kot Kapoora, casus belli of, 238
Kutch, 80–81, 120, 202, 218, 380

Lahore, Treaty of, 245, 252
Lakhiraj, land resumption of, 147
Lambert, Commodore, Resident at
    Burma, 264–69
Lapse, doctrine of, 250, 274–77,
    282–84
Lawrence, Henry, 251, 285, 301,
    347, 348, 350, 357, 417, 418
Lawrence, John, 266, 301, 357, 358,
    360, 364, 391, 408, 496
Lecky, W. E. H., 49, 127, 313
Lincoln, Abraham, 150, 522
Lindsay, W. S., 58, 139
London *Times,* Comments on Tatya
    Tope, 305, 333, 387, 489
Lucknow, 66, 67, 82, 247, 285–88,
    308, 310, 315, 316, 333, 335, 337,
    347–50, 353, 384, 416–39, 442,
    446, 452, 453, 463, 476–77, 482,
    496, 497
Ludhiana, 32, 67, 73, 146, 182, 184,
    234–36, 326, 362–63

Ludlow, 72, 131, 141, 146, 162, 163, 246, 278, 298, 500

Macaulay's work, policy, aims, 152–53
MacNaghten, Williams, 189, 191–93, 197, 198
Mahal, Hazrat Begum, 307–308, 416–17, 432–38, 476, 478–84, 499
Maharajpur, 227
Mahidpur, Battle of, 112–13
Mahmood, brother of Zaman Shah, 27, 28
Mainpuri, 320–21
Malcolm, John, 9, 12, 26–28, 33, 99, 100, 106, 131, 144, 166, 168, 519
Malleson, G. B., 314, 321, 330, 340, 341, 346, 350, 352, 360, 364, 378, 381, 386, 419, 424–27, 429, 439, 446, 447, 460, 464, 484, 489, 490, 491, 496
Mama Saheb, 223, 225
Mangal Pandey, Martyrdom of, 314–16, 347
Mccarthy, Justin, 313, 341
Meerut, 67, 72, 235, 314, 316–22, 325, 327, 348, 356, 359, 367, 368, 496
Metcalfe, Charles, 12, 31–33, 125–27, 130, 131, 144, 145, 182, 286, 295, 357, 377, 510, 512
Miami, battle of, 212–14
Mill, John, 4, 17, 24, 51, 64, 65, 119
Minto, Lord, 13, 16–19, 23, 24, 28–31, 33–36, 38, 119–21, 201
Mir Rustam Khan, 204–7, 209–12, 214–17
Mohammad Hussain, Tehsildar, 430
Mohanlal, Kashmiri Pandit, 178, 183, 188
Mohanlal, K. P., 178, 183, 188
Montgomery, Martin, 408
Moñtgomery, Robert, 301, 359, 388, 391
Mool Raj, 251–53, 256–60
Mudki, battle of, 240, 243
Mueller, Max, 162, 163
Mughal Empire and the English, 284
Mull, Diwan Sawan, 251
Multan, annexation and revolt, 253, 257–59
Murad, Ali, 200, 207, 209, 210, 215
Musran, acquisition of, 81–82

Nagpur, 22, 23, 102–12, 114, 132, 182, 275, 278–81, 298, 324, 469, 490–91
Naik, Raja Enketappa, 471
Nana Dhondupant, 101
Nana Sahib, 101, 304–307, 310, 320, 335–42, 382–84, 386, 387, 414, 419, 420, 423, 425–27, 429, 437, 459, 462, 468, 469, 476, 483, 484, 499
Napier, Charles, 208–15, 218, 219, 259, 488, 492
Nasirabad, 321–22, 486
Nawab Wazir of Oudh, 3, 4, 66, 82, 96, 141, 294
Neill, General, 326, 330, 332, 334, 339, 341, 356, 366, 382, 384, 419, 421–23, 428, 498, 500
  atrocities and butcheries, 366, 428, 500
Nepal, 64–77, 80, 83, 86, 96, 194, 246, 247, 348, 430, 483, 484, 512, 522, 523
Nicholson, General, 235, 360, 396–401
Nizami, Khwaja Hasan, 404, 409, 410, 411
Nizam of Hyderabad, 250, 470
Nolan, S., 19, 302
Nur, Mir Mohammed, 186, 187, 204

Octroi, new methods of, 47, 52–53, 106
Oudh, 3, 4, 66, 75, 82, 96, 132, 141–42, 224, 231, 247, 250, 274, 280, 284–88, 294, 297–98, 307–308, 327, 328, 344–53, 357, 370, 416–39, 453, 468, 476–84, 492, 500
Outram, Major, 211, 212, 313, 424, 425, 432, 433

Paramountcy, doctrine of, 86, 114, 274–75
Patiala, 30, 236, 241–46, 358, 364, 496
Pegu, annexation of, 270
Peshwa, 10, 20, 21, 80, 86, 90–102, 104, 105, 110, 113, 114, 120, 182, 276, 281, 341–42, 345, 462, 463, 469, 486, 490
Peshwa, Bajirao, 20, 92, 110, 114, 276, 294, 298
Phalke, Ramarao, Prime Minister of Gwalior, 225, 227
Phillaur, 359, 362–63
Pindaris, 18–22, 99
  suppression, 86, 89–90
Plassey, battle of-its revenge, 40, 44, 192, 197, 292, 375, 522
Poona, conditions in, 93–96, 101
Prinsep, 73–75, 81, 95, 97, 103
Propaganda, during mutiny, 299, 328
Punjab, declaration of war on, 185
Punniar, 227
Purandhar, 94, 98, 99

Ram, Daya, King of Hathras, 81
Rango Bapooji, 304, 305, 306, 468, 469
Rao, Bheem, 473
Roberts, Lord, 38, 142, 305, 312, 313, 375, 409, 486, 487, 489
Rohilkhand, 284, 322–25, 357, 376, 396, 397, 416–39, 453, 468

Rose, Sir Hugh, 456, 459, 461–65
Roy, Raja Ram Mohan, 133, 142, 295
Russell, Howard, 304, 305, 310
Russell, John, 159, 387

Saloni, 351
Sambalpur, annexation of, 277, 298
Satara, 99, 100, 101, 113, 246, 275–77, 298, 304–306, 308, 468, 469
Sati-Chowra Ghat, Massacre of, 339–41, 382
Sepoy Mutiny
  aftereffects, 501–502
  Background, 13, 35–36
  Christianity as a cause, 302, 303
  Failure of mutiny and reasons, 496–97
  Immediate causes, 293–94
  Revolts of
    Agra, 381
    Aligarh, 320, 321
    Allahabad, 327–29
    Azamgarh, 325
    Banaras, 325–26
    Bareilly, 437
    Barrackpore, 309, 314
    Belgaum, 469
    Bithoor, 335
    Calcutta, 302
    Delhi, 292, 318–20, 372, 401
    Dharwar, 469
    Directives for mutiny, 452–53
    Emblem of mutiny, 309–10
    Emissaries, 348
    Etawah, 320–21
    Farrukhabad, 350
    Firozepur, 362
    Fyzabad, 350–51
    Gwalior, 380
    Hoti Mardan, 360–61
    Indore, 380
    Jabalpur, 469
    Jaunpur, 326–27

INDEX 533

Jhansi, 345, 346
Jullundur, 362–63
Kala-Kankar, 362
Kanpur, 336, 339
Kolhapur, 468, 469
Lucknow, 347
Ludhiana, 362–63
Mainpuri, 319–20
Meerut, 317–18
Nagpur, 469
Nasirabad, 321–22
Oudh, 298, 346, 416
Peshawar, 359
Phillaur, 362–63
Propaganda, 309
Rohilkhand, 322–24
Saloni, 351–52
Satara, 304–5, 469
Sati-Chowra Ghat, 341
Shahganj, 351
Shahjehanpur, 323
Sitapur, 349, 350
Sultanpur, 351
Scindia, Doulatrao
  coercion into new treaty, 87–89
  disputes with English, 2
  treaty with English, 7–8
Scindia, Jayajirao, 222, 380, 462, 464
Scindia, Junkojirao, 142
Seaton, Captain, 29, 429
Sedgwick, W. Major, 55, 61
Shah, Akbar, 82, 132, 133, 142, 295, 296, 413
Shah Alam, 4, 294, 295, 413
Shah, Bahadur, 293, 296, 297, 306, 307, 310, 318, 319, 324, 339, 342, 357, 358, 368, 370–71, 372, 374, 376, 377, 395, 398, 401–405, 413, 414, 417, 460, 498, 499
Shah, Feroze, Prince of Delhi, 470, 492–94
Shah, Moulvi Ahmed, 350, 351, 432–34, 436–39, 476
  death and tributes, 438–39
Shah, Sardar Rustam, 351

Shah Shuja, 28, 29, 33–35, 146, 184–88, 190, 191, 193, 197, 198, 203
Shah, Wajid Ali, King of Oudh, 286, 288, 307, 351, 416, 417, 480
Shah, Zaman, 24–28
Shamsuddin, Subedar, 300, 336
Shastri, Gangadhar, 86, 92–95, 98
Shepperd, Captain, 264–66, 269, 270
Shore, Frederick, 53–54, 136, 137, 512
Sikandar Bagh, Battle of, 424–25
Sikhs, their betrayal, 364
Sindh
  accusations, 209
  after annexation, 207–10
  annexation, 200–219
  before English annexation, 194
  English intrigues, 30
  political background, 200, 208
Singh, Balbhadra, 68–72
Singh, Balwant, 130, 131
Singh, Chatar, Governor of Hazara, 255–58
Singh, Dulip, 230, 234, 235, 237, 240, 245, 246, 251, 262
Singh, Gulab, treachery of, 229, 235, 243, 245, 256, 476
Singh, Gurbaksh, Havildar, 345
Singh, Hanumant, Raja, 352, 476
Singh, Pratap, Raja of Satara, 246
Singh, Raja Amar, 68, 72, 74–76, 449, 451, 452
Singh, Raja Bhagwant, 82
Singh, Raja Kunwar, 443–51
Singh, Raja Lal, 235, 239, 240, 241, 243, 245, 246, 251, 252
Singh, Raja Man, 351, 492, 493
Singh, Raja Shankar, 469
Singh, Raja Sher, 207, 255, 258–60
Singh, Ranjit, 9, 30–33, 35, 36, 81, 144–47, 182, 183, 185, 202, 203, 229, 230, 234, 236, 237, 244, 251, 261, 348
  expansion of Empire, 33, 147

Singh, Teeka, Subedar, 336, 382
Sleeman, Colonel, Resident at
  Gwalior, 224
Snodgrass, 124, 129
Spencer, Herbert, 10, 45, 128, 501
Subsidiary Alliance, 8, 10, 22, 76, 87–
  89, 102, 103, 107, 113, 120, 140

Tafazzul Hussain Khan, 350
Tanjore, 250, 274, 282–84
Tatya Tope
  battles of Charkhari and Kalpi, 457
  Comments from London *Times*, 489
  end, 493–94
  Final efforts, 486–94
  indefatigable struggles, 494
  the man, 490
  siege of Kanpur, 494
  Supreme Commander-in-chief, 492
Tea Estates, creation of, 54–55
Tej Singh, 235, 239–41, 243, 246, 437
Thackeray, William, 136
Thapa, Raja Amar Singh, 68, 72, 74, 75
Treaties, Record of, with East India Co
  Afghanistan, 29, 35

Bhaironwal, 246, 251–53
Holkar, 9–10
Khairpur, 206
Kutch, 202
Lahore, 245, 252
Mandeshwar, 112–13
Nagpur, 104
Ranjit Singh, 30, 31, 33, 146, 203, 236
Scindia, 142
Sindh, 7–8, 29–30, 201, 202, 203
Trevelyan, Sir Charles, 56, 57, 173, 175–78, 299, 341

Vellore, mutiny of, 13
Victoria's Proclamation, Queen, 479, 482, 483, 504–506
  constitutional value, 506

Walpole, General, 428, 429, 436
War of Independence, *see* Sepoy Mutiny
Wellesley, 2–5, 7, 10, 11, 21, 22, 23, 28, 30, 38, 41, 90, 102, 193, 295
  foreign policy, 24–27
Wheeler, Hugh, 316, 335–38, 383
White Soldiers' Mutiny, 35–36
Wilson, General, 378, 394, 399, 404

Zeenat Mahal, Begum, 307, 310, 318, 377, 402, 403

About the Author

Pandit Sunderlal was an eminent Gandhian and freedom fighter. He was originally a revolutionary and belonged to the famous Ghadar party. After coming in close contact with Mahatma Gandhi in the early 1920s, Pandit Sunderlal became a Gandhian and a practitioner of non-violence and Ahimsa. He represented the holistic evolution of a revolutionary to a Gandhian believing in non-violence and worked closely with Mahatma Gandhi in Sevagram Ashram, Wardha. He was imprisoned seven times for participating in the Indian freedom movement.

Pandit Sunderlal founded the Hindustani Culture Society in 1941. He was part of a goodwill mission to the erstwhile Hyderabad state in 1948. He was President of the All India Peace Council during 1950–62 and President of the India–China Friendship Association. He pursued three key missions throughout his life—promoting the essential unity of all religions, promoting communal harmony between Hindus and Muslims, and promoting and practising the composite culture of India.

Pandit Sunderlal's original work in four volumes, entitled *Bharat Mein Angrezi Raj*, was published in 1929, banned by the British, and republished when the ban on the book was lifted. In 1941, he published *Geeta aur Quran* simultaneously in Hindi and Urdu. This book has been translated into many languages. He authored more than 40 books. Pandit Sunderlal launched *Karmayogi* in 1909. He was editor of *Swarajya*, a Hindi weekly in the early part of the 20th century.